Death and the metropolis

Cambridge Studies in Population, Economy and Society in Past Time 20

Series Editors

PETER LASLETT, ROGER SCHOFIELD, and
E. A. WRIGLEY

ESRC Cambridge Group for the History of Population and Social Structure

and DANIEL SCOTT SMITH

University of Illinois at Chicago

Recent work in social, economic and demographic history has revealed much that was previously obscure about societal stability and change in the past. It has also suggested that crossing the conventional boundaries between these branches of history can be very rewarding.

This series will exemplify the value of interdisciplinary work of this kind, and will include books on topics such as family, kinship and neighbourhood; welfare provision and social control; work and leisure; migration; urban growth; and legal structures and procedures, as well as more familiar matters. It will demonstrate that, for example, anthropology and economics have become as close intellectual neighbours to history as have political philosophy or biography.

For a full list of titles in the series, please see end of book

Death and the metropolis

Studies in the demographic history of London 1670–1830

JOHN LANDERS

University Lecturer in Historical Demography and
Fellow of All Souls College, Oxford

CAMBRIDGE
UNIVERSITY PRESS

Published by the Press Syndicate of the University of Cambridge
The Pitt Building, Trumpington Street, Cambridge CB2 1RP
40 West 20th Street, New York, NY 10011–4211, USA
10 Stamford Road, Oakleigh, Victoria 3166, Australia

First published 1993

Printed in Great Britain at the University Press, Cambridge

A catalogue record for this book is available from the British Library

Library of Congress cataloguing in publication data
Landers, John.
Death and the metropolis : studies in the demographic history of London,
1670–1830 / John Landers.
p.   cm. – (Cambridge studies in population, economy, and society
in past time)
ISBN 0 521 35599 0 (hardback)
1. Mortality – England – London – History.   2. London (England) –
Population – History.   3. Family reconstitution – England – London –
History.   I. Title.   II. Series.
HB 1416.L8L36   1993
304.6'4'094212 – dc20   92-10887   CIP

ISBN 0 521 35599 0 hardback

Contents

Contents

Figures and maps

Maps

Tables

Preface

The key to the social history of London is to be found in its changes in
population – its growth and the ratio between births and deaths... For most
of the eighteenth century London is dominated by a sense of the 'waste of
life' recorded in the Bills.

(George 1966: 35–6)

The 'waste of life' recorded in London's Bills of Mortality between the
later seventeenth century and the end of the eighteenth was enormous (see figure P.1). At its worst, in the second quarter of the
eighteenth century, burials exceeded baptisms by more than 65 per
cent, and it is easy to comprehend Dorothy George's sense of death
as an omnipresent shadow falling across the life of the contemporary
metropolis in all its aspects. Judged by the extraordinary standards of
George's encyclopedic *London Life in the Eighteenth Century*, this book
has the relatively limited goal of understanding eighteenth-century
London's recorded burial surpluses as a demographic phenomenon –
as an outward expression of that underlying cat's cradle of relationships which has come to be termed a 'vital regime'.

The scale and nature of the eighteenth-century metropolis is
nonetheless sufficient to make this a very difficult goal to accomplish.
The sources of vital data are abundant, but they are often of uncertain
quality and rarely lend themselves to the techniques which have been
used so successfully on smaller – and more geographically bounded –
populations elsewhere. Measurements such as the precise level of
age-specific fertility and mortality can thus be undertaken only on
restricted sub-populations, or to a very much greater degree of
approximation than has become usual in empirical 'parish register'
historical demography.

These shortcomings are real, but they are more than offset by the
corresponding strengths of the material – its scale and the richness of

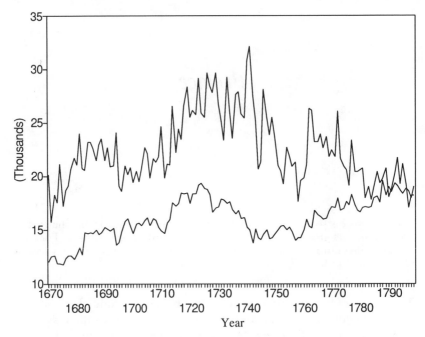

P.1 Recorded burials and baptisms in the London Bills of Mortality

its aggregate details – and by the fact that so many of the theoretically important questions can be posed in terms of orders of magnitude of vital rates and the direction of trends. These are matters on which our sources can be treated with some confidence, but the question of theory raises further difficulties. Facts rarely 'speak for themselves', and this is particularly true of historical demography. Our 'facts' are themselves so often the product of elaborate sequences of adjustment and correction.

Under these circumstances, obtaining data from sources, and information from data, requires the refinement of theoretically informed questions, but historical demography's recent theoretical treatment of mortality has been unduly hampered by the opposition of a narrowly 'economistic', real-wage, determinism to explanations which invoke an 'autonomous death rate' altogether outside the world of human agency.

The first part of the book is concerned with developing an alternative frame of reference, grounding it in the specific circumstances of eighteenth-century London, and carrying out some preliminary empirical tests on the resulting model. This is followed, in part II, by an attempt to measure the level of mortality by means of a family reconstitution study carried out on the vital registers of London Quakers and an aggregative analysis of material from the London Bills of Mortality. Part III is based primarily on numerator statistics and examines the seasonality, short-run instability, and spatial variability, of mortality patterns using material taken from both the annual and weekly Bills, as well as two samples of parish registers.

The model of historical metropolitan vital regimes outlined in part I stands up well to its encounter with empirical data and is likely to have a wider applicability. But such regimes are neither simply imposed by timeless ecological constraints nor inherent in a supposedly homogeneous 'traditional' past. They are grounded in the specificities of time and space, and we have tried to show some of the ways in which the demography of eighteenth-century London was affected by the economic and political circumstances of the time. For all this, however, the volume remains a work of historical demography – concerned primarily with the analysis of aggregate demographic data – and not one of economic or social history.

The broader reality of metropolitan life, and the structures within which it was contained, thus appear only at one remove, as the 'ultimate determinants' of demographic variables. This is particularly true in respect of the dramatic decline of mortality from the 1780s, on which we have had relatively little to say as a topic in its own right. What we have tried to do is to show *how* this process developed – in terms of changes in the proximate determinants of mortality – and how it was that the old demographic regime collapsed. We have then gone on to consider how far this picture is compatible with the existing accounts of changes in the regime's ultimate determinants. The validity of such accounts, and the broader transformation of the capital's economic and social life over our period, remain questions for a latter day Dorothy George.

Acknowledgements

This book would not have been completed without the help, encouragement and advice of many friends and colleagues. Successive research assistants, Anastasia Mouzas, Kim Whatmore and Tessa Rogowski made fundamental contributions to the project. Tony Wrigley was a model supervisor of the Ph.D thesis for which I undertook the family reconstitution reported in chapter 4. I am very grateful to him, and to all the staff of the Cambridge Group for the History of Population and Social Structure, for their help in the technical and other aspects of that research. Roger Schofield in particular has been a never-failing source of essential assistance and enlightenment. I should also like to thank the staff of the library at Friends House in the Euston Road for allowing me access to the source materials, and for their cheerfulness in sustaining me through the psychic travails of family reconstitution.

In developing my ideas on the role of mortality analysis in historical demography, I have benefited particularly from the advice and expertise of Mary Dobson, Irving Loudon and Adrian Wilson. Above all, I should never have been able to carry the project to completion without the continuing encouragement and support of Richard Smith. I have also benefited greatly from conversations with many others including Brian Benson, John Cleland, the late Amanda Copley, Eilidh Garrett, Alan Hill, John Hobcraft, Mathilda P. Katte, Steve Kunitz, Jack Langton, Richard Lawton, Anne Nightingale, Kevin Stapleton, Jenny Wood and Bob Woods.

The family reconstitution study reported in chapter 4 was carried out whilst the author was in receipt of an SSRC research studentship in sociology. The analyses of the weekly Bills of Mortality, and of the parish register samples, reported in chapters 7, 8 and 9, was made possible by a research grant from the Wellcome Trust. The Nuffield Foundation and the Leverhulme Trust both also provided financial support for the analysis of the weekly Bills, and I am very grateful to all these bodies for their generosity.

A version of chapter 4 appeared as 'Age patterns of mortality in London during the "long eighteenth century"': a test of the "high potential" model of metropolitan mortality', in the *Social History of Medicine*. Sections of chapter 6 appeared in Landers and Mouzas, 'Burial seasonality and causes of death in London 1670–1819', *Population Studies* (1988).

PART I

---

*Eighteenth-century London and its
vital regime*

It is not enough to foster a rising tide of substantive demographic studies of demographic behavior in the past. There must also be a complementary development of organising concepts to link population characteristics to their socioeconomic context and to do justice to the mutual interaction between the two. (Wrigley 1981a: 207)

Few fields of scholarly enquiry have been so transformed by the appearance of a single work as was European historical demography by the publication of Wrigley and Schofield's *English Population History* in 1981. This was partly due to the sheer weight of quantitative data which the authors were able to assemble – and their success in 'resolving the conundrum' of eighteenth-century population growth by establishing the leading role of fertility (Wrigley 1981b) – but the book's importance was not simply that it filled an empirical gap in our knowledge of England's demographic history, however valuable such an achievement may have been in itself.

In the *Population History*, and related publications,[1] the authors developed a style of explanation intended to restore population history to its proper place within historical enquiry as a whole, and to its affiliations with economic and social history which had been weakened through the discipline's lengthy preoccupation with questions of methodology and technique.[2] As Wrigley himself pointed out, the success of such a project depended very much on the construction of an appropriate theoretical framework, and the progress of the 1980s has come about as much through conceptual developments as it has through the accumulation of empirical data.

Central to this process has been the elaboration of a more sophisticated concept of the vital regime[3] itself, in which the latter is treated, not as a loosely related collection of vital rates, but as an unbounded network of relationships between the demography of human populations and the structures of their social, economic and political life, as well as their biology and ecology[4]. Such a treatment implies a distinction between two analytical levels – a distinction between the demo-

---

[1] See, for instance, Wrigley 1981b, 1983a; Schofield 1985a, 1989.

[2] This argument is developed, in particular, in Wrigley 1981b. For an earlier critique of the discipline's technical preoccupations see Stedman Jones (1972).

[3] The term 'demographic regime', in its present sense, appears to have been introduced by Scott Smith (1977), although it seems not to have been systematically defined within the historical literature. Kreager (1986), provides an anthropologist's definition, but one whose compass is restricted to fertility and nuptiality.

[4] In this context, and throughout, we use the term 'structure' in the sense employed by Braudel, as 'a coherent and fairly fixed set of relationships' standing 'as limits beyond which man and his experiences cannot go ... certain geographical frameworks, certain biological realities, certain limits of productivity, even particular spiritual constraints' (Braudel 1980: 31).

graphic variables themselves on the 'surface', and an 'underlying' level of structural causality whose long-term stability is nonetheless consistent with substantial movements in the former.[5] As Tilly has remarked in the context of fertility change, the road to explanatory power 'has increasingly seemed to lie in the identification of recurrent causal relationships rather than of straightforward empirical uniformities. . . the work that shows the greatest promise of moving European historical demography from its present plane deals with covariation, not before/after description' (Tilly 1981: 708).

The development of what can usefully be termed a 'structural' approach to historical demography has fostered its reintegration into the broader field of economic and social history, and it is an approach which we shall try to adopt in the present study, but in so doing we at once encounter a major stumbling block. The character of London's vital data is such that the question of mortality – its levels, trends and determinants – inevitably takes the centre stage in such a project, but the recent theoretical development of the discipline has been concerned almost exclusively with fertility and – in particular – nuptiality and has relegated mortality to the conceptual margins.

Thus, while nuptiality is seen as responding in a complex, but structurally consistent, fashion to economic and social circumstances, the failure of classical standard of living models to predict mortality change has led to its being labelled an 'exogenous' variable, one which cannot be explained in social or economic terms. Furthermore, in the light of this conclusion, the primacy of fertility as a determinant of population growth has itself come to be seen as a necessary prerequisite if the latter is to be successfully understood in structural terms.

The aim of this first section is to contest such a view, and to argue that a structural approach to mortality need not confine itself, either to a narrowly 'economistic' conceptualisation of living standards, or to a rigid determinism. In chapter 1 we pursue these points in detail, through a review of theoretical treatments of mortality in historical demography, and try to develop a general frame of reference for its structural analysis. This is followed by a consideration of some

---

[5] For an elaboration of this point see Tilly's distinction between 'continuity' and 'discontinuity' theory (Tilly 1978: 50–1). The juxtaposition of demographic change and structural stability is most explicit in Wrigley and Schofield's 'continuity' interpretation of eighteenth-century fertility increase, developed in reply to the 'proto-industrial' theories of writers such as Levine (1977) and Mendels (1972). Subsequent re-analysis of the nuptiality series (Weir 1984; Schofield 1985b) has recently led Schofield (1989) to a more complex interpretation, whilst Goldstone (1986) has advanced an alternative version of the 'discontinuity' theory.

aspects of social and economic life in London over our period, and of the process of metropolitan expansion.

Our intention here is not to provide an exhaustive coverage of these topics – which would be impossible within the compass of a single chapter – but rather to throw some light on the likely behaviour of the structural mortality variables identified in chapter 1. Finally, in chapter 3, we develop and try to test a conceptual model which employs the general framework and is intended to describe the dynamics of mortality in pre-industrial metropolitan centres.

1

Mortality theory and historical epidemiology

The remarkable progress achieved in historical demography in the 1980s has been accomplished very largely at the price of excluding mortality from the domain of structural analysis. We contend, however, that such a price need not be paid, and that recent work has furnished the material for a structural understanding of mortality patterns in history. In the present chapter we shall try to justify this claim and thereby set out the frame of reference to be employed in the remainder of the volume. In order to do this we must first consider how mortality has been conceptualised as a variable in population history, from classical population theory onwards.

Classical theory

'Classical' population theory can be defined as the body of thought concerning population change and its determinants which first developed in Britain during the later eighteenth century, and acquired its greatest influence in the nineteenth. It was implicated, among other things, in the rise of Darwinian evolutionary theory[1] and has persisted into the present century as an important strand in the 'folk demography' of the industrial west (Ardener 1974). The influence of the classical arguments has been felt primarily through the work of their most distinguished exponent, Thomas Robert Malthus, and such has been his celebrity – or notoriety – that the overall framework is itself often termed simply 'Malthusian'.[2]

[1] Darwin famously remarked of the 'struggle for existence', that it was 'the doctrine of Malthus applied with manifold force to the whole of the animal and vegetable kingdoms' (Darwin 1968: 116). For a discussion of the broader relationship between Darwinism and classical theory see Bowler 1976 and Young 1969.
[2] Varying assessments of Malthus' place in the development of population studies are provided by the contributions to Dûpaquier et al. 1983 and Coleman and Schofield

This is an unfortunate label, however, for at least two reasons. In the first place it 'over identifies' with Malthus a set of assumptions common to his intellectual peers and which he himself advanced in a more flexible and pragmatic form than did some others (Wrigley 1987, 1989). Secondly, the 'Malthusian' label itself has become a source of confusion, especially since the publication of Wrigley and Schofield's *Population History of England* (1981). For whilst these authors interpret their results as vindicating many of Malthus' claims, they situate their apparently 'Malthusian' findings within a conceptual framework which diverges significantly from that of classical theory.

The central assumption underpinning the latter was that population growth was governed by factors lying within the realm of economy and society, and particularly by the level of subsistence resources, chiefly food. The latter exercised their effects through either or both of two possible pathways, of which priority was generally given to the first involving mortality. Classical theory assumed that mortality change occurred because of changing living standards, a relationship which is generally termed, following Malthus, the 'positive check' to population.

For Malthus, demographic regimes dominated by the positive check constituted the 'general case' for the analysis of population movements and their economic correlates. It was his exposition of this relationship, dominating as it did his early writing and coupled with the postulate of diminishing economic returns to demographic expansion, which earned his name the aura of pessimism which still surrounds it. But Malthus also recognised that where levels of nuptiality responded to changing living standards the effects of the positive check might be offset, and in his later work he attached increasing importance to the workings of such a 'preventive check' cycle in western Europe and particularly his native England (Wrigley 1983, 1986).

Classical theory then, in so far as it sought explanations in changing living standards, assumed what modern econometric demography would term an 'endogenous' role for mortality as a demographic variable. But the classical assumptions could also be interpreted in a less strictly 'economistic' fashion and in the early part of the present century writers such as Talbot Griffiths (1926), Margaret Buer (1926) and, in the case of London, Dorothy George (1966), attributed what they saw as a substantial decline in mortality during the later decades of the eighteenth century, to a wider range of

1986. See James 1979 for a biography and Winch 1987 for a brief survey of his intellectual development.

social changes such as the growth in medical knowledge and practice, improvements in social administration, and a growing 'spirit of humanity'.

Arguments of this kind, together with the older variety linking mortality to the level of subsistence resources, were incorporated by Frank Notestein into his formulation of classical demographic transition theory (DTT) in the immediate post-war period.[3] Classical DTT thus assumed that uniformly high levels of mortality would necessarily have prevailed in pre-transitional demographic regimes because of the economic and social conditions characterising 'traditional' societies. Similarly, the sustained decline in mortality (or 'mortality transition') with which the process of demographic transition began, and which set off the phase of rapid population growth, was attributed to changes in such conditions and to the consequences which these had for living standards, public health, and the capacity of the economy to accommodate sustained demographic expansion.

McKeown and the causes of mortality decline

The most prominent post-war exponent of the classical position in the context of English population history has been Thomas McKeown who, from the publication of his first article in 1955, developed a particularly 'strong' variant of the theory. McKeown's argument was eventually extended to cover the whole span of world population growth from the paleolithic down to the present day but remained principally grounded on an analysis of the English experience.[4] The kernel of the 'McKeown thesis' can be summarised in three central assertions:

(i) Population growth over this lengthy period should be treated as a unitary phenomenon throughout the world – the so-called 'modern rise of population'.

(ii) The modern rise of population itself resulted from a decline in mortality and was not due to any change in birth rates.

(iii) The decline of mortality was principally due to an improvement

---

[3] See Notestein 1945 for the central formulation. Woods (1982: 158–84) provides a general discussion of DTT and its influence on demographic theory and research, together with a review of some alternative schemes at a comparable level of generality.

[4] The initial statements of the thesis with reference to English population history are McKeown and Brown 1955, for the eighteenth century, and McKeown and Record 1962, for the nineteenth. For a broader elaboration see McKeown 1976 where the interpretation of the English data differs on some points of detail from that given earlier.

in nutritional levels, with nutrition being, in practice, the sole determinant of mortality decline before the later nineteenth century.

Paying relatively little attention to the historical evidence for changing living standards, McKeown concentrated on the analysis of cause-specific mortality rates from the civil registration period adopting an argument by exclusion or, as he termed it, the 'Sherlock Holmes' procedure. According to this method one must first eliminate the 'impossible', and then accept as the truth whatever explanation remains, regardless of its anterior probability.

McKeown's arguments for the role of nutrition have had a major influence on studies of nineteenth- and twentieth-century mortality,[5] and his denial of a substantial medical contribution to the eighteenth-century mortality decline has been widely accepted, but this effectively marks the limit of his influence among students of the latter period. There are a number of reasons for this, not the least of which was his consistent rejection of parish registers and any vital rates derived from them. But more generally, the beguiling character of McKeown's logic could not compensate for the lack of any convincing evidence for substantial dietary improvements before the later nineteenth century. Furthermore, in the English case, the disproportionate improvement in Peerage mortality seems to pose an insuperable objection to the nutritional hypothesis (see figure 1.1).[6]

The logical basis of McKeown's procedure has also been called into question. As Szreter has pointed out, it relies on an element of 'zero-sum credibility' since the last of the possible explanations to be considered itself benefits from the discrediting of the others without having to be subjected to an equal degree of scrutiny. Hence, where there is insufficient evidence to resolve the issue directly, and the possible explanations are all open to some objection in principle, the result of the analysis will be affected by the order in which the candidates are considered.[7]

---

[5] See Szreter 1988 for a discussion of McKeown's influence on interpretations of mortality decline in the later period, together with a critique of their validity in this context.

[6] The failure of English real wage data to support McKeown's nutritional hypothesis will be discussed at greater length below. For a more general discussion of the latter's shortcomings see Perrenoud 1984 and Schofield 1984. Broadly similar conclusions arise from the individual country surveys contained in Lee 1979.

[7] See Szreter 1988. In this context we should note that the 'order of priority' adopted by students of the parish register period in English demography has differed from that employed in studies of the civil registration era. Researches in the earlier period have generally regarded the nutritional explanation as a primary option to be tested, whereas the latter have been content to treat it as the residual alternative. It is likely

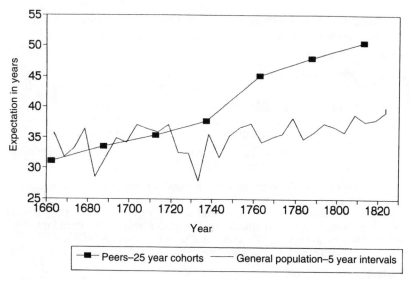

1.1 English life expectation: peerage and general population

In spite of these problems, however, McKeown's 'Sherlock Holmes' logic lends his work a broader relevance to the problem of secular mortality change – above and beyond the validity of the nutritional explanation. This arises from the fact that 'the argument from exclusion is only valid if *all* the suspects have been correctly identified and are separately examined' (Szreter 1988: 11). Hence the initial step in such an analysis must be to specify a unique, exhaustive and non-overlapping set of *a priori* possibilities, and it is this attempt to enforce analytical closure on the problem of explanation which gives a wider importance to McKeown's arguments. If the latter are to be taken seriously then a preliminary requirement must be to list all the factors which might in principle, and at the highest level of generality, affect secular levels of mortality from infectious disease.[8] Hence the options

that this contrast reflects differences in the intellectual genealogies of the two projects, the first being strongly influenced by the legacy of Malthus and the second by that of Engels and other anatomists of the mid-Victorian 'social problem'.

[8] This is the case, at any rate, if the logic of McKeown's method is pursued rigorously and follows from his insistence on the unitary character of mortality decline, and on the need to disregard the anterior probability of the various possible explanations. It is less clear, however, whether it follows from McKeown's own practice since the latter did not always keep to his own procedural canon. For instance, he rejected the genetic explanation for the decline of tuberculosis mortality in nineteenth-century England because – implicitly – of the anterior improbability that a phenomenon of such magnitude should not be related to the social and economic changes going on at the time (McKeown and Record 1962).

Table 1.1. *The possible causes of mortality decline: McKeown's list*

(i) an autonomous decline in the virulence of the micro-organism itself;

(ii) an improvement in the overall environment so as to reduce the chances of
initial exposure to potentially harmful organisms. This could either be:

    (a) as a result of scientific advances in immunisation techniques;
    (b) through a public health policy designed to sanitise the urban
environment – 'municipal sanitation' or 'hygiene improvements';

(iii) an improvement in the human victims' defensive resources *after* initial
exposure to hostile organisms. This could occur either:

    (a) through the development of effective scientific methods of treating
symptoms;
    (b) via an increase in the level and quality of the exposed population's
average nutritional intake, that is better and more abundant food,
thereby improving the individual's own natural defences.

Source: Szreter 1988, p. 7

enumerated must, by definition, constitute the potential explanations
for mortality change in our own study.

Table 1.1 sets out the possibilities considered by McKeown, as
formulated by Szreter, but before proceeding further it is important to
consider the question of ultimate and proximate levels of causality.
The first of these comprises the broadly environmental factors –
whether social, physical or biological – affecting mortality levels in
any given population, whilst the second refers to the intervening
processes through which the latter exercise their effects. The distinction is an important one, since a multiplicity of causal pathways may
run from any given 'ultimate determinant', such as the standard of
living,[9] to the demographic outcome variable, mortality. Thus item
(iia) on McKeown's list, 'scientific advances in immunization techniques', affects mortality in two distinct ways involving both
resistance and exposure to infectious agents. Immunisation increases
the general level of resistance by enhancing individuals' immunological status, but at the same time reduces pathogens' ability to remain
in the population and thus the level of exposure to which the latter is
subject.

A completely general analytical framework for secular mortality

---

[9] McKeown's failure to confront this issue results, as Szreter points out, in the
'standard of living' becoming 'a conceptual, residual catch-all, simply subsuming by
fiat a variety of other possible factors . . . not explicitly addressed in the analysis'
(Szreter 1988: 11).

Table 1.2. *Some proximate determinants*
of mortality levels

(i) Exposure

    (a) Conduction
    (b) Retention
    (c) Autonomous changes in virulence

(ii) Resistance

    (a) Nutritional status
    (b) Immunological status

---

analysis must thus be concerned with this second level – the level of proximate or 'immediate' determination – and comprise a set of intermediate variables lying analytically between mortality and its ultimate determinants, so as to depict the latter's mode of action.[10] Such variables can usefully be grouped under one of two headings, according to whether they act on a population's level of exposure or resistance to infectious agents. The former can be considered a function both of the frequency with which pathogens are encountered and of their potential danger to life and health. As such it is affected by 'autonomous' changes in pathogenic virulence and by two intervening variables based on characteristics of the environment.

The first of these, *retention*, reflects the capacity of the environment to retain pathogens, whilst the second refers to the density of the matrix of potential pathways for infection offered by the environment, whether such infections be airborne, water and food borne, or spread by animal vectors. This density is, of course, affected by a very wide range of factors such as housing conditions, personal and public hygiene, sanitation, and the quality and quantity of water supplies. In the absence of any convenient term already in use we shall refer to the density of this matrix as the degree of *conduction* present in the environment and reformulate McKeown's list using the new terminology as in table 1.2.

In formal terms we can now express the general classical model,

---

[10] The framework of 'intermediate variables' was introduced into fertility analysis by Davis and Blake (1956) and specified in a quantitative form by Bongaarts (1978). For examples of its application see, for instance, Bongaarts et al. 1984 and Hill 1990. Mosley and Chen (1984) have extended the approach to deal with mortality analysis, but their system is concerned with intra-population differences between individuals and households, rather than – as here – synchronic or diachronic variation in the mortality levels of whole populations.

with mortality levels fully determined by social and economic conditions as:

$$M = f \ (Cn, Nu, Re) \qquad \text{where Cn is conduction, Nu nutrition and Re retention,}$$

which reduces in the case of McKeown's version to:

$$M = f \ (Nu)$$

In a subsequent section we shall return to this frame of reference and to the role of the intermediate variables in secular mortality change, but first we must examine an alternative view of the latter topic developed by historians of early modern Europe.

Crisis theory

The decade of the 1950s, which saw the first of McKeown's contributions to English population history, also marked the emergence of a new approach to mortality change which we shall refer to as 'crisis theory'. Centred around the violent short-run disturbances termed 'mortality crises'[11] this had much in common with classical theory but, unlike the latter, recognised that mortality might respond to factors lying outside the domain of economy and society. Nonetheless, the secular propensity of pre-industrial populations to experience crises was seen as a function of the underlying social, economic, and political structures of pre-industrial Europe. From this it followed that the process of mortality decline itself could be seen as a consequence of structural modernisation, and it was through its account of the latter that crisis theory was, in turn, assimilated to DTT.[12]

The growth of interest in 'mortality crises' was due in the first instance to the work of Jean Meuvret (1946, 1965) and, more broadly, to the work of the French *Annales* school, particularly Pierre Goubert's *Beauvais et le Beauvaisis*. Goubert's account of *crises du type ancien* was subsequently generalised to other areas of historical Europe, and thence to pre-transitional populations at large. Outlines of DTT

---

[11] It should be stressed that the schema of 'crisis theory' as we have outlined it is a distillation of the views of a number of writers, and, although the arguments set out here approximate most closely to those of Flinn (1974, 1981), they are not entirely attributable to any single author. The substantive and methodological literature on European mortality crises is very large, but see Charbonneau and Larose 1979 for a representative sample.

[12] See for instance Cipolla 1962, Omran 1971, Woods 1982. The amelioration of crises as a first stage in third world mortality declines was particularly emphasised by Kingsley Davis in connection with the Indian sub-continent (Davis 1950). See McAlpin 1985 and Srikantia 1985 for a discussion of this argument.

offered from the early 1960s onward thus generally characterised the growth pattern of such populations as one in which the modest advances accumulated by the excess of fertility over 'normal' mortality were periodically eliminated by the effects of recurrent crises.

In general terms crisis theory, as it developed from the 1950s to the 1970s, embodied, whether implicitly or explicitly, three main assumptions:

(i) That a qualitative distinction can be made between crisis mortality levels and the so-called 'background' levels of mortality characterising 'normal' years.

(ii) Secular variations in the mortality levels of pre-industrial populations resulted primarily from changes in the incidence and severity of mortality crises, with background levels of mortality varying relatively little in time or space.

(iii) The mortality transition, at least in its initial stages, was caused by a reduction in the incidence and severity of crises, with little change in background levels of mortality.

It is of course on the first of these claims, concerning the definition of mortality crises themselves, that the integrity of the interpretation as a whole depends. At the operational level the question is one of how short-run movements in mortality should best be measured, and of the threshold beyond which they should be recognised as 'crises'.[13] In practice the first of these points can be resolved quite simply by the construction of so-called 'crisis mortality ratios' (CMRs). Indeed crisis theory has been so attractive to historical demographers largely because of the importance it attached to just those quantities most accessible by means of the techniques of 'aggregative analysis' as applied to parish registers and similar sources (Eversley 1966). In such studies there were rarely sufficient population data for mortality levels to be estimated, even as crude rates, but it could usually be argued that their fluctuations could be indexed by corresponding movements in the burial totals.

The problem of definition is more than simply quantitative or operational, however, but has implications reaching to the theory's conceptual foundations. For these imply that the observations labelled 'mortality crises' had an essential character of their own and were more than just the extreme right hand tail of a continuous distribution of annual death rates. Rather, it was assumed that the conditions of

---

[13] On this point, see Flinn 1974 and the contributions to Charbonneau and Larose 1979, particularly that by Dûpaquier.

crisis years were qualitatively distinct from the 'background' mortality which characterised 'normal' years and stemmed from the occurrence of some external shock. From this attribution it followed that the nature of a crisis itself could best be understood by identifying the shock, or 'trigger', which had acted as the proximate cause.

There developed from this a style of analysis which aimed principally at the correlation of environmental triggers with demographic outcomes and paid relatively little attention to the causal pathways through which the latter were realised.[14] Initially both Meuvret and Goubert blamed mortality crises primarily on harvest failures, the latter in particular likening the price of grain to the 'demographic barometer' of early modern Europe (Goubert 1952). But later studies revealed many episodes of crisis mortality which were not accompanied by exceptional price rises; episodes in which the latter did occur but the excess deaths arose from infections owing little to nutrition; and still others where some further disruption to the life of the community had accompanied the upswings in both prices and mortality. Such findings led to the development of a typology in which 'subsistence crises' of the Beauvais variety were only one element. Also recognised were 'epidemic' crises resulting from the apparently spontaneous spread of infectious disease, and 'military' crises brought on by war or civil disruption. These labels, however, proved easier to formulate in principle than to apply in practice. In many instances elements of all three were combined, and, as Flinn pointed out, 'whatever the basic cause of a crisis, epidemic disease generally took over, so that mortality crises of all kinds very commonly appear as great increases in the number of deaths from infectious diseases' (Flinn 1981: 53).[15]

[14] The character of this 'black box' approach to the internal functioning of the vital regime itself is exemplified by Meuvret's discussion of proximate causes of death in subsistence crises:

Il serait donc assez vain de vouloir statistiquément déceler une différence spécifique entre des faits aussi étroitement associés: la mortalité par simple inanition, celle determinée par une maladie mais imputable à la sous-alimentation, enfin la mortalité par contagion cette contagion elle-même étant insepérable de l'état de dissette qui contribuait sans seulement au développement des maladie mais à leur propagation par le déplacement des pauvres mendiants. (Meuvret 1946: 644)

[15] It is, perhaps, partly for this reason that the relative importance of subsistence and epidemic crises, defined in these terms, has been the subject of a vigorous debate among French historians. It should be noted nonetheless that critics of the Meuvret–Goubert position, such as Dûpaquier (1989), have generally not questioned the validity of a basically typological approach to the phenomena in question.

The stabilisation of mortality

Early studies of mortality crises thus attributed them, in the last analysis, to the structural weakness of *ancien regime* society; its low agricultural productivity, poorly developed transport system, political instability, and medical ignorance. This attribution, and the assumption that mortality transition had begun with the amelioration of crises, opened the way to an interpretation of the transition itself in terms of social and economic modernisation. This synthesis of the agenda of *Annales* type historical demography with that of DTT, was associated particularly with the work of M. W. Flinn.[16]

Flinn argued improvements in such areas as transport, food marketing, and social administration – together with military reforms and the growth of 'medical police' – had 'stabilised' mortality and so brought about its secular decline. Subsequent research, however, has failed to substantiate these claims in their original form. Studies such as those of J. D. Post (see below, p. 19) have demonstrated that structural change could avert mortality crises – and true 'famine' crises had been virtually eliminated by the early eighteenth century – but the relationship between secular mortality levels and their short-run stability has proved more complex than was initially assumed.

In Scandinavia, for instance, substantial fluctuations in mortality persisted throughout the early phases of secular decline into the latter part of the nineteenth century, and in the English case, although the national crude death rate both declined and stabilised in the later eighteenth century, the experience of earlier periods was quite different (Perrenoud 1984; Schofield 1984; Anderson 1988). In particular, the later seventeenth century saw a combination of rising death rates and declining fluctuations as mortality apparently 'stabilised' at a new and more severe level. Conversely in mediterranean Europe the association appears more straightforward, and it has been claimed that in this instance the disappearance of bubonic plague brought about both a stabilisation and a decline of mortality, leading to the resumption of population growth.[17]

The relationship between the stability and intensity of mortality has thus proved empirically variable and, contrary to the assumptions of

[16] See Flinn 1974 for an early statement of his position, and 1981 for a general elaboration. For the interpretation of the disappearance of plague crises see Flinn 1979. Perrenoud 1991 provides a recent review of the stabilisation of mortality and its relationship to mortality decline.

[17] See, for instance, Livi Bacci (1978) who has recently reasserted claims for the general importance of mortality crises as determinants of population growth (Livi Bacci 1991).

crisis theory, it seems that levels of 'background' mortality also varied in time and space. Such variability effectively rules out any general interpretation of mortality change grounded entirely on the changing incidence of mortality crises, but further difficulties have arisen with the latter concept itself, and these have forced a revision in the theoretical underpinnings of short-run mortality analysis.

Revisions to crisis theory

The conceptual elegance and methodological benefits of crisis theory together assured the study of short-run mortality change a central place on the research agenda of 'parish register' historical demography. But as such research progressed the 'crisis' concept, as first formulated, became increasingly problematic since the distinction between 'crisis' and 'normal' years was often much more difficult to make than had originally been assumed and often appeared rather arbitrary. Some upswings in mortality, for instance epidemics of bubonic plague, might indeed tower like Himalayan peaks above the plains and foothills of 'normal' mortality, but such cases were more often the exception than the rule, and episodes of unusually severe mortality in a lengthy series of annual burial totals frequently emerged as the elongated right hand tail of a continuous distribution of CMRs. In these circumstances, if one wishes to designate specific 'crises' it is necessary either to take a small number of outlying observations – and thus exclude a number of years whose mortality levels were also substantially above average – or else impose some arbitrary threshold, with the likely result that some 'crises' will manifest CMRs only a little above those displayed in the worst of the 'normal' years.

In comparative studies this problem is further compounded by the difficulty in setting appropriate thresholds for populations of different sizes, given that the stochastic instability of 'normal' mortality will vary according to the scale of the population concerned. Clear-cut distinctions between self-evident mortality crises and the most severe 'normal' years thus occur only in certain cases. Often the division must be imposed on the data according to some, more or less arbitrary, statistical criterion, making the concept of an essential, and generally applicable, dichotomy of 'crisis' and 'background' levels a difficult one to sustain in practice.

The typological approach to the analysis of crises has also proved unsatisfactory. At its most obvious – since most deaths in subsistence crises were caused by infectious diseases – infections themselves, rather than flitting spontaneously between regions were usually spread by humans, particularly by subsistence migrants and marauding armies, and a principal effect of the latter was the destruction of food supplies and the displacement of civilian populations: it is evident that 'single factor' crises were as likely to be the exception as the rule.

In fact the typological approach grants analytical priority to the special case at the expense of the generality of historical experience and in so doing obscures the most valuable insights to have been gained from studies of short-run fluctuations in mortality. These concern precisely the interactions between those structures of pre-industrial communities and their environments which jointly predisposed them to the risk of such fluctuations, and into the density of the causal networks through which such risks were actualised or averted in practice.[18]

These difficulties with the original conceptualisation of crises have fostered the growth of two contrasting styles of short-run mortality analysis. The first rejects qualitative labelling of any kind and restricts itself to the quantitative analysis of long runs of data using statistical time series techniques. In such analyses the interactions between demographic, economic and climatic variables are explored through the medium of statistical associations between movements in the relevant series. The findings of this 'econometric' historical demography, pioneered by Ron Lee, have contributed powerfully to the formulation of 'neoclassical' population theory, but they are couched in terms of coefficients defined over lengthy periods rather than those denoting specific configurations of historical events.[19]

An alternative approach, exemplified by the work of J. D. Post, has continued to focus on specific episodes of unusually severe mortality. Instead of concentrating on their external triggers, however, attention

---

[18] The typological preoccupation, and its consequences, can be seen in Meuvret's comments on the effects of warfare, in the introductory passage to his review of demographic crises in *ancien regime* France: 'although far from negligible, the events connected with war do not fall into categories which make it possible for the demographer to isolate them and to attribute to each a distinctive role. Consequently it is with acute crises arising from epidemics and from dearth that we shall alone concern ourselves.' (Meuvret 1965: 508).

[19] See Lee 1981 for a short-run econometric analysis of the Wrigley–Schofield data, and 1978 for some applications to London. A fuller analysis of the London data is provided by Galloway 1985, who has used a similar methodology to undertake a comparative study of pre-transitional European demographic regimes (Galloway 1988).

is shifted to the networks of intervening variables which lie between these and their demographic outcome.[20] The epidemic mortality accompanying such episodes is now treated as a quantitatively extreme manifestation of characteristics endemic to pre-industrial vital regimes under 'normal' conditions, and seen in the context of, rather than in opposition to, the determinants of 'background' mortality.

Infections such as dysentery, typhus, typhoid and relapsing fever had become endemic among Europe's working population. These smouldering infections could become epidemic under a variety of environmental and social conditions. The stress and wretchedness created by dearth and war were the most common of such circumstances. The pre-existing endemic foci of infection could extend their range and become epidemic under both sets of social conditions. (Post 1984: 24)

Thus mortality in the countries of north west Europe responded differentially to the exceptional weather conditions of the early 1740s. This was not due to variations in either the severity of the weather or the scale of the ensuing price rises, but could be explained in terms of underlying differences in social structure and administration. In demonstrating this Post was led to reconstruct the pathways through which climatic fluctuations affected these variables, and others such as migration patterns and housing densities, in such a way as to transform endemic pools into epidemic currents of infection.

The general structure of Post's model is set out in the form of a flow diagram in figure 1.2. Whereas Goubert and Meuvret had centred their interpretation on the role of malnutrition in reducing resistance to infection, Post's model incorporates a number of mechanisms through which climatic extremes can influence exposure to infectious agents. In particular, shortage of money for fuel and accommodation, and its redirection towards the purchase of food, leads to an increase in effective population densities and a decline in hygiene. Alongside this increase in conduction, however, there is also the potential for a collapse in what we shall term the spatial *bounding* of local regimes, a collapse manifested in the phenomenon of stress-induced migration.

The latter fostered both the diffusion of pathogens and further increases in conduction, since hunger migrants generally forfeited entitlements to shelter and accommodation – even if they benefitted from food handouts – leading to further crowding among the poorer sections of the community at least. In the specific context of the 1740s

---

[20] See, for instance Post 1984, 1990. It is noticeable that studies of this kind favour an implicitly nominalist stance to the phenomena in question, often preferring such relatively non-committal formulae as 'mortality peak', or 'wave', to that of 'crisis'.

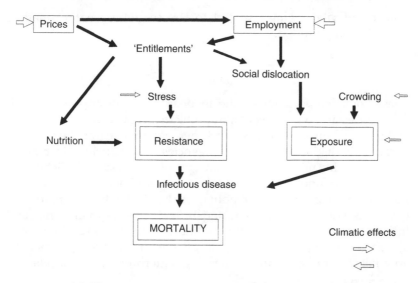

1.2 Climatic stress in a market economy: Post's model

Post concluded that the latter pathways were primarily implicated in the excess mortality: 'the relationship between climatic variability and the higher incidence of infection was social rather than physiological. Epidemics arose more from social upheaval and welfare emergencies than from dangerously lowered resistance to pathogens.' (Post 1984: 5).

Thus the scale of the demographic outcome in any given case reflected, not the intensity of the climatic trigger, but the internal dynamics of the regime itself and the extent to which it possessed 'the ability to adapt to the economic and social consequences of climatic stress' (Post 1984: 20).

The broader relevance of this analysis lies in the relationship established between the mechanisms underlying short-run fluctuations, on the one hand, and those determining the secular level of exposure to infection on the other. The specification of this relationship reopens the possibility that the latter mechanism might be elucidated through short-run aggregative mortality analysis. Furthermore, the model as set out can be generalised from the specific case of climatic fluctuations, to incorporate other sources of external disturbance, simply by specifying the effects of these on the variables it portrays. Hence we can move from a typological approach, based on the 'black-box' juxtaposition of demographic outcomes against clearly differentiated environmental triggers, to analysing the internal function of vital regimes subject to stresses whose nature may be multiply compounded.

Summary

These considerations reveal the inadequacy of an approach which treats crises as isolated events, unproblematically 'given' in our data, and imposed on an otherwise static demographic regime by a variety of mutually distinct external contingencies, whether climatic, biological or politico-military. The concept of an essential dichotomy between crisis and background levels of mortality can be more fruitfully replaced by a broader notion of the 'instability' of mortality, treated as a demographic characteristic that varies both in degree and in form between regimes[21] – the continuity of the latter residing not in a fixed set of vital rates, or even a range within which these necessarily fall, but rather in the underlying pattern of structural relationships governing such rates.

Again – at the level of causation – the more inclusive concept of 'stress' seems preferable to the older typology, since the threads linking a given climatic or military event to its demographic outcome may run through a multiplicity of pathways, and a given pathway may be invoked by a diversity of 'shocks'. It is thus analytically sterile to approach demographic outcomes simply in terms of their external triggers, for this is to ignore the internal, mediating, function of vital regimes themselves, and to impose an artificial separation on the interlocking components of the global stress imposed on pre-industrial communities by prolonged episodes of epidemic disease, warfare or climatic extremes.[22] We shall return to these issues in a subsequent section, but at this point we must look at a third frame of reference which largely supplanted crisis theory in the 1980s.

Neoclassical theory

Wrigley and Schofield's reconstruction of English population history was situated within an overarching 'neoclassical' framework of

---

[21] The crisis: background opposition thus becomes only one of a number of possible *forms* of instability displayed by different regimes (see below, p. x).

[22] We should emphasise here that our concern is with analysis rather than description. Labels such as 'subsistence crisis' or 'military crisis' have an heuristic value in particular cases, but analytically it is the relatively clear-cut instances of this kind which should constitute the special case, rather than those in which the degree of interaction present hinders the application of a simple descriptive label.

population theory. This is recognisably derived from classical theory, but diverges from it in some important respects.[23] In one of these, the enhanced role of nuptiality as a demographic regulator, the difference is largely one of degree. Malthus himself, as we have seen, thought that the peculiar institutional and cultural complexion of western Europe – particularly that of his native England – encouraged the practice of late marriage, or 'prudential restraint', and so enabled the positive check to be held at bay and popular living standards to be kept relatively high. In keeping with this 'Malthusian' contention – though in contrast to the views of McKeown – Wrigley and Schofield see nuptiality as the armature linking population to economic growth in England's 'low pressure' demographic regime. However they carry the argument one step further by concluding that nuptiality was also the principal determinant of variations in growth rates.

Although Schofield has subsequently developed a modified treatment of the relationship between nuptiality and the economy (Schofield 1989), the authors' initial scheme was one in which the former, as measured by a crude first marriage rate, responded homeostatically to fluctuations in the real wage with a lag of roughly a generation. The use of real wage estimates as a proxy for the general level of material well-being is a characteristic feature of neoclassical analyses and allows a formidable battery of econometric techniques to be brought to bear – but the attempt to explain changes in life expectation in such terms has yielded results quite contrary to the assumptions of classical mortality theory.

The autonomous death rate

Wrigley and Schofield's data revealed two long cycles in life expectation, cycles which could not be attributed to corresponding movements in real wages. This supported Lee's earlier contention that secular mortality had been an 'exogenous' variable in pre-industrial England's economic-demographic system (Lee 1973), but the suggestion that mortality change might be independent of living standards considerably pre-dated Lee's pioneering econometric analyses. As early as the 1950s Helleiner had propounded a crisis-theoretic argument along these lines, suggesting that western Europe's 'vital revolution' had been ushered in by a decline in the severity of

---

[23] See references in note 1, p. 7, for basic statements of the neoclassical position. The contributions to Rotberg and Rabb 1986 provide additional consideration of aspects of the theory and its implications.

mortality crises arising in part from factors outside the scope of the economy, or indeed of human agency itself.[24]

The most influential exponent of such arguments in the context of eighteenth-century England, however, was J. D. Chambers who wrote of 'the irrevocable fact which historians have been loath to recognize, the fact of the autonomous death rate, the death rate which could override countervailing influences, such as low prices, an abundance of free land, a shortage of labour, and rising real wages' (Chambers 1972: 82).

It is important at this point to distinguish between Chambers' 'fact of the autonomous death rate' and the concept of 'exogenous' mortality as used by Lee and others. Although superficially similar the two are defined with respect to very different theoretical frameworks and have correspondingly different implications. Of the two the econometric concept of 'exogenous mortality' has a much narrower and more technical interpretation, implying simply that mortality levels cannot be defined within a set of simultaneous equations linking vital rates to population size, wages and prices. Such a usage is silent on the possibility that mortality might be determined by factors lying elsewhere in the domain of economy and society, but this is implicitly ruled out by the concept of the autonomous death rate. Here the causes of secular mortality change are moved altogether outside the sphere of human affairs and attributed to the first item on McKeown's list, spontaneous changes in the virulence of infectious agents.[25] In Chambers' own words:

it is arguable that random biological causes operating in successive onslaughts on an already high death rate were so powerful through to the middle of the eighteenth century that they could initiate long waves of demographic depression independently of available *per capita* resources; and that conversely the absence of such biological factors could result in lowering the death rate and in inducing a population rise . . .[26]

The notion that eighteenth-century mortality declines were 'auto-

[24] Helleiner acknowledged the decline of subsistence crises as a factor in population growth but attached especial importance to the 'obscure ecological revolution among rodents' which had, he believed, banished plague from Western Europe (Helleiner 1957, 1967). For a discussion of Helleiner's work and its significance see Flinn 1970.

[25] Climatic changes have also been invoked in certain cases. This factor, in principle at least, is amenable to empirical investigation, but the results of such studies have generally been equivocal, partly because the relevant data are often very hard to come by (see Galloway 1986).

[26] Chambers 1972: 87. Given the influence of Chambers' argument for the 'autonomous death rate' it is important to remember that he did not himself view the mortality decline of the later eighteenth century in these terms, preferring to attribute it, primarily, to changing living standards and medical advances (pp. 99–104).

nomous', in this absolute sense, has found acceptance among historical demographers working in a number of European countries,[27] but
it has markedly counter heuristic implications. For if the function of
theory is to furnish questions that can be employed in empirical
enquiry, then the concept of autonomous mortality, by moving the
presumptive causes into the realm of microbiology, effectively
stymies any further investigation since these are matters on which
our data can tell us nothing. Given the latter restriction, the
acceptance of the 'autonomy' argument stems from a variant of
McKeown's 'Sherlock Holmes' procedure and follows the failure of
attempts to find convincing evidence for improvements in real wages.
But this failure only compels such a conclusion if we equate the
'autonomous death rate' with the econometricians' concept of
exogenous mortality, and thus conflate the world of human affairs in
its totality with the single dimension of the wage-price ratio.

Exogenous mortality and the neoclassical framework

Neoclassical population theory effectively postulates two types of
demographic regime. The first of these, the 'high-pressure' regime,
corresponds to the classical domination of population growth by
movements in mortality and the determination of the latter by the
availability of subsistence resources. In addition, however, there are
'low-pressure' regimes in which nuptiality is sufficiently sensitive to
changing living standards to keep these above the threshold at which
further declines would bring increased death rates.

In the low-pressure case the determination of secular mortality
levels reverts to a further set of independent variables whose identity
remains unspecified. Although the failure of the classical 'endogenous' mortality relationship does not, as we have seen, necessarily
imply its 'autonomy' in an absolute sense, such an inference has, in
fact, been widely drawn from the success of the neoclassical account
of English population growth. Exogenous mortality fluctuations are
thus widely seen as random, unprogrammed, disturbances to the
smooth running of the demographic-economic system, as events
which in Wrigley's words, 'may have momentous effects, but, like an
earthquake, a typhoon, or a great flood [are] external to the normal
functioning of society. Consequences flow from such events but the
links all run in one direction. Societies may fall victim to such events
but they cannot influence them.' (Wrigley 1981: 207–8).

---

[27] See for instance Perrenoud 1984, and the contributions to Lee 1979 and Schofield et
al. 1991.

Against such a background it is not surprising that Wrigley should view the leading role of nuptiality as a necessary precondition for a structuralist approach to English historical demography, but the prevalence of 'autonomist' interpretations of mortality change has created difficulties nonetheless. The first and most obvious of these is the anomalous position in which it places mortality studies. At the very time when structural approaches to population history have brought such impressive results, mortality change is effectively removed from the domain of structural explanation, and its causes from historical observation.

The role of secular mortality levels as a variable within the neo-classical 'low-pressure' regime is also anomalous as Lee (1986) has pointed out. England's economic-demographic system displayed powerful homeostatic properties over the centuries studied by Wrigley and Schofield, but it was far from a state of equilibrium. In fact 'population size, population growth rates (and their components, fertility and mortality) and real wages, all have a distinctive character-istic: they exhibit a long and deep swing with two or three major turning points over the period from 1540 to 1800' (Lee 1986: 77–8). Behaviour of this kind implies the presence of an exogenous source of disturbance, and where fertility has the homeostatic role proposed by Wrigley and Schofield 'it appears inescapable that exogenous changes in *mortality* drive the long run changes in fertility, population and wages, whatever the proximate decomposition of responsibility; this assertion must be so, because mortality is the only variable with substantial exogenous variation' (Lee 1986: 100). In terms of its sub-stantive importance then mortality has been put out of the door only to come back through the window. But conceptually it has become, to change the metaphor, the 'ghost in the machine', a mysterious entity which drives the system but whose behaviour cannot be accounted for in its terms.[28]

Further difficulties arise when we move from the problem of secular variations in mortality to that of geographical differences, a topic lent particular interest by the neoclassical distinction between high and low pressure regimes. If, as Malthus' own work implied, it was what is now termed the 'north western European marriage pat-tern' (Hajnal 1983) which exorcised the spectre of the positive check from that region, we would expect to find appreciably higher mortality levels prevailing among populations characterised by early

---

[28] Flinn has also pointed out, in his initial review of the *Population History*, that the substantive contribution of mortality change to population growth was rather larger than some of the authors' statements seem to imply; see Flinn 1982.

and universal marriage. This expectation, of course, is based on the lower living standards assumed to follow from such a marriage pattern, and thus implies that the difference in mortality levels between the two regimes is economically determined.

Neoclassical theory thus requires three distinct frameworks to account for large-scale variations in mortality. The first, couched in terms of socio-economic or cultural factors, applies to mortality differences at the inter-regional scale between low and high pressure regimes, whilst a second, based on the classical positive check, explains temporal changes in the high pressure regimes and a third, invoking an unspecified range of non-economic variables, is required for such changes in the low pressure variety.

The lack of a unified framework of explanation capable of encompassing variations in both time and space is a serious handicap and contrasts sharply with the state of nuptiality theory, where a rich and controversial literature has developed around the relationships between marriage ages and proportions marrying on the one hand, and systems of inheritance, kinship and household formation on the other.[29] Indeed the lack of such a framework has meant that mortality analysis – which until recently commanded both analytical and substantive priority in historical demography – remains excluded from the promised re-integration of the discipline into the broader manifold of historical enquiry.

Mortality and spatial structure

The 'exogeneity' thesis has a firm empirical basis. We cannot logically infer from this that secular mortality was thereby 'autonomous', but the success of neoclassical theory – and the predominance it accords to the real wage variable – has led to this inference being widely drawn in practice. A number of attempts have nonetheless been made to develop structural accounts of mortality invoking other dimensions of economic, social and political life. These have characteristically paid particular attention to the role of spatial structure, and to its effects on levels of exposure to infection, through the agency of such factors as population density, migration flows, and patterns of short-range mobility.

[29] See for instance Levine 1977, Berkner and Mendels 1978, Goldstone 1986, Weir 1984, Schofield 1985b, 1989.

Some general surveys

These possibilities were first explored in a review of world population growth by Durand in 1967. Pointing to the remarkably similar experience of widely separated regions of the globe from the sixteenth century onwards, he sought an explanation in the effects of European movements of exploration, trade and colonisation. In its first stages European expansion brought political dislocation to many non-European populations and spread 'new' infections around the world, infections to which recipient populations lacked either immunological defences or cultural means of adaptation. Mortality thus rose generally during the seventeenth century, but after a certain time lag adaptations of various kinds lowered the toll of infectious diseases, whilst the diffusion of new food crops around the globe provided local populations with a resource base that was both richer and more resilient in the face of climatic uncertainties. Hence around the middle of the eighteenth century a new era of world population growth was initiated.

Durand's argument invoked changes both in the levels of exposure to infection and in the levels of resistance. By contrast, Ladurie's contribution, 'The unification of the world by disease' (Ladurie 1981), placed much more emphasis on the role of exposure to infection. In a wide-ranging analysis of patterns of epidemic disease, from the plague of Justinian in the sixth-century Mediterranean to the catastrophic impact of infections on Pacific basin populations in the nineteenth century, Ladurie showed how global movement had merged regional disease pools, and how factors such as population density had facilitated or retarded this process.

McNeill

The most ambitious and best known invocation of spatial structure in this context is that of W. H. McNeill whose book *Plagues and Peoples* (McNeill 1977) attracted a readership enjoyed by few other works of academic population history. In a survey of global mortality trends from the paleolithic to the twentieth century McNeill developed an argument which rested heavily on population distributions, geographical movement, and the effects of these on the levels of exposure to infection prevailing in regional and local populations. Stressing the minimum population size and density required to maintain many varieties of pathogens in a host population, McNeill traced the origin of the majority of killing infectious diseases, first to that of agriculture, and then to those of large urban concentrations.

The emergence of dense population masses in certain regions of the world was accompanied by the development of correspondingly specific regional pools of infectious diseases to which the human population became adapted, both immunologically and culturally. The growth of inter-regional contacts through trade, migration or conquest, then spread pathogens to new 'virgin soil' populations bringing substantial 'die-offs' followed by a period of adaptation and thence a secular reduction in mortality.

McNeill later extended his argument in a manner particularly relevant to the present study (McNeill 1980). This concerned the implications of varying population densities, particularly as between large metropolitan centres and their more thinly settled rural hinterlands. The populations of these two zones, he argued, were characterised by markedly distinct sets of relationships between the level and stability of both mortality and morbidity by age and cause – sets of relationships that we shall refer to as *epidemiological regimes*.

In the metropolitan centres populations were large enough to act as perennial reservoirs of infection, being characterised, in our terms, by a high level of both retention and, given their crowded populations and poor sanitation, conduction. People born into such a population suffered high mortality in childhood but acquired a corresponding level of immunological resistance if they survived to adult life, so that at any one time the pool of susceptibles to a given infection was largely restricted to children and recent immigrants. In these circumstances death rates would be high, especially at the younger ages, but also fairly stable since the scope for epidemics was so restricted. 'Hinterland' populations, however, would be too thinly distributed for serious endemic infections to persist. Hence they would have lower secular mortality levels, but also a reduced immunological resistance which would make them vulnerable to recurrent epidemics of 'metropolitan' infections.

McNeill's account opens the way to a structural theory of 'exogenous' mortality by showing how human agency can promote or retard the spread of pathogens and thus affect levels of exposure to infection. His arguments concerning metropolitan populations bear heavily on our own study and will be considered at length in chapter 3, but at this point we should note that their ambitious scope is not matched by detailed empirical analysis and many of his claims are open to objection in principle. In particular the model relies heavily on the behaviour of the so-called 'crowd diseases', caused by pathogens which are readily transmitted between individuals in close proximity and confer long lasting immunity on their surviving hosts.

Table 1.3. *The influence of nutritional status on infectious diseases*

	Definite	Variable	Slight
Bacterial	Tuberculosis Bacterial Diarrhoea Cholera Leprosy Respiratory infections	Diphtheria Staphylococcus Streptococcus	Typhoid Plague Tetanus Bacterial toxins
Viral	Measles Rotavirus Diarrhoea Respiratory infections	Influenza	Smallpox Yellow fever
Other		Syphilis Typhus	

Source: Lunn 1991, p. 137

Many demographically significant infections, such as smallpox, do display these characteristics, but they are by no means universal. Thus tuberculosis, with its potentially very long interval between infection and death, can persist at a variety of population densities, whilst other diseases displayed a different relationship between childhood morbidity and adult resistance. Thus in the case of bronchitis childhood morbidity apparently lowers adult resistance, whilst in that of typhus children are apparently less susceptible than adults or adolescents amongst whom the disease is generally found (Snyder 1965; Stuart-Harris 1980). Similarly, the existence of animal vectors and reservoirs for bubonic plague – the most notorious urban disease of early modern Europe – gave it a more complex disease ecology which remains to be fully understood (Biraben 1977; Benedictow 1987).

McNeill's arguments also pay relatively little attention to the influence of nutrition on the degree of resistance to infection. In fact, medical evidence suggests that this influence was very restricted in the case of many of the diseases which were of greatest demographic importance in past populations (Livi-Bacci 1990). But nutritional factors are thought to be of considerable significance in other cases (see table 1.3), and where this is so the epidemiology and ecology of the relevant conditions may be substantially more complicated.

In addition models of this kind often provide a more satisfactory account of secular upswings in mortality than they do of the sub-sequent declines. Changes in the genetic composition of populations, whether of host or parasite species, have sometimes been invoked to explain the latter, but to do this is simply to return to the heuristic difficulties of the 'autonomous death rate'. Furthermore, where human hosts are concerned, the scope for genetic adaptation within the relevant space of time is very limited, and the biological evidence that such adaptations have occurred is surprisingly meagre.[30]

Kunitz

Kunitz's account of European mortality trends during the eighteenth and nineteenth centuries confronts the problem of decline directly and invokes changes in both exposure and resistance to infectious agents (Kunitz 1983). Kunitz suggests that the growing density of trading and communication networks in the later seventeenth century and early eighteenth led to the spread of infectious agents and a corresponding increase in mortality. Once a certain threshold had been reached, however, the growing diffusion of pathogens led to a qualitative and quantitative change in their demographic effects. Instead of manifesting themselves in the form of epidemic diseases with a broad age incidence, they were increasingly associated with endemic diseases of childhood leading, Kunitz claims, to lower levels of case fatality and overall mortality. In a subsequent paper the author projected this argument onto a much longer time scale based on an analysis of relationships between adult stature and mortality levels in England from the later Roman occupation to the nineteenth century (Kunitz 1987). Acknowledging the fragility of his data base, Kunitz points to the nonetheless surprising lack of association between stature – taken as an indicator of childhood and adolescent nutritional status – and mortality levels. This discrepancy arises, he suggests, because 'some of the most important infectious causes of death were not made significantly more lethal by the malnourished

---

[30] See Lewontin 1974 for an account of the general difficulties involved in demonstrating the action of genetic selection in natural populations. Among humans a number of attempts have been made to explain inter-population differences in gene frequency – particularly those for blood-groups – in terms of natural selection, but only in the case of malaria and the variant haemoglobins has it been possible to establish an unambiguous relationship. It has been suggested that the 'O' gene – of the ABO system – is associated with a heightened susceptibility to bubonic plague (Harrison et al. 1977: 250–83). If this is so, then the relatively high frequency of 'O' in western Europe suggests that this disease did not exercise a substantial degree of genetic selection, on which basis it would be difficult to make such a claim for any of the other epidemic diseases of medieval or early modern Europe.

state of the population and receded for reasons unrelated to nutrition' (p. 276).

Secular mortality levels were thus long dominated by the degree of exposure to infections such as plague, smallpox or typhus, but with the eighteenth-century mortality decline 'nutritionally sensitive' conditions, such as tuberculosis, pneumonias and diarrhoeas, began to predominate, and diet based variations in resistance became correspondingly important determinants of mortality differentials.[31] The uncertain nature of the data, as the author concedes, renders his conclusions necessarily speculative. But the latter are nonetheless intriguing and, from a theoretical point of view, demonstrate the explanatory power to be derived from a synthesis of both exposure and resistance variables in a unified framework of structural explanation.[32]

Empirical studies

The influence of spatial structure on both the level and the short-run stability of mortality has been explored by a number of writers working in the tradition of empirical parish register demography.

Wrigley and Schofield
The main body of Wrigley and Schofield's text was concerned with the analysis of their data at the national level, but elsewhere they developed an important analysis of the spatial patterning of local mortality fluctuations over their period. In particular they argued that the spatial distribution of these events altered substantially in the decades around 1700. In the earlier period price-related upswings in mortality occurred chiefly in the north-west of England whilst the south-east of England, East Anglia and the southern Midlands were most affected by epidemics of plague and airborne infections. Thus:

before the mid-seventeenth century there would seem to be two Englands: one pastoral and remote, and the other engaged in arable farming but with a

---

[31] As the author points out, the eighteenth-century divergence between the life expectation of the peerage and the general population is particularly significant in this respect and may indicate that once pandemics were reduced by the mid-eighteenth century, the better living conditions, dietary practices, and nutritional status of the peerage began to have a profound impact on their life expectation at all ages (Kunitz 1987: 279).

[32] This employment of both resistance and exposure variables is also found in Mosk and Johansson's interpretation of mortality change in Japan, Italy and England from the later nineteenth century, where the authors attempt an explanation of the social, economic and political factors underlying their changing levels.

high degree of occupational specialisation, reflected in a relatively dense network of small towns. Although access to grain, together with ease of transport and the well developed communications in the south-east made the area much less vulnerable to harvest failures its greater economic integration facilitated the spread of disease. (Schofield 1985a: 91)

Wrigley and Schofield's account of the English case is thus one of a national epidemiological regime divided, or as we shall say *segmented*,[33] into two major functional regions, characterised by varying levels of conduction at the regional level, which stemmed from differences in the geographical relationships between local communities. In the north and west, it is argued, such communities were scattered, with relatively low levels of movement between them. Local epidemiological regimes were thus relatively distinct or, as we shall say, 'strongly bounded'.

Conversely, in the south and east, higher population densities and the closer integration of market networks fostered much higher levels of movement between communities. Local epidemiological regimes thus tended to merge into one another and were correspondingly 'weakly bounded'. From the 1720s, however, this national segmentation apparently disappeared due, Schofield (1985a: 89) argues, to the 'increasing integration of market networks over the seventeenth century and early eighteenth century', and a consequent decline in the bounding of local communities across the old low-conduction region.

Dobson

The configuration of varying epidemiological regimes is pursued further in Mary Dobson's comparative analysis of mortality patterns in the north American colonies and those in south-east England (Dobson 1989a, 1989b). Dobson pointed to the effects of population distribution and mobility, the density of trading networks, and the characteristics of the physical environment, as an explanation for differences both in the absolute level of mortality and in its pattern of short-run instability. Thus in the case of the New England colonies the annual burial series approximate a 'background: crisis' pattern with low and general stable secular levels interrupted by occasional violent upswings.

---

[33] In this instance segmentation is due to regional differentiation, but it may also arise from social, ethnic or other divisions within a population as well as sex-specific differences. The distinction between segmentation and bounding is one of scale, a regional regime will be 'highly segmented' if local communities are strongly bounded and *vice versa*.

This pattern resulted from dispersed settlement and low population densities which reduced the degree of retention in the – strongly bounded – local epidemiological regimes leading to correspondingly low levels of exposure to infection, and thus of mortality. At the same time, however, members of the population had little chance to develop immunities so that the arrival of pathogens across the Atlantic sea lanes brought a heavy toll in epidemic mortality. In southern colonies, by contrast, mortality was high enough to produce a long period of natural decrease, because the low-lying coastal conditions enabled malaria and other old world tropical diseases to become established at an early stage of colonisation. Hence the physical environment conferred a high degree of retention on the regional epidemiological regime, but levels of resistance remained relatively low due to continuing immigration. The burial series were marked by a high frequency of violent disturbances which reflected recurrent malarial outbreaks and prevented the recognition of a 'background' level of mortality in any useful sense.

The south-east of England displayed a third pattern. Here the later seventeenth century was a period in which local communities experienced a high frequency of upswings in mortality. Individually these were of an intermediate scale, but taken together they represented a secular rise in mortality severe enough to lead to demographic stagnation. The impression of stabilisation given by the contemporary national series is thus misleading for, unlike the regionally based bubonic plague outbreaks of the earlier period, local epidemics now usually occurred 'out of phase' with each other, producing a deceptively flat regional aggregate which failed to capture the experience of its component populations. Dobson explains this development in terms of an increase in the density of trading contacts, and thus a reduction in the bounding of local epidemiological regimes, leading in turn to the introduction and diffusion of a variety of 'new' infectious agents.

These findings suggest that the frequency and amplitude of short-run fluctuations can profitably be treated as variables which are analytically independent of each other and can occur in a variety of combinations depending on the characteristics of the epidemiological regime.[34] Dobson's study presents us with three of these, to which

---

[34] In this and the following paragraph a typological approach has been adopted for heuristic reasons, but we should bear in mind that the four combinations or 'types' outlined here refer, in effect, to zones which occupy the extremes of a two dimensional space, and that an infinite number of intermediate combinations can occur. In principle it should be possible to translate this conceptual model into empirical terms

McNeill's (1977) arguments add a fourth. Firstly there is the conjunction of high amplitude with low to intermediate frequencies. Crisis theory implicitly took this combination as the general case, since it yields a relatively unproblematic distinction between 'background' and 'crisis' mortality levels. In New England it arose from the effects of low retention and high bounding, leading to recurrent epidemic crises, but it could also come about through recurrent agricultural failures and the 'subsistence crises' described by Meuvret and Goubert.

The second combination, high frequency and high amplitude, arose in the southern colonies from a combination of high retention with relatively low resistance, although a combination of the latter with low bounding might have similar consequences. Type three, high frequency and intermediate amplitude, arises from a combination of low retention and weak bounding with intermediate levels of resistance, which may be a relatively common condition in 'hinterland' populations as defined by McNeill. Finally we can add McNeill's 'metropolitan' model as a fourth possibility in which both frequency and amplitude take low to intermediate values.

Conclusion: mortality potential and its determinants

Variations in the spatial structure of a population and its economic and social life can thus alter the level of exposure to infection – and thus mortality – to which its members are subject. Nonetheless these variables do not themselves suffice for a general analytical framework. We must also consider changes in the level of resistance to infection, and the possibility of genuinely autonomous changes in the balance between pathogens and hosts. In this concluding section we shall try to construct such a framework, using the intermediate mortality variables introduced in the course of the preceding discussion.

In the first place, we have argued that secular mortality levels reflect the balance between exposure and resistance to infection, each of which is itself determined by two further variables. The level of exposure depends on the number and character of the pathogens present in the environment (a variable we shall term 'pathogenic load'), and on the density of the matrix of pathways through which

by plotting the frequency and amplitude of fluctuations, in any given burial series, on a two dimensional diagram. In practice, however, such an exercise runs up against the difficulty of obtaining an amplitude-independent measure of frequency which does not rely on the use of arbitrary thresholds.

these can move between human hosts and any non-human reservoirs present in the environment. It is important to note that this matrix reflects the structure of the epidemiological regime itself, and its existence is independent of the extent to which its pathways are exploited by the pathogens present in the environment at any given time.

The level of resistance to infection is affected by several variables, amongst which nutritional and immunological status hold pride of place. We can thus express the determination of mortality at time t, in formal terms as:

$$M = f (Cn, Pa, Nu, Im)$$ where Pa is pathogenic load, and Im immunological status

The proximate determinants of nutritional status are the quantity and quality of food intake – or 'diet'[35] – together with the capacity of the gut to absorb nutrients, and the energy demands made by the organism. The latter are themselves both affected by morbidity, and, although immunological status is chiefly a function of prior exposure, the response of the immune system can be impaired by inadequate nutrition (Floud et al. 1990: 225–74; Livi-Bacci 1991).

The elements of our model thus interact, and this interaction extends to the role of the pathogenic load. As Kunitz (1987) points out, the effects of an improvement or deterioration in diet will itself depend on the nature of the pathogens to which the population is exposed. If there is a high level of exposure to infections such as smallpox or bubonic plague, in which nutritional factors play little part, then the effect will be small or even nonexistent. Conversely, in a tuberculosis-ridden population, the effects might be considerable.

Considerations of this kind also apply in the case of conduction. To take a simple example, poor standards of sanitation and water supply place a population at risk of exposure to life-threatening water-borne infections, but the degree to which this risk is realised in practice depends on the presence of, for instance, the cholera vibrio. Likewise, if the scarcity of soap or suitable textiles means that clothes are inadequately washed, or if the cost of clothes themselves induces people to scavenge them from corpses, the structurally determined level of conduction will be correspondingly high, but the extent to which the relevant pathways will be realised as channels of exposure

---

[35] The ultimate determinants of diet are, of course, themselves complex and manifold. An important part is played by real wages, but also by a variety of other factors, such as the marginal propensity to consume food, cultural preferences for foods of varying nutritional quality, and methods of storage and preparation.

to life-threatening infection will depend on the presence of typhus *rickettsiae*.

The structural characteristics which predispose populations to higher or lower levels of exposure and resistance must thus be distinguished from the *realised* levels that arise from the relationship between these and the pathogenic load present at any time. Hence we should write for time t:

$M_t = f (R_t, E_t)$ — where R_t and E_t are currently realised levels of
$R_t = f (Im, Nu, Pa)$ — exposure and resistance
$E_t = f (Cn, Pa)$

The complexities of this system are, however, greatly reduced in the case of secular change. In the first place, levels of morbidity and immunological status are determined within the system, so their effects both disappear[36] leaving diet as the main proximate determinant of changing levels of resistance.

Changes on the exposure side can come about either through those in conduction, or in the pathogenic load. The latter evidently depend on the introduction of new pathogens into the population, and the capacity of the existing ones to perpetuate themselves, whether in biotic reservoirs or the physical environment itself. This, in turn, depends on the ability of the pathogens to exploit those structural features of the epidemiological regime which we have termed its degree of retention.[37]

Introductions can occur in one of two ways. The first is the genuinely 'autonomous' process whereby new viruses, bacteria or other parasites, arise from existing strains by mutation or chromosomal recombination. Alongside this there is the physical introduction of new pathogens due to the movement of people or goods. The likelihood of such introduction is determined by the regime's degree of bounding, a variable which can also affect the level of resistance present in the population if immigrants and indigenes differ in their immunological status.

Change over time thus depends on the action of two sets of factors. Firstly there are the demographic, economic, and other structural

---

[36] Strictly speaking this is only true of immunological status in the absence of vaccination, but the model once formulated can easily be extended to take account of this and other medical interventions.

[37] The degree of retention possesses the same analytical independence of the pathogenic load as does the degree of conduction. Thus the pre-existing 'retentive' properties of south-east England's low-lying coasts and estuaries were only associated with killing infections on a demographically significant scale once vivax malaria had been introduced from continental Europe (Dobson 1989b).

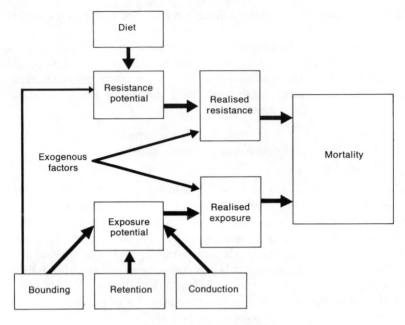

1.3 A structural model of mortality change

determinants which act through the intermediate variables: conduction, retention, bounding and diet. These predispose populations to varying degrees of exposure and resistance to infectious agents, but the extent to which such 'potentials' are translated into 'realised' levels depends on the action of variables that are exogenous to any given regime. These refer to the truly 'autonomous' processes of microbiological change and the characteristics of any 'outside world' populations – their pathogenic load and immunological status – with which the regime is in contact.

We can express the relationships between these variables in the form of a flow diagram, as in figure 1.3, or formally by saying:

$M_t = f (Pa_{t-1}, Mp, e)$ where Mp, Rp and Ep are mortality,
$Mp = f (Rp, Ep)$ resistance and exposure potentials
$Ep = f (Cn, Re, Bo)$ respectively, *e* refers to exogenous
$Rp = f (Di, Bo)$ influences, Re to retention, Bo to bounding
                                  and Di to diet

Hence the mortality level of a population at any time is jointly determined by its structurally determined 'mortality potential',[38] the characteristics of its pathogenic load in the preceding period, and the 'exogeneity operator' e. In subsequent chapters we shall attempt to chart the course of these interactions in the case of eighteenth-century London, but first we must consider some of the social, geographical, economic and other factors which influenced the capital's mortality potential in this period.

---

[38] The concept of mortality potential as used here may appear unfamiliar, but is in fact an extension of the underlying logic of actuarial life table analysis. Just as individuals are placed at a certain mortality risk, measured by life table function $_nq_x$, which may be realised in their death in a given period as a result of factors exogenous to the analysis itself, so a regime's mortality potential predisposes the population as a whole to the risk of experiencing a given level of mortality. The difference between the two instances is that whilst in the first, the outcome variable has only two discrete values, death or survival, in the second it is a continuous variable whose values are the $_nq_x$ experienced by members of the population.

2

Aspects of metropolitan economic and social life

Classical mortality theory saw variations in living standards as the key to differences in the level of mortality. By implication at least, it was nutritionally determined resistance to infection which was the most important proximate determinant of mortality, and the socio-economic component of a demographic regime could, in large measure, be summed up under the heading of diet, its quantity and composition. This orientation was maintained by neoclassical theory with its emphasis on real wages, since the latter were so powerfully determined by movements in food prices. By contrast, recent work in historical epidemiology – which we have tried to summarise in our theory of mortality potential – implies that a much broader range of social, economic and other variables, needs to be taken into account if the dimensions of an epidemiological regime are to be properly understood.

The proximate determinants on the 'exposure side' – conduction, retention and bounding – are affected by a wide variety of factors whose relative importance may vary between populations. Some – such as population density or migration patterns – fall outside the scope of 'living standards' as the term is generally understood, whilst others – such as hygiene, sanitation and housing standards – might usefully be thought of under this heading but are not easily captured in real wage calculations. In this chapter we shall look, in the broadest outlines, at the living conditions of London's population, so as to see how these might have affected the proximate determinants of mortality and the levels which the latter are likely to have assumed over our period. We must begin, however, by considering the growth of London's population and the vital contribution made by immigration.

Migration and the growth of London

London rose to the first rank of European cities in the course of the sixteenth century. Around 1500, the population of what would later be known as 'the metropolis' – comprising the Cities of London and Westminster, together with the Borough of Southwark on the south bank of the river – amounted to some fifty thousand. At this level England's capital was outside the 'top twenty' European cities; around a third the size of Paris or Naples, it was smaller even than such provincial centres as Lyons or Rouen. But by the death of the second Tudor monarch, the population had doubled in size, and when the dynasty ended fifty years later London was a city of around two hundred thousand people, exceeded in size only by Paris and Naples among the cities of Christian Europe.[1]

A further near doubling occurred in the first half of the seventeenth century, but thereafter growth began to slow. The recent estimates of Finlay and Shearer place the total still some little way short of half a million by the year 1700,[2] but this was sufficient, in all probability, to make London the largest city in Europe. The eighteenth century saw another doubling, bringing the population to an estimated 960,000 in 1801, at the time of the first Census.[3] We cannot reconstruct the chronology of this growth with certainty, since there are no contemporary enumerations. We can, however, gain an impression of the likely trend if we follow the practice of contemporaries and use movements in the consumption of basic commodities as an indicator of population trends.

The rising level of coal imports to London is set out in figure 2.1. Their interpretation is complicated by the obvious problem of changing *per capita* consumption, and particularly by the likelihood of secular growth in non-domestic uses, but the overall trend is unlikely to be greatly misleading and follows that suggested by a number of other sources. The century appears to fall into three main sections: an initial period of some three decades, with continuing fairly rapid

[1] These estimates are taken from Mols (1974: 72–3) and Finlay and Shearer (1986: 45). For a comparative database of European urban population estimates see De Vries 1984: appendix 1.

[2] Finlay and Shearer's figure is somewhat below that of Gregory King, who estimated the metropolitan population in 1695 at 527,560. A much higher figure of 674,350 was obtained by Rickman from the Parish Register Abstracts (see Wrigley 1967 and George 1966: 318–20) but its basis is obscure and, in conjunction with his estimate of 676,250 for London's population at mid-century, implies an implausible level of secular stagnation throughout the first half of the century.

[3] Lawton 1978: 331. Corfield (1982: 66) gives the lower estimate of 900,000, although her table I (p. 8), implies a figure of 950,000.

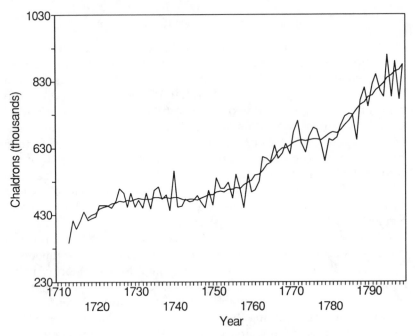

2.1 Coal imports to London: with 11-point moving average

growth, is followed by a period of stagnation which persists into the late 1750s. Renewed growth then sets in, interrupted by a brief set-back around the penultimate decade of the century.

Although London apparently managed a slight increase in its share of England's total population in the course of the eighteenth century its relationship to the country's urban hierarchy changed substantially. In 1700 the capital was still unmistakably a 'primate' city, and it contained the majority of all those Englishmen and women who could be considered town dwellers (Wrigley 1967). Ranking an order of magnitude above the largest provincial cities, such as Norwich or Bristol, it was indeed an enormous head on a very small pair of shoulders, but by 1800 this was no longer true. Urban growth in the preceding decades had created a healthy tier of medium-sized provincial centres,[4] and England's urban population had risen from under six to over sixteen per cent (Finlay and Shearer 1986: 39).

If the pace of expansion was less dramatic than it had been in earlier centuries, London's eighteenth-century growth was nonetheless remarkable given the gloomy demographic context supplied by

[4] See Corfield 1982 and, for a broader European perspective, De Vries 1984.

the Bills of Mortality. Only at the very end of the century did these begin to show a surplus of baptism over burials, and for much of the period the ratio of baptisms to burials (the 'vital index') was below seventy per cent (see below, chapter 3 and *passim*). This ratio had improved substantially in the late seventeenth century, with recorded burials falling as baptisms rose, but shortly after 1700 this decline was reversed, and in the second quarter of the century, as baptisms and recorded burials plateaued, the vital index reached a nadir of little more than fifty per cent.

That population growth continued in the face of such a burial surplus implies, of course, that London was still attracting a large number of immigrants. The importance of this phenomenon has long been recognised, and Wrigley, in a well known calculation, estimated that between 1650 and 1749 the city accounted for the natural increase of a population of some 2.5 million people – equivalent to half the rest of England – and that 'one adult in six had direct experience of London life' (Wrigley 1967: 49). Population movement on such a scale would, he suggested, have fostered the diffusion of new attitudes and values in the country at large, whilst a familiarity with metropolitan conditions 'acted as a powerful solvent of the customs, prejudices and modes of action in traditional rural England' (p. 50).

Furthermore, the burial surplus prevailing in London would have reinforced England's 'low-pressure' vital regime by enabling the countryside to maintain a favourable ratio of births to deaths without having to suffer excessive population growth. The potential repercussions of London's demographic predominance, on the life of the country as a whole, were thus numerous and far reaching, but the scale and extent of the associated migration flows also exercised a profound influence on London's demographic regime itself. Hence to understand the latter we must first examine the former.

Migrant flows

The movement of men and women to London was an integral part of a broader national, and at times international, system of migration and mobility. Studies of this system have tended to concentrate on the century or so before the outbreak of the Civil War. This reflects both the substantive importance of migration in an era of demographic expansion and the relative abundance of documentary sources.[5] By contrast the eighteenth century has been seen as some-

---

[5] See Clark and Souden 1987 for a selection of the most important contributions to the now extensive literature on migration in early modern England.

thing of a 'dark age' where sources are concerned, but what evidence there is suggests that the volume of movement contracted at this time – at any rate where long-range migration is concerned. In this section we shall review some of the available material, looking first at the national matrix and then at the specific question of migration to London.

The national pattern

Migration before the Civil War has been described as an 'almost universal phenomenon' with migrants themselves falling into one of two broad categories. First, there were 'servants, apprentices, would-be spouses and others out to better themselves, travelling fairly limited distances, to a neighbouring town or village, usually within an area defined by notions of a sub-regional "country" ' (Clark 1987a: 215). Alongside such 'betterment' migrants, there were also substantial numbers of 'subsistence' migrants, mainly poor people travelling longer distances under the pressure of immediate economic necessity.

At the national level the geography of subsistence migration was predominantly one of movement from the uplands of the north and west to the south-east, in general, and London in particular. Slack's study of vagrancy records for the first half of the seventeenth century showed that the pastoral 'wood/pasture' districts, with their expanding populations and rural industry, were disproportionately represented among vagrants' places of origin, but that it was, above all, the experience of town life which was 'decisive in the making of a vagrant . . . The further a vagabond had moved, the more likely he was to have come from an urban setting' (1987: 67). It was the towns, and particularly their suburbs and surrounding villages which acted as magnets for subsistence migrants. The making of a 'semi- permanent vagrant', in Slack's words, might thus involve a sequence of moves. 'A short first move to a local town or an area of rural industry could, after an interval of temporary employment in which settlement rights might be acquired, lead to further movement along the roads of England to other towns, often in the direction of London.' (p. 68).

The national pattern of migration was profoundly influenced by the attraction of London in the century of its most rapid growth. The period after the Restoration is poorly documented relative to the one before, but the available evidence suggests a decline in the scale of subsistence migration. Clark's study of court depositions from the decades 1660–1730 revealed that, whilst sixty per cent of deponents claimed to have moved at least once in their lives, only about half of these had moved more than ten miles, and fewer than five per cent over a hundred miles. Townsmen were more mobile than were rural deponents, some eight per cent having moved at least a hundred miles, but there was no evidence of the kind of large-scale, long-range movement which had been seen before the Civil War (Clark 1987b: 223).

In contrast to the earlier period, Clark's urban data showed a tendency for professional men and 'those claiming gentle status' to have moved further than those of a humbler station, together with 'a general bunching of distances travelled, with the great majority of the occupational groups having moved on average between 20 and 35 miles' (p. 225). Clark attributed this reduction both to increased prosperity in the upland regions – as population pressure declined and agricultural output rose – and to the amelioration of urban mortality crises. But beyond these structural factors, he assigned a further role to the attitude of poor law authorities, arguing that

the ruling classes of provincial England launched a pincer attack on the whole problem of long-distance migration, offering incentives – housing, generous relief, work – to those who stayed at home or in a particular area, and ensuring that life was difficult and unpleasant for those who still dared to go tramping the highways of the kingdom. (Clark 1972b: 242)

In spite of these developments, however, migration was never wholly restricted to the short-distance movement of the upwardly mobile or the fashionable journeyings of the elite. In the first place, long-range movement persisted among such marginalised groups as gypsies and certain itinerant trades, whilst the migration of Irish and Scots became increasingly important throughout the eighteenth century and beyond. Similarly, discharged servicemen provided a relatively new category of subsistence migrants who appeared in growing numbers at intervals throughout our period.

The later seventeenth century also witnessed a substantial volume of transatlantic migration. This is estimated to have taken between 100,000 and 150,000 people to the American colonies at this time, many of them doubtless impelled by motives similar to those which had once driven subsistence migrants onto the roads of England.[6] Seasonal migration – apparently of little importance in the earlier period – also seems to have grown up as a replacement for the older pattern of vagrancy, and this form of movement – unlike transatlantic emigration which had passed its peak by 1700 – increased in

---

[6] Clark 1987a: 242–3. See Souden 1978 and Wareing 1981 for further discussion of this point.

importance throughout the following century (Clark 1987b: 242; George 1966: 145–6).

Migration to London

Given the importance of the capital as a node in the national network of subsistence migration, it is unfortunate that the surviving documentary evidence on London migration comes largely from the records of the City Companies and refers to apprentices and freemen – the 'betterment' migrants *par excellence.*[7] Wareing's (1980) review of such material from a number of companies reveals a general contraction in London's migration field between the sixteenth and eighteenth centuries. This is especially marked in the period after the Civil War, but the average distance travelled had already fallen, from around 200 kilometres in the 1550s, to 160 in the first half of the seventeenth century.

This contraction was linked to a sharp fall in the number of migrants coming to London from the northern counties, and a corresponding rise in the proportions from the Midlands and home counties. The proportion of apprentices born in London itself rose substantially – from fewer than one in seven in the late fifteenth century to more than half in the mid eighteenth – but the capital still retained a substantial attraction, and 'apprentices were coming to the capital from every county in England and Wales, the Channel Islands and the Isles of Man and Wight in all periods' (Wareing 1980: 242).

In order to document a wider range of migrants, Wareing employed records of indentured servants bound for the American colonies, from 1683 to the outbreak of the Revolutionary War (Wareing 1981). This migration, he argued, constituted a two stage process, and the first stage – the future servant's initial move to London – was more representative of such movements in general than were those of apprentices. The indenture records suggest that London's migration field was wider than the apprenticeship material would lead us to believe. Wareing attributed this, in part, to the larger 'subsistence' element in servants' migration, but their field also contracted. The proportion of servants coming to London from distances over 170 kilometres fell, from 43.3, to 31.9 per cent over the period as a whole, with the mean distance travelled falling from 166 to 145 kilometres.

In general the servants' migration field seemed to fall into two parts: a 'high sending' zone which accounted for three-quarters of the migrant origins and extended 200 kilometres from the capital, and

---

[7] See for instance Kitch 1986, Smith 1971–3, Wareing 1980.

a 'lower sending' zone beyond this. Even in the later eighteenth century, however, the migration field for servants was still more extensive than the apprentices' field had been in the early seventeenth. The former also differed in its disproportionately large number of urban places of origin. This disproportion suggested 'either a lack of economic opportunity in the major English provincial towns or, more probably, an associated inability of urban economies to absorb an influx of migrants from the rural hinterlands' (Wareing 1981: 371).

Migrants in the City

The structure of migrant flows and the distribution of places of origin are harder to study in our period than they are in preceding decades, but it is possible to obtain some quantitative – and tolerably reliable – information. Questions such as the absolute volume of migration to the capital, or the size and structure of London's immigrant population at any time, are much less tractable – nor are we yet in a position to say much about the important topics of return migration and the emigration of native born Londoners – but scraps of quantitative evidence, together with the opinions of contemporaries, support the expectation that immigrants formed a large proportion of London's population.

From 1774–81 Bland recorded the place of birth of 3,236 married people attending the Westminster General Dispensary obtaining the results given in table 2.1. Overall, the proportion of immigrants is very close to the 75 per cent which Burrington, in 1757, had given as

Table 2.1. *Birthplaces of patients at Westminster General Dispensary 1774–81*

	Percentages (N = 32,326)		
Birthplace	Male	Female	All
London	20.3	30.6	25.5
Elsewhere in England and Wales	58.9	56.6	57.7
Scotland	8.3	4.6	6.5
Ireland	10.0	7.4	8.7
Other	2.5	0.8	1.6
All	100.0	100.0	100.0

Source: George 1966, p. 118

the fraction of London's adult population born elsewhere (George 1966: 118), with twenty per cent of the men and thirteen per cent of the women coming from outside England and Wales. The fact that the proportion of London-born wives exceeded that of their husbands suggests that married people were unrepresentative in this respect. The sex ratio of London burials is generally much below 1.05, imply- ing, a considerable excess of females in net immigration – an excess which can, presumably, be attributed to the large numbers of single women employed in London's labour force – particularly in domestic service. Bland's data tell us nothing about the age-distribution of the immigrant population, but studies of 'sending' districts confirm that adolescents and young adults featured disproportionately in immigrant flows (see Schofield 1970).[8]

The social characteristics, geographical distribution and modes of integration of immigrants into urban society are poorly documented. In the earlier period the institution of apprenticeship is thought to have played a central role in recruiting young immigrants, providing them with food, employment and accommodation, and – in principle at least – setting them on the way to full juridical membership of urban society. Apprenticeship's importance had declined consider- ably by 1700 and, according to a recent estimate, apprentices accoun- ted for only five per cent of the metropolitan population at this date compared with fifteen per cent a century earlier (Finlay 1981: 66–7).

The quantitative 'decline of apprenticeship' continued into the fol- lowing century and was, as we have seen, accompanied by a marked reduction in the proportions of immigrant apprentices. Eighteenth- century apprentices were, moreover, less likely to be accommodated in their masters' homes than were their forebears (Clark 1987b: 270). The 'new world of the eighteenth-century urban migrant' was thus one in which 'one gets only a sketchy idea of the spatial distribution and employment patterns of newcomers within the community: quantitative analysis is virtually impossible' (p. 268). The informal institutions of neighbourhood, kinship and community probably served to integrate many immigrants into the metropolitan society, but these processes are largely hidden from our view.

Informal institutions were probably of particular importance for members of London's ethnic communities. The Irish – numbering over 23,000 (Clark, 1987b: 274) by the 1780s – were the largest of these and were concentrated particularly in the eastern riverside parishes

---

[8] Some demographic evidence concerning the age structure of London's population – and that of migrants in particular – will be considered in chapter 5.

and St Giles. The East End was also the centre of London's Jewish community whom Colhoun estimated at between 15,000 and 20,000, their numbers having increased from an estimated national total of around 5,000 at the middle of the eighteenth century (George 1966: 134). As the two major immigrant communities the Jews and Irish had thus supplanted the Huguenots, large numbers of whom had settled in the East End, around Spitalfields and Bethnal Green, in the later seventeenth century – as had a smaller, and apparently better off, community in Soho. Over time, however, the cohesion of the Huguenot community was eroded, and rapid assimilation into the host population brought a sharp drop in church membership in the course of the eighteenth century (Clark 1987b: 275).

These ethnically distinct groups are easier to locate geographically than is London's immigrant population at large, but it is likely that more recent, and poorer, immigrants were concentrated in the band of extra-mural parishes which ran from the riverside east of the Tower westwards to St Giles-in-the-Fields, and in Southwark and the adjoining parishes south of the river. In these districts proliferated the lodging houses that accommodated a growing proportion of London's immigrants.

Lodging houses first appear as the subject of official concern at the time of the plague scare of the early 1720s, when the Middlesex magistrates lamented:

a common practice in the extreme parts of the town, to receive into their houses persons unknown, without distinction of sex or age, on their paying one penny or more per night for lying in such houses without beds or covering, and . . . it is frequent in such houses for fifteen or twenty or more to lie in a small room. (Quoted in George 1966: 97)

At a penny, or twopence, a night, lodging house accommodation was cheap compared with the two to three shillings, or more, charged for a furnished room in one of the poorer districts. Such properties seem to have grown in number during the central decades of the century, exploiting the substantial volume of derelict and rundown houses in these districts. To understand their proliferation it is thus necessary to examine the processes through which the physical expansion of the built-up area was accomplished.

The building of London

The growth of London's population over our period was matched by an enormous physical expansion of the built-up area (see map 2.1). At the Restoration a ribbon of development along the north bank of the

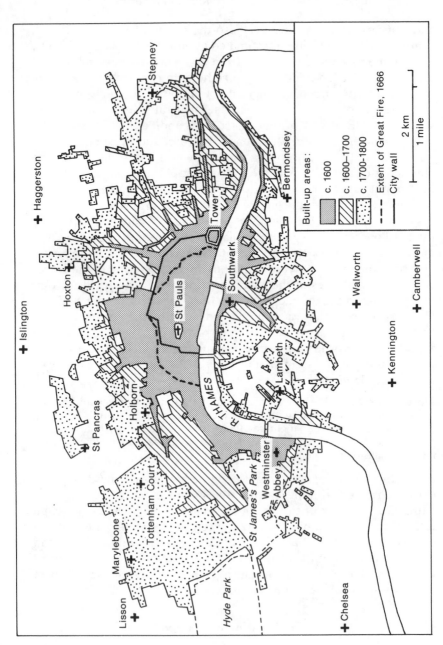

2.1 The growth of London 1600–1800

Built-up areas:

- c. 1600
- c. 1600–1700
- c. 1700–1800

- - - Extent of Great Fire, 1666
——— City wall

2 km
1 mile

Stepney

Haggerston

Bermondsey

Tower

Southwark

Islington

Hoxton

St Pauls

Walworth

Camberwell

St Pancras

Holborn

R. THAMES

Lambeth

Kennington

Marylebone

Tottenham Court

Westminster
Abbey

St James's Park

Lisson

Hyde Park

Chelsea

Thames linked the recognisably distinct metropolitan nuclei of London and Westminster, and a single bridge connected the former to its outlying dependency of Southwark across the river. By the 1830s the metropolis formed a contiguous mass of housing from Limehouse to Chelsea, on the northern side of the Thames, linked by half a dozen bridges to a matching southern expanse stretching to Camberwell and Peckham. At the same time the social geography of the capital had undergone a qualitative transformation.

In the late seventeenth century this geography still retained some classically 'pre-industrial' features, with high status housing in the central district, in this case the old City within the walls, and poorer quarters concentrated around the suburban periphery and the water-front.[9] Despite this overall differentiation the degree of residential segregation was much lower than it later became. Whilst whole districts might be ranked in terms of social and economic status, they remained internally heterogeneous deriving their position from relative differences in the mix of component 'micro-areas' rather than a uniform social character common to the district as a whole. In particular there was still, for much of the eighteenth century, no distinct 'working-class quarter', although the capital retained its 'dangerous districts'. These were situated in a peripheral belt from the East End to St Giles and Drury Lane in the west, and in Southwark around the Mint (George 1966: 91–4; Rudé 1971: 86–7).

A new scale of differentiation had, however, begun to emerge in the later seventeenth century with the development of Covent Garden, St James's and Bloomsbury (Olsen 1976: 18–19). Successive Georgian building booms fostered a growing cleavage between the 'aristocratic' London of relatively self- contained districts to the west and north-west,[10] and a proletarian – or lumpenproletarian – London in the east. As Rudé (1971: 10) remarked, 'a growing gulf was drawn between the eastern and western districts of London. Where, earlier, citizens had sought their recreations and country retreats almost indiscriminately either east or west, the east was now becoming more

---

[9] Finlay 1981: 70–82; Glass 1969; Jones 1986; Power 1978, 1986.
[10] Again, it should be stressed that this 'aristocratic' character reflected the relative proportions of different strata among the inhabitants, rather than social exclusivity in any literal sense. As Olsen remarks:

> By later standards the degree of social and functional differentiation was at best moderate. Even the new districts of the eighteenth century had within them wide variations in population, with the wealthy occupying the squares and the principal streets, the middle classes the adjacent smaller streets, and the poor the back courts and mews: one could speak of fashionable or unfashionable streets, but not fashionable or unfashionable neighbourhoods. (Olsen 1976: 18)

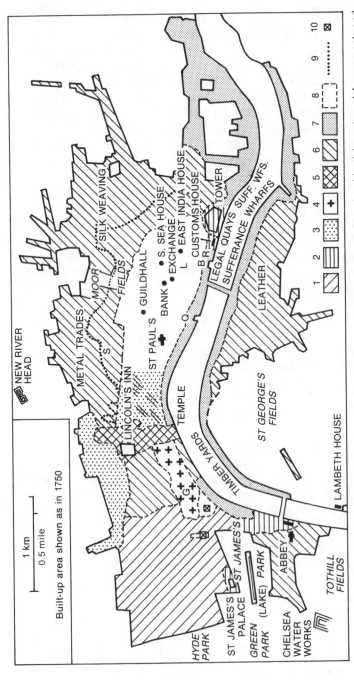

Key: 1 Aristocratic residential quarter 2 Government offices, etc. 3 Middle class and professional residential quarter 4 Amusements and vice area 5 Legal quarter 6 Industrial areas and artisans' dwellings 7 Wharfs, warehouses, waterside trades, including labourers' dwellings, seamen's taverns, etc. 8 'The City' – commerce and finance 9 Boundary of the City Liberties 10 West End shopping and hotel centres round Haymarket and Charing Cross *Principal Markets:* S Smithfield (meat, hay) L Leadenhall (meat, provisions, leather) G Covent Garden Q Queenhithe (corn, meal, malt) B Billingsgate R Roomland (coal). The boundaries shown are only approximate.

2.2 The occupations of London in the eighteenth century

and more the preserve of the industrious poor and the west that of the fashionable and rich.'

This gulf, which reflected both physical geography and the historical accidents of land tenure, was fostered by an accompanying growth in the areal separation of residential and economic functions. The co-residence of employer and work force became less common – and the former was less likely to 'live above the shop' – but the trend's most striking manifestation was an exodus of population from the intramural parishes and the associated conversion of private residences to warehousing and other commercial uses. This exodus embraced both the westward migration of the better off and the movement of poorer craftsmen away from the guild restrictions of the City to the freer environment of the liberties and extra-mural parishes (Beier, 1986; Rudé 1971: 9).

As a result, by the middle of the eighteenth century, the basic east-west division of London was compounded by a large-scale process of differentiation in the central and eastern districts. Here Spate distinguished three industrial sectors (see map 2.2):

very different not only from the nucleus but from one another. Clerkenwell, sprawling up the eastern slopes of the Fleet valley, formed, together with Shoreditch and Bishopsgate, a district of innumerable twisting lanes and alleys, the homes of artisans of many trades but especially those employed – or employing themselves – in the making of clocks and jewelry. To the northeast Spitalfields extended its monotonously regular streets of mean cottages, inhabited by a more homogeneous industrial population of weavers. Finally in the waterside parishes there was the labyrinth of rope-walks, breweries, small foundries, anchor forges . . . Here too were the irregularly built homes and taverns for artisans, sailors, coal-heavers and other waterside workers.

(Spate 1936: 534)

A chronology

The materials for a quantitative history of this process are relatively meagre. In the absence of censuses of production, or of the housing stock available at any time, we must fall back on proxy indicators such as the output of construction materials. These become available at various points in the eighteenth century, as excise duties were extended to materials such as brick, glass, timber and wallpaper. The relevant series have been collected in a convenient form by Ashton (1959), but, being compiled on a national basis, they do not allow us to identify the specific demands of the London market. Some data on the latter can be obtained from the series constructed by Sheppard and colleagues using the records of the Middlesex Land Registry

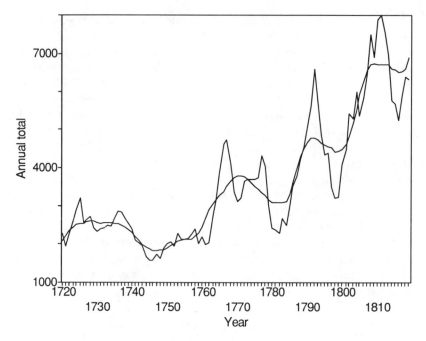

2.2 Deeds registered in Middlesex Land Registry

(Sheppard et al. 1979). Although these document a variety of transactions involving landed property, their annual totals are likely to form
a reasonably accurate indicator of trends in the level of building
activity and the property market generally (see figure 2.2).

The shortcomings of the quantitative material must be set against
the rich literature on the architectural history of the period, and in
particular the magisterial *Georgian London* of Sir John Summerson on
whose narrative the following chronology is largely based. The
nature of Summerson's interest, and of his sources, were such that
for the most part his is necessarily a history of the building of
aristocratic London, with much less attention given to the 'other
Londons' in the south and east. It seems likely, however, that the
tempo of expansion was similar in the 'two Londons' and that Summerson's account thus provides an acceptable chronology for the
capital as a whole.

Summerson saw the physical expansion of London over our period
as a series of waves spaced at roughly fifty year intervals and associated with the transition from war to peace, or in the case of the first

episode with the re-establishment of monarchy after the republican interregnum. Each wave had a character of its own:

a different social character, representing a different stratum of the national wealth and bringing into prominence a different kind of taste. Thus Restoration building actively represented the consolidation of aristocrats in the west end, and, particularly after the Fire, the westward trek of luxury trades; taste was uncertain and retained a vernacular roughness. The next wave had its origins towards the end of Marlborough's wars and broke after the treaty of Utrecht. This time, the central figure was the country lord setting up a town house and calling about him a genteel population of professional men. Taste was strictly Palladian. The third great wave of building began, likewise, in the middle of a war – this time the Seven Years War. It was slow in breaking, and the peak came ten to fifteen years later. The demand in this instance came from two quarters – from the country gentleman getting a foothold in town and from the citizen migrating to the west end. Taste was less assertive, less a matter of class *décor*, and advanced greatly in refinement and maturity. Finally there came the first Napoleonic building boom, the contributory factors to which may be expressed as the sum of those which affected the first two periods with the addition of an enormous impetus from the rapidly increasing shopkeeper, artisan, and labouring classes . . . (Summerson 1978: 24–5)

The data from the Land Registry have nothing to say on questions of sociology or aesthetics, but the scale of both the post-war booms and the lengthy stagnation following the collapse of the 1720s emerge clearly from the annual totals. Sheppard's series also reveals two further episodes of rapid growth, one beginning in the later 1780s and the other around the time of the Treaty of Amiens, and each following a war time trough. We shall now examine these waves a little more closely.

The later seventeenth century
The first 'building boom' of our period followed shortly on the Restoration and was further stimulated by the fire of 1666.[11] Building centred on the development of the Earl of Southampton's Bloomsbury estate and the holdings of the Jermyn family in St James's Fields bordering Piccadilly. New squares also appeared in Soho and Gray's Inn Fields, whilst both Covent Garden and Lincoln's Inn were further developed, and the construction of the Seven Dials 'made a pin point nucleus for yet more building' linking the parishes of St Martin's and St Giles (Summerson 1978: 20). Further south, new private housing replaced the aristocratic hôtels along the Strand, and

---

[11] See Brett-James 1935 and Reddaway 1940 for details of this process.

when the wave of activity spent itself in the closing years of the
century, the two Cities of London and Westminster had merged into
a single conurbation.

This first stage in the evolution of 'Georgian' London saw the
emergence of what would remain the distinctive feature of development throughout the following century. This was the characteristic
partnership between the aristocratic landowner, whose leading
presence was established by the construction of 'his own house in his
square' (Summerson 1978: 42), and the array of speculative middle-
men who arranged, and sometimes executed, the work itself. The
post-Restoration boom also saw the appearance, in both Bloomsbury
and St James's, of a recurrent physical pattern. This was the 'principle
of a complete unit of development, comprising square, secondary
streets, market, and, perhaps church' (Summerson 1978: 42).

The early eighteenth century

The first years of the eighteenth century witnessed a short-lived
revival in building activity, but timber imports had reached their
nadir by the years 1710–11, and the first truly 'Georgian' boom
awaited peace with France in 1713, and the Hanoverian Succession
the following year. This time development centred on four north-
western estates stretching from the present Regent Street to the edge
of Hyde Park. Hanover Square, developed in the years 1717–19 and
embodying, both in name and in its Germanic style (Summerson
1978: 99), a profession of Whig loyalty to the new dynasty, was soon
inhabited by many of the latter's staunchest partisans. The nearby
Burlington Estate to the south was developed in the early years of the
following decade, and at the same time work was begun on the
Grosvenor estate, in the angle between Oxford Street and Park Lane.
This development too was planned as a unit, centred around
Grosvenor Square, but was not completed until the middle of the
century.

North of Oxford Street the Harley–Cavendish estate was projected
in 1717 and backed by members of the former administration as a
Tory riposte to the Whigs of Hanover Square. At its core work on
Cavendish Square itself began in the early 1720s but was not finally
completed for another fifty years. The relative failure of the project
may have been due to the political marginalisation of the Tories in
this period or more generally, in Summerson's words, to the fact that
'members of the aristocracy were not interested in their town houses
to anything like the extent they were in their country dwellings'
(1978: 111).

The boom also saw housing develop around Charterhouse to the north of London and Ratcliffe Highway to the east. It survived the Bubble crisis with only a temporary setback, but by the late 1720s there were clear signs of a slow down. A wave of bankruptcies in 1727–8 was followed by a sharp fall in timber imports, and the 1728 figure was not to be equalled until the close of the Seven Years War. The import statistics and the land registry data both suggest that the crisis of 1728 led to over three decades of stagnation, troughing in the 1740s, and only temporarily interrupted by the upturns of 1734–8 and 1750–4.

The limited activity witnessed in these decades is unlikely to have had much effect on the overall size of the housing stock. For Summerson the 1730s was a decade 'of consolidation and gradual rebuilding in central areas'. Expansion had 'slowed down almost to a standstill' (1978: 111), and the upturn of the mid 1730s was attributable to rebuilding in the intramural parishes, particularly the conversion of private housing to warehouses (Ashton 1959: 95). In 1739 it was estimated that at least 1,500 houses stood empty in St Martin's and adjacent parishes (Summerson 1978: 111–2), but stagnation persisted through the late 1750s despite the development of an evident housing shortage such that, 'we find a nobleman of 1754 complaining that "houses are so difficult to get, and there are so many purchasers, that I am under a necessity of taking the first opportunity"' (p. 112).

The later eighteenth century
The era of stagnation in house building came to a spectacular end following the Peace of Paris in 1763. In the following ten years timber imports ran at more than twice the level of the 1740s, and levels of activity in the land registry rapidly surpassed those of the 1720s. A financial crisis in 1772 produced a substantial crop of bankruptcies in construction, but the onset of severe depression was delayed until the outbreak of the American war. The accumulation of wartime debt delayed the post-war recovery until the late 1780s leading, Ashton (1959: 101) argues, to 'acute congestion' in the country at a time of renewed population growth. By 1788, however, recovery was evidently well under way, and high levels of activity persisted until this last wave of eighteenth-century growth was abruptly terminated by the outbreak of war with revolutionary France.

The bulk of demand for new housing in this period may have been supplied by town-struck country gentlemen and westbound citizens, but as before, it was the aristocratic proprietors who provided most of the land. The first phase began with the development of the Portman

estate on the eve of the Peace of Paris and reached its climax with the
building of Portland Place and surrounding streets in 1774, to bring
the built-up area to the edge of Marylebone Fields. Two years later
agreements were signed for the development of the Bedford estate in
Bloomsbury, and work continued here into the recession years of the
1790s, as it did on the adjoining Foundling Hospital and Skinners'
Company estates and the Portman estate to the west. In the south the
1780s and 1790s saw housing spread from Southwark into St George's
Fields along the new roads which linked Blackfriars and Westminster
Bridges (opened in 1748 and 1769 respectively), and London Bridge,
with Walworth and Lambeth at St George's Circus.

The nineteenth century
Sheppard's data imply that the wartime recession troughed at the end
of the century, with brick output reaching its lowest point in 1799.
According to Summerson the period after the resumption of war with
France was one of continuing stagnation during which 'for six or
eight years, the picture scarcely moves. Prices are high; invasion
threatens. Bankrupt builders desert the brick carcasses too hopefully
begun. Depression reigns . . .' (Sheppard et al. 1979: 22). He acknowledged, however, that dock building after 1801 had stimulated the
spread of housing eastwards into Essex, and the Sheppard series rises
steadily after 1800 to reach a new peak at the end of the decade. But a
trade crisis in 1810 led to a collapse in activity (Summerson 1978: 179)
which was not reversed until the post-war boom.
    Already in 1811 the reversion to the Crown of the Marylebone
estate at a time of improving credit had allowed the inception of a
great plan of 'improvement' under John Nash. A plan

which embraced the Regent's Park layout in the north, St James's Park in the
south, the Regent Street artery connecting the two, the formation of Trafalgar
Square and the reconstruction of the West End of the Strand, and the Suffolk
Street area; as well as the cutting of the Regent's Canal; with its branch and
basin to serve Regent's Park . . . which gave a 'spine' to London's inchoate
West End and had a far-reaching effect on subsequent northward and south-
ward expansion. (Summerson 1978: 177)

Constructed for the most part in the 1820s, the development
stretched from the Park Villages and the new working class housing
on the Marylebone Estate to the east, southwards along the 'Royal
Mile' to St James's Park and the newly reconstructed Buckingham
Palace, where its proximity stimulated Cubitt's development of Bel-
gravia and Pimlico.
    In the north building resumed in Bloomsbury towards the New

Road, where parts of Euston Square and Fitzroy Square were already standing. The development of the Bishop of London's Paddington Estate pushed the boundaries of the conurbation beyond the Edgware Road in the west, whilst a little to the north-east the Eyre Estate in St John's Wood 'was the first part of London, and indeed of any other town, to abandon the terrace house for the semi-detached villa – a revolution of striking significance and far-reaching effect' (Summerson 1978: 176).

In the east the pattern of development was more fluid. From the Gray's Inn Road a series of estates stretched as far as that of St Bartholomew's Hospital around King Square, but from there:

> the map becomes inextricably confused in small and tentative developments, the back-wash of the great westward drive ... In the west the speculator played for big stakes, and thither went capital and the planner's skill. In the east the rewards were unimposing. Nobody thought of planning the great manors of Hackney and Stepney when the East End began to creep and seep towards them. All comers were served with their cuts from those two great territorial joints. The resulting jig-saw is a monument to the economic assiduity of the little man. (Summerson 1978: 197)

In the south development continued along the roads radiating from St George's Circus, further stimulated by the construction of Vauxhall, Waterloo and Southwark Bridges, and 'all the wedges were loosely filled with small developments of the same sort, mostly rather poor architecturally' (Summerson 1978: 283). By 1836 the ' "middle distance" suburbs were bounded by Peckham, Camberwell, Dulwich, Brixton, Clapham, and, possibly South Lambeth' (Dyos 1954: 77).

The building industry: structure and finance

The peculiar character of London's physical growth over this period is familiar to historians. Piecemeal in space and irregular in time, metropolitan expansion was driven neither by a single political will, nor the systematic investment of large-scale mercantile or industrial wealth. Rather it depended on a partnership between landowners, themselves generally unwilling – and sometimes unable – to provide other capital, and – frequently underfunded – speculative builders who gambled on their ability to forecast waves of demand and match them against movements in the price and availability of both credit and raw materials.[12]

[12] For a general discussion of housing and construction in London during this period see George 1966: 73–115; Summerson 1978: 65–83; Ashton 1959: 84–105; on which this and the ensuing paragraphs are chiefly based.

The tempo and quality of construction in the capital reflected both the character of this partnership and the chronically unstable economic – and, more particularly, financial – environment within which it operated for most of the period. The effect of this instability, and some of its determinants, will be considered in a subsequent section, but at this point we must look at the structure of the partnership itself, and the constraints to which its members were subject, to see just why levels of activity were so sensitive to external shocks.

The basis of the partnership, as far as the landowner was concerned, was the 'building lease' granted to a master-builder, either directly or through the intermediary of a 'land-jobber', and under which the latter agreed to build, at his own expense, a number of houses of a specified character which would revert to the leasor when the lease fell in. This arrangement enabled the landowner to obtain profits from his estate, whilst retaining the legal title and without the need to raise capital either by selling, or encumbering, lands elsewhere. Given the social and political significance of landed property to contemporaries, these were important advantages, but they were crucial where, as was so often the case, the existence of an entail meant that land could not be alienated without considerable difficulty.

For the builders the arrangement dramatically reduced the scale of early cash outlays, and these could be cut still more by the granting of 'peppercorn' rents in the early years of the lease. The majority of master-builders were themselves working tradesmen, usually bricklayers or carpenters (Summerson 1978: 76), who sometimes undertook a substantial house for a wealthy customer but were more often to be found in the speculative market. As Ashton pointed out, building entrepreneurs in general were unusually dependent on others for their working capital (Ashton 1959: 85), but the speculators were remarkable in their ability to reduce cash requirements to a very low level.

Raw materials could generally be obtained on credit, but the master-builder still required the expertise of others to carry out the work itself. The solution to this problem was the development of networks of reciprocal sub-contracting between tradesmen which 'eliminated any considerable need for cash payment. It was, in effect, a remarkably effective system of barter' (Summerson 1978: 77). Unavoidable outlays might be met by mortgaging the building in the course of construction (Ashton 1959: 85), but ideally the house would be sold as a half-built brick shell and finished at the customer's own expense before the expiry of the peppercorn period. In this way landowners might obtain substantial incomes from their estates without breaking them up, and working tradesmen could speculate without having to accumulate prior capital. The system was capable of producing large numbers of houses in a short time, but its inherent dangers were well recognised by contemporaries. It encouraged very low standards of workmanship and was very vulnerable to changes in the economic climate.

Fluctuations in building activity are, in Ashton's words, 'to be explained . . . by changes in expectations of profit and in the resources made available to those who directed production' (1959: 84). The first of these factors remains obscure, but it is clear that violent fluctuations occurred in the availability of both raw materials and finance. At the opening of our period England was already heavily dependent on Baltic timber for both houses and ships, and the disruption of imports was an ever-present danger. Short-term interruptions, such as those caused by bad weather, might be met from stocks, but the prolonged wartime interdiction of shipping lanes could lead to serious shortages and a subsequent decline in the level of activity (Ashton 1959: 85).

Whilst the problem of timber supplies had broadly historical and strategic causes, that of finance reflected the nature of the building trade itself. The heavy dependence on credit, and the meagre working capital employed, meant that changes in the price or availability of the former could have very serious consequences. In Summerson's words:

It was reckoned that a man needed £100 capital to set himself up as a master-builder, but in fact any clown of a bricklayer with a guinea or two in his pocket could plunge into the speculative business. Many did, with the result that bricklayers and carpenters stand high in the bankruptcy lists of the eighteenth century. (Summerson 1978: 78)

The waves of bankruptcy which accompanied the recurrent tightening of credit in the eighteenth century explain much of the construction sector's volatility and left their mark in the rows of abandoned half-built houses so familiar to contemporaries. If we are to understand the context and implications of this phenomenon it is necessary to say something about the general structure of economic life in London at this time.

Production and consumption

The centrality of the capital in the nation's economic, social and political life is a familiar theme in the historiography of early modern

England.[13] London's demographic primacy was bound up with its role as the country's administrative and judicial centre, and as its principal port, whilst the pull of the London market promoted both areal and functional specialisation and stimulated the development of transport and communications. This stimulus was reinforced by the capital's continuing growth after 1650, but its role in the national economy was not confined to consumption. As recent accounts have reminded us (Beier 1986; Earle 1989a), London was also Europe's largest manufacturing centre and, in this respect, its importance relative to the rest of England was at a peak in the early eighteenth century.

Production

The Port of London in the early eighteenth century accounted for nearly sixty per cent of the total tonnage of English shipping and three-quarters of its foreign trade. The expansion of other centres had reduced the latter proportion to sixty-five per cent by 1792, but the absolute volume of London shipping involved in foreign trade quadrupled in the course of the century. At the same time the city's entrepôt functions fostered its rise as a financial centre, with the growth of banking and insurance, and by 1810 the value of insured risks engaged in foreign trade had increased to £465 million, from a base of only £2.3 million in 1720 (Rudé 1971: 32).

Data on the composition of the London labour force are hard to come by, but recent estimates put the proportion employed in manufacturing at between forty and sixty per cent, as many as half of them being found in the clothing and textiles sectors (Beier 1986: 150; Earle 1989a: 18–34). Earle suggests that building should be placed next in importance, followed jointly by leather and metalwork which each employed some 10,000 people. Woodworking, coachmaking, hatmaking, baking, and shipbuilding and its associated trades also accounted for several thousand people each. Apart from these, domestic service, catering, carriage, and the sale of drink may each have accounted for 30,000 to 40,000. The importance of domestic service as an employment for unmarried women emerges from a sample of London deponents from the years 1695 to 1725. Three-fifths of employed spinsters gave domestic service as their employment,

---

[13] London's role in the growth and integration of the national economy was stressed by Fisher (1936, 1948, 1971), whilst the argument was broadened, and applied to a later period, by Wrigley (1967). For critical evaluations see Daunton 1978 and Chartres 1986.

compared with some five per cent of married women and ten per cent of widows, of whom a further seventeen and ten per cent respectively were working as domestic cleaners or laundresses (Earle 1989b).

London's importance as a manufacturing centre also declined in the course of the eighteenth and early nineteenth centuries, but in this case relative decline reflected an absolute reduction in levels of activity and a 'flight' of production to the provinces (Rudé 1971: 28–9; George 1966: 195). The reasons for this were complex and included both the avoidance of guild restrictions and the search for a wider range of cost advantages. Lower wage costs were an element of the latter, but so too were the high costs of physical space in London and, increasingly, of transporting fuel for energy-intensive processes. The latter grew in importance with the development of factory production, but the exodus of textile manufactures was already under way before the final quarter of the eighteenth century.

Thus, in the case of framework knitting, London's 2,500 frames represented over a third of the national total in 1727, but by 1750 the number had fallen to 1,000. Thirty years later of England's 20,000 frames only 200 remained in the capital (Rudé 1971: 28). The precise chronology of this movement is, however, difficult to establish and varied greatly between sectors. Certainly, it would be wrong to overstate the 'de- industrialisation' of eighteenth century London, for the capital retained a substantial manufacturing sector into the first quarter of the nineteenth century (Sheppard 1971: 158–201; Stedman Jones 1976: 19–32).

Thereafter the movement apparently accelerated, and by mid-century London's occupational structure had become very different from that postulated by Earle (1989a), with textiles and clothing now accounting for barely a tenth of the employed male labour force (Sheppard 1971, appendix). In spite of this the organisation of production retained some distinctly 'pre-industrial' characteristics throughout our period. This was particularly true in respect of its scale. Small-scale production seems to have remained the rule in London late into the nineteenth century: three-quarters of all employers who made returns to the 1851 Census had five workers or less, and fewer than two per cent employed more than fifty (Stedman Jones 1976: 374).[14]

---

[14] There are no data of this kind for the eighteenth century, but the figures can be compared with those for Spitalfield weavers a hundred years earlier. In 1745, a sample of 133 masters each pledged the militia service of an average of 23 journeymen, but 6 pledged over 60, and 2 more than 100, each (Rudé 1971: 25).

Consumption

The importance of London as a centre of demand for both luxury and subsistence goods and services was forcefully demonstrated by Professor Fisher in the 1930s and has since become a theme of early modern English economic history. The size and scope of the London market exercised a powerful influence on much of lowland England, and further afield as early as the sixteenth century when 'corn growers of Cambridgeshire, south-east Essex and north-east Kent, the dairy farmers of Suffolk, the graziers of the south Midlands, all looked to the London market as the hub of their economic universe' (Fisher 1935: 57).

These arguments have primarily concerned themselves with the scale of London's aggregate demand or with the structure of consumption among the elite and the 'middling sort' (Earle 1989a: 269–301; McKendrick et al. 1983). Much, by contrast, remains to be discovered about average living standards and about consumption patterns among the population at large. In this section we can thus do no more than outline the current understanding of the former topics, and provide a brief discussion of those aspects of the latter that seem most relevant to the problem of demographic change.

The standard of living

Early modern living standards are most commonly measured by the construction of real wage series. These have the advantage of being defined in relatively unambiguous terms, and a number of relevant series are available for London. Nonetheless they present several problems of interpretation. The main sources of money wage data are to be found in the building sector, and, although only a small proportion of London's labour force was to be found in this sector, it is thought that the wages of labourers and artisans in building were comparable to those at similar skill levels in other sectors.[15]

Money wages were higher in London than elsewhere in eighteenth-century England. It is generally assumed that the same was true of real wages, although the cost of living differential is unknown, and accommodation, in particular, appears to have been

---

[15] It is unlikely that building workers, in the eighteenth century, accounted for more than the ten per cent or so of London's adult labour force which they constituted in the Victorian censuses; see Stedman Jones 1976: 37 and appendix tables 1–5. The relative availability of wage data for this sector, however, has led to their being widely used as indicators of real wage levels, among the population at large, in accounts of the relationship between population and economy in pre-industrial England: see, for example, Schofield 1985, Wrigley 1983.

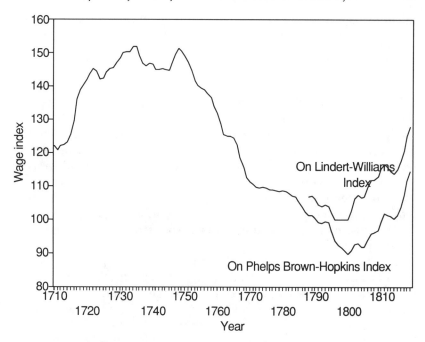

2.3 Real wages of London bricklayers: 11-point moving averages

more expensive in the capital (George 1966: 166–73; Schwarz 1985). The trend in living standards over our period is one of the most controversial issues in English economic history, but the available real wage data for London depict the early eighteenth century as a time of relative plenty, money wages remaining steady in the face of falling food prices. Subsequently, real wages fell as prices increased in the latter part of the eighteenth century, with a subsequent recovery in the second decade of the nineteenth (see figure 2.3).

The interpretation of real wage data is fraught with difficulties. It is not always clear exactly what relationship the stated wages bore to the money actually handed to the workers. The builders' wages recorded in the eighteenth century are curiously inelastic, and the recurrent depressions plaguing the London industry from the late 1720s to the 1750s leave little trace in the series. Phelps Brown and Hopkins thought that was partly an artefact of their nominal wage data, suggesting:

that there are fewer falls among our kind of wage-payments than elsewhere, since for most of our period these payments were made not by employers to wage-earners but by customers to craftsmen working on their own account and these employers were generally institutions and not private persons who had to put their hands into their own pockets. In later years, again the recognised or negotiated rates we follow will have been secretly cut, in not a few engagements, when trade was slack. (Phelps Brown and Hopkins 1962: 174)

The published series may thus give too optimistic a picture of real wages during the decades of stagnation, but greater difficulties surround the relationship between real wages and earnings. If money wages were 'sticky' in the face of falling demand, then the burden of recession will have fallen all the more heavily on employment. Unfortunately, very little is known concerning hours worked, or levels of unemployment in London at this time, but it seems likely that the growing 'proletarianisation' of London's labour force from the later seventeenth century was associated with a substantial decline in the security of employment.[16]

An alternative approach to the problem of living standards has recently been developed, based on the analysis of nutritional status from data on mean stature at different stages in the life cycle. The method has been applied to England by Floud and others (1990), using military records for cohorts born from the middle of the eighteenth century. The general trend of young adult stature is one of modest improvement in the early decades of the period followed by a period of stagnation – a decline in the heights of men born at the end of the eighteenth century – giving way to renewed and more rapid improvement in the early nineteenth century (see figure 2.4).

A study of regional contrasts revealed an appreciable height disadvantage on the part of recruits born in London up until the end of the Napoleonic Wars, suggesting that the high wages in the capital were more than offset by 'urban disamenities, disease, unemployment, crowding and high costs of living' (Floud et al. 1990: 202). A more dramatic picture of deprivation emerges from the heights of London slum children who passed through the hands of the Marine Society. The trend in these data was an exaggerated version of that seen among the soldiers, but their most striking feature was the smallness of the values recorded (see figure 2.5. As the authors remark:

The boys of the Marine Society were extraordinarily short, particularly in the eighteenth century. Thirteen-year-olds born in 1753–1780 average 51.4 in

---

[16] Beier (1986: 162), stressing the importance of 'proletarianisation' in London at this time, concludes that the process 'had social costs, gone was the security of guild membership, which had included the defence of one's employment, a measure of community solidarity and assistance in old age and other family crises. In its place grew up a system of casual labour in which security was minimal'.

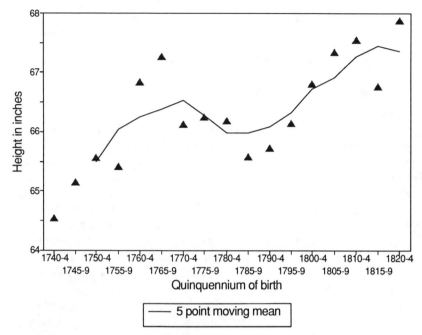

2.4 Stature of military recruits: mean at ages 21–3

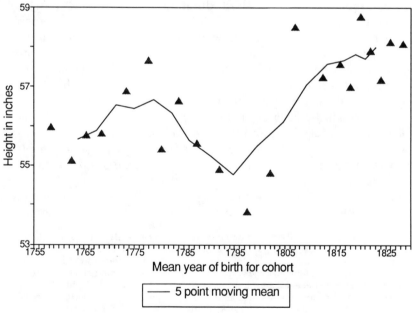

2.5 Stature of Marine Society recruits: mean at age 15

(130.6 cm), a full 10 inches (25.4 cm) less than the children of London measured by Tanner and others in the 1960s . . . if a Marine Society boy were miraculously transported into a doctor's surgery in 1987, his next step would be into hospital as a sufferer from undernutrition or child abuse. (Floud et al. 1990: 165–6)

Housing standards

The structural weaknesses of the construction sector and its system of finance had important consequences for housing standards. The tightening of credit could bring building activity to a halt, but, 'it was not only the quantity of production that suffered: when rates of interest rose, builders would be tempted to economise in land, reduce the depths of foundations, and make use of inferior bricks and timber. Jerry-building was partly, at least, a consequence of dear money.' (Ashton 1959: 86). The poor physical quality of many of the buildings in London was notorious, and it seems to have been fairly common for houses to fall down around their inhabitants (George 1966: 83–4). This was partly due to the large number of badly maintained old structures which 'were patched together and let as tenement houses, common lodging-houses or brothels or were left empty and derelict, inhabited "only by such as paid no rent" ' (George 1966: 83). But new construction was often little better and things were particularly bad where the lease was of short duration or the title to the land uncertain.[17] Here, in the words of a contemporary 'the outside appears to be of brick, but the wall consists only of a single row of bricks, these being made of the first earth that comes to hand, and only just warmed at the fire' (quoted in George 1966: 85–6).

The houses built under this system, however irregular their fabric, followed a remarkably regular design, varying little according to the size or overall character of the building (Summerson 1978: 65–7). The plot was typically long and narrow, so that the largest number of houses could be built on a given frontage, and the internal plan consisted of a front and rear room with a staircase and passage on each floor. Such terraces housed all but a handful of magnates and a rather larger number of destitute 'rookery' dwellers, being differentiated by the width of their rooms and the number of storeys they

---

[17] The granting of short leases and life interests, combined with their disposal to third parties and the appropriation of scraps of building land, generated a great quantity of uncertain and bad titles. The effect of this was compounded by the practice of charging the initial tenants large entry fines together with a nominal rent. Occupants might thus live effectively rent free, but with little or no security, whilst the owner was deprived of any interest in maintaining the property. See George 1966: 83–6 and, for the consequences of this 'system' in the Covent Garden district, p. 338.

contained – all but the poorest having some kind of cellar or basement.

This regularity was formalised by the Building Act of 1774 which, in consolidating a variety of earlier provisions, laid down minimum standards for the construction of various classes, or 'rates' of new housing defined in terms of their floor area and value. The 'real importance of this system', in Summerson's (1978: 126) view, 'was not so much that it facilitated the enforcement of a structural code but that it confirmed a degree of standardisation in speculative building' and 'laid down minimum standards for working class urban housing'. Surveyors were appointed, and the Act seems to have been effectively enforced, but its scope was restricted to issues such as the correct alignment of streets, and the reduction of fire risks. Overcrowding and sanitation were not addressed.

According to Summerson (1978: 82), in the larger houses of the better-off sanitary 'accommodation consisted of a spacious 'bog-house' built either at the end of the garden or attached to the back of the house. A brick lined circular pit was constructed under it and connected to the main drain.' Elsewhere – and particularly in the tenements – privies were more often located indoors at the foot of the stairs,[18] but the major sanitary problem was that of disposal. In Rudden's words:

The supply of water could be carried on for reward, but its removal after use was not a service that any individual would willingly pay for. Consequently any water which was drunk then found its way through the customer's body either directly into the New River or into a cesspool which lay boarded up under the feet of the family. Solid excrement went the same way, or into ancient rectangular sewers through which flowed an occasional trickle of water, or into heaps to be conserved, ripened and sold. The polite name for this substance was 'dust'. (Rudden 1985: 151)[19]

Overcrowding seems to have been endemic, and the 'impression given by accounts of housing conditions in London is of a floating population living largely as weekly tenants in furnished rooms' (George 1966: 102).[20] At the bottom of the scale were the common

[18] See Creighton 1894: 87 and references. It may be significant that the available descriptions of domestic sanitation among the population at large appear to date from the period of mortality decline at the end of the century.

[19] Summerson (1978: 82) states, more optimistically, that a 'brick drain was laid under the house and carried to the public sewer beneath the road – or if no public sewer were handy, to a cesspool in the garden', but the former arrangement would have been illegal in the eighteenth century, since public sewers were intended only for surface water and the connection of domestic drains was only allowed in 1815 (Hardy 1984).

[20] This impression is reinforced by the apparent decline in the frequency with which

lodging houses, often semi-derelict and located in notorious 'rookeries', whose numbers apparently increased in the course of the century and which housed the most mobile and destitute for twopence a night. For the more stable – or 'respectable' – of the labouring population, paying a weekly rent, the vertical matrix of the London terraced house offered an inverted image of the occupational hierarchy. Status, or income, rose with the descent from garret to street level – but here the symmetry broke down, for the cheapest accommodation was to be found in the cellars.[21]

A proportion of shopkeepers and artisans were householders in their own right – as were a certain number of labourers[22] – their living conditions were hardly less cramped since all but one or two rooms were usually let out to lodgers. Under these circumstances it is not surprising that Londoners were said to spend little of their waking time at home. The arena of social life was the street, together with a growing network of institutions such as coffee-houses, clubs and alehouses, many of which developed important economic functions.

Water supply

At the opening of our period London's water supplies were drawn from three main sources.[23] A series of shallow wells served the local requirements of many of the poorer districts. Thames water was supplied through a number of conduits – and to low-lying districts of the City – by the London Bridge Waterwork's pumping engine. The principle supplier of piped water was, however, the New River Company which brought its water through an open conduit from Hertfordshire, distributing it to 'tenants' through a network of wooden pipes.

The New River was joined in the 1690s by the York Buildings Company, which piped water from the Thames along the Strand, and by the Hampstead Aqueduct bringing spring water from Hampstead

apprentices and others were accommodated under their employers' roof (Rudé 1971: 87).

[21] Grose, on whose 'table of precedency' these remarks are based, rated 'sheds and stalls' along with cellars as the homes of the lowest class (quoted in George 1966: 96–7). George, however, suggests that the former 'were more characteristic of the seventeenth than of the eighteenth century', by which time they 'were probably most common in the outskirts of the town'.

[22] See Rudé 1971: 87 for the socio-economic position of householders in the Westminster poll books.

[23] For aspects of London's water supply at this time see, for instance, Hardy 1984, Ormsby 1928, Spate 1936. Rudden 1985 is concerned primarily with administrative and legal matters but also contains some information on the operations of the New River and other companies engaged in water supply.

through Camden Town, but its principal rival – and the only one of the early companies to avoid eventual takeover by the New River – was the Chelsea Company. This was chartered in 1722 to supply the newly developed West End with water from the Thames at Chelsea, which was stored in reservoirs at Green Park. The network extended to match the residential development of west London, and the Company was also technically the most innovative. It experimented with iron piping as early as 1757 and introduced filtration in the late 1820s.

Elsewhere, in Spate's words, the 'huge and formless expanse of the East End had to wait nearly until the nineteenth century to secure anything like an adequate supply of water' (Spate 1936: 540). The East London Water Company, founded in 1807, expanded rapidly through the East End into Shoreditch and Islington. The Company adopted an aggressive commercial policy – precipitating a price war with the New River – but was highly selective in its choice of customers. It avoided the poorer streets and courts which continued to rely on standpipes. Quantitative data on water supplies are lacking for the eighteenth century, but it is clear that the geographical disproportion was at least as great as that documented in 1827. In this year the average West End house received 218 daily gallons, compared with 182 in north London, and only 143 in the East End despite the latter's industries. This volume was, however, greater than that supplied south of the river which amounted to only 93 gallons per house (Spate 1936: 540).

The question of water quality is also difficult to resolve. The quality of Thames water began to draw adverse comment early in the nineteenth century, and it evidently deteriorated rapidly after 1815, when the effects of urban growth and new industrial processes were compounded by the spread of the water closet and the connection of domestic drains to the common sewers. The Chelsea Company, drawing its water from as far upstream as Hammersmith, was least affected by this deterioration. The New River ought to have been immune, but in practice 'its out-take from the Lea took in Hertford's sewage and the water then ran almost forty miles in an open channel which was used by the neighbours for many purposes' (Rudden 1985: 150). South London seems to have had the poorest quality – as well as the most meagre – supply, its three companies taking their water from the heavily polluted stretch of the Thames between Vauxhall and Southwark.

The methods of water transmission and storage also compromised its purity. Individual houses were supplied for a limited number of hours per week, and the water was pumped into ground floor or basement storage tanks. The state of domestic sanitation doubtless posed serious risks of contamination for the water in the tanks, but a worse problem was the condition of the Company's own pipes. In the eighteenth century these were made of wood and were not water-tight. As much as a quarter of the supply entering the system was estimated to be lost in transmission, and where the pipes ran through contaminated soil there was a serious danger of pollution. The invention of the spigot and socket joint in 1785 made a network of iron pipes technically feasible, but iron remained twice as expensive as timber (Rudden 1985: 99). In spite of this the New River replaced its four hundred miles of wooden pipes with iron in 1811, and six years later iron became compulsory for all new mains. This is likely to have improved both the quantity and the quality of water supplies, although most of the latter benefit was probably lost through deterioration at the source.

The 'gin-craze'

One element of popular consumption which has received considerable attention in the literature is, of course, gin drinking. The 'gin epidemic' of the 1730s and 1740s was the subject of contemporary polemic – studded with numerical assertions as to the scale of the 'problem' and its baleful consequences – but quantitative data on the structure of the trade, the level and social context of consumption, and, above all, its impact on life and health, have proved much harder to obtain.[24] Clark, in a recent review of the available evidence, has concluded that 'the spirits trade was more limited in scale and more conventional in its organisation than alarmist propaganda attested' (Clark 1988: 71), and was focussed predominantly on a limited number of districts in the East End and Southwark.

Gin shops do not seem to have been 'poorer and meaner' establishments than alehouses, nor, apparently, was the gin trade dominated by 'the impoverished and disorderly'. It did, however, contain an unusually large proportion of women, who seem also to have been prominent among consumers, and this may have contributed to the opprobrium which the trade attracted (Clark 1988: 70–1). Despite the failure of repeated attempts to restrict gin drinking by legislation in the 1730s and 1740s, the habit waned rapidly after mid-century.[25] This

---

[24] In 1725 a committee of Middlesex justices enumerated 6,187 premises retailing spirits in the extra-mural parishes north of the river. Ten years later this had risen to 7,044, but on both occasions the justices argued that the true figure was much higher (George 1966: 44–7); for a discussion of the political background to such claims see Clark 1988.

[25] The annual output of spirits, which averaged 7.2 million gallons nationally from 1740

was part of a broader set of changes in consumption patterns which included a revival in brewing and a secular increase in the consumption of other commodities such as tea, soap and cotton textiles (McKendrick et al. 1983: 9–33).

Conclusion: consumption and deprivation
In this brief review we have stressed the limits of current knowledge concerning the pattern of popular consumption. Nonetheless there are scattered – and often qualitative – pieces of evidence which suggest that pressure on budgets took a rather different form in London than was the case elsewhere in eighteenth-century England. A London labourer might spend as much as forty per cent of his income on bread, but, in general, food supplies – despite some well publicised deaths from starvation – seem to have been more reliable in the capital as witness the conspicuous absence of food riots for much of our period.[26]

Another suggestive indicator of a distinct structure of popular deprivation in London is to be found in Beattie's comparative analysis of eighteenth-century larceny indictments (Beattie 1986: 181–92). As a proportion of all indicted thefts, small items of food for immediate consumption were only about a third as important in Southwark as they were in a sample of rural parishes from Surrey and Sussex. This material is subject to obvious interpretative difficulties, and differences in the opportunities for theft are likely to have made a substantial contribution to the results. But the contrast is nonetheless striking and sufficiently large to suggest a genuine underlying difference. In London the immediate pressures of bodily subsistence seem to have made relatively smaller demands, compared to those for a variety of other goods and services available for cash.[27]

---

to 1749, had fallen to below a third of this amount by the 1760s (see Ashton 1955: 243).

[26] As Stevens (1979: 99) remarks, 'London would have seemed to present a potential danger spot for popular food rioting, but in fact the most striking feature of these waves of food riots is their relative absence there. London shared in the major periods of high prices ... but witnessed only minor incidents'. The importance Londoners attached to the *quality* of their bread supplies, even in times of scarcity (Wells 1988: 14), may also be of some significance in this regard.

[27] For the years 1660–1800 food was the largest category in both rural Surrey and Sussex, comprising 26.5, and 29.2, per cent of the total respectively. In Southwark, however, food – at 11.4 per cent – was only the fourth item on the list. Furthermore, over 20 per cent of these thefts – twice the proportion in the rural parishes – were valued at more than two pounds, suggesting that the motive was sale rather than consumption. The main item stolen in Southwark was clothing (27.4 per cent) – which ranked second in the rural sample at a little over 20 per cent – followed by household goods (14.4 per cent) and worked metal (13.2 per cent).

Clothing evidently featured prominently among the latter, but the evidence suggests that adequate housing and shelter were also beyond the means of an appreciable proportion of London's population, at least some of the time. If this is so, it reinforces our earlier suggestion that the peculiar lethality of London's epidemiological regime was rooted in the determinants of exposure, rather than resistance, to infection. In order to pursue this point we must examine the temporal stability of economic and social life in the capital and their implications for demographic patterns.

The rhythms of economic and social life

The temporal unevenness of life in a pre-industrial economy forms one of its main contrasts with that in an industrial economy. This unevenness prevailed at a number of levels, from seasonal cycles of employment and unemployment in the short-term, through the irregular occurrence of 'crisis' years at the annual scale, to the broader movements of expansion and recession to which the term 'conjuncture' has sometimes been applied.[28] Unevenness of this kind was, as we saw in chapter 1, matched by a corresponding instability in vital processes which loomed large in historical demographic research, both empirically and theoretically. The instability of mortality in London will form the subject matter of a chapter in its own right, but if these movements in death rates are to be understood we must first examine the fluctuations in economic and social life which underlay them.

In the case of agrarian communities most of these fluctuations – certainly at the shorter-terms – arose from the effects of weather on food production and can be captured in the movements of agricultural prices, but for metropolitan centres the position was more complex. At the shortest time-scale, the metropolitan economy retained a strong seasonal rhythm into the nineteenth century. Many trades – particularly those associated with the construction sector – experienced a substantial slow down, or outright cessation, in activity during the winter months, although others benefitted from the autumn and winter 'season'.[29] On an annual time scale, the rhythms

---

[28] In historical usage, the term 'conjuncture' is particularly associated with the work of Braudel (1980) and is often used interchangeably with 'cycle'. In the present context, however, it is important to distinguish these looser, wave-like, movements of growth and recession, from the more narrowly-defined economists' concept of the 'business cycle', whose existence in this period has been a subject of controversy (Hoppitt 1987, pp. 116–121).

[29] George (1966: 262–312) provides a general discussion of seasonal and other interrup-

of economic life were partly determined by the state of the harvest – and thus at one remove by climate – and climate could also influence the metropolitan economy directly through its effects on transport and construction, and on the levels of demand for items such as fuel.

Nonetheless, the economic and political centrality enjoyed by a city such as London offered its food supply a degree of protection against the kind of weather-related disruption which could be so damaging elsewhere. Substantial upswings in food prices did occur in eighteenth-century London, but it is likely that the short-run course of popular welfare depended at least as much on movements in employment as it did on prices.[30] In this respect, the very openness of the metropolitan economy enhanced its vulnerability to the behaviour of markets on a wide geographical scale and to a broader constellation of disturbances.

Thus, in the short-term, economic 'shocks' most often materialised as financial crises – whether generated 'endogenously', by the peculiar character of England's fiscal arrangements, or 'exogenously' by events such as warfare or bad weather – whilst the medium-term was dominated by political events through the alternation of war and peace. We shall thus look first at the question of financial crises, and the impact of war on economic and social life, before turning to the problem of longer-term movements.

Financial crises

Financial crises of varying magnitude were endemic to the eighteenth-century economy. They were exacerbated by the work-ings of the Usury Act which set the upper limit to interest rates at six per cent until 1714 and then at five per cent for the remainder of the century (Ashton 1955: 27–9). A sudden increase in the demand for cash, accompanied by the calling in of loans, due to the prior over-

---

tions to trade. Detailed studies of the seasonality of employment in eighteenth-century London are lacking, although it is likely that Stedman Jones's account of the position in the following century (1976: 33–51) is also substantially applicable to our period. See Snell 1985: 15–66 for some data on the seasonality of rural employment, in the adjacent counties, which is likely to have had some 'knock on' effects on the London labour market.

[30] Thus Beattie (1986: 231), comparing the position in London with that in rural Sussex and Surrey, argued that 'for many in London there were fewer cushions against serious adversity than in the countryside. In circumstances in which the worker had no access to the produce of a garden, no right to relief from the parish, and perhaps little neighbourly support, unemployment was devastating – much more devastating than the adjustments that a rise in the price of food would force on everyone who depended on the market'.

extension of credit, over-trading, or a war scare thus placed bankers in a serious dilemma. Unable to restrict demand by the 'natural' mechanism of raising interest rates, they risked undermining confidence – and provoking a 'run' – if they refused to lend, but might fatally over-commit themselves if they did not. Under such circumstances the solution was for:

the monetary authority (the Bank of England or the government itself) to make an emergency issue of some form of paper which bankers, merchants and the general public would accept. When this was done the panic was allayed; rates of interest (which, legally or not, had been driven up) were reduced; and men regained trust in each other. But the recovery of trade and industry took time: the duration of the period of recovery was usually proportioned to the intensity of the preceding crisis. (Ashton 1959: 111)

The bankruptcy statistics suggest a pronounced degree of uncertainty in London for much of the eighteenth century.[31] The capital contributed a disproportionate share of the national totals and, for the first sixty years at least, annual fluctuations were more violent in the capital than elsewhere (Hoppit 1987: 63–74). Hoppit suggests that some of this volatility may reflect the relative ease of taking proceedings in London, but it was substantially a product of the enhanced opportunities for risk taking in the metropolitan economy and the uncertainties inherent in the overseas trade on which so much of it depended. Fluctuations in demand were heightened by London's role as a centre of fashion, but the city's vulnerability to such fluctuations reflected 'the greater financial interdependence of businessmen in the capital. Credit networks were larger, more powerful and more common there. Collapses sent out shock waves and rumours through the coffee houses and marts of the hive-like city.' (Hoppit 1987: 73).

Financial crises arise from dramatic failures of confidence in some underlying mechanism (Hoppit 1987: 130) and are thus difficult to capture statistically, but statistical data are nonetheless essential whether for the purposes of chronology or analysis. Ashton himself (1959) identified thirteen crises in the course of the century (1701, 1710, 1715, 1720, 1726, 1745, 1761, 1763, 1772, 1778, 1788, 1793 and 1797). Hoppit (1986) classifies the last five of these as crises of private finance, associated with a substantial increase in bankruptcies and widespread distress. Earlier crises, by contrast, were concentrated in the spheres of public or corporate finance and do not seem to have

---

[31] See Hoppitt 1987: 42–55 for a discussion of the problems and pitfalls of eighteenth-century bankruptcy statistics. The following paragraphs are largely based on this author's work.

disrupted business nationally. Only in 1710,[32] after a disastrous harvest, and again in 1726 did the bankruptcy totals register a major impact.

The circumstances of the latter year display a unique concatenation of misfortunes:

As in 1710, in 1726 the crisis in the area of high finance was unmistakable . . . The depression was intensified in 1727 and 1728 by harvest failure and mortality crises. High numbers of bankruptcies throughout 1727–8 reflect not just financial pressures but deep depression arising from a series of unhappy coincidences. What the crisis of 1726 shows, moreover, is that war could precipitate a simultaneous crisis in public, corporate and private finance. (Hoppit 1986: 49)

The threat, or reality, of military action also triggered crises in 1701, 1715, 1745, 1761, 1778, 1793 and 1797, whilst both the crisis of 1763 and the financial difficulties of the early 1780s arose directly from the problems of wartime finance. Only in 1772 and 1788 was the collapse of a banking or industrial venture enough to precipitate a crisis in an atmosphere of tranquillity. Hoppit argues that business's increased vulnerability to financial crises after 1770 arose from a greater integration of private finance and from a growing use of credit instruments, such as bills of exchange, at home. The former was also responsible, he claims, for the closer relationship visible between the London and national bankruptcy series in the latter half of the century.

A comparison of these series suggests that the impact of the earlier crises was largely confined to London. It is difficult to measure the scale of their broader effects on economic life in the capital, or on its population at large, but the scale of the differential is impressive nonetheless. In 1715, bankruptcies were 40 per cent below trend nationally (by Hoppit's method of calculation) but 8 per cent above in London, whilst the years 1739–40 saw little deviation from trend in the national series but London bankruptcies were 33 and 43 per cent, respectively, above this level (Hoppit 1987: 73).

The impact of war

It was the cities that felt the first impact of events in the sphere of high politics, and this was above all true of the alternation of war and peace. The major wars of our period were fought abroad, or at sea, by forces representing a tiny proportion of the nation's population, but for all this they brought substantial dislocation to the economic and

---

[32] In fact the main wave of bankruptcies followed directly on the harvest in the autumn of 1709.

social life of the country.[33] London felt the impact twice over. It was itself directly affected, but it also received shock waves generated elsewhere in the country, both by wartime conditions and the transition from war to peace.

War and the economy

War affected both foreign and inland trade as well as domestic production as a result of military operations themselves – whether directly or indirectly – and government measures to meet the enormous costs thus incurred. As a result 'War substantially destabilised the eighteenth-century economy, producing prosperity and depression in an unpredictable mix. Certainty was eroded, confidence ebbed and the prospect of stability vanished.' (Hoppit 1987: 129). Land Tax and import duties were both increased to meet wartime expenses, but the majority of these were met by borrowing,[34] and particularly by short-term borrowing of a kind which Ashton (1959: 67) regarded as fostering instability and speculative tendencies. On a larger scale wartime borrowing deflected money 'from other channels, and in particular from investment in building and construction reducing the production of capital goods. The production of capital goods was relatively low in most years of war.' (Ashton 1959: 65).

In London this relationship can be seen in movements in the land registry series and the yield on 3 per cent Consols. Figure 2.6[35] reveals a strong negative association between these movements for the period after the outbreak of the American war, explicable in terms of wartime increase in a yield which was already historically high. Yields on stock ran at, or close to, 5 per cent in the years 1779–86 and 1795–1801, a level at which builders and contractors were prevented from competing as a result of the Usury Laws.

The position earlier in the century is less clear. The yield on Funds remained below the critical 5 per cent from the end of the War of

---

[33] The deleterious economic effects were stressed by Ashton (1959). A contrasting view, arguing for beneficial effects on economic growth, had earlier been provided by John (1954–5), who nonetheless conceded the extent of wartime disruption of London's economic life. The extent of any directly beneficial effects of war-related expenditure in the earlier part of our period have recently been questioned by Jones (1988: 308–11), who also points to the importance of British *victories* in securing export markets. The use of criminal statistics as indicators of the extent of social and economic disruption was pioneered by Hay (1982).

[34] For most of our period loans accounted for 30 to 40 per cent of total expenditure in wartime, but 70 to 80 per cent of the incremental expenditure compared with that in peacetime (Kennedy 1989: 81; O'Brien 1988: 4).

[35] Both series are expressed as percentage deviations from the long term trend estimated by exponential regression.

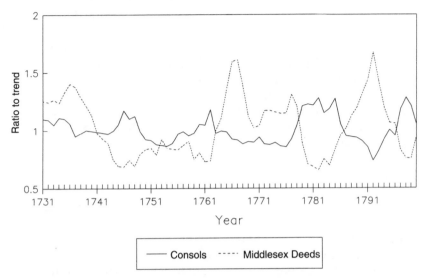

2.6 Middlesex Land Registry Deeds and yield on consols: exponentially de-trended

Spanish Succession until 1760, and Ashton attributed the depressions of the 1740s and 1750s entirely to interruptions in raw materials or low expectations of profit. The latter were, no doubt, of great significance, but we should not ignore the low risks attached to government borrowing, a factor which makes it difficult to compare wartime rates of interest in the public and private sectors. Certainly there is a noticeable tendency for the two series to move against each other in the years 1740–60, suggesting that the competing lure of the public sector may also have contributed to the stagnation which afflicted construction.

The extent of wartime disruption to foreign trade varied with a number of factors including the Navy's success in controlling the major shipping lanes. An initial decline in exports was usually followed by a recovery which might lift them to a new peak especially if, as in the Seven Years War, overseas demand was boosted by subsidies to continental allies. Recovery conspicuously failed to materialise, however, during both the American war, and the Spanish war of the late 1720s. Imports generally fared worse than exports, partly because of the rise in duties. This was particularly true in 1702–13 and 1739–48, however, the years from 1793 to 1800 saw substantial growth in imports.

The effects of war on domestic industry were uneven. Those

supplying the armed forces or who, like the Spitalfield weavers, suffered from French competition often prospered, but others were harmed by shortages of credit or imported materials. London markets benefitted from the provisioning of fleets in the Thames estuary and troop concentrations in the surrounding region, but economically the city suffered from the disruption of coastal shipping brought about by requisitioning and the threat of privateers. Some trade was redirected from coastal to inland transport but London's coal supplies apparently suffered in each of the wars before the 1790s.

War and society
The disruption wrought by war on the life of the capital extended beyond its immediate effects on finance, trade and industry. The dramatic expansion and contraction of the armed forces themselves disrupted the lives of first tens, and then hundreds, of thousands of young men and, indirectly, of an incalculable number of their dependents. The authorities depended on a mixture of volunteering, inducement and coercion in order to fill the ranks of both the army and the navy, and it 'was among the down-and-outs, the semi-employed and the criminal classes that the recruiting squads and press gangs did most of their business' (Ashton 1959: 51).[36]

It is thus likely that wartime conditions deflected many potential subsistence migrants away from London and into the armed forces, but the flow reversed dramatically on demobilisation. Con-temporaries were familiar with the sharp increases of reported crime in and around London following rapidly on the heels of peace and generally attributed to discharged soldiers and sailors.[37] Beattie's study of indictments for property offences in Southwark, rural Surrey and Sussex provides some quantitative evidence of this process (1986: 202–37).[38] In general, argues the author, the alternation of war and

---

[36] For a detailed review of the 'history and historiography' of military recruiting in this period, together with some quantitative estimates of the numbers involved, see Floud et al. 1990: 30–83.

[37] This was a theme of contemporary comment from the time of the anonymous *Hanging Not Punishment Enough* in 1701. As the title of the pamphlet implies, however, the problem was conventionally attributed to moral failings on the part of servicemen themselves, rather than to structural features of economy or society (George 1966: 30–1; Beattie 1966: 225–9).

[38] The quantitative analysis of indictments in this manner has drawn criticism from some historians (see Innes and Styles 1986 for a review of the relevant issues). The main thrust of this criticism, however, has been that, at times of social and economic disruption, the numbers of indictments might be inflated for reasons other than an underlying rise in 'real' crime, and thus it does not seriously question the validity of indictment statistics as an indicator of disruption of this kind.

peace operated as a 'ratchet' in the metropolitan series: 'the making of peace was invariably followed by a strong increase in prosecutions for property crime that then tended to remain at roughly that higher level until another war supervened and diminished the numbers of charges being laid in the courts' (p. 215).

The post-war increase in crime reflected a 'jarring and rapid return to normal peacetime circumstances' of structural underemployment and unemployment 'which had been temporarily relieved by the boon of war' (p. 229) when the armed forces had absorbed the labour surplus. Pointing to the association between property indictments and high prices, Beattie argues that the former generally rose when 'unfavourable economic circumstances made it more difficult than usual for large numbers of the working poor to support themselves' (p. 235).

A comparison of data from the three areas underlines the relationship between London's crime figures and both price levels and the state of war or peace, but it is remarkable that the second of these is effectively confined to London. Beattie divided his observations into four categories – according to whether prices were 'high' or 'low' (that is above or below the trend expectation) and whether the prevailing condition was one of war or peace – and counted the numbers of years in each category with indictment totals above or below trend ('high' or 'low crime' years) as in the upper panel of table 2.2.

In the lower panel of the table we give the proportion of 'high crime' years in each category, and the ratio that this bears to the proportion observed under 'base' conditions of war and low prices. In Southwark there are almost no 'high crime' years under the base conditions, but the proportions in wartime years of scarcity, and peacetime years of plenty, are similar at around 60 per cent. By contrast, in rural Surrey the ratio is hardly affected by peacetime conditions without high prices – although it is doubled by high prices in wartime – whilst in Sussex it actually falls below the base level under these circumstances.

The direct effects of such post-war disruption might be relatively short-term. Their severity depended in part on the smoothness of the transition to a peacetime economy, and London's post-war building booms are reminders of the success with which this could be accomplished. Its indirect effects, however, are likely to have lasted much longer. These are much more difficult to measure and lay particularly in the sphere of education and training – in the economists' phrase 'human capital formation'. The unsuitability of ex-servicemen for regular employment was a common theme in contemporary

Table 2.2. *Economic circumstances and indictments for offences against property 1660–1820*

Circumstances	Place	Number of 'high crime' years	Number of 'low crime' years
War and low prices	Urban Surrey	1	24
	Rural Surrey	7	19
	Sussex	4	13
War and high prices	Urban Surrey	10	6
	Rural Surrey	9	7
	Sussex	10	0
Peace and low prices	Urban Surrey	22	16
	Rural Surrey	12	26
	Sussex	2	17
Peace and high prices	Urban Surrey	16	1
	Rural Surrey	13	3
	Sussex	6	3

Circumstances	Place	Proportion of 'high crime' years (and ratio to 'base' proportion)
War and low prices ('base' condition)	Urban Surrey	0.04
	Rural Surrey	0.27
	Sussex	0.24
War and high prices	Urban Surrey	0.63 (×15.6)
	Rural Surrey	0.56 (× 2.1)
	Sussex	1.00 (× 4.3)
Peace and low prices	Urban Surrey	0.58 (×14.5)
	Rural Surrey	0.32 (× 1.2)
	Sussex	0.11 (× 0.4)
Peace and high prices	Urban Surrey	0.94 (×23.5)
	Rural Surrey	0.81 (× 3.0)
	Sussex	0.67 (× 2.8)

Source: Beattie 1986, p. 236, table 5.2

accounts, and at a time when the acquisition of skills was so closely tied to the life-cycle, it is probable that the life chances of many tens of thousands of young men were permanently damaged by their participation in the armed forces.[39] As Ashton (1959: 52) put it many 'boys

[39] See Ashton 1959: 52–3 and references. The relationship between life-cycle stages, the acquisition of skills, and the formation of social personality in general, was

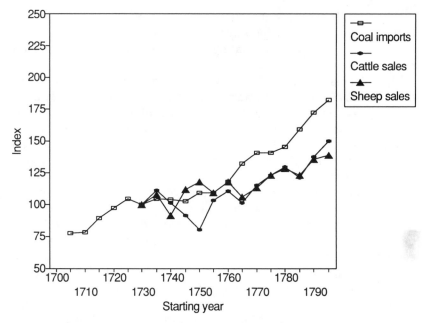

2.7 London coal imports and Smithfield livestock sales: quinquennial indices

went into the forces before they had acquired knowledge of a trade: they left the army and navy totally unskilled except in the arts of war'.

The longer term: growth and stagnation

In the longer term – at the level of the conjuncture – evidence from a number of consumption and price series suggests that the rhythm of London's physical expansion corresponded to the waves of growth and recession in general levels of metropolitan economic activity (see figure 2.7). An initial period of expansion was apparently terminated by a series of inter-related crises in the latter part of the 1720s, leading to some thirty years of stagnation interrupted only by sickly and short-lived recoveries.[40] Activity seems to have troughed some time

embodied in the systems of apprenticeship and 'life-cycle service' (Laslett 1977), and has been chiefly examined through its relationship with marriage and family forma-tion (Kussmaul 1981; Weir 1984; Goldstone 1986).

[40] For a general discussion of this phenomenon and a review of the available data see Schwarz, in press, chapter 3 'Trends, cycles and wars'. Schwarz's interpretation of the causes of the recession differs in certain respects from that advanced here.

in the 1740s, but it was not until the aftermath of the Seven Years War that the secular trend turned decisively upward, after which growth was maintained at an accelerating rate, broken only by war-related depressions.

The explanation for this hiatus in what had so often struck contemporaries as London's inexorable progress, could conceivably lie in a failure of population growth and thus of internally generated demand. It is overwhelmingly likely that demographic expansion virtually ceased in the 1730s and 1740s, and the population of 1750 probably exceeded that of 1730 by less than 3 per cent. Why this should have been the case is not entirely clear, but a review of the possibilities suggests that some are much more likely than others.

The first candidate is a worsening in natural decrease due to increased mortality. Material to be reviewed in chapters 4 and 5 suggests that mortality did rise in the second quarter of the eighteenth century, but the increase in the crude death rate is unlikely to have been anything like the seven to ten per thousand which would have been needed to arrest the secular growth of the previous decades – indeed we cannot demonstrate unequivocally that it increased at all.[41] Alternatively, it is conceivable that the birth rate fell. This may have happened in the 1740s – certainly the recorded baptisms for the decade fell below 170,000, compared with over 200,000 in the 1720s – but our estimates (see chapter 5) suggest that birth rates were higher in both the 1730s and 1750s than they would ever be again. Moreover, at the level of explanation, a birth rate hypothesis – even if successful – merely invites the further question of why such a reduction should have occurred.

A narrowly 'demographic' explanation thus appears unconvincing, and this leads us to the second component of population growth – migration. If the changing balance of births and deaths cannot account for the whole of the stagnation then this implies a failure of net migration to make good the deficit – and thus a reduction in the volume of immigration, or in the length of stay, or both. Once more, a purely demographic explanation based on the size of the 'migration-prone' age groups is hard to sustain. It is true that the national population growth of the early eighteenth century was halting and uncertain, but the years 1730–49 were no worse than the previous half century in this respect – and much better than the decade of the

---

[41] Annual total burials in the Bills of Mortality averaged around 26,500 in the period 1725–49, compared with 25,750 in the ten years to 1724.

1660s, when immigration rapidly made good a huge volume of plague losses.[42]

This implies that London became less attractive to long-term
immigrants, and the most plausible explanation for this is a decline in
perceived opportunities stemming from the decline in economic
activity. If this is so, then demographic stagnation was a consequence
of economic slow down, rather than *vice versa*, although, once the
recession had set in, an element of feedback may have come into play
with demographic stagnation further depressing internal demand.
The origins of London's recession itself were presumably related to
whatever factors underlay the slow down which has been detected in
the contemporary national economy.[43] An analysis of the latter is
outside our remit, but there is sufficient evidence for a plausible
speculation.

The years of stagnation coincided roughly with the era of abundant
harvests and low food prices, circumstances benefitting consumers
but tending to reduce income from land. The macroeconomic consequences of such transfers of resources depend on the nature and
distribution of marginal propensities to consume across the social
structure. These were much debated at the time and remain to be
fully resolved,[44] but it is probable that the volume of landed income
available for the purchase of non-essential goods and services (the
notorious 'luxuries' of eighteenth-century discourse) fell appreciably
in these decades.

If this is so then the consequences would have been felt disproportionately in the London market, and the rise in real wages brought by
cheaper food achieved at the cost of a secular fall in employment –
and consequently earnings – in the relevant economic sectors. At the
same time the increased purchasing power generated in other sectors, and the growth in demand for labour accompanying the fitful
recoveries of the period, exacerbated the short-run instability already
endemic to the system. It is, as Mathias argues, against such a background of irregular earnings and unpredictable prospects that the

---

[42] Wrigley and Schofield's estimates imply that the population aged 15–24 years grew
at an annual rate of 0.44 per cent from 1730 to 1749, compared with 0.15 per cent in
the years 1680–1729, and −0.22 per cent in the 1660s (see Wrigley and Schofield
1981, table A3.1).

[43] For general reviews see Little 1976, Cole 1981, pp. 45–56.

[44] See Ashton pp. 40–8 for a general discussion of the problem and the views of
contemporaries. Wrigley has recently pointed out that the question is further complicated by the possible divergence of net and gross yields under fluctuating conditions (Wrigley 1989).

supposed 'gin craze' requires to be seen: 'If higher wages came unexpectedly, spasmodically and might disappear as quickly as they came, increased permanent commitments . . . might prove disastrous . . . pouring away a surplus in drink or leisure could thus be defended as a rational response to context'.[45]

Conclusion

The picture emerging from this brief survey of London life in our period corresponds in many respects to McNeill's model of a metropolitan epidemiological regime. London's exposure potential was evidently very high. Substantial immigration and large-scale trade – both national and international – kept levels of bounding low, whilst conduction and retention were both promoted by population density and very poor sanitation. At the same time, however, immunological resistance would have been correspondingly high among long-term residents, and food supplies for the bulk of the population relatively secure – if not more abundant – when compared with those elsewhere in the country.

Many of these characteristics were, as McNeill's arguments imply, generic to pre-industrial metropolitan centres, though London was no doubt unusual in the scale of its international trade and national food base. Others, however, were specific to their time and place reflecting the characteristics of contemporary English economy and society. This is above all true of housing and construction whose peculiar organisation and funding we have already considered at some length, but whose significance in this context cannot be over-stressed. Classical theory saw food as the resource whose scarcity promoted high mortality, but living space is more likely to have fulfilled this function in eighteenth-century London, and it was the construction sector that produced and distributed such space.

This question takes on a particular importance in relation to the second peculiarity to emerge from our survey – the lengthy period of stagnation in the central decades of the eighteenth century. This was accompanied by high – and probably rising – levels of mortality, but food prices were unusually low, and it is hard to argue that popular nutrition was much worse than in either the later seventeenth, or eighteenth centuries. Indeed, the opposite is equally likely to have been the case. Thus it is in these years above all that a structural

---

[45] P. Mathias, 'Leisure and wages in theory and practice', in *The Transformation of England* (1979), p. 165.

explanation of London's mortality must look to the exposure variables, and particularly conduction.

The extent to which the supply of living space – and thus the level of house building and maintenance – kept pace with the needs of London's population is therefore central to our understanding of mortality trends in the capital for a large part of the eighteenth century. The data from the land registry reveal very low levels of activity over most of these decades, whilst the surveys of Ashton and Summerson suggest that construction virtually ceased for extended periods. It might be argued that this simply reflects demographic stagnation, which had rendered further expansion of the housing stock redundant. Certainly the evidence of falling property values suggests that – even at this diminished level – supply exceeded demand, but to assume that this was also true of popular housing needs is to overlook the complexity of the processes by which the latter were met.

In much of the metropolis the housing stock appears to have expanded 'from the top down', and incremental popular accommodation was generated, not through new building for that purpose, but by an involutionary process of 'internal colonisation' – properties being divided and sub-divided as they were abandoned in the westward migration of the elite and the 'middling sort'.[46] Sheppard, describing the process at work in the years after 1800, noted

the absence, except in parts of East London, of new building specifically for the working class, for most early nineteenth- century landlords, being anxious for the maintenance of the value of their property, intended that their estates should be occupied by the upper or the middle classes. But . . . many houses intended for the 'respectable' classes often degenerated into slums within a decade or two of their erection. Once this process had begun it was almost impossible to reverse it. Decaying houses intended for occupation by a single family, with cellars, large rooms and an inadequate water supply, were invaded by half-a- dozen or more families, for whom they provided utterly unsuitable accommodation. (Sheppard 1971: 94)

The literature suggests that much housing was badly built to begin with and in a chronically poor state of repair. The funds necessary for adequate maintenance are unlikely to have been forthcoming on a substantial scale, and many buildings were evidently allowed to deteriorate until they became fit only 'for such as pay no rent'. Such a situation might be tolerable as long as the stock was replenished 'from the top' by the new tranches of construction generated by

---

[46] This process can be seen at work particularly in the decline of the Soho and Covent Garden districts (Phillips 1964: 119–42, 231–9; George 1966: 92–3, 338–9).

London's physical growth – but this ceased to be the case in the decades of stagnation, and expenditure on maintenance is more likely to have declined than increased.[47]

Under these circumstances the stock of accommodation available to the bulk of London's population would have declined in quality, and shrunk in volume, as more and more buildings deteriorated to the level of lodging houses and night shelters. Hence the effective density of population is likely to have increased, at any rate in those districts most affected by this process, with all that that implies for levels of potential exposure to infection. It is important to bear this possibility in mind when examining the specific trend and structure of eighteenth-century mortality in London, but before doing this we must consider how far the aggregate vital data bear out the characteristics of the generic model of metropolitan epidemiological regimes which we have outlined.

[47] This problem would have been compounded by the way in which the uncertainty of title and the use of entry fines reduced the owners' interest in maintaining older buildings. See note seventeen.

3

The 'high potential' model: a preliminary test

For much of the eighteenth century the relative movements of baptisms and burials in the London Bills of Mortality sketch the outlines of a grim picture, and one need not be a demographic determinist to share Dorothy George's sense of a metropolis dominated by the waste and destruction of lives which they imply. But London was not the only city in early modern Europe to display consistent burial surpluses, and in chapter 1 we considered a general model – put forward by W. H. McNeill – which attempts to explain the phenomenon in terms of the maintenance of endemic foci of infection. These result from a set of structural characteristics endowing such centres with what we have termed a 'high exposure potential' – characteristics which eighteenth-century London seems to have possessed in an exaggerated form. In this chapter we shall try to specify our model further and to make a preliminary test of its predictions against some aggregate vital data.

The high potential model of metropolitan mortality

For McNeill the large dense populations of metropolitan centres enabled immunising infections to persist, whilst their frequent contacts with the outside world promoted a two way traffic in pathogens between them, their relatively thinly settled hinterland, and the more remote places with which they maintained trading connections. They were thus characterised by high levels of conduction and retention, and by weak bounding, all of which contributed to a high exposure potential. At the same time, those fortunate enough to survive the hazards of childhood acquired substantial immunological protection, resulting in a population whose resistance potential was relatively high by the standards of the time. It is also likely that the political and economic centrality of a city such as London ensured a food supply which, in the face of all but the most severe crises, was more secure, and perhaps also more abundant, than that enjoyed elsewhere.

For these reasons we shall refer to McNeill's formulation, from now on, as the 'high potential' model of metropolitan mortality, or HPM. The model, as we have seen, predicts that metropolitan mortality will be high, especially in childhood, but that substantial fluctuations in the death rate will be relatively rare and of comparatively modest amplitude, producing what we termed a 'type IV' pattern of instability. At the same time the city's epidemiological regime will display a degree of segmentation along demographic lines because, if the assumptions are correct, members of the population will have differing levels of immunological protection according to their age and migratory experience. These can be schematised as follows:

(i) *Infants.* Nursing infants acquire maternal antibodies and thus a degree of protection against infection. On weaning they become particularly vulnerable to gastric disease spread by contaminated food and water.

(ii) *Children.* Children, whether native born or immigrant, initially lack a wide spectrum of immunity and thus experience high mortality from infectious disease, but the survivors acquire immunity and take on the characteristics of group (iii).

(iii) *Native born adolescents and young adults.* This group possess a wide spectrum of immunity and are expected to have relatively low mortality, although they may display a degree of susceptibility to typhus which increases with age.

(iv) *Recent immigrants.* Immigrants have restricted immunities and thus have an epidemiological resemblance to group (ii).

(v) *Older adults.* This age-group have had prolonged exposure to immunising infections but become increasingly vulnerable to other conditions such as bronchitis, to which surviving native-born individuals may now have less resistance than have immigrants.

The metropolitan surplus should be concentrated among groups (i), (ii) and (iv), although the extent of the infant mortality differential will depend on the method of infant feeding. The levels of mortality among groups (ii) and (iv) should also be the most volatile in the short term, since it is here that 'mini- epidemics' can occur among the susceptible element. The aggregate burial totals for group (iv) may be further destabilised by sudden changes in the volume or composition of migration through the latter's contribution to the immunologically 'naive' component of the population, as well as the composition of the pathogenic load.

The conceptual elegance and explanatory power of the HPM are attractive, but we must beware of over simplification. In particular, the nature of the postulated 'urban' or 'metropolitan' diseases needs to be examined more closely since pathogens capable of producing the effects predicted by the model, particularly the sharp qualitative contrast between metropolis and hinterland, must possess certain specific properties. They should be transmitted directly from person to person, without the agency of a free-living animal vector,[1] must not be retained in animal reservoirs and must either kill or immunise their victims within a fairly short period. It is important to bear these points in mind since, as we saw in chapter 1, there are a number of conditions which might have claimed more lives in cities than they did elsewhere without necessarily displaying all the characteristics predicted by the model.

The elements of the HPM are thus structural mortality potentials whose full realisation depends on the character of a population's pathogenic load at any time. The infections with which it is concerned are primarily the airborne 'crowd diseases' such as smallpox, measles, and some of the respiratory conditions. Hence the model's applicability in any given instance depends very much on the relative importance of these causes of death in the relevant population, and we shall thus try to pursue this question using aggregate vital data from the London Bills of Mortality.

The London Bills of Mortality

The Bills possess both advantages and disadvantages in such a context. Their principal advantage is one of scale since they purport to document the capital as a whole in a single set of tabulations. On this basis, as Appleby (1975: 7) concluded, 'the data in the London Bills are probably more complete and more accurate than any available elsewhere in England at the time'. But their corresponding shortcomings should not be minimised and have led some observers, including a number of contemporaries, to dismiss the information they contain as worthless.[2]

The first difficulty is one of geographical coverage. In the latter part of the eighteenth century, as we have seen, the expansion of the metropolis engulfed a number of hitherto rural parishes, particularly

---

[1] This qualification is necessary because in cases, such as typhus, where the vector – in this instance the body louse – is dependent on close proximity to a human host it is not, in practice, necessary to consider the existence of animal reservoirs in order to understand the behaviour of the infection at the population level.

[2] For a sample of contemporary and current opinions see George 1966: 35–6; Appleby 1975; Forbes 1974; Ogle 1892.

those lying to the west and north-west such as St Pancras and
Marylebone. Although new parishes do appear at intervals in the
published tabulations, these are sub-divisions of those already
included at the beginning of our period. Geographically, the area
documented by the scope of the system – an area itself sometimes
referred to as 'the Bills' – remained, in Dorothy George's phrase, the
'greater London of the seventeenth century' (1966: 35).

The limits of London in 1800, then, reached beyond those of the
Bills, but even at this date the latter retained the greater part of the
capital's population.[3] Hence the published data should be broadly
acceptable indicators of metropolitan conditions as a whole providing
they are also an adequate record of events within the districts
covered. It is this latter question which presents the greatest difficulty
we encounter in working with the Bills, and it is useful to consider it
under two headings; systematic omissions and 'negligence'.

The treatment of non-conformist burials provides the main area
where there is likely to have been systematic omission, but the position here is ambiguous. The figures appearing in the Bills were based
on returns obtained from 'searchers' in each parish, whose task it was
to report deaths as they occurred and to ascertain the cause of death,
and the age of the deceased, by 'viewing the corpse'. The searchers
reported to the parish clerks who, each week, took the information to
the headquarters of the Parish Clerks Company which was responsible for producing the printed Bill. Officially, burials outside Anglican grounds were excluded from the Bills, and although the searchers
were called out to view casualties of other denominations, such as
Quakers,[4] the parish clerks were supposed to discard such cases from
their returns.

Assuming that they did in fact do so, the published totals would
thus exclude growing numbers of dissenters in the course of the
eighteenth century, as well as persons buried in civil burial grounds,
but the problems this presents are akin to those posed by the
diminishing geographical coverage of the Bills and similar considerations apply.[5] The experience of the omitted groups is unlikely to have

[3] Parishes outside the Bills contributed 12.6 per cent of the total 'metropolitan' burials
for 1800 in the Parish Register Abstracts, having risen from 7.9 per cent in 1770 and a
mere 1.4 per cent in 1700. By 1820 the figure had reached 17.6 per cent (Marshall
1832: 62).
[4] In practice, however, the Quaker burial registers sometimes report that the searchers
had refused to 'view the corpse' owing to the former's non-payment of church rates.
[5] At mid-century Maitland estimated that around 10 per cent of London burials took
place in grounds which were not included in the Bills' totals (Maitland 1756: 719–20,
740–4); see also Hollingsworth 1976: 145–8.

differed sufficiently from that of the general population at large for the structure of the burial totals as a whole to have been greatly distorted.[6]

The problem of 'negligence' on the part of the searchers, resulting in the more or less random omission of events, was much discussed by contemporaries. In fact it is as unlikely that the searchers were always resolute, in either scrupulousness or efficiency, as it is that every death in London's crowded courts and alleys could ever have been brought to their attention. Such problems may well have multiplied as the plague epidemics that provided the system with its initial *raison d'etre* receded, first into memory and then history, but such 'under-registration' is a familiar feature of sources of this kind and can be dealt with in one of two ways.

The first of these is to offset the effects of under-registration by constructing appropriate correction factors. There are a number of techniques for doing this but most of them, as we shall see in Part II rely on nominal record linkage and so are unsuitable for use with aggregated data. The methods usually adopted in such 'aggregative analyses' are based on the assumption that shortfalls in the recorded totals are essentially random[7] and will 'even out' on a monthly, or even weekly, basis. In the absence of evidence to the contrary it can also be assumed that secular changes in the level of under-registration will occur too slowly to distort short-run comparisons.

This strategy limits the range of topics that can be investigated, and studies of this kind generally concentrate on short-term fluctuations in the relevant series and on their relative magnitude over restricted time periods. Fortunately such topics are closely related to the question of HPM's adequacy as a description of London's epidemiological regime, and the Bills provide material well suited to such an approach. We shall begin by looking at the composition of the burial series.

The annual burial series

The Bills provide burial totals for individual parishes and a global total which is broken down by cause of death, throughout our period, and by age after 1728. In both cases the searchers made their classi-

---

[6] The possible inclusion of dissenters and others in the burial totals, whilst being excluded from baptisms, does however present considerable difficulties if we wish to relate the two series to each other, as we shall see in chapter 4.

[7] This assumption is, of course, often violated by the systematic omission of early infant deaths, but it is rarely necessary to make a specific allowance for this in the calculations.

fication on the basis of visual inspection and talking to people present at, or near, the time of death. The cause of death categories thus lean heavily on visible signs and symptoms, such as 'fever' or 'consumption'. These present obvious difficulties of interpretation, and only in a few special cases, such as smallpox, can we be reasonably certain of the disease responsible.[8] The age classification presents fewer problems of this kind. The accuracy of the assignment is open to question, but there is little reason to expect systematic bias apart from a likely tendency to overstate the age of the elderly.[9]

Causes of death

The numbers of burials falling in the major cause of death categories are plotted as an area graph in figure 3.1, and expressed as proportions of the total, for twenty-five-year periods, in table 3.1. The majority of burials always falls into one of four categories: 'consumption', 'fevers', smallpox, and a group of causes classified by Marshall[10] as 'diseases incidental to infancy' (henceforth simply 'infancy'). This last always accounts for the largest fraction of the total, with consumption and fevers claiming roughly equal shares until the middle of the eighteenth century, when the former rises and that of the latter declines. Smallpox deaths show a slow but consistent relative increase from the late seventeenth century to the third quarter of the eighteenth, declining somewhat after 1775. In the early nineteenth century deaths from both smallpox and fevers fall substantially as a proportion of the total.

The proportion of infancy burials rises substantially from the seventeenth century into the eighteenth, but there is an accompanying fall in that ascribed to a further cause of death, 'griping in the guts'. Large numbers of casualties were attributed to this cause in the seventeenth century, but it declined rapidly throughout the early decades of our period and had effectively disappeared by the second

[8] The smallpox figures may, in fact, understate the 'true' mortality from the disease to a certain extent. This is because victims of its severest form, 'fulminating smallpox', could die before developing the characteristic rash and so might be listed under the heading of 'convulsions' in the Bills (Razzell 1977: 105).

[9] See Coale and Kisker 1986 for a general discussion of this problem and the distortions it can introduce into measures of mortality. Some estimates of age-misstatements in nineteenth-century English data are provided by Lee and Lam 1983.

[10] John Marshall's *Mortality of the Metropolis*, published in 1832, is an invaluable digest of the figures from annual Bills of Mortality over our period, together with data from the Parish Register Abstracts and a variety of other material from the early censuses, such as poor law statistics. Marshall's tabulations form the basis of the annual Bills' series used in this analysis.

Table 3.1. *Contribution of causes of death to total burials in Bills of Mortality (in percentages)*

	1675–99	1700–24	1725–49	1750–74	1775–99	1800–24
Consumption	16.7	12.6	15.7	19.5	24.5	23.2
Fevers	15.2	14.9	15.3	13.9	11.3	6.9
Infancy	29.9 (37.9)	39.2	37.6	35.0	32.2	29.2
Smallpox	6.4	7.3	7.8	10.0	9.3	5.4
Griping in the guts	10.7	—	—	—	—	—
All other	21.1 (23.8)	26.0	26.0	21.6	22.7	35.3

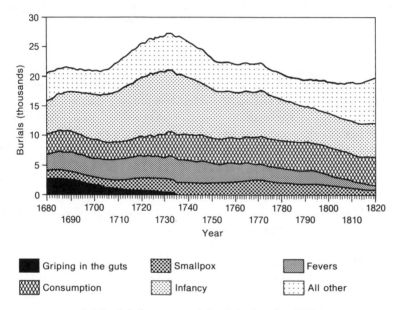

3.1 Burials by cause of death in London Bills

quarter of the eighteenth century. Although Marshall excluded griping in the guts from the infancy category, Creighton argued in his *History of Epidemics* that the disease was in fact a form of infantile diarrhoea, pointing out that the decline in griping in the guts deaths was balanced by an increase in those ascribed to 'convulsions'.

A closer analysis of the later seventeenth-century data (see table 3.2) reveals a more complex picture since changes also occurred in the distribution of deaths between the different causes grouped under

Table 3.2. *Breakdown of burials from 'Diseases incidental to infancy' (in percentages)*

	Decade		
	1670–9	1680–9	1690–9
'Convulsions'	43.2	58.3	63.0
'Infants and chrisoms'	9.7	3.8	2.3
'Teething'	23.7	18.7	18.4

'diseases incidental to infancy', with both 'teething' and 'infants and chrisomes' declining at the expense of 'convulsions'. Hence in order to evaluate Creighton's assertion the burial registers of the six London Quaker Monthly Meetings were examined and the age distribution of 'griping in the guts' burials determined. Approximately three quarters were found to be of individuals below the age of two, and the percentages in parenthesis next to 'infancy' and 'other causes' in table 3.1 were obtained by distributing the 'griping in the guts' totals in the appropriate proportions (see below for a discussion of the age incidence of 'diseases incidental to infancy').

Table 3.3 analyses changes in the fraction of total burials falling under each of the main headings (henceforth 'burial fractions'), and the contributions that these make to changes in the global figure. In each case two comparisons are made; between the periods 1675–99 and 1725–49, and between the latter and the years 1800–24, with griping in the guts burials distributed as indicated above. Over the first interval the burial fractions remain practically unchanged, with the exception of the smallpox fraction which increases by about a fifth of its initial value. The latter is relatively low however, and the increase explains less than 15 per cent of the rise in total burials between the two periods.

Substantial changes occur in the second interval however. The fever and smallpox fractions decline by about one half and one third of their 1725–49 values, respectively. The 'infancy' fraction drops by about one fifth, and those for 'consumption' and 'other causes' increase correspondingly by about half their initial value. The decline in 'infancy' burials accounts for nearly 60 per cent of the reduction in the overall total, that in fevers for a further third and smallpox for about 15 per cent, whilst consumption and 'other causes' show small absolute increases.

We shall not try to interpret these movements at this point beyond

Table 3.3. *Percentage changes in burials: by cause of death category*

	Change[a]	Change[b]
1675–99 to 1725–49		
Consumption	11.6	–6.1
Fevers	15.6	0.5
Diseases incidental to infancy	35.4	–1.4
Smallpox	13.4	21.8
Other causes	24.0	0.2
1725–49 to 1800–24		
Consumption	–3.6	47.5
Fevers	36.8	–54.6
Diseases incidental to infancy	59.4	–22.4
Smallpox	14.2	–31.7
Other causes	–6.8	49.9

Note: [a]Change in absolute number of burials (as % of change in total burials)
[b]Change in percentage share of total burials (as % of share at start of interval)

stressing the uncertain nature of the categories themselves. In the nineteenth century the term 'consumption' became a synonym for respiratory tuberculosis, and it seems reasonable to assume that the great bulk of eighteenth-century deaths due to the latter are listed under this heading. But it would be dangerous to assume that the converse is also true, since contemporaries sometimes claimed that the searchers used the term 'consumption' as an indiscriminate catch-all.[11] Thus Fothergill thought that:

if the body is emaciated, which may happen from an acute fever, it is enough for [the searchers] to place it to the account of consumption, though the death of the party was perhaps owing to a disease specifically different: and thus a monstrous account is formed by the ignorance of the searchers, to the disgrace of our country, even so far as to discourage some foreigners from coming to visit us. (Fothergill 1821: 167)

The interpretation of 'fever' is equally problematic, for the term could be applied to a variety of conditions united only by their febrile symptoms. The category lasted as long as the Bills of Mortality themselves and was retained in the early decades of civil registration. Only from 1869 were separate totals published for typhus and typhoid fever, and it is likely that the majority of fever deaths in earlier

---

[11] For a discussion of the interpretative problems posed by this term see Hardy 1988 and Landers 1986.

decades of the nineteenth century should be attributed to one of these causes. The position in the earlier period, however, is much less clear, and even after 1869 substantial numbers of deaths were, for several years, allotted to 'simple continued fever' a category which Longstaff (1884–5: 78) took to comprise 'in addition to typhus and enteric fevers . . . general tuberculosis, septicemia, pneumonia, [and] intermittent fever'.

The age distributions

The age classification of burials includes three categories below the age of ten: nought to one, two to four, and five to nine years, with ten year age-groups beyond this. These extend beyond the age of a hundred, but we have grouped all those over seventy into a single category. The overall distribution changes relatively little over the eighteenth century, as can be seen from the area graphs in figure 3.2 and the proportions in table 3.4. Slightly less than half of all deaths occur below the age of ten, and rather more than a third of the remainder fall into the modal adult categories of 30–49 years. The relative size of the youngest age-group falls a little between the second and third quarters of the eighteenth century, but it does so substantially after 1800, with offsetting increases in the older age-groups, most markedly in those above fifty.

Table 3.5 repeats the analysis carried out in table 3.3, looking at changes in the age distributions over the second of the two intervals. Only two age-groups, 0–1 and 20–9 years, show any substantial reduction in their share of the total, with a more modest reduction at 30–9 years. A comparison of the absolute figures for these two periods reveals that the youngest age-group accounts for nearly three-quarters of the overall reduction in burials, and the younger adult ages (20–39) for most of the remainder.

The level of mortality

The distribution of burials by age enables us to make an indirect, and very rough, measurement of the level of infant mortality. Other things being equal the higher the level of mortality in a population the larger the proportion of deaths which occur in infancy and early childhood. In particular, in a stationary population, the fraction of deaths falling in the first year of life is equal to the infant mortality rate.[12] London's population was not of course stationary during our

---

[12] Technically the life table mortality probability at age zero.

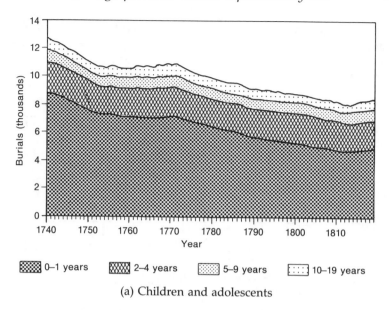

(a) Children and adolescents

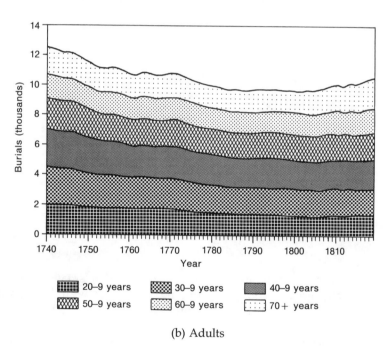

(b) Adults

3.2 Burials by age at death in London Bills

Table 3.4. *Age distribution of total burials*

Age-group	1728–49	1750–74	1775–99	1800–24
0–1	36.3	33.6	33.2	28.4
2–4	8.6	9.1	10.1	10.6
5–9	3.6	3.6	3.8	4.2
10–19	3.1	3.4	3.5	3.3
20–9	7.8	8.0	7.2	6.9
30–9	9.5	9.3	9.0	9.4
40–9	9.8	9.7	9.9	10.3
50–9	7.9	7.9	8.5	9.2
60–9	6.2	8.1	7.2	8.1
70+	7.2	7.3	7.6	9.6

Table 3.5. *Percentage changes in burials*
1725–49 to 1800–24: by age-category

Age-group	Change[a]	Change[b]
0–1	74.0	–22.0
2–4	–0.9	23.3
5–9	0.5	16.7
10–19	2.3	6.1
20–9	12.0	–11.5
30–9	9.9	–1.1
40–9	7.3	5.1
50–9	1.4	16.5
60–9	–2.3	30.6
70+	-4.2	33.3

Note: [a]Change in absolute numbers of burials
(as % of change in total burials)
[b]Change in percentage share of total burials
(as % of share at start of interval)

period, but it is more likely to have contained a smaller, than a substantially larger, proportion of infants compared with the stationary population defined by the appropriate life table.[13] The ratio of

[13] This assertion is based on the likely role of migration in boosting the numbers in the reproductive age-groups. For some comments on the demographic 'efficiency' of migration in this respect see De Vries 1984: 97–8.

infant to total burials should thus serve as an approximate lower limit to the prevailing level of infant mortality.[14]

The absence of an age-breakdown in the earlier part of our period, can be met by recourse to the cause of death distribution, since a comparison of the figures in table 3.5 with those in table 3.2 reveals that the numbers of deaths in the 0–1 age-group are approximately equal to those attributed to 'diseases incidental to infancy'. It thus seems reasonable to use the latter (suitably inflated to take account of 'griping in the guts' deaths) as an indicator of the numbers of deaths under two years of age prior to 1728. Over the first half of our period deaths below the age of two thus constitute a little under 40 per cent of the total, falling to below 30 per cent in the early nineteenth century.

By comparison q_0 for the two most severe levels of the Princeton model south life table (sexes combined) are 0.321 and 0.298 corresponding to expectations of life at birth of 19.96 and 22.40 respectively. If we follow Brownlee in assuming that 75 per cent of deaths under the age of two occur in the first year of life, then these proportions suggest that, for much of our period, the level of infant mortality was close to the upper limit of those embodied in the model tables, and substantially in excess of those reported in family reconstitution studies from contemporary English parishes outside London.

Conclusion

Mortality levels in London thus seem to have been substantially higher than those prevailing in the country at large, as the HPM requires, and for all their shortcomings the aggregate burial data are sufficient to demonstrate the heavy toll of childhood diseases. Many difficulties attend the interpretation of the cause of death figures, but the importance of smallpox in the epidemiological regime of eighteenth-century London emerges clearly from our material.

The overall decline of mortality was bound up with a dramatic reduction in smallpox deaths, as well as those from fevers and the diseases of infancy. The age-composition of the burial totals suggests that infant and early adult mortality fell disproportionately, but the

---

[14] An alternative rationale for this procedure, as applied to the decades 1730–49, lies in the fact that in these years the crude birth rate, regardless of under-registration, cannot plausibly have exceeded the death rate (see chapter 4), and thus the global burial total can be taken as the effective upper limit to the denominator of the infant mortality rate.

former of these two reductions would have enhanced the rate of survival into childhood thus increasing the numbers at risk in these age-groups. Hence the constancy of the latter's burial fractions is consistent with a disproportionate decline in their absolute level of mortality.[15]

The instability of mortality

The HPM makes predictions about the short-run stability of mortality as well as its absolute level, and these are relatively easy to test by means of aggregative analysis. The first step in this procedure is to eliminate the effects of medium and long-term trends in the series of annual burial totals by transforming them into crisis mortality ratios (CMRs). There are a number of ways in which this can be done, some more complex than others, but the technique employed here is the relatively simple one employed by Flinn (1974) which takes each year's trend value to be the mean of the annual totals observed in the quinquennia on either side.[16] The CMR is then obtained by expressing the burial total actually recorded for the year in question as a percentage of this figure.

Once we have obtained a CMR series there are at least two ways of measuring short-term instability: either by calculating the mean absolute deviation (MAD) of the CMRs from the trend value of a hundred over a given period,[17] or by counting the number of occa-

---

[15] This point can be simply demonstrated with reference to some stable population calculations. For instance, we can compare stable populations which correspond to the Princeton model west life tables at levels one and five and have similar levels of fertility – gross reproduction ratio equal to 4.2 in the former case and 4.3 in the latter (Coale and Demeny 1983). In this case, as mortality declines from a life expectancy at birth of twenty years to one of thirty years, the proportion of all deaths occurring at ages one to nine completed years rises from 23.0 to 25.2 per cent, whilst that occurring between the ages of twenty and thirty-nine falls from 13.3 to 11.6 per cent. But the risk of mortality falls by 30.6 per cent of its initial value in the first of the two intervals, as against only 26.5 per cent in the second.

[16] This measure is technically equivalent to an eleven point de-centred moving average and has gained wide acceptance in the literature. A widely used refinement to the technique employed here (e.g. Dûpaquier 1979) is to express the observed deviations from trend in a standardised form. This, however, hampers the comparison of values from different series, where the variances of the latter differ greatly, and so was not done here. Hollingsworth 1979 has defined an alternative measure of crisis mortality, incorporating additional parameters including absolute mortality levels and duration. The latter has conceptual advantages but requires data which are rarely available from historical populations. For more sophisticated approaches to both trend estimation and the construction of crisis thresholds see Wrigley and Schofield 1981: 646–9.

[17] It follows from the method of calculation that the CMR values would all be equal to a hundred in the absence of short-run fluctuations.

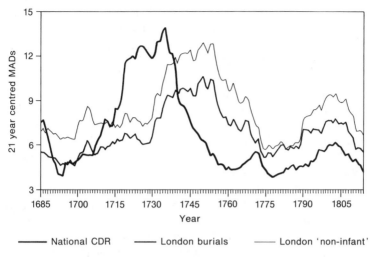

3.3 English CDR and burials in London Bills: short-run instability

sions on which the CMRs exceed a specified threshold. Since numbers of deaths in the youngest age-group are generally less volatile,
from year to year, than are those at older ages, the fact that infant
deaths form a larger proportion of the total in London than elsewhere
will tend to bias the comparison of levels of instability between the
capital and the country at large. Figure 3.3 thus plots twenty-one
point moving MADs[18] constructed from the Wrigley–Schofield
national CDR series (for calendar years), along with two sets of
figures based on the London Bills – the first referring to total recorded
burials and the second to a 'non-infant' series constructed by sub-
tracting the numbers of infancy deaths from the latter.

The results for the period up till 1750 confirm the expectations of
the model to a remarkable extent. In this context it is important to
bear in mind that the larger the geographical area covered by a vital
series the greater the degree of short-term stability we should expect
it to display, for both statistical and substantive reasons. Furthermore
a CDR series possesses an inbuilt tendency to lower instability when
compared with one based on aggregate burials. This is because a
sharp upswing in mortality will reduce the size of the population at
risk in the following period. The crude rate is 'buffered' against this
since population size is used as the divisor, but no corresponding

[18] In other words each annual point represents the MAD calculated from the CMRs for
the year in question and the decades on either side.

adjustment is made to the burial totals.[19] It is thus striking that the national MADs are actually larger than those for the Bills' total burial series, for the first half of the period, and only slightly below the 'non-infant' values, although there appears to have been a reversal of this pattern after 1750.

An examination of extreme CMR values leads to similar conclusions. In figure 3.4(a) we have plotted the three sets of CMRs calculated for the years in which the national series registers its fifteen highest values, whilst in figure 3.4(b) we have done the same for years which fall into the 'top fifteen' in either of our London series without doing so nationally. The designation of 'mortality crises' has, as we have seen, an arbitrary character in situations of this kind, but Flinn has suggested a CMR of 130 as the appropriate criterion when working on a regional scale. If we adopt this, for purposes of demonstration, we find that there were no 'crises' in London at any time during our period, using either of our two series, although the threshold is passed once in the national series. The level of 120 is reached on only six occasions in the 'non-infant' series, and three times in the total burials. The national series also contains six values above this level but passes the 40 per cent mark in the crisis year of 1729.

It is interesting to note once more that London's 'advantage' appears to have been most marked in the earlier part of the period, when absolute levels of mortality were most severe. Of the fifteen worst years in the national series, eight occur before 1740, but only in 1681 and 1729 does the London CMR pass the 110 mark. Similarly only four of the years excluded on the national criterion, for this part of our period, feature among the fifteen worst years in London. Furthermore, in two of these cases – those of 1710 and 1719 – the divergence is probably less marked than appears at first sight, since both prefigure major upswings in the national series and the 1719 CMR for the latter is, in any case, of comparable magnitude to the London non-infant figure. The position after the mortality wave of the early 1740s is, however, very different. The London CMRs are now close to, or above, the national figure in each of the remaining five national crises, and six major upswings which are included on the national criterion.

[19] The fact that the national series incorporates the aggregated experience of a diversity of regions will tend to dampen fluctuations even more, and means that the heuristic value of our comparisons is very limited. But in the absence of comparable data on a regional scale, the Wrigley–Schofield material forms the only available bench-mark against which to judge the level of instability in our own series.

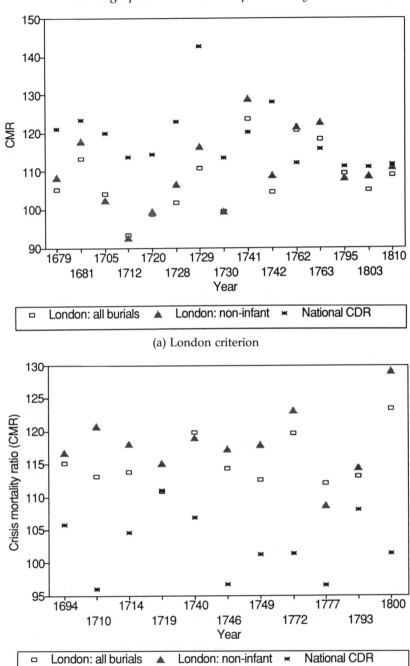

(a) London criterion

(b) National criterion

3.4 Extreme values for crisis mortality ratios

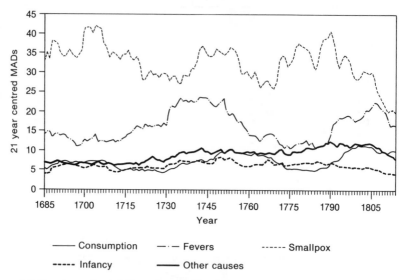

3.5 Short-run instability of mortality in London Bills by cause of death

Causes of death

The construction of cause-specific CMR series reveals substantial differences in levels of instability as measured by the MADs (see figure 3.5). Smallpox, as we might expect, is generally the most volatile whilst fever burials are intermediate between the former category and the remaining three. The volatility of the fever series increases in the second quarter of the eighteenth century and again at the close of the century, before declining after 1800. The relationship between major fluctuations in total burials and those in the cause-specific series is investigated in figure 3.6 which plots the mean cause-specific CMRs, for each of the main categories, in the worst five, ten and fifteen years for total burials.

Smallpox stands out with CMRs of more than 150 in the latter two calculations, although the average is a little below this in the worst five years, whilst the figure for fever is around 130, and the means for the remaining series are close to 115 in each case. Figure 3.7 partitions the total burial surplus for the worst fifteen years taken together into fractions attributable to each of the causes of death. The shares of smallpox and fevers are roughly equal at a quarter each, but the absolute volume of infancy deaths is such that this category accounts for a further fifth of the total. Consumption, by contrast, accounts for less than one in eight of the total surplus.

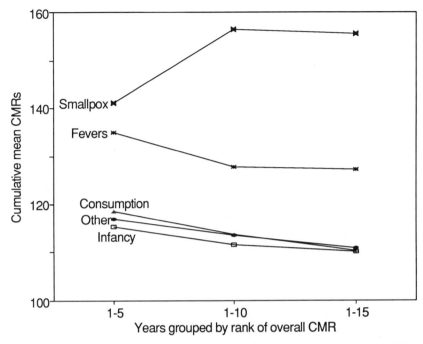

3.6 London cause-specific CMRs in 15 years with highest total burial CMR

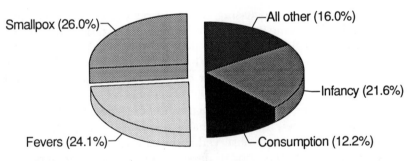

3.7 Composition of Bills' burial surplus in 15 years with highest CMRs

The HPM, as we have indicated, assumes a substantial degree of interaction between the metropolitan and hinterland epidemiological regimes. Major fluctuations in the London burial totals seem, however, to have had a very weak relationship to those in the national death rate. We shall now try to determine whether this was also the case for the cause-specific totals. In figure 3.8 we repeat the

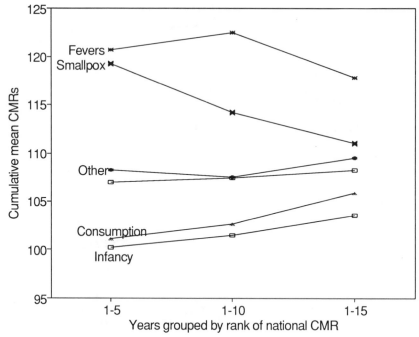

3.8 Cause-specific London CMRs in 15 years with highest national de-
trended CDR

analysis of figure 3.6 focussing this time on years with unusually
severe CDRs. This time it is the fever series which stands out with an
average burial surplus of around 20 per cent in each case, whereas the
smallpox value is intermediate and is only clearly distinguished from
that of 'other causes' if we restrict our attention to the ten highest
CDRs.

The foregoing analysis was limited to the detection of 'immediate'
relationships between the series, that is relationships between movements both of which were observed in the same year. But the interactions embodied in the model depend on physical movement –
whether of susceptible individuals, pathogens, or both – and this
raises the possibility that a delay, or 'lag', might have intervened
between demographically significant stresses in the 'hinterland' and
the response of mortality levels in London. One very simple way of
searching for such an effect is to include in the analysis the London
CMR, either for the same year as the national mortality peak, or that
for the following year, depending on which is the larger. The inclusion of these 'lagged' observations (see figure 3.9) results in a very

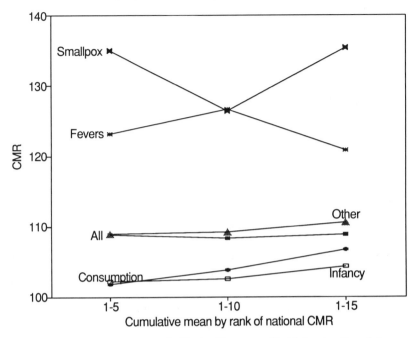

3.9 Cause-specific London CMRs in 15 years with highest national de-
trended CDR (including effects lagged 1 year)

large divergence between the mean CMRs for fever and smallpox and
those for the remaining series, which remain substantially
unchanged, a finding which suggests that some kind of geographical
movement may indeed have played an important part in triggering
the upswing of fever and smallpox mortality in London.

Age-groups

The HPM predicts that immunological differences between age-
groups will result in differences in the short-run instability of their
mortality levels. This prediction can easily be tested by examining
CMR series based on the age-specific burial totals. Figure 3.10 plots
the MADs which were calculated from the latter series, and the
results generally bear out our expectations since it is the childhood
and adolescent age-groups which display the greatest volatility. Taking the period as a whole, the MAD rises sharply with age from the 0–
1 to the 2–5 year age-groups and displays a generally U-shaped pattern thereafter. The sharp reduction from the 5–9 to the 10–19 year

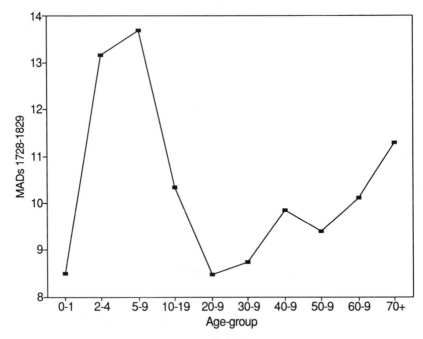

3.10 Short-run instability in London Bills' cause-specific burial series

age-groups is striking, but the latter value is itself above that for any succeeding age-group below the age of 70.

If we examine the figures for sub-periods, given in table 3.6, differences emerge between the age-groups in the trend of instability over time. The MADs for the oldest and youngest age-groups show relatively little change, apart from the very high value for the 70+ group in the 1740s, but each of the intermediate values declines substantially over the period as a whole. The timing of this 'stabilisation', however, differs markedly between age-groups. The 2–9 year old burial series stabilise in the first quarter of the nineteenth century, whereas those for the 40–59 year olds have already done so in the last quarter of the eighteenth. The MADs for the younger adult burials also decline at this point, but this age-group displays a further substantial reduction in instability between first and second sub-periods.

In figure 3.11 we examine the behaviour of the age-specific CMRs during the major mortality peaks. The age profile of CMRs in the five most severe years for total burials is relatively flat over the main range of ages, with the youngest age-group having a noticeably low value and the oldest age-groups being much worse affected, indeed the

Table 3.6. *Mean absolute deviations from trend in age-specific burial series (in percentages)*

Age-group	1735–49	1750–74	1775–99	1800–24	1735–1824
0–1	8.1	10.1	7.7	9.0	8.8
2–4	14.4	15.3	14.7	8.6	13.0
5–9	16.8	15.1	14.6	9.2	13.5
10–19	10.8	10.4	10.4	9.9	10.4
20–9	13.7	9.2	6.0	6.7	8.4
30–9	13.4	9.8	6.7	6.6	8.7
40–9	13.3	12.1	8.2	6.9	9.8
50–9	13.4	11.3	7.0	7.2	9.4
60–9	12.0	10.4	9.2	9.4	10.0
70+	15.9	10.8	9.2	10.7	11.2

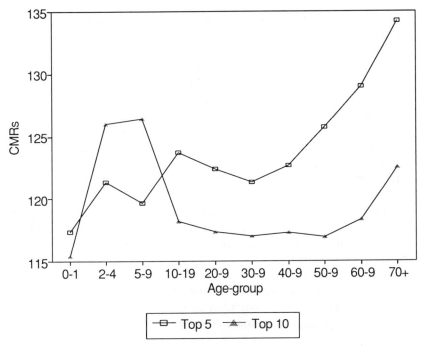

3.11 Mean age-specific London CMRs in years of exceptional mortality

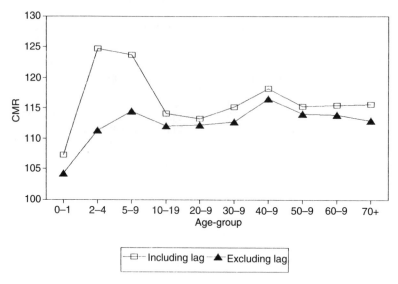

3.12 Age-specific CMRs in 10 years with highest national de-trended CDR

mean CMRs rise monotonically from ages 30–9 years, after a local maximum in adolescence. The inclusion of the values for the years ranked sixth to tenth according to the magnitude of the total burial CMRs changes the profile substantially. The childhood ages now stand out sharply from the others, with a secondary peak in old age, a finding which suggests that these 'second order' mortality peaks resulted primarily from upswings in mortality from the childhood infections whose impact, though severe among the age-groups directly affected, was too restricted to equal the worst of those registered by the total burial CMR.

In figure 3.12 we look at the relationship between movements in the age-specific CMRs and those in the national CDR estimates. If we consider the 'immediate' relationships there are few age-differentials apart from the very low figure for the youngest age-group. Indeed, in the case of the 'top ten' years, the profile is almost entirely flat above the age of 2. The inclusion of 'lags', however, has a marked effect on the figures for the 2–9 year olds, presumably reflecting the import-ance of smallpox as a cause of death in this age-group. We must now examine the relationships between movements in the cause of death and the age-specific series more generally.

Age and cause of death interactions

If London's epidemiological regime was segmented according to age and migratory status in the manner that we have postulated, we should expect to find high short-run correlations between movements in the burial series for adjacent age-groups since the latter would have generally similar profiles of resistance. But groups containing a substantial proportion of recent immigrants might deviate from this pattern because of their internal heterogeneity with respect to immunological status, and because fluctuations in the numbers of recorded deaths would partly reflect those in the volume of immigration.

We should also expect to find systematic variations in the relationships between age and cause of death. The material in the London Bills does not allow us to examine such relationships directly, since it lacks the necessary two-way classification of burials, but we can approach the problem indirectly through the statistical associations between annual movements in the relevant burial series. Even here, of course, we are hampered by the unsatisfactory nature of the cause of death categories which appear in the Bills. The smallpox category is quite straightforward but this is certainly not the case with either 'consumption' or 'fever'. In a later chapter we shall try to throw some light on the likely range of conditions embraced by these terms, but at this point we shall treat them as 'black boxes', restricting our attention to the investigation of statistical differences in the behaviour of the relevant burial series. We shall begin by examining the relationship between the age-groups.

Age-group associations

In this analysis we shall employ a set of series constructed in the same manner as were the CMRs but based on the age-specific burial fractions, rather than the absolute burial totals. Each annual figure thus measures the extent to which the age-group's contribution to that year's burial total is above, or below, the average proportion for the quinqennia on either side. The reason for adopting this procedure is to remove the effects of fluctuations in the general level of mortality and thus enable the underlying relationships between age-groups to emerge more clearly. In table 3.7 we give the resulting product-moment correlation coefficients between adjacent age-groups. The number of observations is such that each coefficient is statistically significant, but it is noticeable that the teenage series displays values

Table 3.7. *Correlation*
coefficients between adjacent
age-groups in burial series

Age-groups	Correlation
0–1/ 2–4	0.275**
2–4/ 5–9	0.760***
5–9/10–19	0.369***
10–19/20–9	0.256**
20–9/30–9	0.664***
30–9/40–9	0.671***
40–9/50–9	0.770***
50–9/60–9	0.737***
60–9/70+	0.720***

Note: **Significant at 1 per cent
confidence level
***Significant at 0.1 per cent
confidence level

only a third to a half the magnitude of those for the other age-groups
(with the exception of the youngest whose correlation with the 2–4
year olds is also relatively low), a result which may reflect the effects
of immigration in this age-group.

The overall configuration of these relationships can conveniently be
described by means of a principal components analysis carried out on
the matrix of pairwise correlation coefficients. The results in figure
3.13 reveal a first component, accounting for half the total variance,
which splits the age-groups into two clusters, children and adults,
with the teenage score falling between them but rather closer to the
former than the latter. A second component explains a further fifth of
the variance, and the scores here reveal an entirely different pattern.
The age-groups falling in the 5–39 year interval all have very similar,
negative, scores, whilst those on either side increase in value progressively as we move to the extremes of the age range. We shall
consider this pattern at greater length below, but at this point it is
sufficient to note that, apart from the 0–1 year olds, those age-groups
which seem to have experienced the largest mortality decline all fall
into the low scoring group on the second component.

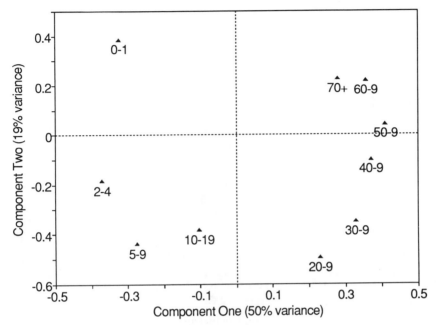

3.13 Short-run instability in age-specific series 1733–1824: principal
components analysis

Age and cause of death

We shall approach the question of age and cause of death interactions
using a variety of techniques. The first of these is a principal components analysis carried out on the correlation matrix between the
age-specific CMRs and those for the five main causes of death, with
the burial series split into two overlapping fifty-year periods.[20] In
each period the first component accounted for a little under 70 per
cent of the total variance, and the second for around 25 per cent, but
there were some differences in both the coefficients and the component scores.

In the first of the two periods (see figure 3.14), the coefficients on
component one distinguish the effects of smallpox from those of the
other non-infant causes of death,[21] whilst the second component

---

[20] This periodisation was necessary in order to obtain comparability between the two
sets of correlation coefficients whilst ensuring that each was based on a reasonably
large number of observations.

[21] In this analysis the components were standardised in order to take account of the
much greater variance of the smallpox correlations which would otherwise dominate
the analysis entirely.

Death and the metropolis

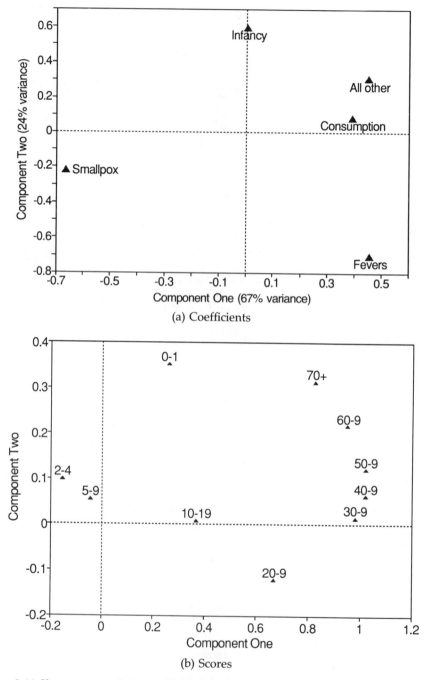

(a) Coefficients

(b) Scores

3.14 Short-run correlations of burials by age and cause of death: principal
components analysis 1733–82

opposes fever burials – with a strongly negative coefficient – to infancy, consumption and other causes, with smallpox occupying an intermediate position. The pattern of component scores on the first – 'smallpox' – component reveals a split between the age-groups below 20 and above 30 years, with the 20–9 year olds falling between the two, though rather closer to the latter. On the second – 'fever' – component it is the 20–9 year olds who have the lowest score with a pattern of monotonic increase as one descends through the child-hood, and ascends through the adult, ages. The pattern of coef-ficients is broadly similar in the second period (see figure 3.15), the main change being that smallpox and infancy now have very similar values on component one. Where the scores are concerned, the split on this component is now between childhood age-groups – below the age of 10 – and the adults, with the teenagers falling between the two. The main changes to the pattern of scores on the second coefficient are an increase in the value for the teenage group – which is now much closer to those for the extreme age-groups – and a relative decline in that for the older children (5–9 years), who now have the lowest score suggesting a possible shift in the age-impact of fever mortality.

Z scores
The use of product-moment correlation coefficients is a familiar and convenient way of measuring statistical associations between series, but they are only one among many possible types of measurement and they have their limitations. Such coefficients are not, for instance, appropriate in cases where the underlying relationships are strongly non-linear, and their use of absolute values can cause problems where, as here, the observations are likely to incorporate a substantial measurement error. Nor do they take account of the possibility of serial autocorrelation in the data.[22]

We have thus supplemented our correlation analysis with a further investigation using Goodman's Z, a non-parametric coefficient which measures the relative frequency of concordant movements in two series so as to take account of any autocorrelation detected in either of them.[23] This results in a characteristic profile of age-associations for each cause of death (see table 3.8). The consumption profile is

[22] The main effect of such autocorrelation, however, is likely to be the indication of a spuriously high level of statistical significance.

[23] A 'concordant' movement occurs where both series move in the same direction on the same occasion. For details of Goodman's Z and its method of calculation see Goodman 1963, and for an example of its application in historical demography, Wrigley and Schofield 1981: 342–53.

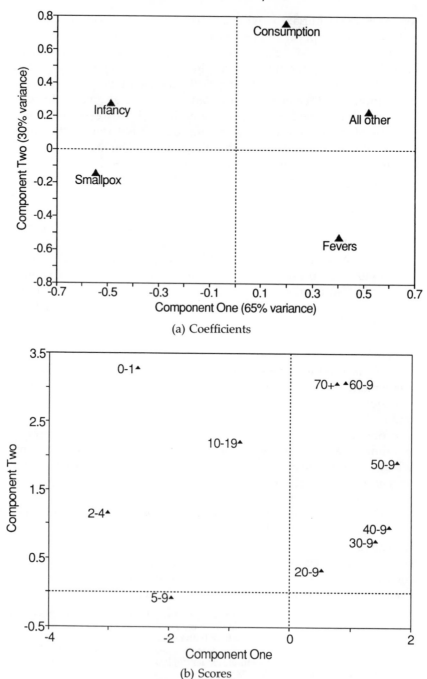

3.15 Short-run correlations of burials by age and cause of death: principal
components analysis 1775–1824

Table 3.8. *Z scores between age-specific and cause-specific burial series*

Age-group	Consumption	Fevers	Smallpox	Other causes
0–1	3.08**	1.83	3.86***	1.54
2–4	2.52*	1.70	3.65***	1.31
5–9	0.82	3.23**	4.49***	0.40
10–19	1.60	2.74**	3.52***	1.12
20–9	4.08***	3.68***	1.40	3.66***
30–9	4.66***	4.87***	0.37	3.81***
40–9	4.73***	3.81***	−0.80	4.86***
50–9	5.54***	2.37*	−1.72	5.28***
60–9	4.83***	0.31	0.63	4.84***
70–9	6.16***	1.76	0.28	5.55***

Note: *Significant at 5 per cent confidence level
**Significant at 1 per cent confidence level
***Significant at 0.1 per cent confidence level

roughly U-shaped with high values below age 2, and above 20, rising irregularly to peak in the 70+ age-group. The values for 'other causes' show a somewhat similar pattern above age 20 but are markedly lower in early childhood than are those for consumption.

Mortality from 'fevers' by contrast is significantly associated with burials in the central range of ages, roughly 5–59 years, with the highest values in the 20–49 year groups. Smallpox, as might be expected, displays a very marked pattern of significant age-associations extending from the youngest age-group into the 'teens and then falling to very low, or negative, values above age 30. At ages below 20 it is smallpox, of the four series, which shows the strongest associations whereas either consumption or the residual category generally predominates above this age.

This divergence is reflected in the results of a principal components analysis carried out on the matrix of Z coefficients (see figure 3.15). The first component, with a negative coefficient for smallpox and positive coefficients for both consumption and other causes, accounts for about four-fifths of the total variance. The pattern of scores on this component reveals distinct childhood and adult clusters, the teenagers this time lying clearly inside the former. The second component explaining nearly 15 per cent of the variance is once more dominated by a large negative coefficient for fevers, but the pattern of scores is rather different from that seen in the earlier analysis since it is now the age group 30–9 years which has the lowest value.

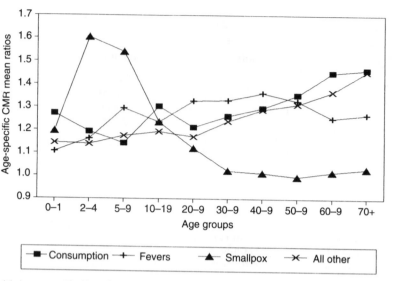

3.16 Age-specific London CMRs in years with extreme cause-specific CMRs

Extreme values

Alongside these analyses of relationships between movements in the series as a whole, we have also investigated the behaviour of the age-specific CMRs in years when the CMRs for the various cause of death series display extreme values. The procedure adopted was to rank the annual CMRs for each of the non-infancy causes, over the period 1733–1824, in order of magnitude so as to identify the ten years with the highest and lowest values. Taking each cause of death series in turn as our criterion, we then calculated the mean CMR for each age-group in the highest and lowest ten years for each of the cause of death series, and plotted the ratios of the two as in figure 3.16.

The results are generally in line with those of the previous analyses. The importance of smallpox as a determinant of fluctuations in childhood and adolescent mortality stands out clearly, but the CMRs for ages 20–9 years are also about 10 per cent higher in the 'top' smallpox years than they are in the 'bottom' years. The fever figures by contrast show a rough plateau between the ages of 20 and 59 years, with a noticeable 'spike' in the older childhood age-group. Both consumption and the residual category show a progressive increase in the ratios throughout adult life reaching a maximum in old age, but the former also displays high values early in life and in adolescence.

Discussion

Movements in the cause-specific burial series, whatever the uncertainties associated with the cause of death categories themselves, thus display systematically distinct sets of associations with those broken down by age. In the case of consumption the pattern is sufficiently close to the age-incidence of nineteenth-century respiratory tuberculosis for us to be reasonably confident that the latter was an important contributor to this category of burials, whatever else it may have encompassed. The association of fever mortality with the lower part of the adult age range is also consistent with the behaviour of typhus and typhoid in Victorian London (Murchison 1858), but its relationship with the 5–9 year totals suggests an important contribution from febrile childhood conditions. The principal components analysis by sub-periods suggested that these may have become more important after 1775.

In many ways it is smallpox which presents the most intriguing pattern. Smallpox, of all the causes of death recorded in eighteenth-century London, is closest to McNeill's (1980) model 'metropolitan' infection, and it has featured prominently in the debate on eighteenth-century population change in England.[24] Contemporaries appear to have thought that the disease was a universal childhood affliction in the capital at this time. Lettsom, for instance, argued that children borne in the city at this time would have contracted the disease by the age of eight, but its prevalence in the country at large is less certain.[25]

Our results suggest that smallpox had a significant effect on overall mortality into the teenage years and, possibly, beyond the age of twenty. If it was indeed the case that London children all caught smallpox before reaching their teens, then it follows that the deaths in this age group and above were those of immigrants from populations elsewhere in which the disease did not have same ubiquity it enjoyed in the capital. This would also explain the importance of the smallpox coefficients in clustering the principal components scores of both the childhood and young adult age-groups' CMRs. A further inference from this might be that the behaviour of burial totals in the second of

[24] Smallpox's 'model' status in this respect reflects the absence of either animal reservoirs or immune carriers, the direct 'person to person' mode of infection, apparent indifference to the nutritional status of the victim, and the existence of lifetime immunity among survivors. The main partisan of its importance in the process of mortality decline has been Razzell (1965, 1977); see also Chambers 1972: 100–2, Mercer 1985 and 1990: 46–73.

[25] See Razzell 1977: 71 for a discussion of this point.

Death and the metropolis

Table 3.9. *Z scores between cause-specific burial series in London Bills*

	Fevers	Infancy	Smallpox	Other causes
Consumption	2.02*	4.83***	0.29	7.09***
Fevers		3.38***	1.56	2.97**
Infancy			0.86	4.01***
Smallpox				–0.14

Note: *Significant at 5 per cent confidence level
**Significant at 1 per cent confidence level
***Significant at 0.1 per cent confidence level

these age ranges was, as we predicted, strongly influenced by the consequences of migration. Again, however, the analysis by sub-periods suggests that the association between smallpox and child-hood mortality became stronger, relative to its association with that at the older ages, after 1775.

The distinctive behaviour of the smallpox series emerges clearly when we calculate Z scores between the cause-specific series for the period as a whole (see table 3.9). Movements in the numbers of deaths in the infancy, consumption, fever and residual categories are all significantly associated with each other, but none of them displays a statistically significant association with movements in the smallpox series. There are, no doubt, a number of reasons for this, but one of them is likely to be found in the age composition of the population at risk to the disease: a population apparently consisting of infants, children, and a section of the adolescent/young adult age-group, but excluding the great majority of older adults from whom consumption and the residual category of causes drew most of their victims, and more heavily weighted towards the bottom end of the age-range than was mortality from fevers.

Conclusions

The structure of London's mortality regime, as it emerges from these aggregate data, conforms broadly to the expectations of our model. For much of the period the overall burial totals for the capital show less short-term instability than do the English crude death rate estimates, striking testimony to the relative importance of endemic infections among causes of death in the capital. Absolute levels of mortality cannot, strictly speaking, be determined from the type of analysis we have been pursuing, but if we take the proportion of total burials constituted by infants to be a rough indicator of mortality levels in the capital, then these appear to have been substantially above those prevailing elsewhere in England throughout the period.

The structure of the age-specific burial totals also tends to bear out the 'high potential' interpretation since the figures for the childhood age-groups, whose members are expected to have relatively low levels of immunity, are substantially more volatile than are those for higher ages. The levels of such volatility themselves vary in the longer term, but this variation lends only very limited support to the 'stabilisation of mortality' thesis. The apparent decline in mortality at the end of the period is associated with a reduction in short-term fluctuations, but the levels of instability recorded in the early nineteenth century are no lower than those of the late seventeenth and this development might equally well be interpreted as a return to 'normal' conditions after a period of unusual disturbance in the middle decades of the eighteenth century.

The age-specific burial series suggest that the young adult age-groups (20–39 years) were particularly affected by this disturbance in the period 1735–49, but all the adult series below the age of 60 show markedly higher levels of instability before 1775 than they do subsequently. The stabilisation of mortality at the childhood ages after 1800 can plausibly be linked to the substantial reduction in smallpox deaths, but does not itself give rise to any fall in the age-group's share of total burials. On this latter basis the main beneficiaries, apart from the youngest age-group, are the young adults whose declining share of the total is associated with a substantial fall in the numbers of deaths from 'fevers'.

The vital regimes of London and its hinterland were mutually inter-related as a result of the migration streams which the city required if its numbers were to be kept up in the face of recurrent burial surpluses. The HPM assumes that many of these migrants would have lacked immunological resistance to urban diseases and experienced correspondingly more severe mortality. Paradoxically, the presence of substantial immigration would itself thus have contributed to the mortality 'penalty' experienced by metropolitan populations. The aggregative evidence suggests, however, that the inter-relationship between migration and mortality went beyond a simply additive contribution to the death rate.

Smallpox and 'fevers' are both likely to have made a substantial contribution to immigrant mortality, but smallpox in particular was also a major cause of death among London children. The short-run correlations between the mortality of different age-groups suggest that, on this time scale, mortality among older children, adolescents and younger adults responded to an interrelated set of factors, amongst which smallpox and fevers were strongly represented. Again, in the longer term it was at these ages, together with infancy, that the decline in mortality was apparently most pronounced, and amongst causes of death, it was fever and smallpox which displayed the most substantial reduction. It is thus possible that – in these age-groups at least – the mechanisms governing short-term fluctuations in mortality were cognate with those which determined its secular decline, and that the effects of migration were implicated in the behaviour of mortality in a broad range of age-groups, through pathways enabling the transmission of smallpox and 'fever' pathogens.

Summary

The failure of classical 'standard of living' models to predict secular mortality variations in past populations has led many historical demographers to see these as 'autonomous' and determined by variables lying wholly outside the world of human affairs. Ironically this has coincided with the development of a much closer relationship between historical demography and other areas of social and economic history, a relationship fostered by the success of economic and social structural explanations of variations in population growth. Such explanations have, however, been couched in terms of nuptiality and fertility, leading to the marginalisation of mortality as a demographic variable both conceptually and in substantive terms.

This marginalisation, however, reflects a failure to distinguish adequately between mortality shifts which are genuinely 'autonomous' with respect to economy and society – reflecting climatic or microbiological change – and those which are simply 'exogenous' in the more limited econometric sense of independence from the level of real wages. Accounts which invoke further dimensions of the human world – especially those relating to spatial structure – have proved successful in incorporating a number of such 'exogenous' movements in mortality within a framework of structural explanation.

Models of vital regimes constructed along these lines are concerned with a population's structurally determined 'mortality potential', rather than the 'realised' level of mortality prevailing at any time which results from an interaction between the mortality potential, the realised level in the recent past, and exogenous factors such as microbial mutation and the epidemiological characteristics of the outside world. Mortality potential is itself ultimately determined by a diversity of ecological, economic and social factors, but the range of pathways through which these exercise their effects is relatively restricted, and the most important can be captured by a set of 'intermediate' variables which we have termed 'bounding', 'conduction', 'diet' and 'retention'.

The conditions prevailing in pre-industrial metropolitan centres are likely to have endowed these variables with a characteristic set of values, leading to a configuration which we have described in terms of the 'high model' of metropolitan epidemiology. This predicts that, relative to more thinly settled regions, mortality in such populations is likely to be high – especially in childhood – due to the maintenance of endemic foci of infection, which will also reduce the level of short-run instability displayed by mortality levels. Such high mortality may lead to natural decrease among the population and thus to a dependence on immigration if numbers are to be maintained, but the immigrants themselves are likely to lack immunological defences against many 'metropolitan' infections and suffer substantially higher mortality than their 'native' peers.

A review of the literature on social and economic conditions in eighteenth-century London suggests that the city experienced many of the conditions associated with the high potential model. The population was large and densely settled, with inadequate housing causing widespread problems of overcrowding. Standards of sanitation and water supply were low in much of the city, although the food supply was apparently more reliable than was the case elsewhere in England. Recorded real wage levels were relatively high, but these are very difficult to translate into actual earnings, and the heights of working-class Londoners were low by the standards of rural England. A number of these characteristics, however, reflected the action of factors specific to their time and place, rather than generic to pre-industrial populations. In particular the difficulties with housing were due in part to the undercapitalised and overspeculative character of the construction sector, conditions themselves linked to a particular regime of fiscal legislation and the means adopted to finance the state's recurrent war-making.

The available aggregate vital data are generally consistent with the predictions of the model for most of the period. Burials substantially outnumber baptisms until the end of the eighteenth century, and the burial series itself is relatively stable in the short term. Analysis of short-run movements in the age-specific burials revealed two statistically independent components, one distinguishing children from adults, whilst the second picked out older children, adolescents and young adults in a manner that may be associated with the epidemio-logical consequences of immigration. The cause of death data sug-gested that both smallpox and – in particular – 'fever' were associated with the latter component, although smallpox was also strongly asso-ciated with childhood mortality. At the same time, however, it would be wrong to adopt too static a view of London's vital regime, for its character altered considerably in the closing decades of our period, a development manifested most dramatically in the disappearance of the aggregate burial surplus.

PART II

The level of mortality

What is now known about the pre-nineteenth century urban population of Europe? The short answer to this question must be: surprisingly little. The meagreness of the existing literature is surprising because historians and social scientists have never been hesitant to make sweeping statements about the historical evolution of urban populations. (De Vries 1984: 17)

The predictions of the HPM have withstood a number of preliminary tests based on the aggregate vital data, but the central question we must answer, in order to determine the adequacy of the model in the present context, is that of absolute mortality levels. The amount of information available on mortality levels in pre-industrial European cities is, as De Vries implies, remarkably meagre. The widespread prevalence of burial surpluses in the aggregate vital data for such populations has often been taken to reflect the effects of elevated mortality levels, but this attribution is not conclusive and other explanations – such as depressed fertility – have also been advanced.[1]

This deficiency in our knowledge is partly due to the inherent difficulty of the topic, in the absence of adequate data on population size and structure, but it is also a paradoxical consequence of the growing methodological refinement of historical demographic research itself. As De Vries points out, the latter has been based on techniques which either lend themselves – like family reconstitution – more readily to the study of villages and small towns than to cities, or else – like aggregative back projection – are pitched at the level of national aggregates. Consequently, whilst the new methodological rigour has discredited many older estimates of the death rates in large towns and cities, little of the resulting research has been directed at such populations.

The present study is based on a combination of two approaches which are intended to complement each other. The first of these is a detailed analysis of age-specific mortality patterns, in a restricted population, obtained by means of family reconstitution. Family reconstitution, based on the nominal linkage of entries from vital registers, is potentially very powerful, since as well as yielding age-specific schedules of vital rates, it can also perform a limited range of internal checks on the accuracy and consistency of the source materials used in the analysis (Wrigley 1966a). These advantages, however, are purchased at a substantial price, for the method is laborious and makes considerable demands on the quality of the vital registers, which must be sufficiently detailed to permit the reliable identification of individuals over lengthy periods. Furthermore it

---

[1] See below chapter 4.

129

restricts attention to a limited, geographically stable, 'reconstitutable fraction' of the population and yields no information on the size or structure of the population at large or on crude demographic rates.

Limitations of this kind are particularly relevant to the study of metropolitan populations and, whilst some parish registers from seventeenth-century London have been subjected to a modified form of reconstitution (Finlay 1981), eighteenth-century registers are thought to have suffered too much from popular anti-clericalism, clerical laxity and the growth of religious non-conformity to be suitable for this purpose. We have tried to overcome some of these difficulties by taking as our source, not parish registers as such, but an analogous body of material maintained by two of London's six 'Monthly Meetings' of Quakers.

The Quaker records are of a generally high quality, but the population they document is small in size and can hardly be said to 'represent' that of London as a whole. We have thus complemented the family reconstitution results with a further analysis of the Bills of Mortality intended – in the first instance – to furnish us with a set of infant mortality estimates. The latter task requires us to estimate a number of unknown quantities, of which the most important is the relative under-registration of births and baptisms. The dearth of information on this topic is such that any estimates are subject to substantial uncertainty and, rather than try to improve on those produced by Wrigley and Schofield (1981), our strategy has been to take the latter, with minor alterations, and then to assess the resulting mortality series in terms of its plausibility and its sensitivity to likely sources of error.

A strategy of this kind implies a much lower level of reliance on the absolute values of the mortality estimates than is usual in historical demographic research, and it is thus correspondingly important that we specify hypotheses testable in terms of large-scale trends and orders of magnitude. Fortunately the adoption of the HPM enables us to do this, and it is possible to demonstrate that, in both the relevant respects, our mortality results are robust within the range required for hypothesis testing. The infant mortality series can also be used as the starting point for the calculation of a variety of other demographic indicators including the age-structure of net migration, and crude birth rates. The former is of central importance to our interpretation of the HPM, whilst the level of the birth rate is relevant to the latter's applicability, and it is fortunate that both sets of estimates are relatively robust since most of the likely sources of error involved in their calculation are self-cancelling.

4

Mortality among London Quakers

The maintenance of vital registers was a central part of the Quaker religious practice or 'discipline', throughout the period with which we are concerned, associated as it was with their rejection of the established church and its parochial institutions (Lloyd 1950). Quakers were strictly endogamous throughout our period and their meetings conducted marriages, whose validity was recognised in law (Lloyd 1950: 51), buried their dead in Quaker burial grounds and maintained a sophisticated system of poor relief. The vital registers grew out of this system and differ from Anglican Parochial materials chiefly in their registration of births rather than baptisms (Rowntree 1902).

The quality of the vital registers maintained by the London meetings was generally high, the birth registers providing information on residence and occupation of parents, whilst before about 1800 the burial registers generally specify age and cause of death in addition to occupation and place of residence of the deceased or their parents. The information on age and cause of death was provided by the same 'searchers' who gathered material for the Bills of Mortality, and the cause of death categories in the Quaker registers are the same as those appearing in the latter.

The two meetings selected for analysis, those of Southwark and 'Peel', were both suburban. Southwark covered the built-up area south of the river including Rotherhithe and Bermondsey, as well as Southwark itself and the parishes of Lambeth, Camberwell and Newington Butts, initially rural areas which became urbanised in the latter decades of the eighteenth century. Peel meeting covered a less well defined area taking in the parishes lying in a north western quadrant outside the City walls (see maps 4.1 and 4.2).

The size of the meetings is hard to ascertain prior to the appearance

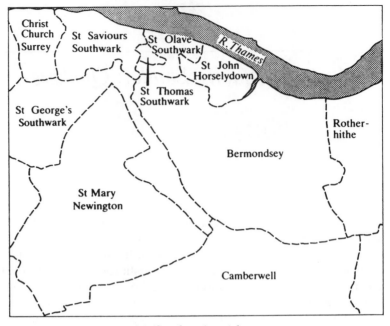

4.1 'Southern' parishes

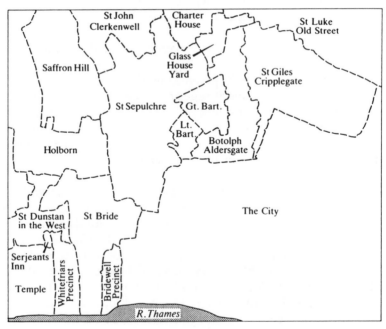

4.2 'Northern' parishes

of formal membership lists. Southwark produced the first of these in 1737, including 809 names, and Peel in 1770 with 230. By 1850 these had dwindled to 499 and 178 respectively (Landers 1984: chapter 3). Some idea of the size of the study population, relative to that of London Quakers as a whole, can be obtained from the numbers of recorded marriages. Between 1650 and 1749 Peel and Southwark accounted for roughly 19 per cent of the 3095 marriages recorded in the digests of the London and Middlesex Quarterly Meeting, and in the period 1750–1849 for 24.6 per cent of a total 1443 marriages (Landers 1984: 123, n. 4).

A more detailed picture of the geographical structure of the two meetings can be obtained from the residential information contained in the birth and burial registers. This is displayed for the two sources separately (from a 79 per cent sample in the case of the burial registers) in table 4.1. In both cases the results suggest little change prior to the latter part of the eighteenth century when a marked shift away from the older 'core' areas, towards the newer suburbs such as Islington, Camberwell and Newington, becomes visible.

The social composition of the meetings seems, especially during the first century of their existence, to have been heterogeneous. In Southwark, for instance:

analysis of the subscriptions for the building of Horsleydown Meeting-House in 1738 shows it to have had a fair number of prosperous members. Out of the total subscription of £717 9s, £642 4s was raised by 104 subscribers as follows:- sixteen Friends gave amounts varying from £2 to £5; thirty-one gave between £5 and £10; six gave £10 10s each; thirteen gave £15 15s, whilst three gave £20 and one . . headed the list with £35. (Beck and Ball 1869: 226)

On the other hand, the cost of maintaining numerous poor Friends was a continuous source of complaint on the part of both meetings well into the eighteenth century. Quantitative data on this topic are scanty, and the social and economic position of the early Quakers remains a topic of debate (Reay 1980). One source of evidence is the occupational information included in the vital registers but this needs to be interpreted with care as the same term, for example 'baker', may be used of individuals working in a given trade without regard to their actual role, still less their relative wealth.

The figures in table 4.2, which are taken from the burial entries with initial letter 'B', and classified according to the scheme developed by John Patten (Patten 1977) should thus be treated as no more than a broad indicator of trends. Overall the proportion of servants and apprentices falls appreciably up till 1800,[1] whereas that of

---

[1] The very high frequency of the terms 'servant' and 'apprentice' in the seventeenth-century registers probably reflects the relative scarcity of occupational descriptions

Table 4.1. *Distribution of events between parish groups within Northern and Southern areas (in percentages)*

Groups[a]:	Northern				Southern				Number observed	
	1	2	3	4	5	6	7	8	North	South
(a) Births										
1650–99	50	15	6	29	27	25	5	43	354	759
1700–49	44	13	17	26	26	27	7	40	446	1,305
1750–99	31	18	27	24	24	25	22	29	361	744
1800–49	7	11	52	30	11	13	70	6	405	728
(b) Burials										
1650–99	35	17	16	32	29	19	9	43	1,022	1,275
1700–49	31	18	21	30	27	30	13	30	1,426	2,115
1750–99	22	14	33	31	21	29	19	32	531	840
1800–49	11	9	49	31	14	14	66	6	288	651

Note: [a]Key to Parish groups

Northern
1 St Botolph Aldersgate, St Bartholomew Great and Less, St Sepulchre
2 St Brides, St Dunstans, Holborn
3 Clerkenwell, Islington
4 St Giles Cripplegate, St Lukes

Southern
5 Bermondsey, Rotherhithe
6 Christ Church Surrey, St Saviour Southwark
7 St George Southwark, Lambeth, Newington Butts, Camberwell
8 SS John, Olave, Thomas Southwark

'artisans and artisan-retailers' tends to rise. In general, however, there is little evidence of a major discontinuity before the nineteenth century when the sharp increase in the 'professional' group suggests that 1800 marks a watershed in this, as in the geographical, respect.

The family reconstitution results for mortality in infancy and childhood (technically 'mortality probabilities', corresponding to the life table function q_x) are set out in the upper panel of table 4.3.[2] The

in the early decades of burial registrations. These two terms seem to have been treated as indicators of household affiliation, on a par with 'wife' or 'child', rather than as 'occupational' categories as such, and so individuals in these positions were more likely to be described as such than were heads of households (see Landers 1984: 123, n. 4).

[2] For convenience the data have been grouped into fifty year cohorts, beginning in 1650, with results also being calculated for 25 year cohorts where there are enough observations to make this viable. The numbers of events recorded for the years before 1675 and after 1824 are, however, relatively small and the effective boundary

Table 4.2. *Occupational descriptions in sample of Peel and Southwark Burial Register entries (in percentages)*

Period	Occupational Categories						N
	1	2	3	4	5	6	
1650–99	8.4	5.3	1.0	1.5	74.6	9.2	131
1700–49	21.4	27.2	2.9	7.8	33.5	7.2	206
1750–99	26.2	40.2	3.6	17.3	5.6	7.1	196
1800–49	31.3	35.1	22.3	3.0	2.3	6.0	134

Note: Categories: 1 Distributors and distributor-processors. 2 Artisans and artisan-retailers. 3 Professional and services. 4 Transport. 5 Servants and apprentices. 6 Others.

overall trend of mortality is similar to that of the vital index obtained from the Bills of Mortality. The infant mortality rate for the last cohort is comparable to those obtained by the Registrar General for London in the 1840s. These were close to the national average (Wrigley 1977: 299), but the scale of London's excess mortality before the nineteenth century emerges starkly from a comparison of our results with those obtained from other English reconstitutions which are set out in the lower panel of the table.[3]

This excess is particularly severe in the 1–4 year age-group, as the high potential model would lead us to expect, since at this point the children's immunological defences are still relatively weak. We should also note that the trend of London's mortality, at all ages below 10 years, apparently differed from that in the country at large. Infant mortality in the 13 parish sample rose a little after 1700, but the childhood rates changed scarcely at all throughout the period. The heightened severity of mortality in early eighteenth-century London

dates for the study are 1665 and 1840. The infant rates for the cohorts 1650–1749 have been adjusted to take account of the practice of some parents who registered the burials, but not the births, of their children with the two meetings. The resulting corrections are relatively minor for the eighteenth-century cohorts, but those for the seventeenth are substantial, of the order of 30 per cent. The rationale for these adjustments is given in Landers 1984: appendix, together with a detailed examination of the reliability of the data. They are unlikely to be greatly in error, but the corrected rates for the seventeenth century may be a little too low. The numbers of risks on which the infant rates are based are 1743, 1852, 907 and 601 for the cohorts born 1650–99, 1700–49, 1750–99 and 1800–49.

[3] The parish register infant mortality rates quoted in the table embody Wrigley and Schofield's proposed corrections for under-registration. The uncorrected rates for the four cohorts are 161.3, 166.7, 169.2, 133.4.

Table 4.3. *Age-specific mortality in Peel and Southwark Quaker Meetings
and in thirteen English parishes (rates per thousand at risk)*

(a) London Quakers

	Months				Years			
Cohort	0	0–2	3–5	6–11	0	1	2–4	5–9
1650–74	108	152	51	70	251	103	190	66
1675–99	115	158	46	82	263	113	132	69
1700–24	125	197	59	130	342	145	177	89
1725–49	112	204	58	121	341	143	186	109
1750–74	96	168	82	119	327	150	159	91
1775–99	81	114	38	80	231	101	141	32
1800–24	40	53	41	95	194	93	85	79
1824–49	33	33	37	76	151	77	93	—

(b) Age-specific mortality rates (per thousand)

Cohort	Age-group	English parishes	London Quakers
1650–99			
	0	170	260
	1–4	101	244
	5–9	40	67
	1–9	137	295
	0–9	284	478
1700–49			
	0	195	342
	1–4	107	298
	5–9	41	95
	1–9	143	365
	0–9	310	582
1750–99			
	0	165	276
	1–4	103	253
	5–9	33	57
	1–9	133	296
	0–9	277	490

Source: Wrigley and Schofield 1983, and Reconstitution Tabulations

thus seems to have been a specifically metropolitan phenomenon and
not a reflection of any substantial deterioration in conditions over a
wider area. We shall now examine the level and trend in the rates
under three main headings: infant mortality, mortality in childhood,
and adult mortality.

Infant mortality

Although the Quaker Registers, like the Bills of Mortality, do contain information on causes of death, the categories used by the searchers to classify such causes are hard to translate into those of scientific medicine and this is particularly true in the case of infant mortality. Labels such as 'teething' or 'convulsions' might denote deaths from any of a number of distinct diseases and we cannot even guarantee that they were always employed in a consistent fashion. Our analysis of infant mortality must thus be based on the techniques developed for use with sources in which explicit references to causes of death are absent. These rely chiefly on the distribution of infant deaths within the first year of life and on their seasonal incidence. As a first step, however, it is useful to look at some comparative data from other studies so as to place our own results in a broader context.

Flinn (1981: appendix table 10) has tabulated the results of reconstitution studies from a number of regions of early modern Europe which serve to emphasise the unusual severity of London's mortality throughout much of the eighteenth century. Of the sixteen rates obtained from English studies prior to 1750 none is in excess of 250 per thousand and of eighty French cases for the appropriate period, 20 per cent lie between 250 and 299 per thousand, with only five in excess of 350. Knodel's studies (1968, 1967, 1988: chapter 3) of a number of villages in south-western Germany are alone in reporting levels of this kind on a consistent basis, a finding the author ascribed to the practice of artificial feeding from birth.

Studies of urban populations are, as we have indicated, less numerous, but such as are available also suggest that mortality in London was unusually high. Perrenoud (1985), calculated a rate of 296 per thousand for Geneva in the period 1580–1739, whilst the figures for the insalubrious Le Havre suburb of Ingouville, in the period 1730–70, was only 186 (Terrisse 1961). Galliano's (1966) study of nineteen parishes on the southern outskirts of Paris in the last quarter of the eighteenth century yielded a mean rate of 177 although the figures for individual parishes varied between 134 and 296.

Early in the following century, however, our study population began to overtake the Parisians. The estimates of infant mortality for the Seine department prepared by Preston and Van de Walle (1978) fluctuate between 179 and 200 per thousand over the first half of the century, suggesting that the London Quakers were experiencing appreciably lower levels of mortality by mid-century, having entered the post-Napoleonic era in a roughly similar position. The contrast

Table 4.4. *Infant mortality in six London
parishes (rates per thousand)*

Parish	−1653	1690s
1 Allhallows Bread Street	111	209
2 St Peters Cornhill	129	215
3 Christopher Le Stocks	88	155
4 St Michael Cornhill	133	169
5 St Mary Somerset	272	182
6 St Botolph Bishopsgate	211	176
Mean	157	185
Mean of parishes 1–4	115	187

Source: Finlay 1978

between London and other European capitals later in the century was dramatic.

In the 1860s the published infant mortality rate for Berlin (Knodel 1974: 159) was 297 per thousand whilst that for Stockholm in the preceding decade was 322 (Fridlizius 1979: 392). Mortality in London had thus improved dramatically, in both absolute and relative terms, since the middle of the eighteenth century, but for how long had the already high levels detectable in the late seventeenth century prevailed? Finlay's (1978) study of six London parishes indicates a sharp rise in infant mortality in the second half of the seventeenth century (see table 4.4), but the figure he obtained for the 1690s was still below 200 per thousand.

Inspection of the results for individual parishes, however, suggests that the latter figure may be something of an underestimate since the two poorest parishes in Finlay's sample, SS Mary Somerset and Botolph Bishopsgate, show an apparent improvement against the general trend. Had the rates for these parishes remained as they were at mid-century, then the rate for the sample as a whole in the 1690s would have been a little over 200, whilst it would have exceeded 250 per thousand had the two exhibited the same trend as the other four.

In view of this rather suspicious improvement one is tempted to suspect that the 'true' figure for the sample as a whole may have been closer to that obtained from the Quaker registers than it was to the 185 per thousand given by the author. This suspicion is strengthened by the rates of 246 and 333 per thousand quoted by Wrigley (1977) for the parishes of St Vedast and St Michael's Cornhill in the 1680s. Taking these figures together it seems safe to conclude that London in the late seventeenth century was experiencing levels of infant mortality which were higher than had been the case in earlier decades. In the following century the position worsened still further and London seems to have become appreciably less healthy than a number of continental towns and cities.

Endogenous and exogenous mortality

Analysis of changing patterns of infant mortality in the past have been strongly influenced by the biometric model formulated by Bourgeois-Pichat (1951) which partitions the overall mortality rate into components arising from so-called 'endogenous' causes, present at birth, and 'exogenous' causes arising from subsequent encounters with the external environment. These quantities are determined by calculating the cumulated deaths sustained by a cohort at successive intervals during the first year of life and plotting the resulting totals against a logarithmic transformation of age in days. In principle the totals should increase linearly against transformed age after the first month of life, reflecting the action of exogenous causes, and the numbers of deaths arising from endogenous causes can be obtained by projecting this increase back to the origin at age zero days.

Our own data, as set out in the first four columns of table 4.3, reveal that substantial changes occurred in the age incidence of infant mortality over the period. In particular, the overall reduction from the early eighteenth-century peak is primarily a consequence of the great diminution of risks associated with the first three months of life. This conclusion arises even more strongly from a comparison of the figures for the 1800–24 cohort with those for the first cohort in the series. Mortality at ages less than three months falls by more than 60 per cent, whereas that at ages above six months remains at a higher level in the early nineteenth century than it was at the beginning of the study period.

The application of the biometric model yields estimates of endogenous mortality (see table 4.5) which remain at a high level, similar to that observed in other English studies, until the middle of the eighteenth century when a sharp decline sets in. This decline continues into the nineteenth century and takes the final figure to the 14 per thousand given by the Registrar-General for London as a whole in the late 1840s (Wrigley 1977). The exogenous component, by contrast, rises sharply after 1700 and remains at a high level until the last

Table 4.5. *Exogenous and endogenous components of infant mortality (rates per thousand)*

Cohort	Exogenous	Endogenous
London Quakers		
1650–74	175	76
1675–99	183	80
1700–24	267	75
1725–49	260	81
1750–74	284	43
1775–99	183	48
1800–24	167	27
1825–49	137	14
Four English Parishes (means)		
1650–99	70	75
1700–49	79	100
1750–99	48	85

Source: Wrigley 1977, and Reconstitution Tabulations

quarter of the century, showing some increase after 1750, before falling to a level around 80 per cent of that prevailing in the later seventeenth century.

The scale of this phenomenon is hard to account for in terms of a rigid interpretation of the biometric model, which has also yielded unexpected findings when applied to reconstitution data derived from English parish registers. Estimates of endogenous mortality have proved both high and variable, relative to exogenous mortality, in studies of material from the sixteenth and early seventeenth centuries whereas the reverse has held true in recent periods.[4] An alternative interpretation based on changing patterns of infectious disease has been advanced by R. E. Jones (1980) to explain the findings of his study of registers from some 60 parishes in north Shropshire from the sixteenth to the nineteenth centuries.

This period witnessed both a substantial reduction in the level of infant mortality and also a major change in its structure. In terms of the biometric model:

[4] See Schofield and Wrigley 1979 and Wrigley 1977 for a review of the relevant data and a discussion of the interpretative problems they pose.

this transformation had three major aspects – a very large decline in endogenous mortality, taking place between the mid-seventeenth and the mid-eighteenth centuries, a halving of exogenous mortality during the first three months of life, taking place mainly in the late eighteenth century, and a doubling of mortality during the second half of the first year of life, taking place around 1710. (Jones 1980: 244)

Jones argued, however, that such an explanation would be misconceived and that the initially high estimates of endogenous mortality were an artefact of the analysis. The period between the middle of the seventeenth century and the opening decades of the eighteenth should, he suggested, be seen as one of epidemiological transition in which an historically older pattern, dominated by high neonatal mortality arising from respiratory infection, gave way to a 'modern' incidence of high mortality later in the first year of life, due to the familiar 'childhood' infections such as smallpox and measles.

Jones grounded this claim on two features of the data from the earlier period: firstly, the curve of accumulated deaths within the first year of life was not linear under the Bourgeois-Pichat transformation and secondly, there was evidence of marked seasonal variation in the incidence of the supposedly 'endogenous' neonatal deaths. The curve of infant deaths obtained during the period of high neonatal mortality was markedly convex, a shape which made the estimation of a 'true' rate of endogenous mortality a matter of some difficulty but which strongly resembled those obtained in several reconstitutions from Atlantic coastal parishes of France (Blayo and Henry 1967) where the authors suggested that respiratory infections were responsible for an accelerated 'build-up' of infant deaths in the early months of life.

In our own case, however, the shape of the mortality curve (see figure 4.1) obtained by pooling data from the cohorts 1650–1749 shows no appreciable deviation from linearity, a slight convexity up to 90 days being offset by a tendency to kink upwards thereafter. But Jones derived additional support for his argument by demonstrating a marked winter peak in the neonatal mortality rates derived from the earlier Shropshire registers, a finding hard to reconcile with the action of endogenous causes of death but entirely consistent with that of respiratory infection.

The seasonality of burials

The seasonal distribution of infant burials at successive infant ages in our London Quaker sample was thus examined and appropriate

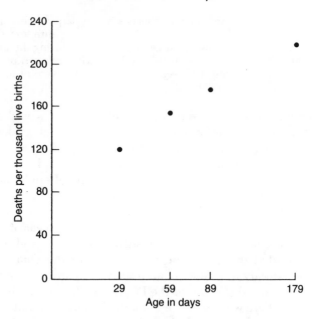

4.1 Biometric analysis of infant mortality, 1650–1749

Table 4.6. *Seasonality of infant burials:*
numbers of observations by age and cohort

Age in Days	1650–99	1700–49	1750–1849
0–30	321	302	119
31–89	120	176	85
90–179	115	114	83
181–	197	237	158

seasonality indices constructed.[5] The figures for the cohorts born after 1750 were pooled in view of the relatively small number of observations in this period (see table 4.6) and the seasonal indices for burials at ages below 90 days weighted to take account of the seasonality of

---

[5] The seasonality indices were constructed in the conventional manner and express the proportion of events falling in a given season relative to the length of the season in days. Thus if the incidence of events was distributed evenly across the year each seasonal index would be equal to 100. Conversely a figure of 200 for a given season would indicate that twice as many events had occurred in that season as would be expected on the basis of an even distribution.

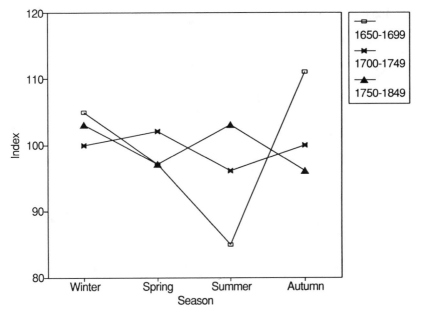

4.2 Birth seasonality in Peel and Southwark Vital Registers

births (see figure 4.2).[6] The analysis revealed substantial variations in the seasonal incidence of infant death, but these did not in general conform to the expectations of the Jones hypothesis. Deaths in the 0–29 day age-group (see figure 4.3) show a strong seasonal peak in the summer months (June–August) throughout the period, although this peak weakens somewhat in the second cohort (1700–49). The index for Autumn (September–November) is close to 100 for all cohorts and those for Winter and Spring (December–February and March–May respectively) fall below this level, the Spring index being particularly low after 1750.

The seasonality of deaths in the 30–89 day age-group changes rather more over the period (see figure 4.4). Cohorts born before 1700 and after 1750, display a strong summer peak with the latter cohort also showing a clear spring trough, but the excess summer mortality

---

[6] The indices for burials at ages below 31 days were weighted by the reciprocal of the relevant birth seasonality index. In the case of burials at ages 30–89 days the reciprocal of the combined birth indices for the season in question and the preceding season, weighted in the relative proportions two to one, was employed. These procedures, although necessarily inexact, should remove most of the disturbing effects of seasonal variations in the numbers of births. For a more sophisticated procedure, employing nominal record linkage, see Knodel 1988: 60–8.

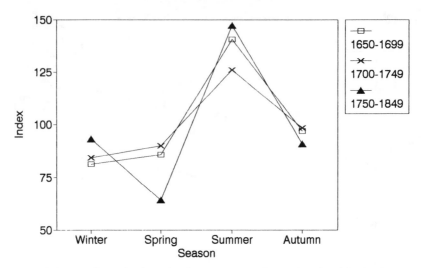

4.3 Seasonality of infant deaths: ages 0–29 days (weighted by birth seasonality)

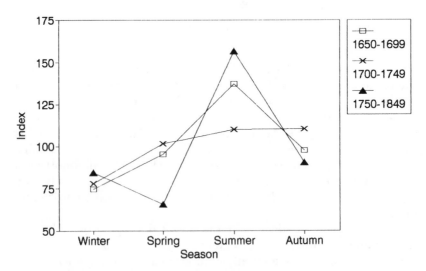

4.4 Seasonality of infant deaths: ages 30–89 days (weighted by birth seasonality)

almost disappears in the middle cohort (1700–49) in the face of a small rise in the autumn index. The results for the 3–5 month age-groups, by contrast, do show substantial excess mortality in the winter, and particularly in the spring, until 1750 (see figure 4.5).

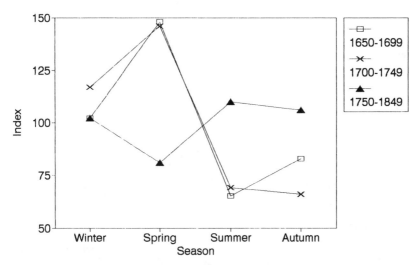

4.5 Seasonality of infant deaths: ages 90–179 days

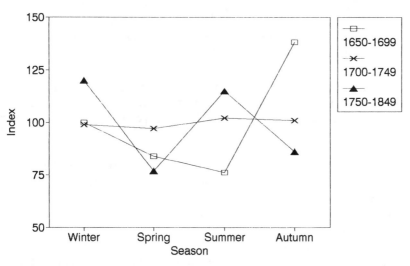

4.6 Seasonality of infant deaths: ages 180+ days

This pattern is consistent with the action of the respiratory infection postulated by Jones, but its disappearance after 1750 is associated with only a modest reduction in mortality, which suggests that the amelioration in this cause of death was largely offset by the effects of others acting later in the year. The seasonal profile of deaths in the oldest age-group (see figure 4.6) evolves from one of excess autumn

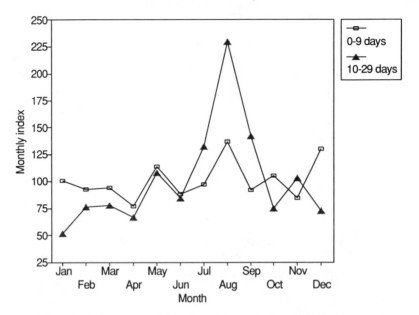

4.7 Monthly incidence (weighted) of infant deaths, 1650–1749: ages 0–29 days

mortality in the first cohort, combined with a pronounced spring and summer trough, through an almost flat pattern between 1700 and 1749, to a bimodal distribution in the century after 1750, with excess mortality in both winter and summer and a deficit in the spring and autumn.

The data for the first two cohorts taken together are sufficiently numerous to bear analysis on a monthly basis. In figure 4.7 we have split the first month of life into ages 0–9 and 10–29 days calculating separate indices for each with appropriate allowance for the monthly distribution of births. The scale of the August burial peak in the older of these two age-groups is striking, but infants under 10 days also suffer an excess August mortality of some 25 per cent suggesting a significant level of artificial feeding from very close to birth, if not from birth itself. The monthly pattern of mortality at ages between 30 and 179 days (see figure 4.8) broadly reflects that seen in the indices for the four seasons although the scale of the July trough is unexpected.[7] In the case of the oldest age-group, however, the autumn excess

[7] Such a trough contrasts strikingly with the seasonality of infant mortality in Victorian London, but is in keeping with that of infant burials in the contemporary Bills of Mortality, where the July index for 'infants and chrisomes' falls below 100 in the

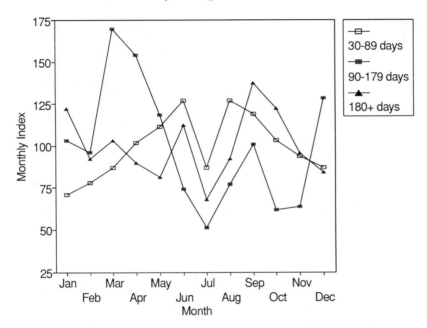

4.8 Monthly incidence of infant deaths, 1650–1749: ages 30+ days

proves to be heavily weighted toward September, the index value having fallen below 100 by November, and might thus be more accurately labelled as 'late summer/early autumn'.

The interpretation of these diverse movements is far from straight-forward, and is complicated by the occurrence of substantial shifts in the overall seasonal distribution of burials in London over this period,[8] but we can attempt some explanations. In the first place, the strong seasonality observed in the mortality of the youngest age-groups suggests that it was infectious diseases, rather than endo-genous causes of death, which were chiefly responsible for the high levels of neonatal mortality observed in the early cohorts. The fact that the peak mortality occurred in the summer months, however, is not compatible with the effects of respiratory disease so much as with

late seventeenth century – as does the early eighteenth-century figure for convul-sions burials, to which the former series was assimilated after 1700 (see chapter 6). Data on the seasonality of burials in Victorian London are tabulated in Buchan and Mitchell 1875.

[8] These changes seem, however, to have affected mortality at childhood ages more than they did infants or adults (see chapter 6). Substantial spatial variations in the seasonality of childhood mortality also developed in the latter part of our period, but seem to have been relatively unimportant before 1750 (see chapter 8).

exposure to the risks of water-borne, and particularly food-borne, infections.

This conclusion in turn suggests that artificial feeding was widely practised from an early age. Such a practice has, as we have seen, often been linked to severe neonatal mortality in historical Europe and it seems a plausible explanation for the high levels observed in the present study.[9] If this attribution is correct, however, the fact that the summer excess continues undiminished into the second half of our period, despite the steep reduction in neonatal mortality, implies that such artificial feeding continued among an ever-diminishing fraction of the reconstituted families, who in turn experienced the bulk of neonatal deaths.

The behaviour of the figures for the older age-groups is consistent with a changing pattern of mortality from airborne infections, but in the present case reductions in deaths from respiratory disease do not seem to have played the decisive role detected by Jones in his Shropshire study. The decline in mortality at ages 30–89 days after 1750, is associated with a fall in the Spring index of a kind that might be expected from the amelioration of respiratory infection, but this effect is altogether too modest to account for the observed fall in mortality to less than a sixth of its peak level.

The seasonality data for the 90–179 day age-group are consistent with a substantial reduction in respiratory deaths, but one which was largely offset by a 'replacement' infection acting particularly in the summer and autumn. The early eighteenth century rise in the mortality of infants at ages over 180 days, however, was associated particularly with an increase in deaths in spring and summer. The precise nature of these 'replacement' infections remains unclear, but we should not lose sight of the central role played by changing levels of early infant mortality in the overall decline and it is to this that we must now return.

Postpartum insusceptibility

The possibility that a 'replacement' airborne infection may have been an important cause of such early infant deaths returns us to the question of methods of infant feeding. Breast-fed babies generally obtain a degree of immunity to such infections through the secretion of maternal antibodies in milk, and so the existence of widespread vulnerability among young infants in this respect would further

---

[9] See for instance Brändström 1988; Knodel 1988: chapters 3 and 4.

imply the prevalence of early artificial feeding, whether permanently or only during the secretion of the maternal colostrum. Fildes (1980) found that the latter procedure was recommended by some contemporary medical authorities and advice books, but direct evidence as to Quaker practices is lacking (Frost 1973: 71–4).

An indirect estimate of the mean length of lactation is possible, however, because of the strong association between this interval and the duration of the postpartum nonsusceptible period (nsp). The technique is based on a comparison of the mean interval from marriage to first birth (the 'protogenesic interval') with that between the first and second births (the 'first intergenesic interval'). Since the major difference between these two is that the protogenesic interval excludes the nsp, the difference between the means should provide a rough indicator of the latter's duration and thus, indirectly, of the length of lactation.

The method suffers from some technical problems (see Wilson 1982: 137–41) but all these will tend to exaggerate the estimate of nsp and so the results can safely be treated as an upper limit on its length. The possibility of systematic under-registration of first births relative to those of higher orders presents greater difficulties. Wilson argues that, where Anglican parish registers are concerned, delayed baptism together with the practice of baptising the first child in the mother's natal parish, leads to a spurious extension of the right hand 'tail' of the distribution of protogenesic intervals biasing the mean estimate upward.

In his study Wilson dealt with this problem by excluding intervals of more than two years duration and working with the resulting 'trimmed' distributions. In the present case, however, we do not have the problem of baptismal delay whilst, in the latter periods particularly, the importance of birth-right membership makes it unlikely that parents would fail to register their child's birth with their own meeting. We have thus adopted a more moderate criterion excluding protogenesic intervals of more than three years and intergenesic intervals over four years in duration, resulting, for the period 1650–1749 in means of 15.1 months for the protogenesic interval and 20.2 for the first intergenesic interval: a mean difference of 5.1 months.

This is similar to results obtained by Finlay for his two 'rich' City parishes, SS Michael and Peter Cornhill, in the period 1580–1650, and to those found in a number of French studies reflecting the influence of wet-nursing (Finlay 1981: 134 and appendix table 3), but contrasts sharply with Wilson's estimates, of approximately eleven months, for the mean nsp in a dozen English reconstitutions over the period

1650–1799. Our result for the period 1750–1849 is only 3.5 months but this implied reduction in mean nsp must be treated with great caution for the birth interval distributions in this period display unusual features which suggest artificial prolongation and thus render them unsuitable for our present purpose (Landers 1990).

Spatial variations

Some additional light can be thrown on the relationship between infant mortality, infant feeding and hygiene by an analysis of spatial variations in the ratio of recorded infant deaths to births using the residential information reviewed above. An index of infant mortality was constructed for each group of parishes, by 50 year cohorts, such that $I_i = 100$ where the ratio of infant burials to births in the ith group was equal to that obtained by pooling the observations from all groups. The results in table 4.7 reveal generally higher levels of mortality in the northern parishes than in those south of the river prior to 1800.

In the nineteenth century, however, the picture changes; the

Table 4.7. *Index figures for ratio of infant burials to births by parish groups*

	1700–49	1750–99	1800–49
Group 1	100	91	—
Group 2	159	67	—
Group 3	134	117	60
Group 4	142	147	125
Groups 1–4	127	107	85
Group 5	88	79	118
Group 6	124	140	176
Group 7	117	88	89
Group 8	64	120	186
Groups 5–8	91	96	108
Index Base	0.527	0.276	0.136 (=100)
Base if no spatial changes	—	0.298	0.174

Note: See table 4.1 for composition of parish groups

southern parishes now have higher mortality than do the northern and, within each of these two major divisions the newly expanding outer parishes have lower indices than do the inner parishes – although the number of events in some of the northern parishes is too small to bear detailed analysis. In the lower panel of the table an attempt is made to assess the responsibility of residential movement for the mortality trends observed in the reconstitution study.

For each of the two periods 1750–99 and 1800–49 the overall infant burial ratio was computed using the observed ratios in each group of parishes for that period, but weighting these according to the spatial distribution of births observed in the period preceding it. The results suggest that changes in the spatial distribution of the population had little effect on the overall trend in infant mortality before 1800, but that movement to the suburbs beyond this date produced a level of mortality some 20 per cent below that which would have prevailed otherwise.

These results are of interest for two reasons. In the first place they confirm that the reduction in infant mortality visible in the family reconstitution results after 1750 was 'genuine' and not an artefact of geographical movement. Secondly they give some hints as to the causes of death which were in operation. In particular, the higher mortality south of the river, and the greater contrast between 'old' and 'new' areas here than in the north may reflect differences in the quality of the water supply. After 1800 London's expansion was greatly affected by the development of piped water.

Much difficulty was encountered in maintaining a supply, which was taken from the Thames and inadequately filtered, to the low lying areas immediately south of the river. Districts further south, however, such as Camberwell were supplied with water from springs in the gravel hills. Hence the mortality differentials in the early nineteenth century may reflect the contrast between domestic water supplies which were pure and relatively abundant and those which were polluted and liable to disruption (Dyos 1961: 36–7, 143–5; Hardy 1984: 250). Ecological variation of this kind is, in turn, consistent with the hypothesis of gastric diseases as the major mortality factor among certain age-groups in this period.

Summary

The high potential model of metropolitan mortality is compatible with a wider range of mortality in infancy than at older ages. This is because of the way in which breast-feeding can insulate the young infant from food- and water-borne diseases, as well as provide a degree of vicarious immunological protection against airborne infection. Hence, where such feeding is practised, levels of early infant mortality need not differ greatly from those in lower density 'hinterland' populations. Such protection, however, is lost on weaning, and so the 'weanlings' and older infants would be expected to display the elevated levels of mortality characterising the childhood age-groups in such environments.

In the present case it appears that the degree of conduction present in London's epidemiological regime was seriously aggravated by the artificial feeding of young infants, which exposed them to the pathogenic hazards of contaminated food and water, whilst simultaneously robbing them of immunological protection and thus lowering their degree of resistance to airborne infections. It seems likely that a substantial decline in this practice played a larger role in reducing early infant mortality over the period than did an amelioration in the effects of respiratory disease, but we have no direct evidence as to infant feeding methods among the study population.

In terms of seasonality the effects of gastric diseases as causes of death can be seen among the 6–11 month age-group throughout the study period, with the exception of the cohorts born 1700–49, and there seems little reason to believe that their severity varied greatly over the period. It seems most likely that the 'hump' in the mortality rates of this age-group, visible in the first half of the eighteenth century, were the result of some 'new' airborne infection whose effects were sufficiently severe to obscure those of the underlying seasonality of water- and food-borne infection. Such a development may also have had some effect on childhood mortality rates and it is to these that we shall now turn.

Smallpox and childhood mortality

The rates of childhood mortality obtained from the reconstitution study were even more in excess of those found elsewhere in eighteenth-century England than was the case with infant mortality, a finding consistent with the expectations of the high potential model. The trend in mortality rates at ages one year and over among the London Quaker families also differed from that experienced by other communities outside the capital. The study of mortality at these ages is simplified by the predominance of a single cause of death – smallpox. The behaviour of smallpox mortality has, moreover, a particular theoretical interest since, as a highly infectious disease which

Table 4.8. *Age distribution of smallpox burials in London Quaker Meetings (in percentages)*

Age-group	Peel and Southwark			All London Meetings		
	1650–99	1700–49	1750–99	1650–99	1700–49	1750–99
0–1	29.2	17.6	28.2	26.5	17.7	31.3
2–4	23.2	31.2	25.9	24.5	31.2	29.4
5–9	10.3	14.6	18.5	10.6	14.1	13.4
10–19	11.9	10.5	6.5	15.3	10.6	7.0
20–9	18.4	16.9	14.5	15.7	17.2	11.4
30–9	4.3	4.1	4.0	4.9	4.2	3.2
40–9	2.2	2.7	1.6	1.9	1.6	2.3
50+	0.5	2.4	0.8	0.6	3.4	2.0
N	191	300	124	470	615	343

confers lasting immunity on survivors, this is likely to depend heavily on the density of population.

Smallpox thus exemplifies to a high degree the characteristics of those causes of death on whose behaviour the high potential model is chiefly based, and it is thus fortunate that smallpox was also one of the few diseases reliably identified as such by the searchers. The Quaker registers are uniquely valuable in this respect, since they allow a double classification of deaths by both age and cause, and a special study was undertaken taking the smallpox entries from the burial registers of all six of the London Quaker monthly meetings. This material was used to examine the age distribution of smallpox mortality and then, by linking these results to those obtained from family reconstitution, it was possible to estimate age-specific mortality rates for the disease and thus to assess its impact on overall levels of mortality in childhood.

The recorded totals of smallpox casualties, classified by age, are given in table 4.8 for the six meetings and for Peel and Southwark separately. In both cases children under five form the majority of entries in each of the fifty-year periods, but between 25 and 35 per cent of cases are in the adolescent or young adult age-groups. These figures, however, require some adjustment, for the cause of death is sometimes absent and the likelihood of its being omitted itself varies with age. This difficulty was overcome, in the case of the Peel and Southwark registers, by examining a sample of some 2000 burial

Table 4.9. *Smallpox burials – Peel and Southwark*

(a) Corrected distributions

Age	As percentage of burials by age			As percentage of total in age-group		
	1650–99	1700–49	1750–99	1650–99	1700–49	1750–99
0	15	16	14	3	7	4
2–4	36	45	48	10	29	26
5–9	10	13	16	16	44	29
10–19	13	9	5	15	23	14
20–9	18	11	11	12	18	16
30–9	5	3	4	5	4	4
40–9	2	2	1	—	3	1
50+	1	1	1	—	1	—

(b) Age-specific mortality rates (per thousand) eliminating direct effects of smallpox

Age	1650–99	1700–49	1750–99
6–11 months	71	97	85
1 year	102	123	87
2–9 years	185	171	155
1–9 years	268	273	229

entries for the two meetings and determining the proportions lacking cause of death information in each age-group. These were then used to calculate appropriate adjustment factors and thus obtain the corrected proportions given in table 4.9.

The proportion of casualties falling in the younger age-groups is now somewhat greater than before, since it was here that causes of death were most often omitted, but the fraction aged over ten years remains substantial. A significant proportion of adolescents and young adults in London's population thus lacked immunity to smallpox. The most plausible interpretation of this finding is that these individuals were immigrants from the countryside, since the disease may well have been universal among children born in the capital: in no case was it possible to link the burial entry of a smallpox casualty aged more than ten years, in the Peel or Southwark burial register, to an entry in the birth registers of either meeting. Such results indicate both the very high levels of immunity to be found among the native born adults, and the importance of the weak bounding of London's epidemiological regime, for mortality in the adolescent and young adult age-groups.[10]

The adjusted distributions of casualties classified by age, as taken from the Peel and Southwark registers, can be used to determine the probability of dying from smallpox in childhood. As a first step we must retabulate the results so as to indicate the proportions of all deaths at each age which are due to the disease. This can be done using the distributions of ages taken from the 2000 burial slip sample to indicate the age distribution of all deaths in the population, leading to the distribution in the right hand columns of table 4.9.

The latter strikingly demonstrates the importance of smallpox as a mortality factor among children in the first half of the eighteenth century. Nearly half of all lives lost in the 5–9 year age-group, at this time, were due to the disease, but smallpox was evidently an important influence on death rates at all ages between one and thirty years throughout the period covered by the data. The next step is to apply these proportions to the mortality probabilities calculated from the family reconstitution data.

Such a procedure is justified on the assumption that the share of smallpox in the deaths occurring among the reconstituted families was equal to that observed in the burial registers as a whole. The differing susceptibilities of natives and immigrants makes this assumption untenable for adolescents and young adults, but it is unlikely to be too far out where children under ten are concerned. In the case of infant deaths we have related smallpox burials to the deaths at ages 6–11 months since it has been claimed that vulnerability to the disease below this age is minimal (Razzell 1977: 105–6).

The effect of smallpox on childhood mortality among the reconstituted families was estimated on the assumption that the probability of death from the disease was independent of that from other causes. It is unlikely that the prevalence of other causes of death aggravated the risks from smallpox on any significant scale, but the converse may well have been the case if survivors of the disease were so weakened that they succumbed to maladies which would not otherwise have proved fatal. If this were so then our calculations would tend to

[10] The very low proportions of smallpox burials falling in the age-groups above the age of 30 imply a substantial concentration of immigration in the 10–29 age group, whilst the findings as a whole indicate that a substantial proportion of the adult population outside London had managed to avoid infection. The latter contrasts sharply with the position in other contemporary populations, such as Sweden, where the proportion of smallpox burials above the age of ten was of the order of 5 per cent or below, implying near universal childhood infection (see Landers 1984: 198–201). I am grateful to Dr R. S. Schofield for drawing my attention to these points.

underestimate the overall contribution of smallpox to mortality levels.

We can calculate mortality probabilities (q_x) eliminating the effects of this disease by assuming that those whose lives are thus saved are thereby exposed to the same risks of death from all other causes as was observed among those surviving the risk of death from smallpox among the reconstituted families. If we divide the life table deaths at age x into two groups: $d(1)_x$, who die of smallpox and $d(0)_x$, who die from all other causes then:

$$q_x = [d(0)_x + ((d(1)_x . d(0)_x)/1_x)]/1_x$$

The results in the lower panel of the table suggest that the increase in childhood mortality observed after 1700 is entirely attributable to smallpox. Only between the ages of six months and two years does this increase persist once the direct effects of the disease are removed. This removal lowers the overall risk of mortality between the ages of one and ten years by about 25 per cent in both halves of the eighteenth century, but only by some ten per cent in the period prior to 1700. In the second year of life this reduction is much smaller and the adjusted rate rises by about 20 per cent in the early eighteenth century.

Smallpox cannot, therefore, be the sole explanation for the increased mortality between six months and two years of age, but it does account for a substantial fraction of it. The decline in the mortality of children over two years of age, after 1750, is likewise explicable mainly in terms of smallpox, but a substantial decline in the mortality of the one-year-olds persists when the effects of the disease are removed. Above this age the estimates of childhood mortality in the absence of smallpox show a very modest reduction in each period, the hypothetical 'smallpox free' rate for the cohort 1750–99 being close to the childhood rates actually observed in the first quarter of the nineteenth century. Smallpox mortality itself evidently rose sharply in the early decades of the eighteenth century and fell again after 1750. The spread of inoculation may well explain the latter development and it is particularly frustrating that the absence of cause of death information in the nineteenth-century registers prevents us from following its progress beyond 1800.[11]

---

[11] The spread of inoculation and its demographic effects are discussed by Razzell 1977. For a recent review of the problem, including a discussion of the later impact of vaccination, see Mercer 1985.

Adult mortality and the expectation of life

The third and final age category which we shall examine is the 'adult' series, a heading under which it is also convenient to consider the question of overall life expectancy. There are two ways in which we can estimate adult mortality rates from family reconstitution data, both of them yielding results of a more approximate character than is the case with the younger ages. The first method is based on the recorded burials of husbands and wives in the reconstituted families. Only a proportion of deaths among this group are recorded however, and so assumptions must be made about the fate of the 'survivors' who pass out of observation in other ways.

This results in a range of estimates falling between 'optimistic' and 'pessimistic' limits. The latter is given by the assumption that these survivors are immediately exposed to the same risks of mortality observed among those whose deaths are recorded, whereas the former is based on the assumption that such persons all survive to the age of sixty before they encounter the observed risks of mortality. Since the observed distribution of deaths is biased downwards, Wrigley (1968) suggests that the 'true' rates of adult mortality will lie closer to the optimistic than to the pessimistic end of the interval.

The reliance on recorded burials of married persons necessarily restricts our calculations to age-groups in the mid 20s and above, hence we must look elsewhere for data on the mortality of adolescents and younger adults. These can be obtained from model life tables fitted to the observed infant and child mortality rates. Model life tables can also be used as a basis for estimating mortality at all ages above 15, the second of the two methods referred to above, but we shall employ the first method which makes more use of the actual observations.

The Princeton Regional Model Life Tables constructed by Coale and Demeny (1983) were used in the analysis as they have the advantage of providing four 'families' of tables based on the experience of populations denoted 'West', 'East', 'North' and 'South'. The 'West' tables are based on survival curves found in a series of particularly well documented European countries, whereas the others describe particular divergent patterns. Of these the 'North' and 'South' families have particularly high rates of mortality in childhood relative to those in infancy. The former generally give the best fit to English reconstitution results (Wrigley and Schofield 1981: 708), whilst the latter have successfully been applied to data from other metropolitan populations (Perrenoud 1985; Preston and Van de Walle 1978). In the

Table 4.10. *Estimated life expectation for London Quakers*

	Mid-range		Range	
	Males	Females	Males	Females
At birth				
1650–99	27.3	30.2	25.9–28.7	28.7–31.7
1700–49	20.6	21.9	19.7–21.5	20.9–22.9
1750–99	29.7	29.9	28.5–31.0	28.5–31.2
1800–49	34.2	36.7	32.3–36.1	34.6–38.9
At age 30				
1650–99	28.0	29.3	24.8–31.2	25.8–32.7
1700–49	26.2	26.5	23.4–29.0	23.6–29.5
1750–99	30.9	32.6	28.2–33.5	29.7–35.5
1800–49	31.3	32.5	27.9–34.8	28.6–36.3

Estimated life expectation at birth in England
(medians of quinquennial estimates for combined sexes)

1650–74	34.1	1750–74	35.6
1675–99	34.1	1775–99	36.8
1700–24	36.4	1800–24	37.9
1725–49	32.4	1825–49	40.2

Life expectation at age 30: means of 12 English reconstitutions

Cohort	Males	Females
1650–99	28.4	28.9
1700–49	30.4	30.2
1750–99	32.1	32.4

Source: Wrigley and Schofield 1977, tables 7.15 and 7.21

present case, the North tables provided a good description of the observed rates for the 1800–49 cohort whilst the South series did better before this date and the appropriate 'bridging rates' were selected accordingly (Landers 1984: 154–6).

The results in table 4.10 suggest that life expectation at the age of 30 was relatively static throughout the period when compared with the experience at younger ages, the major change being a decline of some two to three years after 1700, followed by an improvement of some five to six years in the second half of the eighteenth century. Life expectation at birth was more volatile, falling from around thirty years in the later seventeenth century to little more than twenty in the first half of the eighteenth. The later eighteenth century saw a major rise in life expectation at birth for both sexes, the male figure rising to a level above that of the later seventeenth century. Substantial improvement continued into the nineteenth century but this did not apparently affect adult mortality.

A comparison of the adult estimates with figures obtained from other English reconstitution studies, in the lower panel of the table, shows very little difference in levels of mortality for the period as a whole. This finding is in line with the expectations of the high potential model since metropolitan dwellers in these age-groups, whether immigrant or native-born, have now acquired a high degree of immunological protection against infection. The main contrast between the two sets of results lies in their trend since the rates for the parish sample show a progressive improvement throughout the period, whereas those for the London Quakers deteriorate after 1700, which leads to a differential of some four years in e_{30} for the 1700–49 cohort. The contrast in the e_0 series, however is dramatic – the national figure being nearly twice that for the London Quakers in the 1700–24 cohort. After 1750 the latter recover disproportionately and the differential remains at some five to six years for the remainder of the study period.

Conclusions

The outstanding feature of these results is the exceptional severity of infant and child mortality throughout much of the period, a severity which substantially bears out what we have termed the 'high potential' interpretation of metropolitan epidemiological regimes in early modern Europe. From the latter part of the eighteenth century these levels of mortality declined dramatically and by the end of the period there appears to have been little difference between the experience of our reconstituted families and that of the population nationally.[12]

The limited spatial analysis which we were able to undertake suggested that whilst some of this reduction might be attributable to residential movement, this was only the case after 1800 and was of secondary importance even then. Our analysis of occupational labels in the vital registers also found no evidence of major structural change before the nineteenth century. A full explanation of these developments would need to draw on a broad range of external

---

[12] Our mid-range estimates of life expectation in the last cohort are also comparable with, though slightly higher than, Woods' estimates for London as a whole which rise linearly from 30 years in 1811 to 33 in 1841 (see Woods 1985).

evidence as to social, economic and epidemiological changes both in the capital and in the country at large.

The present chapter has, by contrast, a much more restricted ambit, being limited to a detailed scrutiny of the mortality rates themselves and of their internal structure, but this framework has enabled us to identify a number of partially independent factors underlying the high levels of mortality. Gastric disease, apparently linked to deficient water supplies, seems to have been a major killer of older infants and 'weanlings' throughout the period and before the latter part of the eighteenth century it may also have claimed many lives among the newborn.

It was a reduction in the rate for the first three months of life which accounted for most of the long-term decline in infant mortality but gastric diseases are unlikely to have been wholly responsible. There is evidence of deaths from respiratory infections in the 3–5 month age-group before 1750 and, though we have not been able to establish this definitively, it is probable that these also took their toll among younger infants during the earlier part of the period. The overall rise in infant mortality in the early eighteenth century was due to an increase in the rate for the 6–11 month age-group.

Mortality in the second year of life also increased at this time and in both cases much of the increase was attributable to smallpox, with a substantial minority of the excess deaths coming from some other disease. We have not been able to identify the latter, but it is unlikely to have been food- or water-borne since the early eighteenth century sees a temporary disappearance of the characteristic Summer peak in the mortality of older infants.[13] A parallel rise in mortality at ages between two and ten years at this time reflected an increased incidence of smallpox deaths, but the overall difference between the levels of childhood mortality found in the present study and those found in other eighteenth-century English reconstitutions is too great to be accounted for by this disease alone.

Eighteenth-century London was evidently an extremely unhealthy place even for those who escaped the ravages of smallpox, but the prevalence of the latter evidently constituted a particular threat to the lives of immigrants many of whom seemed to have lacked immunity to the disease. The relatively narrow gap between metropolitan and national mortality levels above the age of thirty is consistent with the

---

[13] The seasonality of burials in the Bills of Mortality, particularly those attributed to 'fevers', reveals the severe impact made by a 'new' infection characterised by a marked Autumn peak, possibly a form of scarlet fever, particularly in the second quarter of the eighteenth century; see chapter 6.

HPM's attribution of excess metropolitan mortality to the action of density dependent immunising infections, but we should beware of over simplifying what was evidently a highly complex mortality regime. Many of the excess deaths, for instance, were due to gastric diseases in infancy and the heightened prevalence of these arose from an interaction between patterns of infant care and feeding, the particular hazards of an urban environment, and the effects of population density.

Mortality levels in England as a whole improved from the last quarter of the eighteenth century, and the London Quakers apparently shared in this improvement to an exaggerated degree. Before this, however, the trend of mortality among our study population seems to have differed from that of the country at large. The parish register reconstitution results suggest that the level of child mortality in the first half of the eighteenth century was essentially unchanged from that of the previous fifty years, whilst adult mortality may have improved slightly.

The life expectations from the aggregative back-projection reveal a rather more complicated picture, but again there is a noticeable divergence in trend from the Quaker results. The back-projections for the first two decades after 1700 yield an e_0 more than two years higher than the late seventeenth-century figure (which averages 33.1 for the years 1670–99). In 1720–39 e_0 falls by about a year below the latter level, but it recovers to 33.5 in the 1740s, and the levels for the third quarter of the eighteenth century are clearly above those for the last decades of the seventeenth. The persistence of a stubborn 'plateau' of mortality for the first three quarters of the eighteenth century, at a level substantially above that prevailing before 1700, thus appears to have been a distinctively London phenomenon. We must now determine whether it can also be seen in data for the capital's population as a whole.

5

Mortality levels among the general population

The question of mortality levels among London's population at large returns us to the aggregate data contained in the Bills of Mortality. Although it would be a formidable – probably an impossible – task to determine the absolute shortfall in registration embodied in the latter such a labour is, fortunately, unnecessary, for the key demographic indices can be calculated without reference to such absolute levels, providing only that we can gauge the relative deficiency of baptism registration relative to that of burials. It would be rash to claim that even this 'relative under-registration' can be measured with a high degree of precision, but the work of Wrigley and Schofield (1981) provides us with a basis for such an exercise.

These authors developed correction factors intended for use with their national sample of parish register data, and although they incorporate material from the Bills, and the London Parish Register Abstracts, they do not bear directly on conditions in the capital, which are likely to have deviated from those in the country at large.[1] Nonetheless, the figures have the advantage of a substantial empirical and analytical base, and any alternative 'improved' series would – given the material at our disposal – have a more uncertain foundation. Hence, rather than trying to adjust the Wrigley–Schofield factors to cater for the peculiar circumstances of London we shall – with minor exceptions – take them as they stand and then try to assess the general credibility of the vital indices obtained with their aid.

---

[1] Only a brief outline of Wrigley and Schofield's correction factors, and their rationale, can be given in the present chapter – details of their derivation can be found in the first hundred and fifty pages of the *Population History*. The corrections appear to have gained general acceptance (Lindert 1983 is an exception), though this may be due in part to the relative insensitivity of the authors' main results to differences in their values; see Wrigley and Schofield 1981: 269–77.

Correction factors

The correction factors constructed by Wrigley and Schofield were intended to offset the various sources of under-registration detected, directly or indirectly, in the vital registers from their sample of 404 English parishes. The first stage in our procedure must thus be to convert the Bills' baptism and burial figures into 'parish register equivalent' (PREq) totals to which these corrections can be applied.

'Parish register equivalents'

The PREq totals were obtained by taking the figures given in the Parish Register Abstracts (PRA)[2] for the parishes falling within the geographical scope of the Bills and assuming a level of under-registration equal to that detected in the initial analysis of the registers from the 404 parish sample (Wrigley and Schofield 1981: 30–2). PRA totals are available annually after 1780, but before this only for years ending in zero. Hence figures for the earlier decades were obtained on the assumption that the ratio of Bills' totals to parish register totals varied in a linear fashion between the known values, and that the ratio observed in 1700, the first date in the PRA series, held good in the preceding period.

For most of the period the ratio of PREq to Bills' totals is appreciably greater where baptisms are concerned than it is in the case of burials (see table 5.1). This is particularly true in the first half of the eighteenth century when the Bills' burial total exceeds the PREq for a number of decades. The vital index calculated from the new figures is thus correspondingly more optimistic than that derived from the Bills for these years, but this ceases to be the case from the 1780s when the numbers of additional parish register burials increase substantially and the effect is sufficiently great to bring the index below unity in the first decade of the nineteenth century.

Inflation factors

Wrigley and Schofield constructed three series of inflation factors for use with their parish register totals. These were intended, respect-

---

[2] This refers to the material collected by Rickman from incumbents of Anglican parishes in conjunction with the early censuses, and was the staple of English historical demography before the development of family reconstitution and aggregative analysis. See Flinn 1970 for a discussion of their origins and historiographic significance, and Wrigley and Schofield (1981: 66–76, 597–630) for a detailed technical review.

Table 5.1. *'Parish Register Equivalent' baptisms and burials for parishes within the Bills of Mortality*

	Baptisms	Burials	Vital index
1680s	154103	225846	0.68
1690s	162995	213360	0.76
1700s	162829	202186	0.81
1710s	182079	228821	0.80
1720s	201961	256749	0.79
1730s	193101	248896	0.78
1740s	168628	259388	0.65
1750s	169426	213328	0.79
1760s	178531	236577	0.75
1770s	191311	227682	0.84
1780s	194465	212778	0.91
1790s	202286	211953	0.95
1800s	218833	240677	0.91
1810s	264506	238605	1.11
1820s	300408	279935	1.07

Source: see text, p. 163

ively, to 'take into account the increase in nonconformity . . . to offset the effects of the interval between birth and baptism and . . . to cover any remaining gap between the totals produced by earlier changes and the "true" totals of births and deaths' (Wrigley and Schofield 1981: 89). In the present study we have used the first and third of these, the inflation for non-conformity and the 'final inflation factor', as they stand but modified the second, the factor designed to offset the effects of delayed baptism, a little.

The delay of baptism resulted in under-registration because a certain proportion of infants died before the rite could be carried out. Where, as was increasingly the case in the eighteenth century, the burials of unbaptised children were omitted from the register, the registration of both events would be affected. The overall degree of under-registration resulting from delayed baptism thus rises with the length of the birth–baptism interval and with the level of mortality in the early weeks of life. Analysis of these two variables in data from national samples led Wrigley and Schofield to calculate a series of corrections whose magnitude increases throughout our period, around inflection points in 1675, 1725, 1775, and 1825 (see upper panel, table 5.2), reflecting a lengthening birth-baptism interval and a

Table 5.2. *Correction factors for*
delayed baptism (inflection points)

	Baptism	Burial
Wrigley–Schofield values		
1675	1.041	1.000
1725	1.051	1.020
1775	1.074	1.045
1825	1.090	1.070
London Quaker values		
1725	1.077	1.037
1775	1.013	1.074
1825	1.038	1.034

reduction in the propensity to register the burials of unbaptised infants.

In the case of London, however, it seems likely that the effects of a substantial fall in early infant mortality, between the mid-eighteenth and nineteenth centuries, would have offset those of the concurrent extension in the birth–baptism interval. We have thus constructed a revised series of correction factors taking the Wrigley–Schofield values for 1675, but substituting new ones at the subsequent points of inflection (see lower panel, table 5.2). These values were calculated using the mortality rates observed in the London Quaker families, and assuming a level of pre-baptismal mortality equivalent to 60, 80 and 100 per cent of the overall rate for the first month at the three dates 1725, 1775, and 1825.

In addition it was assumed that 50, 25, and 10 per cent, respectively of these casualties appeared in the burial register. The resulting corrections are inevitably arbitrary to some degree and they are especially prone to understate the shortfall in burial registration relative to that of baptisms in the early eighteenth century. Overall, however, it seems likely that, where London is concerned, they capture the trend in this source of under-registration more accurately than do the figures derived from the national data.

The full set of correction factors are given in table 5.3. In the case of delayed baptism the degree of inflation rises to the 1770s and then declines to the end of the period, the reduction being more rapid in the case of baptisms than burials. The Wrigley–Schofield burial inflation factors fluctuate over the early decades, whilst those for baptisms rise consistently. After 1780 both sets of factors increase substantially

Table 5.3. *Correction factors applied to 'Parish Register Equivalent' baptisms and burials in London Bills*

| | Delayed Baptism | | Non-Conformity | | 'Final Inflation' | |
	Baptisms	Burials	Baptisms	Burials	Baptisms	Burials
1680s	1.0477	1.0070	1.0111	1.0116	1.0276	1.0110
1690s	1.0548	1.0144	1.0129	1.0113	1.0321	1.0128
1700s	1.0619	1.0217	1.0140	1.0109	1.0350	1.0140
1710s	1.0690	1.0291	1.0154	1.0105	1.0382	1.0153
1720s	1.0760	1.0364	1.0159	1.0095	1.0397	1.0159
1730s	1.0815	1.0439	1.0161	1.0090	1.0409	1.0164
1740s	1.0868	1.0513	1.0184	1.0086	1.0459	1.0183
1750s	1.0921	1.0588	1.0204	1.0086	1.0511	1.0204
1760s	1.0974	1.0663	1.0227	1.0081	1.0567	1.0229
1770s	1.1009	1.0722	1.0248	1.0085	1.0620	1.0248
1780s	1.0906	1.0665	1.0316	1.0109	1.0980	1.0490
1790s	1.0776	1.0585	1.0396	1.0145	1.1266	1.1081
1800s	1.0646	1.0504	1.0483	1.0269	1.2172	1.2078
1810s	1.0516	1.0424	1.0563	1.0203	1.2870	1.3109
1820s	1.0379	1.0340	1.0623	1.0222	1.2262	1.1756

until the last decade of the period, with the burial factors now rising more rapidly. The 'k' ratio, measuring the overall inflation factor applied to baptisms relative to that of burials thus rises throughout the seventeenth and eighteenth centuries, but falls sharply in the two decades after 1800 (see figure 5.1).[3]

The overall results

The vital index which results from applying the 'k' ratio to the PREq totals (see figure 5.2) rises from the 1680s to the 1700s and then fluctuates until the last quarter of the eighteenth century, with a noticeable dip in the 1740s. After 1770 the index rises substantially and the level of unity is attained in the 1780s, but the setback in the

[3] This reversal – which produces a marked 'notch' in the curve of figure 5.1 – is largely due to the behaviour of the 'PREq' figures and, in particular, to the appearance in the 1811 PRA of a substantial number of burials (5,753 as against only 1,345 baptisms) which had apparently been omitted from the main tabulations. In the light of the longer term trend, the behaviour of the ratio in these decades is rather suspicious, and it is tempting to assume a linear increase in the 'true' value between 1800 and the end of the period. But it should be borne in mind that, even on this latter basis, the existence of the 'notch' inflates the infant mortality estimate only by some 4 to 5 per cent of the 'true' value.

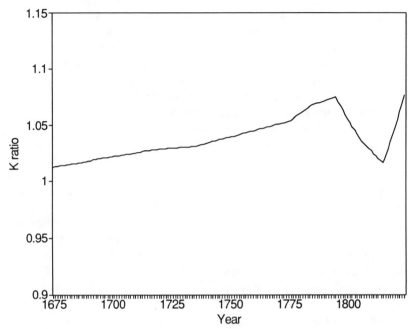

5.1 Ratio of correction factors ('k') applied to baptisms and burial totals in London Bills

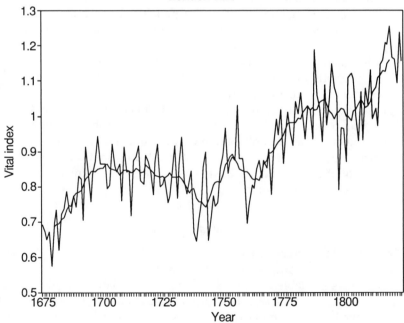

5.2 London Bills' Vital Index – corrected for under-registration

years around 1800 is still visible when the correction factors are applied. The degree to which the 'k' series, based as it is on data from a national sample, accurately represents the relative shortfall in the recording of baptisms in London itself is of course open to question and this presents us with a difficulty which cannot easily be dismissed, although it should be borne in mind that we do not have to be concerned with differences between the absolute levels of under-registration in the capital and elsewhere.

The prevalence of non-conformity and the presence of civil burying grounds in the capital may perhaps have affected burial registration more severely there than was the case in the country at large, but we should not ignore the possibility of countervailing factors. The recording of baptisms is based entirely on an ecclesiastical ceremony, whereas burial registration reflects a further range of necessities and proprieties. Hence a greater degree of popular indifference, or hostility, to the ecclesiastical establishment in London than elsewhere might have affected the baptismal registration more than it did burials. Certainly Linebaugh's (1975) study of the Tyburn riots suggests a fierce devotion to the fundamental 'decencies' of interment among a section of the population who might not have been so scrupulous over baptisms.

Given the inevitable uncertainties which surround the question of levels of under-registration, and the paucity of our information on many of the relevant points, the most profitable strategy seems to be to proceed to the calculation of some estimated vital series and then to examine the internal consistency, and overall plausibility, of these in the light of other evidence. These calculations generally rely on data, or estimates, concerning the age-breakdown of the total burial figures. Since such figures are available directly for the years after 1728, our results will be correspondingly more robust. Before this date, however, we can only obtain very limited and indirect estimates of burial ages by using the cause of death information. Hence the results for the two periods have a very different character and we shall consider them separately.

Vital rates after 1728

The correction factors constructed in the previous section can be used to calculate a set of mortality rates, on the basis of the age-specific burial totals available after 1728. Of these, the infant mortality rate is the easiest to estimate directly, since it is possible to derive the size of the relevant population at risk from the number of baptisms. Where older age-groups are concerned this information is unrecoverable, but it is possible to make some inferences from the level of infant mortality with the aid of a model life table system. The resulting mortality rates can then themselves be used to generate some estimates of crude vital rates and population structure.

Infant mortality

In principle we can construct an infant mortality rate (IMR) from the material at our disposal by means of the formula:

$IMR = p * Bu/(Ba * k')$ where:

p   = burials under one year of age as a proportion of recorded burials under the age of two

Ba = recorded baptisms

Bu = recorded burials under the age of two

k' = under-registration of baptisms relative to burials in the youngest age-group.

In practice, however, apart from the uncertainties associated with the components of the k' ratio, we immediately encounter difficulties in attempting to determine the numbers of infant burials. Although age-specific burial totals are available from 1728, the youngest category embraces both the first and second years of life. It was thus necessary to estimate the proportion p which was set, following Brownlee (1925), at a constant 75 per cent.[4] The numbers of stillbirths and 'abortions' were also subtracted from the burials in the 0–1 year age group from the 1730s, although it is likely that these included a number of early neonatal deaths.

The potential sources of error in this procedure are evident, and the resulting estimates of infant mortality need to be assessed with corresponding caution. We shall try to do this in the final section of this chapter, but at this point we should note that, as they stand (see

---

[4] This is a clearly arbitrary proportion, but it is difficult to improve on it as the two most obvious alternatives are also open to objection. The first of these would be to use the corresponding proportion from the Quaker registers, but, since this system revolved around births rather than baptisms, it is likely to have missed fewer infant casualties, and thus to have generated a different ratio of deaths in the first and second year of life from that registered by the parishes. An alternative approach would be to use ratios derived from civil registration data in nineteenth-century London, but this runs up against the problem of the disproportionate decline in infant mortality since the early eighteenth century, when it is likely to have been higher, relative to that in the second year of life, than it was in Victorian times. Under these circumstances the simplest course seems to be to retain Brownlee's ratio unaltered and then assess the plausibility of the infant mortality rates as a whole.

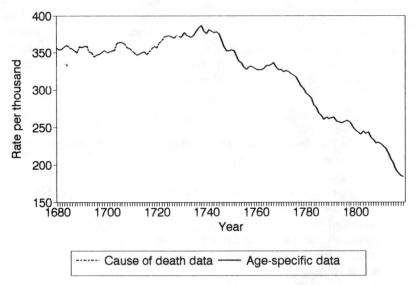

5.3 Infant mortality rate in London Bills: 11-point moving average

figure 5.3), the figures suggest a trend very similar to that observed among the Quakers over this period, although the absolute level is rather higher. The infant death rate appears to have been relatively stable at a very severe level until the middle of the eighteenth century. In the crisis years of the 1740s infant mortality was affected, but less so than that at older ages, resulting in a reduction in the proportionate contribution of the youngest age group to the total burials. The following decade then saw a substantial decline in infant mortality which continued until the end of the period, with interruptions in the 1760s and 1800s. By the final decade of the period our estimated rate is less than half that calculated for the 1740s, and close to the 163 per thousand embodied in the Registrar-General's 'metropolitan' life table for 1841.

Overall mortality

The construction of infant mortality estimates from the London Bills is, in principle, relatively straightforward although there are many practical difficulties to be encountered along the way. But where mortality at older ages is concerned the material presents problems of an altogether different order, since it contains no information on the size of the population at risk in the different age-groups. It was thus

Table 5.4. *Bills of Mortality: model life*
table parameters and estimated life
expectation at birth

Decade	Alpha	Beta	Expectation of life
1730s	0.0370	0.9704	18.2
1740s	0.0659	0.9670	17.6
1750s	−0.0285	0.9502	20.1
1760s	−0.0362	0.9330	20.5
1770s	−0.0666	0.9155	21.6
1780s	−0.1954	0.8990	25.5
1790s	−0.2529	0.8877	27.5
1800s	−0.2657	0.8806	28.0
1810s	−0.4021	0.8735	32.4
1820s	−0.4584	0.8665	34.4

Source: see text below

necessary to proceed by inference using a model life table system developed by Brass (1971) and based on the equation:

$$Y_x = \text{alpha} + \text{beta} \times Y_{Rx}$$

where Y_x denotes the logit transformation of the life table survival function 1_x, and 1_{Rx} refers to the proportion of survivors to age x in the life table selected as a standard, in this instance level one of the Princeton Model North family.

Given this standard table, and a series of values for the 'slope' parameter beta, we can use our decadal infant mortality estimates to derive corresponding values for the constant alpha, using the formula:

$$\text{alpha} = Y (1 - q) - \text{beta} \times Y_{R1}$$

where q is the decadal infant mortality estimate. Decadal estimates of beta were obtained by linear interpolation, between points of inflection calculated from the eighteenth-century Quaker family reconstitution values and the Registrar-General's 1841 London life table (*5th Annual Report*, p. 48). These estimates were then used to generate life tables for each decade, yielding estimates of life expectation at birth which are set out in table 5.4 together with the corresponding values of alpha and beta.

As might be expected the early estimates are very low with a pattern of consistent improvement over time, but in the early decades this is little more than proportional to the improvement displayed by the Wrigley–Schofield national estimates, and the London figure remains around 60 per cent of the latter until the final quarter of the eighteenth century. From the 1780s, however, life expectation in London rises by more than a third, some nine years, in contrast to the figure for England as a whole which shows an increase of only 4.2 years, much of it a recovery from the uncharacteristically low levels observed in the 1780s. By the last decade for which our estimates can be calculated the London figure has thus risen to a level equal to 90 per cent of national life expectation, and close to the 36.6 years embodied in the Registrar-General's 'Metropolitan' life table of 1841.

The decline of mortality by age
The construction of model life tables can also furnish us with some insights into the age-structure of mortality decline. In table 5.5, and figure 5.4, we examine this question by comparing our estimated life table mortality probabilities for the period 1730–49, with those derived from the 1841 London life table. Given the numerous assumptions which we had to make in order to construct our estimates it would be a mistake to place too much faith in any single comparison, but it seems unlikely that the very distinct pattern of age-specific mortality decline revealed by the table is entirely an arte-fact of our method. Mortality rates at all ages show some reduction over the century or so separating the two sets of figures, but this reduction is heavily concentrated in the childhood, adolescent, and younger adult age-groups.

The proportional declines in q_x for the fifteen year age-groups below 45 years are at least twice those observed above that age. Thus the proportion surviving from birth to age 35 rises from 241 to 538 per

Table 5.5. *Age-specific mortality probabilities*

Age	London Bills 1730–49	Registrar-General 1841	Percentage reduction
1–14	0.442	0.242	45.4
15–29	0.227	0.108	52.4
30–44	0.316	0.183	42.1
45–59	0.455	0.355	21.9
60–74	0.823	0.648	21.2

Source: see text above

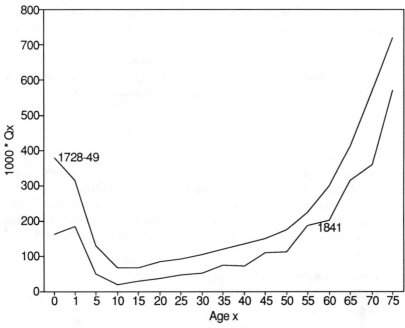

(a) q_x, 1728–39 and 1841

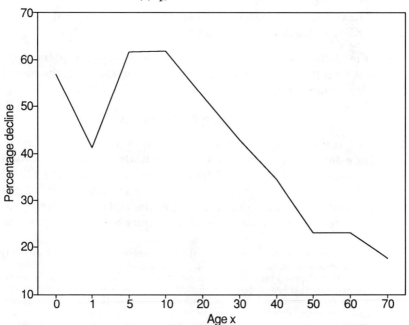

(b) Percentage decline in q_x, 1728–39 to 1841

5.4 Age-specific mortality probabilities (q_x) in London

thousand, whereas the corresponding figures for ages 35 to 70 are 172 and 304, representing increases of 120 and 70 per cent respectively. The changes in the composition of age-specific burial totals over this period, which we observed in chapter 3, thus seem to have had their origin in a substantial shift in the underlying age-structure of mortality risks, rather than that of the population itself.[5]

Crude vital rates and population structure

The existence of an age-breakdown of burials from the 1730s onwards means that we can construct some estimates of crude birth and death rates (CBR and CDR) without having to assume anything about either population size or the absolute shortfall in the registration of baptisms and burials. This is possible because of the relationships between the various quantities which feature in the relevant formulae:

$$CDR = SUM (Bu_x * KBu_x) / SUM P_x$$
and $CBR = Ba * KBa / SUM P_x$
where Ba = total baptisms
Bu_x = burials at age x,
P_x = population aged x,
KBu_x = inflation to offset under-registration at age x,
and KBa = inflation to offset under-registration of baptisms.

P_x, the estimated population size in each age-group, is itself obtained from the age distribution of burials, together with the model life tables, using the formula:

$$P_x = Bu_x \times KBu_x / m_x$$

Where m_x is the age-specific death rate at age x. Hence in the case of the CDR estimates the correction factors for under- registration cancel out, whereas in that of the CBR they appear as the ratio $KBa / SUM KBu_x$ which we have already encountered in the calculation of our infant mortality estimates and of the model life table parameter alpha. The accuracy of our estimated crude rates thus depends only on the

---

[5] It should of course be borne in mind that the postulated age-pattern of mortality decline is based, in part, on the age-profile of mortality at the opening of the interval. Its validity thus depends on the assumptions underlying the model life table system used to generate this age-profile, and the latter themselves include a tendency for pre-transitional mortality levels to be particularly high in childhood, adolescence and early adult life (Vallin 1991; Preston 1976). The Quaker reconstitution results, however, lend support to this assumption in the case of eighteenth-century London.

Table 5.6. *Crude vital rates in England and London*

Decade	National		London Bills of Mortality		
	CBR	CDR	CBR	CDR	I* f
1730s	34.8	31.4	43.1	48.6	0.422
1740s	33.2	29.3	34.4	46.0	0.325
1750s	33.3	26.0	40.5	44.8	0.391
1760s	34.1	28.4	36.5	42.2	0.360
1770s	36.1	26.5	40.2	42.1	0.410
1780s	36.6	27.9	37.4	36.0	0.386
1790s	38.9	26.4	37.4	34.6	0.351
1800s	39.1	25.9	33.1	33.2	0.358
1810s	40.7	25.5	34.0	28.9	0.343
1820s	39.8	23.8	32.2	26.7	—

Source: see text below

adequacy with which we have gauged the relative shortfall in baptism registration, together with the 'slope' of mortality with age as measured by the beta parameter.

The figures in table 5.6 were calculated using this procedure, after applying a set of correction factors for burial age misstatements which were taken from the work of Lee and Lam.[6] Both the birth and the death rate series begin at high levels and tend to decline throughout the period. In the case of the death rate this decline is continual and brings the figure from a level equal to 155 per cent of that for England as a whole in the 1730s, to only 112 per cent in the 1820s. The reduction in the birth rate, by contrast, is irregular and is substantially complete by the end of the eighteenth century. For the first fifty years of the period the birth rate estimates for London are higher than the national figures, but the latter increase steadily from the 1770s, whilst the former tend to decline, and by the 1820s London's estimated birth rate is only 80 per cent of that for England as a whole.

The CBR itself is, of course, an inadequate measure of fertility, since it is affected by population structure. We do not have enough data to disentangle the effects of nuptiality from those of marital fertility and illegitimacy, but we can get some idea of the contribution of the effects of age-structure by means of standardisation. The most

[6] The adjustments used are based on a comparison of the 1821 and 1841 Census age-structures and an assumed inter- censal mortality schedule equivalent to level eleven of the Wrigley–Schofield life table system (Lee and Lam 1983: 457).

widely applied technique, in this context, is the one developed by Coale for the Princeton European Fertility Project (Coale and Treadway 1986: 153–62). Coale's index of overall fertility, I_f, expresses the observed number of births as a ratio to that expected from a population which combined the observed age-structure with the age-specific marital fertility rates of the North American Hutterites.

To be used properly this technique requires census data for five year age-groups. Although we do not possess such detailed information it is possible to produce estimates for ten year age-groups (see below). We can thus manage a crude approximation to Coale's index – which we shall term I'_f – by averaging the Hutterite rates for the two five year age-groups, in each of the ranges 20–9 and 30–9 years, and arbitrarily assuming that half of the population aged in their forties fall into the 40–4 year age-group. In the absence of any reliable data on sex ratios we shall assume equal numbers of males and females in the population. These assumptions are too crude for the results to give anything other than an indication of the order of magnitude of fertility in London at this time. But, as such, the values in the last column of the table are sufficiently high to refute any suggestion that the magnitude of the CBR in the early decades is an age-structure effect.[7]

The reliability of the rates
The validity of our CDR estimates – in terms of their absolute levels – depends on that of the values for alpha and beta, the nature of which we have already considered. The CBR figures, however, are arrived at by an indirect route which involves the calculation, as an intermediate stage, of 'internal' estimates of population size, which we shall call P, and are given by $SUM(Bu_x/m_x)$. As the values of m_x, the estimated mortality rates, decline, P will tend to increase – for a given set of burial totals – and *vice versa*. It follows from this that an underestimate of mortality levels at any age will result in a corresponding inflation in the value of P_x, and thus an artificial depression in the estimates of both the CDR and the CBR.

Such under-estimation may arise in either of two ways; through a miscalculation of the underlying 'base' level of mortality, as measured by the constant alpha, or of the rate at which mortality increases with age, as measured by the coefficient beta. In the first case, since our values of alpha themselves depend indirectly on estimates of the

---

[7] Such an effect could, in principle, arise as a result of the age-composition of net migration; see De Vries (1984: 97–8) for a discussion of this possibility and its importance.

relative inflation of burials and baptisms, any such underestimate of the 'base' level of mortality will be associated with a correspondingly excessive inflation of the baptism totals, tending to offset the effect on the estimated CBR.

Paradoxically then, given the doubts which surround the level of baptism under-registration in London, our birth rate estimates should be relatively robust against disturbances from this source. But no such stabilisers will operate where errors in the coefficient beta are concerned, and if we have overestimated the slope of the mortality curve above age ten – and thus the magnitude of adult m_xs relative to those in infancy and childhood, this will result in an artificially inflated birth rate estimate. Since the HPM predicts that mortality will be particularly high early in life, relative to the older age-groups, this is a possibility that we need to take seriously, but it is easy to show that, in practical terms, the scope for distortions of this kind is very limited.

For the sake of illustration we shall take the period 1730–49 and assume that the 'true' mortality levels at age twenty and above are those given by the female rates of the Princeton Model West table level five. These combine an e0 of thirty years with a temporary life expectancy from ages twenty to sixty of 29.1 years, compared with approximately 17.8 and 26.3 for our own mortality estimates. Applying the model rates to the burial and baptism totals used above results in a CBR estimate of 36.1 and an I^*_f of 0.33, compared with unweighted decadal means of 38.7 and 0.37 for the original estimates.[8]

It thus seems safe to conclude that during the decades when the baptism shortfall was at its worst, both the CBR and the underlying level of fertility were at least as high – and very probably higher – as they were in the rest of the country. How seriously we should take the medium-term decadal movements in both the CDR and CBR estimates is another question, however, and arises particularly in connection with the 1740s. Here the birth rate falls sharply. The death rate falls by around three per thousand from the level of the 1730s, but estimated life expectation also deteriorates slightly, whilst the birth rate falls sharply.

In principle, we could throw some light on the matter if we had access to figures for population size. Denoting the latter as P^*, it follows from our calculations so far that:

---

[8] The relative insensitivity of the fertility estimates to changes in the value of k can be seen in the fact that substituting the model values at all ages leads to estimates of 36.7 for the CBR and 0.40 for I(F).

$$B = Ib * Ba / P^*$$
$$\text{and } D = Id * Bu / P^*$$

where B and D are, respectively, our estimates of crude birth and death rates, Ba and Bu are the PREq baptisms and burials, and Ib and Id are estimates of the absolute shortfall in the latter two series

For most of the period, any values that we might obtain for P^* would themselves be too weakly founded for the absolute levels of either Ib or Id to bear interpretation, but the conjunction of marked decadal fluctuations in these series with anomalous CDR and CBR estimates might imply that some at least of our assumptions have broken down.

We saw in chapter 2 that there is a dearth of reliable population figures for eighteenth-century London, but that movements in coal consumption have sometimes been taken as a proxy indicator of the general trend. Population size itself cannot, of course, be deduced directly from materials of this kind, but they can reasonably be used to set upper and lower bounds to the range of credible estimates. Given our benchmark totals of 490,000 for 1700, and 950,000 for 1801, what is needed is a set of estimates for the growth of *per capita* consumption in the intervening century. The results plotted in figure 5.5 were derived on the basis of two alternative assumptions. These were:

I Linear increase 1700–29 and 1750–1801, static level 1730–49
II Static level 1700–49, linear increase 1750–1801.

The artificiality of these two sets of assumptions is obvious, but they should nonetheless serve to define a reasonably acceptable 'interval of plausibility' for the purposes of our calculations. The general impression of economic stagnation encountered in the London of the 1730s and 1740s is such that consumption is scarcely likely to have risen over these decades. In other respects scenario I seems more likely than II, although growth was presumably more rapid in the fourth quarter of the century than it had been in the first. We shall, in any case, take the mean of the two resulting figures as our estimated population size for each decade. Inspection of the results for the 1740s (see table 5.7) reveals a conjunction of the kind indicated above, since the implied baptism inflation falls sharply and then rises again into the 1750s.

The unusually low value of both Id and Ib (the implied burials and baptism inflation factors in columns two and three of the table) observed in the 1740s may be due in part to a violent increase in young adult mortality – resulting from the contemporary fever epi-

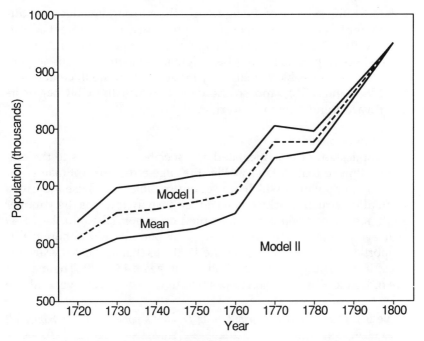

5.5 Population estimates for London: 2 models, 11-point moving averages

Table 5.7. *Crude vital rates: implied inflation factors*

Decade	Estimated population	Burial inflation	Baptism inflation
1730s	660	1.28	1.47
1740s	670	1.18	1.36
1750s	680	1.43	1.62
1760s	730	1.31	1.50
1770s	780	1.44	1.63
1780s	820	1.39	1.58
1790s	910	1.48	1.67

demics – above the levels predicted by the values of alpha and beta. Conversely, the high values observed in the 1750s may indicate a 'recovery' period of correspondingly low mortality in the older age groups. If we were to take the 'true' value of Ib for the years 1740–59 to be 1.51, the average of the figures for the surrounding decades, this would imply a CBR of 39.4 per thousand, whilst an equivalent adjustment to the CDR would take the figure to 52.8 per thousand. These figures seem preferable to the original estimates[9] but it is not, unfortunately possible to make any judgement on the fluctuations of the 1760s and 1770s, and so the date at which the CBR began its downward trend remains uncertain.

Population structure and migration
The application of our calculated age-specific death rates to the corresponding burial totals yields the age-structure estimates for London's population which are set out in table 5.8. These indicate a population structure which is weighted heavily towards the younger adult ages. Nearly 60 per cent of the population falls into the 20–49 year age-groups in the first twenty year period[10] and although this proportion declines a little after the 1790s, as that of the 2–9 year-olds rises, it remains at more than half in the years 1810–29. The median age of London's population appears to have been several years above

Table 5.8. *Estimated age distribution of London's population (per thousand)*

Age-group	1730–49	1750–69	1770–89	1790–1809	1810–29
0–1	46	47	50	47	46
2–4	59	63	67	83	79
5–9	69	69	71	83	88
10–19	111	119	140	119	136
20–9	195	197	187	171	172
30–9	205	198	187	193	185
40–9	165	160	155	158	149
50–9	98	95	94	98	94
60–9	37	39	37	37	38
70–9	16	15	14	13	15

[9] The alternative to accepting them, since an actual improvement in baptism registration seems unlikely, would be to argue that we have overestimated population size in London at this time. On such an argument the fall in the birth rate would be a genuine phenomenon, reflecting economic disruption, sex ratio disturbances, or both, and the marginal improvement in the death rate would result from a fall in the proportion of very young children in the population. Such an explanation is possible but implies a continuing rise in coal consumption into the 1740s, which may not be plausible.

[10] The argument of the preceding section implies that, for the 1740s, this proportion is likely to be a slight overestimate resulting from an underestimation of younger adult mortality. This may be offset, however, by a slight underestimate in the figure for the 1750s.

Table 5.9. *Estimated median ages:*
London and England

Decade	London	England
1730–9	30.3	25.1
1740–9	31.7	24.7
1750–9	30.9	24.5
1760–9	29.7	24.3
1770–9	29.3	23.7

Source: see text below

that calculated from the Wrigley–Schofield estimates for England as a whole throughout the period. Decadal figures (unweighted means for quinquennia in the case of the Wrigley–Schofield data) for the period before the substantial decline of mortality in London are given in table 5.9.

The principal difference lies in the proportions aged 5–14 years, where the London value is only 60 per cent of that for the country at large, although those for the adjacent age-groups are almost the same in the two populations. Such a contrast is consistent with the very severe levels of childhood mortality in the capital, combined with an elevated birth rate and high levels of in-migration among adolescents and young adults. However, the relatively low mortality levels which characterise teenagers make this a particularly difficult age-group to reconstruct, since relatively small absolute changes in our estimates of the relevant age-specific death rates will produce proportionally large variations in the size of the multipliers which are applied to the burial totals.

The age-structure estimates can also be used to obtain some information on the age pattern of net migration to London. In order to do this it is necessary to adopt a rather crude methodology, but the results are quite robust. To begin with we assume that the estimates for the 1730s describe the population pyramid at the beginning of 1735. We then derive a set of age-specific survival rates for the following ten years, using the methodology described above, and project the starting age-groups through to 1745. The discrepancy between the projected age-groups and those previously estimated for the 1740s is then assumed to reflect the effects of net migration, and we can repeat the process for the interval 1745–55. In table 5.10 we set out the results in terms of the implied net immigration in each cohort over

Table 5.10. *Estimated net immigration (as percentage of initial cohort size)*

Decade	Age-Group				
	10–19	20–9	30–9	40–9	50–9
1735–45	71.4	30.4	12.2	−5.5	−28.1
1745–55	71.4	22.4	−0.1	−23.1	−40.2
1755–65	77.1	24.3	5.3	−16.4	−31.0
1765–75	54.8	18.6	5.8	−15.2	−30.1
1775–85	46.8	19.4	6.1	−15.3	−38.7
1785–95	37.9	25.9	9.7	−13.3	−36.2

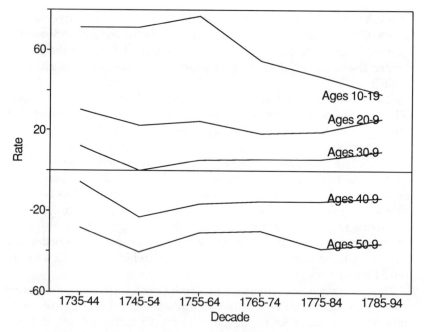

5.6 Estimated net immigration by age: annual rate per thousand

each ten year interval, expressed as a percentage of the size of the cohort at the opening of the interval.[11]

The results bring out dramatically the importance of migration in

[11] The oldest and youngest age-groups have both been omitted from these calculations – the latter because of the problems of estimating initial birth cohort size, and the former because of the serious distortions that age-mistatements are likely to impose on estimates of mortality at advanced ages (Coale and Kisker 1986).

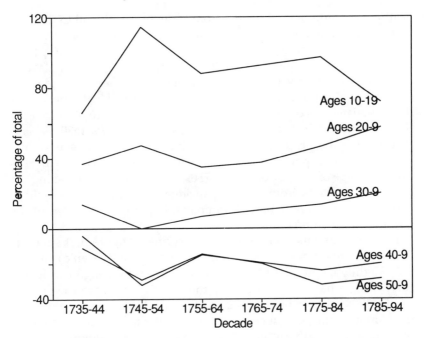

5.7 Estimated net immigration by age: as percentage of total

the 'teens and twenties, as well as suggesting a net outflow above the age of forty. The absolute numbers on which these percentages are based were obtained from the median population estimates discussed above and should be treated with corresponding reserve, but their age-pattern will not be affected by distortion from this source. In addition, because the decadal population structure estimates derive from the same assumptions concerning the age curve of mortality, they will not be affected by errors in the latter unless the relationship between mortality at the different adult ages change violently from decade to decade. No doubt some such changes did occur but the overall age-pattern is too stable to be an artefact of such effects (see figures 5.6 and 5.7).

The period before 1728

The results we have been considering so far depend heavily on estimates of infant mortality, and thus on the numbers of recorded infant burials. In the absence of an age-breakdown before 1728 it is necessary to proceed indirectly by means of the cause of death classification. The numbers of deaths from 'diseases incidental to infancy' (deducting 'childbed' deaths, stillbirths and abortions) are approximately equal to those in the 0–1 year age category, over the period 1730–49, but by this point the toll exacted by 'griping in the guts' had dwindled to insignificant proportions, and so it is necessary to make some special additional allowance for these deaths in the earlier decades. This was done by examining the age structure of 'griping in the guts' deaths in the Quaker registers for the years 1670–99, and determining the proportion falling within the first two years of life. This came to 78 per cent and so the numbers of recorded burials under the age of two, prior to the 1730s, were estimated by taking the numbers of deaths from 'diseases incidental to infancy' (less 'childbed' deaths, stillbirths, and abortions and adding 78 per cent of the 'griping in the guts' total.

The result of this exercise (see dotted line in figure 5.3) suggests that the infant mortality rate over the period was fairly stable at a level only slightly below that of the second quarter of the eighteenth century. It is, perhaps, reassuring that the infant mortality rate estimated for the 1720s should be so similar to that for the 1740s, for which age data are available, but such reassurance must fade as we move back into the seventeenth century. The estimates now rely quite heavily on the assumed age-incidence of the 'griping in the guts' deaths and, unlike those for the 1700–24 period, diverge substantially from the Quaker infant mortality rates. The seventeenth-century figures thus require more detailed investigation using an alternative approach.

Infant mortality in Gregory King's London

The level of infant mortality in London at the end of the seventeenth century and thus, by implication, the trend in infant mortality over the second half of that century was investigated further by means of a record linkage study using registers from a sample of City parishes for the period 1690–1709, the era of Gregory King. The criteria which parishes had to meet in order to be included in the sample were that the baptism registers should specify the age of the infant when the event occurred, and the burial registers should give enough information for at least half of the entries to be distinguished as children or adults.

These criteria were met by five intramural parishes during the decades in question, and the details of each child burial (predominantly those described as 'son' or 'daughter', together with foundlings and chrisoms) were transcribed onto slips and linked,

Table 5.11. *Parish Register infant mortality estimates (known infant burials only)*

Parish	Age in Months						Number of risks
	0	1–2	3–5	6–11	1–11	0–11	
St Benet Paul's Wharf	74	49	43	69	153	216	820
St Peter Paul's Wharf	68	17	48	54	115	191	324
St Mary Aldermary	107	18	40	42	98	193	367
St Mary Woolnoth	62	28	29	23	79	136	487
St Vedast Foster Lane	86	55	49	54	149	223	521
Weighted mean	81	38	42	51	125	195	

Source: see text, p. 184

where possible, to a corresponding entry in the baptism register. By this means, and taking the numbers of baptisms to indicate numbers of risks at the opening of the first month of life, age-specific mortality probabilities (life table q_x) were calculated for the first year and for subdivisions of this interval (see table 5.11).

Rates calculated in this way will of course understate the 'true' level of infant mortality, since some of the child burials which remain unlinked, and are thus excluded from the calculations, will in fact be those of infants for whom no baptismal record exists in the relevant parish. Such cases fall into two groups. In the first place there are the 'immigrants'. These infants were baptised in another parish from the one in which their burial was recorded, either because their parents were then living there, or because they chose to baptise their off-spring elsewhere. The second group comprises infants who died unbaptised and can also be split into two sub-groups, or 'popula-tions'. The first of these remained unbaptised by reason of their early death (population I), whilst the second consists of infants who would not have been baptised in any case and thus fell outside the scope of the registration system (population II).

The treatment of unbaptised infants in the burial registers of this period is, as we have already seen, uncertain and does not appear to have been entirely consistent. In earlier periods appreciable numbers of burial entries are recognisably those of unbaptised infants, generally described as 'chrisoms', and lacking a first name. Finlay (1981), for instance, found that the recorded baptisms in his sample of early seventeenth-century City registers should be inflated by a factor of 1.0405 to take account of these so-called 'dummy baptisms',

Death and the metropolis

Table 5.12. *Parish Register infant mortality rates*

| | Age in Months | | | |
Parish	0	1–11	0–11	Risks
Allhallows Bread Street, 1538–1653	77	37	111	1,562
St Peter Cornhill, 1580–1650	76	58	129	1,769
St Christopher le Stocks, 1580–1653	64	26	88	1,115
St Michael Cornhill, 1580–1650	86	52	135	2,261
St Dunstan in the East, 1605–53	201	67	255	3,103
St Mary Somerset, 1605–53	186	106	272	2,079
Allhallows London Wall, 1570–1636	157	81	225	1,839
St Botolph Bishopsgate, 1600–50	129	94	211	2,809
Weighted mean	138	73	200	

Source: Finlay 1981, pp. 28–9, table 2.2

inferred from entries in the burial register. A smaller sample of registers from the 1690s, however, yielded an inflation factor of 1.0176, and the comparable value from our own study was only 1.0032.

The virtual disappearance from the burial registers of 'chrisoms' and related entries implies that early deaths of this kind were either going unregistered, or that a first name was being placed in the register even though the infant had not been baptised before it died. It seems reasonable to assume that the latter might have occurred in instances where the infant should be treated as falling outside the scope of registration altogether (population II), but that parents who conscientiously baptised their surviving children (population I) would have been less likely to specify a 'Christian' name where this had not been properly bestowed. Hence in the majority of such cases the burial went unrecorded.

If this assumption is correct then our method is chiefly prone to understate the level of mortality in the first weeks of life, a conclusion reinforced when we compare our results with those obtained by Finlay earlier in the century (see table 5.12). The weighted mean infant mortality rates for the two samples are closely comparable, but a strikingly different picture emerges if we calculate separate rates for the first month of life and for the remainder of the first year. In our sample the latter figure is nearly twice that observed in the early seventeenth century, whereas the rate for the first month is substantially lower. If we assume that most, if not all, of this apparent decline in neonatal mortality is spurious then the overall comparison suggests that infant mortality had risen appreciably over the latter half of the seventeenth century.

The magnitude of this rise, however, is obscured by the consequences of under-registration and of our failure to identify correctly all of the infant burials which were recorded in the registers. The infant mortality rate we have calculated from the latter is substantially below that previously obtained from contemporary Bills of Mortality. We shall try to remedy these deficiencies in our results, but before doing this we must consider how far the comparison between our sample of registers, and that used by Finlay, is a fair one. The simplest way of doing this is to compare the relative wealth of the two samples as measured by the proportion of 'substantial' houses recorded in each parish in the tax listings of 1638 and 1695 (see table 5.13). In neither case has the material for all the parishes in the two samples survived, but such comparisons as can be made suggest that our sample is rather wealthier than Finlay's and so, other things being equal, would be expected to display lower levels of mortality than would the latter.

The information we have available does not allow us to determine the exact shortfall in our parish register estimates of infant mortality, but we can be reasonably confident in setting a lower bound to the 'true' value. In order to do this, we need to shift our attention from the logic of record linkage to that of aggregative analysis, and from the strictly defined life table measure q_0 to the looser measure of infant mortality furnished by the ratio of infant deaths to births. We can set an effective lower bound to the latter by assuming that burial registration was complete, but that baptism registration was defective due to deaths in the birth–baptism interval. This is equivalent to assuming that all of the infant deaths omitted from our calculations were overlooked because of the absence of a corresponding baptism entry, and that the shortfall in our estimate of total infant mortality is wholly attributable to the rate for the first month.

On this basis the ratio of infant deaths to births can be obtained by gauging the 'true' number of infant deaths in the burial register, since the required correction to the recorded baptisms will be equal to the difference between this figure and the number of infant burials obtained from record linkage. When we estimated infant mortality rates from the London Bills of Mortality we calculated the numbers of burials under two years of age by using the cause of death breakdown. Since the present analysis is intended as an independent check on those results, however, we must arrive at a burial total by a

Table 5.13. *Percentage of 'substantial' households in two samples of City parishes*

	Number of households (houses)		Substantial households (%)	
	1638	1695	1638	1695
Finlay's sample				
Allhallows Bread Street	—	80	—	60.0
St Peter Cornhill	129	—	59.7	—
St Christopher le Stocks	63	86	40.1	43.0
St Michael Cornhill	165	136	34.5	39.7
St Dunstan in the East	285	312	22.8	44.5
St Mary Somerset	144	117	8.3	6.0
Allhallows London Wall	196	278	2.5	9.7
St Botolph Bishopsgate	1,471	1,760	1.2	5.8
Weighted means				
(1)			10.5	19.4
(2)			17.2	28.2
Landers' sample				
St Benet Paul's Wharf	—	120	—	45.0
St Mary Aldermary	91	95	29.7	30.5
St Mary Woolnoth	88	85	59.1	31.8
St Peter Paul's Wharf	80	—	32.5	—
St Vedast Foster Lane	128	—	34.4	—
Weighted means				
(1)			38.5	36.7

Note: Weights employed:
(1) numbers of enumerated households, or houses, in parish
(2) numbers of risks observed in Finlay's parish register sample.
Source: Finlay 1981, pp. 168–72, table A3.1; Jones and Judges 1935, pp. 58–62, table 3

different method. This is based on the proportion of recorded child burials in our sample and employs two further assumptions. These are: (i) that the numbers of such burials are equivalent to the total for burials under the age of ten; and (ii) that, of the latter, the proportion which occur under two years of age in our sample is equal to the corresponding proportion observed in the London Bills during the decades 1730–49.

In practice, the latter proportion is likely to have been rather lower in 1730–49 than it was in the decades 1690–1709, because of the

Table 5.14. *Adjustments to infant mortality
estimate for five parish sample 1690–1709*

Parish Register sample
Total recorded burials	=	2,772
Total 'child' burials	=	1,470
Known infant burials	=	492
Known births	=	2,519

Bills of Mortality 1730–49
Total burials – 9 years	=	241,819
Estimated infant burials	=	133,819 (= 55.34%)

Estimated number of infant burials in Parish
Register sample:
= 0.5534 * 1470
= 814
Estimated omitted births:
= 814 – 492
= 322
Estimated 'true' infant mortality rate:
= 814 / (2519 + 322)
= 0.287

---

heightened incidence of smallpox, which is likely to have had a proportionately greater effect on the mortality of older children given the
importance of the disease as a cause of death in later childhood. In
other respects, however, the assumptions do not seem unreasonable
and they yield the results set out in table 5.14. The overall infant
mortality rate, incorporating the corrected figure for the first month,
now shows a large increase from the early seventeenth-century
levels, although the rise in the neo-natal estimate remains substantially below that observed in the 1–11 month period.

In reality of course the registration of infant burials was certainly
not complete at this time, and not all of the infant burials overlooked
in our record linkage analysis will have lacked corresponding baptismal entries. Hence it seems safe to assume that our corrected figure
still underestimates the prevailing level of infant mortality to some
degree. Glass (1972) estimated that burials and baptisms in the registers of the intramural parishes, for the years 1696–8, should be
multiplied by 1.271 and 1.335 respectively to allow for under-registration. If we apply these inflations to our observed baptismal total, and
to the estimated number of infant burials, we obtain an infant burial:
baptism ratio of 308 per thousand.

This is equivalent, in terms of the above calculations, to adding about forty per cent of the additional infant burials to the observed baptisms, which seems plausible, and since mortality in the intramural parishes appears to have been rather lower than elsewhere, it is also compatible with the estimates derived from the contemporary Bills. It thus seems safe to conclude that the level of infant mortality prevailing in London around 1700 was indeed in excess of 300 per thousand, and had thus risen steeply since the period studied by Finlay, although the precise chronology of this increase remains unclear at this point due to the difficulties surrounding use of the Bills in the last decades of the seventeenth century.

A concluding assessment

These results suggest a level of infant mortality which was about twice that found in other English reconstitutions for most of the period, but which declined rapidly from the last quarter of the eighteenth century. The birth rate was also about 20 per cent higher than the national figure at the opening of the period for which such calculations can be made and this rate also declined in the later eighteenth century, although the timing of the decline is harder to date with any precision, given the fluctuations evident in the 1760s and 1770s. The calculations underlying such results are necessarily less exact than is usually the case in historical demographic work, and they required us to make several assumptions whose validity cannot be directly investigated. This is unfortunate, but it should be borne in mind that our primary concern here is not to produce statistically robust point estimates of fertility and mortality for their own sake, but to test the predictions of a general model and thus to answer questions which are couched in terms of orders of magnitude and of secular trends.

We should thus consider how far our results are acceptable in such terms, and here the central issue is that of the infant mortality series, since it is these figures which underlie most of the other calculations we have carried out. The infant mortality estimates for the final decade of our period are sufficiently close to the early civil registration figures to give some confidence in their adequacy as a broad indicator of the levels prevailing at that point. Similarly, it seems unlikely that our figures for the first half of the eighteenth century greatly overstate prevailing levels of infant mortality, since were this the case it would imply both that the Quaker rates were correspondingly higher than those of the surrounding population, which does not appear very plausible, and that there was a truly enormous shortfall in the registration of baptisms relative to that of burials.

At least one contemporary observer – Daniel Defoe – did, however, advance such an explanation for London's burial surpluses in the early eighteenth century, and it requires some investigation at this point since, given the apparently high level of the birth rate, deficient baptism registration is the only remaining alternative to high mortality. For the purposes of analysis we shall consider the possibility that the underlying totals of births and deaths occurring in London were in balance, but that baptismal registration was grossly deficient relative to that of burials (the 'Defoe hypothesis'). In this case the 'true' infant mortality rate would be equal to the proportion of infant burials among the global figure, a proportion which we have estimated as about 28 per cent for the 1730s and 25 per cent for the 1740s.

It is worth noting that such rates would still be substantially higher than those estimated from English parish register reconstitutions at this time, but it can also be demonstrated that, leaving the comparison with the Quaker rates aside, they are unacceptably low. We can do this by applying life table model m_xs to the age-specific burial totals so as to determine the underlying population size implied by any given level of mortality. For simplicity of calculation we shall take the Princeton Model North tables. The Defoe hypothesis, as we have called it, would imply a set of mortality rates roughly equivalent to level four, with an infant mortality rate of 264 per thousand.

This procedure yields mid-decadal population totals of 688,750 and 712,850 for the 1730s and 1740s respectively. If we inflate these figures by 15 per cent to allow for under-registration, and such an inflation seems the plausible minimum, we get estimates of around 792,000 and 820,000, which are much too large to be acceptable. The level three table, with a q_0 of 289 per thousand, yields inflated population totals of 698,000 and 749,000 for the two decades, as compared with the median estimates of 639,000 and 648,000, and upper limits of 698,000 and 706,000, which we derived from the coal figures. The upper limits, based as they are on the unrealistic hypothesis of no *per capita* change in consumption, are themselves implausibly high. Moreover, if London's population in 1745 was as large as 749,000 this would imply a long-term annual growth rate of 0.95 per cent from 1701, as against only 0.45 per cent *per annum* between 1745 and the end of the century, an imbalance which seems quite incompatible with such evidence as we possess on this topic.

It thus seems safe to conclude that London's infant mortality rate was somewhere above 300 per thousand in the 1730s and 1740s, and that our estimates for these decades are of the correct order of magnitude at least. If this is accepted then it follows that infant mortality in London fell by rather more than half in the century after 1740, and the general similarity of the trend in the estimates based on the London Bills of Mortality to that in the Quaker reconstitution results suggests that the two series give a reasonable indication of the chronology of this reduction. A relatively modest decline in the third quarter of the eighteenth century[12] apparently gave way to a rapid and continuing fall from around 1770, with only a temporary interruption in the 1790s.

This interruption in the decline of infant mortality is associated with an abrupt reversal in the rising trend displayed by our estimates of relative baptism under-registration, as measured by the 'k' ratio, a conjunction which raises the suspicion that the 'k' series itself may be in error at this point, and the underlying mortality decline continuous. We do not have sufficient evidence to resolve this question definitively, but it is interesting to note that the smallpox fraction displays a similar trend at this time, with a secular decline beginning in the 1770s and being temporarily reversed in the 1790s. Hence it is possible that the improvement in infant mortality in London was temporarily halted by a renewed upsurge in deaths from this cause.

The period before 1728 raises greater difficulties. The Bills' estimates for the first quarter of the century are similar to the Quaker figure, and compatible with the parish register estimates for the decades around 1700. It thus seems safe to conclude that infant mortality had reached something approaching its early eighteenth-century level by the end of the preceding century. This in turn implies a sharp increase from the levels detected by Finlay a hundred years before, but the timing of the former is not entirely clear. Our results suggest that it had occurred by the late 1670s, at least, and that there was little change in infant mortality thereafter. The apparent stability of the late seventeenth-century infant mortality rate may, however, be deceptive, for it conceals offsetting movements in the vital index and the estimated proportion of infant burials, both of which increase substantially between the 1670s and 1700. Furthermore, there is a considerable gap between the Bills' mortality estimates for the later seventeenth century and the corresponding Quaker figure.

This raises a number of possibilities. If the Bills' series are correct

---

[12] The Bills' infant mortality estimate actually falls below the Quaker figure at this point, suggesting that we may have over-estimated the relative shortfall in baptism registration and thus exaggerated the scale of this first phase of mortality decline.

then either mortality at older ages declined sharply from the 1670s, or else there was a substantial rise in the birth rate. Alternatively, it is possible that the recovery in the vital index is factitious, arising from a progressive improvement in baptismal registration after the Republican period.[13] The first of these possibilities seems very unlikely, given that Quaker child and adult mortality apparently increased from the later seventeenth to the early eighteenth century, but the second cannot be entirely dismissed as the Quaker infant mortality rates may themselves be too low before 1700.

The gap between the latter and the contemporary Bills' estimates, however, seems too large to be accounted for entirely in these terms, and the case for the third possibility – improving registration – is strengthened by some calculations undertaken using Finlay and Shearer's (1986) estimates of contemporary population size. Taking these, the 'PRE equivalent' baptism totals, and the inflation factors from table 5.3, we obtain CBR estimates of 31, 35, and 37 respectively for the three decades.[14] The figures going into these calculations are too uncertain for the results to bear much interpretation in terms of their absolute levels, but the implied increase of nearly 20 per cent in the birth rate is suspicious under the circumstances. It thus seems most probable that some, at least, of the difference between the two sets of mortality rates arises from our having under-estimated the relative shortfall in baptismal registration, and that London's infant mortality was still rising in the last decades of the seventeenth century.

Summary

The two sources of data employed in the foregoing chapters both have their strengths and weaknesses. The Bills of Mortality have the virtue of breadth, but their pre-aggregated character limits the range of techniques that can be employed, and they are subject to a level of

[13] Other explanations are theoretically possible but do not seem at all likely. We may, for instance have miscalculated the proportion of infant burials, but the trend in the proportion remains very similar if all the 'griping in the guts' burials are counted as under two years of age, and it is hard to see why there should have been systematic changes in the age-distribution of deaths from this cause over the period. Similarly the movements in the two series seem too large to be explained in terms of changes in population age-structure independent of increases in fertility.

[14] Population totals of 467, 481, and 487,000 for the three decades in question were obtained by linear interpolation from the figures given in Finlay and Shearer's tables 3 and 5. 'PRE equivalent' baptism totals, and inflation factors, for the 1670s were obtained by applying the relevant ratios observed in 1680–9 to the Bills' baptisms for the former decade.

under-recording which cannot be determined with any precision but is likely to have been substantial. Conversely, the Quaker material allows analysis in depth with the aid of nominative techniques. Its reliability is also relatively assured at any rate after 1700, but against this must be set its restriction to a limited sub-section of London's population whose demographic 'representativeness' cannot be assumed.

The general agreement between the two sets of results is thus reassuring. Both suggest that mortality was much higher in London than elsewhere, and that it declined rapidly from the last quarter of the eighteenth century. The levels of infant mortality in the two series are generally similar, whilst the Quaker data reveal an exceptionally severe level of mortality in childhood. The importance of adolescent, and young adult, immigration emerges clearly from Bills, whilst the Quaker material suggests an interaction between migration and smallpox mortality of just the kind that our earlier aggregative analysis led us to expect.

These patterns of mortality and immigration in combination gave rise to a population structure weighted in the younger adult age-groups. This in turn fostered a birth rate which was high by English standards, but the age-standardised general fertility level seems also to have been relatively high. In the absence of nuptiality data it is not possible to partition general fertility into components due to nuptiality and marital fertility, but the Quaker data suggest that birth intervals were short owing to limitations on breast feeding.

There is some disagreement between our two sources in terms of the trend of mortality, but this is limited to the earliest decades of our period. The Quaker data imply an increase in mortality, at all ages, from the later seventeenth to the early eighteenth century, whereas the Bills suggest that eighteenth-century levels of infant mortality had been largely attained by the 1680s. We have suggested that the latter is probably an overestimate, and that the Quaker results are likely to provide a more reliable guide to general conditions at this time, but it is not possible to resolve this issue with certainty.

What is certain, however, is that the trend of mortality in eighteenth-century London differed from that in the country at large until the 1780s. Even if life expectancy in the capital did not deteriorate after 1700, there is certainly no trace of the improvement displayed by the back-projection results for the first twenty years of the eighteenth century. London's medium-term response to the stresses of the next three decades also differed from that of England as a whole. National life expectancy apparently fell by more than 4.5 years from 1715–9 into the 1720s, and by the same amount again into the early 1730s, but this was followed by a recovery of over 7.5 years in the second half of the decade.

Crisis conditions returned in the 1740s, but their impact on life expectancy was apparently restricted to the quinquennium 1741–6. The average e_0 for the entire decade was equal to that for the years 1670–99, whilst the figure for the 1750s marked a return to the early seventeenth century. In London, by contrast the response of mortality was more protracted, and conditions apparently deteriorated into the 1740s. Only a very limited recovery is visible in the following thirty years and it is not until the 1780s that conditions have clearly improved beyond the levels of the preceding century. In the following chapters we shall try to understand the reasons for this delayed recovery and for the dramatic transformation of London's vital regime which it ushered in.

PART III

Dimensions of London's epidemiological regime

There has as yet, however, been little detailed research into the explicitly quantitative incidence of disease, or of specific infections, in the late eighteenth and nineteenth centuries. (Luckin 1980: 54)

In the preceding sections we have considered the pattern of aggregate vital data from eighteenth-century London and tried to estimate the prevailing levels of fertility and mortality. The results generally bore out the 'high potential' interpretation of metropolitan epidemiology, but if we are to pursue this question any further we must move from a study of the 'output' variable – the medium-term level of mortality – to one of the 'internal' character of the regime itself. This involves a consideration of the intermediate mortality variables, their structure and inter-relationships, together with London's pathogenic load over our period.

The latter is, of course, crucial for the proximate explanation of mortality patterns in any population, but assumes prime importance when we consider relationships between metropolitan epidemiological regimes and those of their hinterlands. The HPM portrays the former as endemic reservoirs of infection – sources of epidemic crises in the hinterland – whose distinctive character reflects quantitative differences in the incidence of infections common to both metropolis and hinterland, rather than the action of diseases peculiar to the former. In particular, the model implies that excess urban mortality arose substantially from infections communicated from person to person, either directly or by the action of arthropod vectors.

Historical demographers by contrast – to the extent that they have considered the problem of causes of death – have more often posited a qualitative difference between metropolitan and hinterland regimes, with the former determined principally by the physical environment of towns and cities and the problems of water supply, sanitation and sewage disposal which they experienced. In this view it was the presence of water- and food-borne gastric diseases which gave metropolitan vital regimes their distinctive character and were primarily responsible for variations in their levels of mortality. Preston and Van de Walle thus found the 'most appealing candidate' for the explanation of urban mortality trends in nineteenth-century France to be:

the quality of the water supply and techniques of sewage disposal, since water-and food-borne diseases, spread by faecal contamination are a prominent feature of high-mortality disease profiles and are the group to which exposure was most readily altered prior to the bacteriological revolution of the 1880s and 1890s. (Preston and Van de Walle 1978: 279)[1]

[1] Wrigley and Schofield (1981: 295) also suggest that, in the English case, 'the combina-

199

This 'naturalistic' treatment of metropolitan demography accords mortality a powerful and independent influence on urban society, but one whose historical evolution is largely restricted to the axis of sanitary reform and whose sole action on the surrounding population is that of a demographic drain.[2] Although metropolitan mortality levels in early modern Europe have been the subject of recent debate among demographic historians,[3] the causes of death which underlay these have in fact received little attention. Luckin's observations on the dearth of late eighteenth- and nineteenth-century studies holds with equal – or greater – force for the preceding hundred years.

The reasons for this lie, of course, in the character of the source materials, which are such as to make any form of mortality analysis difficult and are often silent on the question of cause of death. The London Bills do provide cause of death information, but, as we have seen, few of the terms employed can be equated with those known to present day medicine. In chapter 6 we thus adopt an alternative approach to the problem, based on an analysis of burial seasonality. The difficulties involved in inferring causes of death from the seasonality of burials are obvious, but we are fortunate in that the central questions we need to resolve are – at least in the first analysis – couched in terms of the means of transmission of infection, rather than the identity of the pathogens themselves. Variations in the former do give rise, statistically at least, to differences in the seasonality of mortality, and, as we shall see, burial seasonality in London alters sufficiently over our period to allow some reasonably firm inferences as to the means of transmission involved and the primacy of person to person infections.

The evidence suggests that these changes in seasonality are not wholly explicable in terms of 'autonomous' pathogenic variation but also reflect changes in the structure of the epidemiological regime itself. The latter is largely determined by the network of pathways which it affords to pathogens to move between members of the population, and by the relationships between the latter and the outside world. In the absence of sufficient data for a direct analysis of these questions much can be learned from the response of mortality to external stress, from whatever source. The London data are par-

---

tion of high density and imperfect sanitation that was typical of the towns of pre-industrial Europe magnified the normal seasonal prevalence of fly borne diseases, which particularly affected children, to such an extent that the overall seasonal pattern of mortality was substantially affected'.

[2] The classic argument for the importance of this effect, in the case of London, is Wrigley 1967. For a critique of the argument's general assumptions see Sharlin 1978.

[3] For a recent review of the urban mortality debate see J. de Vries 1984: chapter 9.

ticularly valuable in this context, allowing us to examine variations in the response of mortality from different causes of death and in different age-groups.

The analysis of extreme conditions is one way of looking at the relationship between demographic 'output', and 'input' from the economic or physical environment. Crisis theory posited radical discontinuities between the response of mortality to such conditions and the 'background' mortality of 'normal' years, emphasising the effect of food shortages on resistance to infection, but as we have seen this approach has proved of limited value in eighteenth-century studies. As an alternative, Post (1984; 1985) has argued that 'mortality peaks' represented a quantitative exaggeration – rather than a qualitative transformation – of 'normal' mortality patterns and located their origin in the determinants of exposure to infection.

Neoclassical historical demography, by contrast, has more often avoided the analysis of specific configurations of events, employing statistical analysis of demographic, economic and meteorological series in their entirety in order to distinguish 'high- and low-pressure' demographic regimes. Both of these approaches are pursued in chapter 7. The time series analysis suggests that mortality was sensitive to price movements in the short-term, but that the relationship was relatively weak and not consistent with a strong 'resistance' effect. Fever and smallpox mortality, however, both show severe responses to extreme conditions, and the evidence strongly suggests that the underlying relationships involved the determinants of exposure to infection.

Spatial structure, particularly housing and migration patterns, seems to have been intimately bound up with these determinants and forms the subject matter of chapter 8. Unfortunately, there are serious methodological difficulties in the way of such a study. The parishes which served as the basis for vital registration bore an awkward and uncertain relationship to any 'natural' social areas in early modern London, and our sources give only impressionistic and coarse-grained accounts of spatial differentiation in contemporary social and economic life. That such differentiation existed is not, however, in question, and there is general agreement as to its principal axes.

The aggregate vital data do display differences in levels and forms of instability – and apparently in cause of death patterns – between districts with different ecological and migratory characteristics in a manner which provides general support to our hypotheses. Furthermore, a limited parish register study reveals growing spatial differences in both the level and seasonality of mortality during the eighteenth-century decades of economic and demographic stagnation, suggesting that the deterioration of conditions was largely restricted to a belt of 'unhealthy districts' in the older suburbs. These were the districts, we argue, in which recent immigrants were concentrated, and where housing conditions suffered disproportionately as a result of economic stagnation.

6

The seasonality of mortality

The importance of cause of death patterns for the understanding of mortality in the past has been widely acknowledged, but has not generated a corresponding body of demographic literature on the subject. The diseases of eighteenth-century London have, however, attracted some attention from contemporary and later writers alike who have generally concentrated on two conditions that seem to have worsened in the course of the century: smallpox and typhus.[1] The first of these was only too familiar to contemporaries and it is one of the few instances of a cause of death category in the Bills which can be reliably equated with a condition known to twentieth-century medicine.

Smallpox, as we have seen, appears to have been a universal childhood affliction in the capital. It was particularly prevalent in the third quarter of the century, accounting for 10 per cent of all recorded burials, but from the 1780s its share began to decline substantially, and the disease was responsible for little more than 5 per cent of burials in the years 1800–24. The earlier proportions are more likely to understate the relative significance of the disease than to exaggerate it. A certain number of victims of 'fulminating smallpox' may have been wrongly classified, but more important is the apparent role of smallpox morbidity in enhancing the risks of death from other conditions.

The term 'typhus', by contrast, was not used until mid-century and then only as a generic label to distinguish a range of 'slow', or

---

[1] A wide ranging review of the available data on the incidence of smallpox in this period can be found in Razzell 1977; the demographic implications of the decline of the disease are discussed by Mercer 1985. For the classic account of the historical development of typhus fever see Zinsser 1935. Clinical and epidemiological aspects of the disease are discussed in Snyder 1965.

'nervous', fevers from the 'inflammatory', or 'choleric', conditions described by writers such as Sydenham in the preceding century (Risse 1985). But by the 1760s a number of medical practitioners had described 'the unmistakable characteristics of the disease that physicians today consider to be louse-born typhus' (Risse 1985: 177) and pointed to its association with poverty and overcrowding. This, petechial, typhus was widely regarded as a new disease by medical opinion in the later eighteenth century, but despite this the Bills of Mortality continued to treat 'fevers' as a single category, a practice maintained in the early decades of civil registration.

The inclusion of typhus under the general heading of fevers in the Bills exemplifies the central difficulty encountered in using material of this kind to study causes of death. The categories in which it deals – such as fevers, convulsions, and even consumption – denote external symptoms whose character was very loosely defined, and which might arise from a number of different pathological conditions. Given data of this kind we can realistically hope to identify specific causes of death in only a small number of instances, but this is not as much of a handicap as might first appear. Many of the key theoretical questions with which we are concerned refer to the mode of transmission of the relevant pathogens rather than to their specific identity – in particular the relative importance of diseases directly transmitted from person to person rather than by contaminated food or water.

In the body of this chapter we shall approach the question of causes of death by looking at variations in the seasonality of recorded burials.[2] The logical and empirical difficulties involved in thus moving from observed patterns of seasonality to imputed patterns of disease are considerable – and the results must be treated with corresponding caution – but the procedure should allow us to distinguish with some confidence between the effects of broad groups of diseases, and particularly between gastric and respiratory conditions.

We shall begin by examining the seasonality of the total and cause-

---

[2] In what follows we assume that seasonal variations in the numbers of burials follow those in mortality levels, rather than changes in the size of the population at risk. Such an assumption is generally reasonable, but partially breaks down in the case of infant burials, which are affected by birth seasonality. In order to correct for this effect we should require detailed knowledge of the level, and age incidence, of infant mortality in London throughout the period, and this is not available. But a comparison between the seasonality of baptisms in the 1670s, when birth-baptism intervals were short (see Berry and Schofield 1971), with that of births in the period 1845–74 (see Landers and Mouzas, 1988, appendix table 4) suggests that there was little change in birth seasonality over our period and that the changing seasonality of infant burials can therefore be safely attributed to changes in the seasonal risks of mortality.

specific burial series from the London Bills, before attempting some inferences on the subject of causes of death. We shall then turn to the problem of variations in burial seasonality by age, and the relative stability of different age-specific seasonalities over time. Finally we shall return to the question, considered briefly in chapter 3, of the relationship between age and causes of death.

The seasonality of burials 1670–1819

The burial totals were taken from the weekly Bills of Mortality for London for the years 1670–1819. Monthly aggregates were then calculated[3] for the total burials, smallpox, and convulsions series for the years 1670–1819; for consumption and fever for 1670–1799; and, on a more limited basis, for some additional series concerned with infant deaths, as explained below.[4] The first step in the analysis was to transform the absolute totals into index numbers showing the relative frequencies of burials in the different months. These 'monthly burial indices' (MBIs) are constructed to take a value of 100 where the number of burials observed in a month is exactly proportionate to its length in days, with values above or below this implying a corresponding relative surplus or deficit.

Total burials

The resulting indices for the total burials series (see table 6.1) suggest that disease patterns in London were anything but static throughout these years, since the pattern of seasonality altered markedly over the period as a whole. There appear to be two main changes, of which the first, accomplished between the late seventeenth and mid-eighteenth centuries, is the more far- reaching. This transforms an initial summer peak, strongly centred on August, into a much broader 'cold weather plateau' stretching from November to April; the months of June and July now representing a trough in mortality, with only a moderate excess remaining in September. In the second phase, from 1775 to the end of the period, a markedly bimodal pattern emerges. The cold

---

[3] For details of the method employed, together with the techniques of interpolation and estimation required to correct shortcomings in the original material see the appendix to Landers and Mouzas 1988.

[4] The collection of weekly Bills held in the Guildhall Museum was used in the present analysis, together with the more restricted holdings of the British Library which run up to the 1770s. It was necessary to terminate the aggregation of the consumption and fevers series in 1799 as the material for more recent years was temporarily removed from public access during the course of the study.

Table 6.1. *Weekly Bills of Mortality: seasonality of total burials*

	Monthly Burial Indices					
	1670–99	1700–24	1725–49	1750–74	1775–79	1800–24
Jan	102	109	110	112	116	117
Feb	104	109	112	110	114	114
Mar	101	105	105	107	104	105
Apr	96	99	104	102	99	97
May	92	94	97	96	94	92
Jun	92	89	87	89	93	87
Jul	104	91	83	85	87	89
Aug	119	103	94	90	93	91
Sep	105	106	104	97	94	96
Oct	92	98	100	97	95	101
Nov	96	97	102	108	115	120
Dec	97	102	104	106	99	95

weather plateau is much reduced – becoming clearly focussed on the months of January and February – whilst a new burial peak emerges in November.

These movements in seasonality were summarised in the form of a principal components analysis (Everitt and Dunn 1983), as in figure 6.1, in which 97 per cent of the variation between the indices for the six periods was accounted for by the first two components. The plot of scores on the latter suggests that the first should be thought of as an axis of secular change – a change which continues throughout the period though at a substantially reduced rate after 1750. Inspection of the coefficients reveals, as we might expect, a pattern of strong negative associations with the indices for the months in the third quarter of the year, especially August.

The second axis, by contrast, separates the 1700–74 periods from the remainder. The coefficients here are harder to interpret, but the combination of relatively strong positive values in December and April, with weak or negative ones for the intervening months, is consistent with the prevalence of the cold weather plateau of mortality at this time. The first three quarters of the eighteenth century thus stand out with a distinctive seasonal pattern of burials, over and above the longer term movement from a summer to a winter peak of mortality.

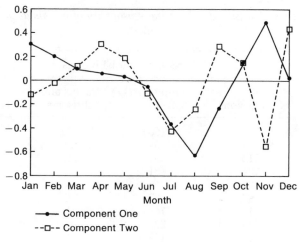

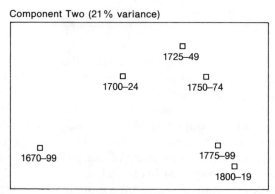

(a) Coefficients

Component Two (21% variance)

Component One (76% variance)

(b) Scores

6.1 Seasonality of total burials in London Bills: principal components
analysis

Burials by cause of death

These changes in the seasonality of total burials were pursued further
by examining the cause-specific seasonalities.

Infant deaths

The burial classification adopted by the London Bills of Mortality
presents a number of obstacles to the analysis of infant deaths, as

Table 6.2. *Weekly Bills of Mortality: seasonality of burials at young ages*
(1670–9)

| | Monthly Burial Indices | | | |
Month	Convulsions	Griping in the guts	Infants and chrisoms	Teething
Jan	111	60	120	87
Feb	119	64	126	107
Mar	112	61	114	109
Apr	104	61	97	108
May	92	65	86	99
Jun	97	97	92	106
Jul	110	168	96	133
Aug	110	231	103	144
Sep	86	175	100	98
Oct	75	88	83	66
Nov	88	66	81	66
Dec	97	60	104	77

demographers now define that term, since the youngest age-category groups together all deaths under the age of two. The lack of a comprehensive age breakdown before 1728 is even more serious, but can be met in part from the cause of death classification. After 1728 the numbers of burials grouped by Marshall under the heading 'diseases incidental to infancy' are approximately equal to those in the youngest age-group, and for most of our period this total is dominated by the single category of convulsions.

The decades prior to 1700 present a more complex picture. 'Infants and chrisomes' and 'teething' both account for a substantial proportion of the 'infancy' totals, whilst a large number of deaths are ascribed to griping in the guts which is excluded from this heading. We have thus used the convulsions series as the basis for the infant MBIs after 1700, whilst before this the convulsions totals were added to those for teething, infants and chrisomes, and 76 per cent of the griping in the guts figure. Before considering the resulting series we must examine the late seventeenth-century material in more detail to see how far the changing prevalence of the different causes of death should be ascribed simply to diagnostic fashion.

The best way to do this is to take the cause-specific seasonalities for the 1670s, the one decade when appreciable numbers of deaths are ascribed to each category. The results in table 6.2 reveal markedly

distinct patterns. Deaths from griping in the guts are heavily concentrated in the third quarter with an August peak. The teething
deaths also peak in July and August – falling to below average levels
by September – but display a generally lower degree of seasonal
variation. Infant and chrisomes burials, by contrast, display a maximum in January and February, whilst the seasonality of convulsions
mortality falls between this series and the teething deaths.

Thus 'convulsions' apparently includes deaths which might
otherwise be attributed either to teething or to infants and chrisomes,[5] and its increased prevalence is probably due to diagnostic
fashion. The seasonality of griping in the guts, however, is very
different from that of the other causes of death, and we cannot
assume that the term was interchangeable with any of them.

The seasonality of the modified convulsions (henceforth simply
convulsions) series varies much less, over the first half of our period,
than does that of total burials (see table 6.3 for the seasonality of
burials in the main cause of death categories). The main feature is a
shift in the summer peak from July and August to August and
September, a movement associated with a striking reduction in the
index for July.[6] In the second half of the period a January–February
maximum emerges as the previous late summer peak gives way to a
more broadly based pattern of excess autumn mortality with a
secondary maximum in November.

Smallpox
Mortality from smallpox is concentrated in the latter half of the year in
each of the six periods. The indices for 1670–99 show a marked third
quarter peak, resembling that for infant burials, but thereafter there is
a tendency for the peak to move back into the fourth quarter, a
tendency which becomes particularly strong as the level of mortality
from the disease declines after 1775.

Consumption
Mortality from consumption was predominantly a winter
phenomenon throughout our period. At all times the December to
April indices are above 100 and those for June to October below this.

---

[5] This conclusion concerning the nature of 'convulsions' as a category is apparently
supported by contemporary observations. Thus Creighton refers to 'the testimony of
Willis. Speaking of convulsions, he says they occur at two special periods of life –
within one month of birth . . . and during teething' (Creighton 1894: 749).

[6] The indices given here for convulsions burials 1670–99 differ from those appearing in
Landers and Mouzas (1988: 66, table 5), which are in error. However the correct
figures were used in all calculations reported in the latter.

Table 6.3. *Weekly Bills of Mortality: monthly burial indices*

Month	1670–99	1700–24	1725–49	1750–74	1775–99	1800–19
Convulsions						
Jan	95	99	102	107	110	111
Feb	99	104	107	107	110	112
Mar	98	105	104	107	105	101
Apr	91	97	102	100	98	97
May	88	92	95	93	89	89
Jun	92	90	87	85	87	87
Jul	121	99	88	91	98	95
Aug	147	120	108	104	110	102
Sep	114	115	116	110	101	102
Oct	85	95	100	99	91	104
Nov	82	91	95	101	106	108
Dec	86	95	96	96	95	94
Smallpox						
Jan	91	97	90	99	98	92
Feb	83	86	87	82	80	68
Mar	75	73	78	83	67	55
Apr	80	87	82	84	70	54
May	89	89	98	93	84	63
Jun	104	92	105	102	101	79
Jul	125	107	111	107	115	100
Aug	131	115	118	105	118	115
Sep	115	117	119	105	121	133
Oct	107	118	108	107	118	151
Nov	104	115	105	117	131	175
Dec	94	108	97	115	95	113
Total burials (excluding smallpox and convulsions)						
Jan	107	115	115	116	120	121
Feb	110	113	117	115	120	118
Mar	105	109	109	111	110	109
Apr	101	102	107	106	103	100
May	95	95	97	98	97	95
Jun	91	88	85	89	93	88
Jul	92	85	77	80	79	86
Aug	103	95	84	82	83	86
Sep	99	100	96	91	88	91
Oct	93	97	99	95	93	96
Nov	103	97	105	109	116	118
Dec	103	104	108	108	101	94
Consumption						
Jan	109	113	115	117	126	
Feb	111	116	117	118	122	
Mar	119	111	112	113	111	

Table 6.3. *(Contd.)*

Month	1670–99	1700–24	1725–49	1750–74	1775–99	1800–19
Apr	102	101	110	108	103	
May	98	98	98	100	96	
Jun	87	90	87	85	93	
Jul	94	86	76	77	79	
Aug	93	88	83	79	80	
Sep	92	97	91	90	83	
Oct	91	94	98	95	91	
Nov	100	99	105	110	116	
Dec	104	106	109	112	101	
Fevers						
Jan	91	97	101	108	109	
Feb	97	94	99	106	108	
Mar	95	92	98	103	98	
Apr	93	100	100	101	95	
May	97	101	98	103	94	
Jun	94	94	89	94	99	
Jul	99	97	86	87	89	
Aug	115	107	99	90	91	
Sep	111	111	112	96	97	
Oct	102	106	108	99	103	
Nov	107	101	107	109	122	
Dec	98	100	105	106	97	
Other causes						
Jan	113	123	121	119	119	
Feb	114	120	126	118	122	
Mar	102	114	112	113	112	
Apr	104	103	109	108	106	
May	92	92	96	95	99	
Jun	91	86	83	91	92	
Jul	88	80	74	78	74	
Aug	102	92	79	81	83	
Sep	97	97	92	90	88	
Oct	91	94	96	94	90	
Nov	102	95	104	109	114	
Dec	105	104	109	107	102	

Nonetheless, changes occur which resemble those in the total burials series. The MBIs for July and August fall steeply over the first half of the period, and those for November to February continue to rise into the third quarter of the eighteenth century. After 1775 the familiar bimodal pattern emerges with maxima in January and February and in November.

Fever
The seasonality of fever burials changes substantially over the period.
The late seventeenth-century figures show a clear maximum in
August and September, with a moderate excess in the late autumn
and a deficit in the months December to June. By the second quarter
of the eighteenth century, however, the MBI for August has fallen
below 100, whilst those for the fourth quarter have risen appreciably,
the September index remains virtually unchanged. A further shift is
visible after 1750, with the maximum moving from September back
into November and a secondary peak emerging in January and
February.

All other causes
The behaviour of this series resembles that for consumption, the
index values peaking in January and February throughout the period
of the study. A substantial reduction in the third quarter indices
occurs over the first half of the period, with corresponding increases
in the first quarter. After 1750 there is little alteration in the seasonal
pattern apart from a reduction in the December value, and a corresponding rise in November, resulting in a secondary maximum.

Summary

The cause-specific burial seasonalities thus vary considerably[7] at any
given time, but most of them display the central trends identifiable
for total burials. Each series shows a relative decline in the number of
summer burials as we move from the seventeenth to the mid-
eighteenth century. For convulsions burials this is associated with a
corresponding rise in the autumn indices, whereas for smallpox the
increase is broadly diffused across the year. Elsewhere, however, it is
generally the winter values which rise, forming what we have termed
the cold weather plateau of mortality.

After 1750 the excess mortality is generally focussed on the late
autumn and mid-winter months, smallpox deaths being unusual in
manifesting only a single, very pronounced, maximum in the late
autumn. Indices for the fever, consumption and 'all other causes'
series could only be calculated up to 1799, but the latest figures show
the mid-winter peak predominating in the latter two as in the convul-

[7] This statement should be qualified in respect of the close similarity between the
seasonalities of consumption and 'all other causes', which supports contemporary
claims that the former was used as a catch-all diagnosis for much of the eighteenth
century; see Landers 1986: n. 22.

sions series. The November peak is the more substantial in the case of fevers.

The relative fall in summer deaths over the first half of our period is striking, but its interpretation is hampered by the fact that we are dealing with index numbers rather than mortality rates. We cannot thus be certain whether absolute levels of summer mortality fell, or those in winter rose. Absolute mortality levels are not our principal concern in this chapter, but we must form some estimate of the trends in winter and summer levels between the seventeenth and eighteenth centuries before turning from seasonality change to variation in causes of death.

We saw in the preceding chapters that London's mortality may have been at a similar level in the second quarter of the eighteenth century to that prevailing in the last quarter of the seventeenth, although it seems more probable that some deterioration had occurred. Nonetheless, for purposes of demonstration we shall adopt the conservative hypothesis of a static crude death rate. Under these circumstances, the amount of change in monthly cause-specific death rates is indicated by the ratio of the increase in the corresponding absolute burial total to that in the annual total for burials from all causes.[8]

The resulting ratios, for non-infant causes of death, are given in the upper panel of table 6.4.

(i)   The consumption series stands out from the others with no appreciable increase in the totals for any month, whilst the July and August rates fall by 22 and 14 per cent respectively.

(ii) The 'other causes' series falls substantially in August, and rather less so in July, reflecting the proportion of seventeenth-century griping in the guts burials allocated to this category. There is a corresponding rise, of between 10 and 20 per cent, in each month from October to May, the figures for the first quarter each rising by at least 15 per cent.

(iii) The fever burials show a small proportionate decline in July and August with increases in each of the other months. These are concentrated between December and April – when each figure rises from 10 to 20 per cent – although there is also a 13 per cent increase in October.

(iv) In the case of smallpox the shift in seasonality apparently reflects a differential rise in mortality, since there is no evidence of an

---

[8] This is because, if the hypothesis is correct, the inflation in the annual totals for the two periods will indicate the amount by which the burials must increase to take account of population growth in the presence of a constant death rate.

Table 6.4. *Relative inflation of monthly burial totals: 1670–99 to 1725–49*

Month	Consumption	Fevers	Smallpox	Other causes
		Burial Series		
Jan	1.03	1.18	1.16	1.15
Feb	1.02	1.10	1.25	1.18
Mar	0.91	1.10	1.21	1.19
Apr	1.04	1.15	1.21	1.13
May	0.97	1.09	1.30	1.12
Jun	0.97	1.01	1.19	0.97
Jul	0.78	0.93	1.04	0.90
Aug	0.86	0.92	1.06	0.83
Sep	0.96	1.08	1.22	1.02
Oct	1.05	1.13	1.19	1.14
Nov	1.03	1.07	1.18	1.10
Dec	1.02	1.16	1.22	1.12

Month	Estimated inflation of infant mortality
Jan	1.14
Feb	1.15
Mar	1.12
Apr	1.18
May	1.14
Jun	1.00
Jul	0.77
Aug	0.78
Sep	1.08
Oct	1.24
Nov	1.22
Dec	1.17

Infant mortality estimates:	1670–99	353
	1725–49	374

absolute decline in any month. The figures for July and August rise only slightly, but elsewhere the increase is spread fairly evenly across the year with the majority of months displaying a relative increase of between 20 and 30 per cent in recorded burials.

In the case of the infant burial series we can be more explicit about absolute mortality levels since we were able to construct a series of estimated infant mortality rates. In the lower panel of table 6.3 we have calculated ratios for the values of each MBI in the two periods, weighted by the change in the global estimate of infant mortality. Once more, it seems likely that the calculations tend to underestimate the rise in the overall level of infant mortality, but even so the scale of the deterioration in the months between October and April is remarkable. This time the focus is on October and November, when mortality rises by nearly a quarter of its initial level, but there is an increase of at least 10 per cent throughout.

Seasonality and cause of death

The changing seasonal incidence of mortality in London over the 'long eighteenth century' provides strong, albeit indirect, evidence of changing patterns of disease. Our results suggest that absolute summer mortality – other than that due to smallpox and fever – actually declined over the first half of the period, whilst autumn and winter mortality increased. This increase was particularly steep in the case of fever and convulsions. We shall now try to identify the diseases – or groups of diseases – that were responsible for these changes by means of statistical comparisons between the Bills' MBIs and similar indices based on the seasonality of deaths from known diseases.

The choice of an appropriate set of cause-specific mortality data is evidently critical to the success of this enterprise and a matter of some difficulty. In order to allow sensible comparisons data must be drawn from the temperate latitudes of the northern hemisphere, but the main diseases with which we are concerned are now rare in such environments, being found predominantly in tropical climates. Furthermore the seasonal incidence of a disease may possibly vary over time in a single environment, reflecting changes in the pathogen concerned, or in the seasonality or prevalence of other diseases with which it is associated.

We should thus take our data from a population as close as possible, in both space and time, to that of the study, and with this in mind we have used figures from London published by the Registrar-General for 1845–74,[9] suitably converted into monthly indices (see

[9] The data were taken from the tabulations in Buchan and Mitchell 1875. They cover the major causes of death in mid-Victorian London, with the exception of measles which appeared as a cause of death in its own right in the Bills, and was evidently of minor importance throughout most of our period. In the case of typhus and typhoid, which do not appear as such in the Registrar-General's figures until 1869, the data cover the years 1868–84 and are taken from Longstaff 1884–5. Diphtheria and scarlet fever have been taken together, since the former was not treated as a separate category until 1861. In analyses carried out using the MBIs for the two diseases

Table 6.5. *Cause-specific seasonality of mortality in London 1845–74: monthly burial indices*

Cause of death	Month											
	Jan	Feb	Mar	Apr	May	Jun	Jul	Aug	Sep	Oct	Nov	Dec
Bronchitis, pneumonia and influenza	150	137	135	99	72	56	45	42	57	94	154	161
Diarrhoea	29	29	25	26	31	104	350	318	152	62	36	28
Diphtheria and scarlet fever	88	78	69	70	73	82	87	105	138	152	143	112
Dysentery	69	73	67	64	72	90	148	199	166	101	77	73
Non-respiratory tuberculosis (Scrofula and *Tabes mesenterica*)	83	89	93	97	93	102	131	131	114	98	86	82
Respiratory tuberculosis	104	105	111	109	102	101	96	91	89	93	102	99
Typhoid	96	92	92	76	71	72	81	99	125	146	138	112
Typhus	114	109	107	115	89	94	90	78	99	97	107	103
Whooping cough	132	135	140	129	111	93	78	62	58	65	88	111

Product Moment Correlations

	(1)	(2)	(3)	(4)	(5)	(6)	(7)	(8)
(2)	-0.74							
(3)	0.04	0.08						
(4)	-0.73	0.89	0.34					
(5)	-0.87	0.96	0.04	0.90				
(6)	0.59	-0.65	-0.67	-0.85	-0.64			
(7)	0.30	-0.11	0.94	0.16	-0.15	-0.45		
(8)	0.78	-0.73	-0.13	-0.74	-0.74	0.69	0.10	
(9)	0.64	-0.65	-0.72	-0.81	-0.67	0.93	-0.48	0.70

Source: see text, p. 215

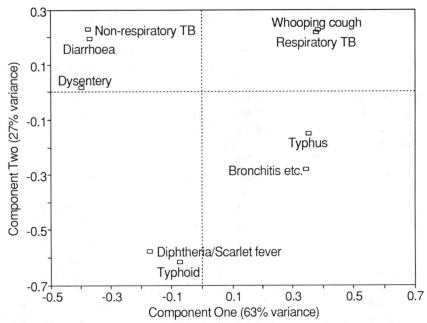

6.2 Mortality seasonality in Victorian London: principal components of correlation matrix

table 6.5). For illustrative purposes these were subjected to a principal components analysis revealing that about 60 per cent of the variance was accounted for by the first component and a little under 30 per cent by the second.

Inspection of the coefficients (see figure 6.2) indicates that the diseases fall into three main clusters, of which the first two are distinguished by their coefficients on component one: diarrhoea, dysentery and non-respiratory tuberculosis have strongly negative values, whilst those for bronchitis, pneumonia and influenza (henceforth for convenience the 'respiratory diseases'), together with typhus and whooping cough are correspondingly positive. The third cluster consists of typhoid and diptheria/scarlet fever, and is distinguished by strongly negative values on component two. Inspection of the seasonality indices suggests that we should label these three groupings as 'summer', 'winter', and 'autumn' respectively.

Principal components analysis

The changing relationships between the seasonality of burials in the Bills, and those given by the Registrar-General, were investigated using a two stage procedure. Firstly, a matrix was calculated for each Bills' series (with the exception of smallpox) giving the Euclidean distance[10] between it and each of the Registrar-General's series in each period. Each matrix was then standardised and subjected to a principal components analysis[11] with the results[12] in figures 6.3 to 6.7. In each case the first component accounted for at least 75 to 80 per cent of the total variance rising to nearly 100 per cent in the case of convulsions. The pattern of coefficients, however, differs between the series:

(i) In the case of the convulsions series these differentiate between the 'summer' group of gastric diseases, and the remainder. The component scores, as we would expect, show a clear move between the two from the late seventeenth century to the second quarter of the eighteenth, most of which is accomplished by 1700.

(ii) Where fever burials are concerned the first component distinguishes the summer and autumn diseases from the winter group. The component scores show an increasingly rapid movement in this direction until the 1775–99 period (the last for which we have data) when there is an abrupt reversal in the trend. The second component, accounting for 14 per cent of the variance, has high positive coefficients for the autumn diseases, and here the score for the quarter of the eighteenth century stands out strongly.

(iii) The coefficients on the first component for the consumption burials are similar to those for 'all other causes', with the respiratory diseases and whooping cough standing out from the remainder. The pattern of scores, however, is rather different in

---

separately, the behaviour of the scarlet fever indices approximated those of the diphtheria/scarlet fever series, whilst those for diphtheria alone were poorly correlated with any of the Bills' burial series.

[10] The Euclidean distance between two sets of seasonality indices is equal to the square root of the sum of squared difference between the indices for corresponding months in the two sets.

[11] If the variables in a principal components analysis have different variances the results will lend greater weight to the behaviour of the variables with the larger variance. Under these circumstances standardisation ensures that each variable assumes equal importance in the analysis, but by employing standardisation we are implicitly assuming that the differences in variances arise from purely random, or 'error', effects and thus contain no useful information about the phenomena in question. It is a matter of judgement whether this is a reasonable assumption in any given case – it does not for instance seem appropriate where differences in the variance of burial indices for given months is concerned – and we have not employed standardisation except where stated.

[12] Since the analysis was carried out on measures of dissimilarity the signs of the coefficients on each component have been reversed so that high positive values indicate a positive association and *vice versa*.

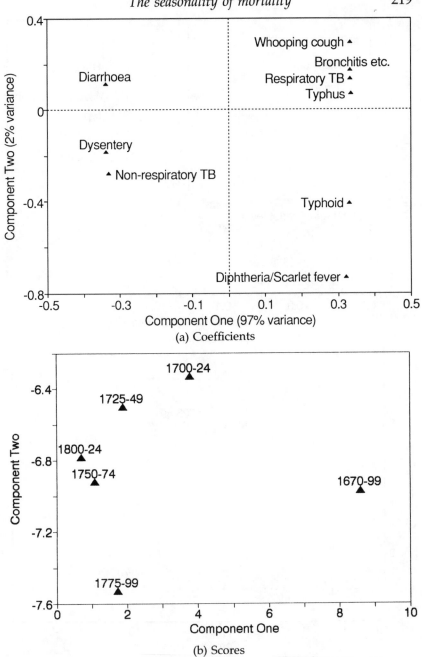

(a) Coefficients

(b) Scores

6.3 Seasonality of convulsions burials in London Bills: principal components analysis

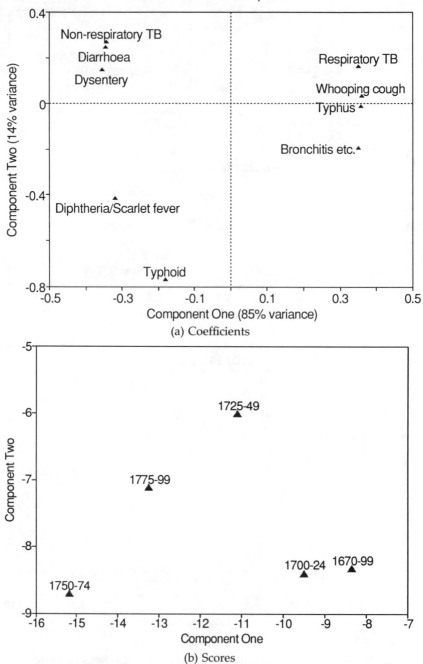

(a) Coefficients

(b) Scores

6.4 Seasonality of fever burials in London Bills: principal components analysis

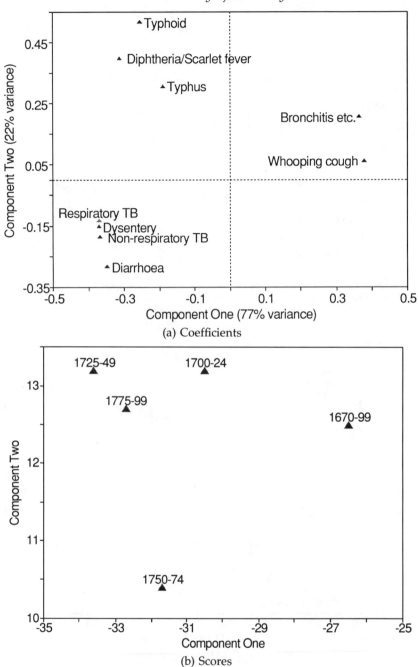

(a) Coefficients

(b) Scores

6.5 Seasonality of consumption burials in London Bills: principal components analysis

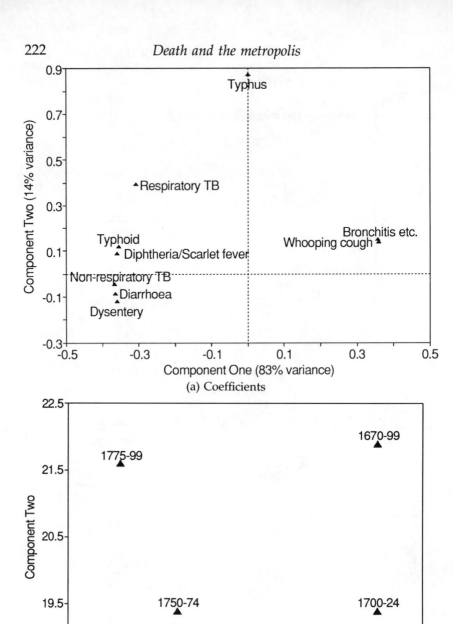

(a) Coefficients

(b) Scores

6.6 Seasonality of 'other causes' burials in London Bills: principal components analysis

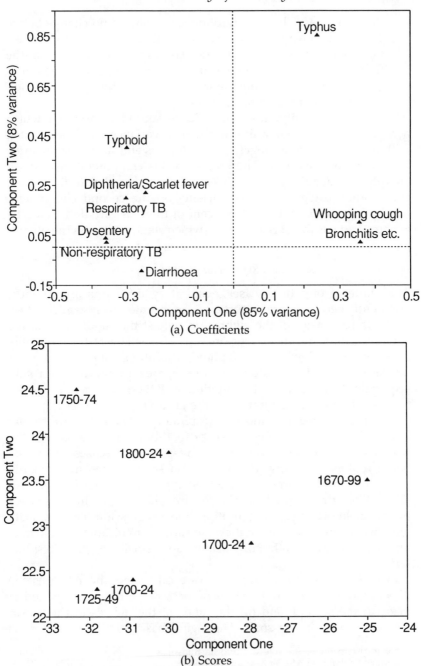

6.7 Seasonality of total burials excluding smallpox and convulsions in London Bills: principal components analysis

the two cases. The consumption series shows no change before 1700, and then a progressive movement in the 'respiratory' direction, whereas the residual series shows a sharp move from the first to the second periods – probably reflecting the fraction of 'griping in the guts' burials included under this heading – followed by an oscillation.

The consumption series also yields a second component which accounts for more than a fifth of the total variance and is associated with the autumn group together with typhus and, to a lesser degree, the respiratory diseases. The scores on this component distinguish sharply between the years 1700–74 and the remainder. In the case of the residual category, the coefficients on the second component, accounting for just under 15 per cent of the total, are dominated by typhus, and it is the period 1750–74 which stands out from the others.

Regression analysis

The winter group of diseases, respiratory infections and typhus, apparently became more important from the late seventeenth century to the third quarter of the eighteenth, whilst the significance of the summer group declined. Our analysis also suggests that mortality from some combination of typhoid, diphtheria and scarlet fever increased around the middle of the eighteenth century and subsequently declined. The interpretation of all these results is, however, hampered by the broad nature of the groupings concerned.

Diarrhoea, dysentery and non-respiratory tuberculosis are similar in that they all result from water- or food-borne pathogens, but the winter group includes both airborne respiratory diseases and louse-borne typhus. Similarly, diphtheria and scarlet fever are primarily airborne, 'droplet', infections, whilst typhoid is water-borne.[13] An attempt was thus made to implicate particular diseases in the process of seasonality change using multiple linear regression. For simplicity only two series were used in the analysis: (i) convulsions; and (ii) total burials excluding both convulsions and smallpox (the 'residual series').

In each case two sets of ratios were calculated and taken as the dependent variables: (i) the ratios of the MBIs in the fourth period to those in the second; and (ii) the ratios of the indices in the fourth period to those in the sixth. The logical basis for this procedure is

[13] For a discussion of the role of airborne transmission of infection in nineteenth-century England see Mercer 1986; on water-borne transmission see Bradley 1974; on the transmission of typhus see Snyder 1965.

that, should mortality from certain diseases have varied disproportionately over either of these intervals, then there should have been a
corresponding variation in the share of annual mortality accounted
for by those months in which such diseases were most prevalent.
Hence there should be some correlation between the MBI ratios and
the seasonalities of the relevant diseases, although it would be
unwise to treat the results as anything more than suggestive.

Apart from the substantive limitations of our material, there are
two technical difficulties in the way of the analysis. Firstly, the
method can only detect relative changes in cause-specific mortality
and so we cannot distinguish the effects of an absolute rise in
mortality from a given condition from those of a moderate decline
coinciding with more substantial reductions elsewhere. Secondly, as
in multiple regression generally, several different combinations of
independent variables may provide a reasonably good fit to the data,
a problem aggravated where, as in the present case, some of the
former are significantly inter-correlated (Everitt and Dunn 1983: 124–
6). Our method is thus a very 'blunt instrument' analytically, but the
coefficients of the best fitting models (see in table 6.6), are interesting
nonetheless.

1750–74 to 1800–19
The ratio of smallpox MBIs was included as a further independent
variable to take account of the possibility that 'survivors' of the infection were predisposed to fatal attacks of diseases such as respiratory
tuberculosis. Changes in smallpox mortality might thus be expected
to have effects on the seasonality of other burial series, and the results
of the regression analysis bear out this expectation for the period of
declining mortality from 1750–74 to 1800–19.

The ratio of smallpox indices features significantly in the models for
both series: at the 0.1 per cent confidence level for convulsions, and
the 1 per cent level for the residual burials. The latter model, explaining over 80 per cent of the variance in the MBI ratios, also includes a
significant positive coefficient for the respiratory group and negative
coefficients for both respiratory tuberculosis and whooping cough,
implying that the latter two underwent a disproportionately small
decline – or perhaps an increase – in their absolute levels.[14]

---

[14] It is interesting to note in this context that Preston, in his analysis of mortality data
from 165 populations, found that 'the cause of death which declines the most when
death rates from all causes decline is "influenza, pneumonia, and bronchitis". About
25 per cent of the change in death rates from all causes can, on average, be ascribed
to changing death rates from this cause' (Preston 1976: 19). The 9 per cent contribu-

Table 6.6. *Monthly burial index ratios: multiple regression models*

Index Ratios 1750–74:1670–99
Y_1 = 0.975 – 0.036 X(2)*** – 0.083 X(4)** + 0.142 X(8)*
R^2 = 0.984
Y_2 = 1.052 – 0.069 X(2)* + 0.224 X(3)** – 0.182 X(4)*
R^2 = 0.962

Index Ratios 1800–19:1750–74
Y_1 = 1.893 + 0.675 X(S)** + 0.385 X(1)* – 1.552 X(6)* + 0.471X(9)*
R^2 = 0.826
Y_2 = 0.502 + 0.405 X(S)*** + 0.235 X(4)** + 0.238 X(3)** – 0.422 X(5)**
R^2 = 0.878

Key to Variables

Dependent
1 Total burials excluding smallpox and convulsions
2 Convulsions

Independent
1 Bronchitis, pneumonia and influenza
2 Diarrhoea
3 Diphtheria and scarlet fever
4 Dysentery
5 Non-respiratory tuberculosis (Scrofula and *Tabes mesenterica*)
6 Respiratory tuberculosis
8 Typhus
9 Whooping cough
S Ratio of monthly burial indices for Bills' smallpox burials

Note: *Significant at 5 per cent confidence level
  **Significant at 1 per cent confidence level
***Significant at 0.1 per cent confidence level

The convulsions model implies that deaths from dysentery and the diphtheria/scarlet fever group underwent a disproportionately large decline, whilst those from non-respiratory tuberculosis increased in relative terms. The amount of variance explained increases to 97 per cent if positive coefficients for diarrhoea and typhus are included. Conversely, the substitution of typhoid for diphtheria/scarlet fever reduces this amount from 88 to 82 per cent. The seasonalities of

tion made by respiratory tuberculosis to English nineteenth-century mortality decline was thus 'quite exceptional', the average contribution of this disease being little more than 10 per cent (p. 20).

typhoid and diphtheria/scarlet fever are so similar that we cannot distinguish adequately between them on this basis alone, but the condition of London's water supply in the early nineteenth century makes a relative decline in typhoid mortality most unlikely at this time.

1670–99 to 1750–74

The ratios of monthly indices over the first of the two intervals – 1750–74 to 1670–99 – are such that positive coefficients imply relative increases in mortality and *vice versa*. On this basis 98 per cent of the change in the indices for the residual series can be explained by a rise in typhus mortality and a decline in that from diarrhoea and dysentery. Similarly, 95 per cent of the change in convulsions seasonality was due to a decline in dysentery and an increase in typhoid, although substitution of diphtheria/scarlet fever for the latter reduces the proportion only slightly to 92 per cent. The difficulty of distinguishing between these two categories on the basis of seasonality alone has already been mentioned. As in the period of mortality decline, however, other evidence suggests that it was scarlet fever, or a related condition, rather than typhoid which was responsible for the trend of mortality from the 'autumn diseases'.

Summary

There are obvious limits to the amount of cause of death information that can be extracted from seasonality data, and the detail of our conclusions must necessarily remain tentative. Nonetheless, many of the major groups of infections have seasonalities which are sufficiently distinct for us to be reasonably confident of the major features of our results. In particular, as the HPM led us to expect, the high levels of mortality prevailing in London do seem to have been due primarily to the same 'winter diseases' that accounted for the bulk of national mortality,[15] rather than to specifically 'urban' conditions relating to the quality of water and food.

A less expected result, however, was the extent of the shift in burial seasonality visible over our period. The cause of death analyses suggested that this arose from a series of underlying movements in disease patterns and, picking our way gingerly through the principal

---

[15] See Wrigley and Schofield (1981: 294, table 8.3) for data on English burial seasonality in this period. A comparison of the monthly burial indicators for the Bills' total burials 1670–99, with those constructed from the Wrigley–Schofield data, suggests that even in these years, when summer mortality in London was relatively high, nearly half of London's excess mortality occurred between October and March.

component and regression coefficients, it is possible to extract what seem to have been four main trends:

(i) The disappearance of the summer burial peak between the late seventeenth and early eighteenth centuries. This apparently reflects an absolute reduction in July and August mortality and corresponds to the virtual disappearance of 'griping in the guts' as a recorded cause of death in the London Bills.

(ii) A secular increase – apparently continuing throughout the eighteenth and early nineteenth centuries – in the importance of the 'winter' group of infections, respiratory tuberculosis and the bronchitis group. In the latter decades of the period this may represent a disproportionately slow decline rather than an absolute increase.

(iii) A substantial rise in the importance of typhus in the first three quarters of the eighteenth century with a subsequent reduction.

(iv) The appearance of an 'autumn disease' in the second quarter of the eighteenth century. This is particularly marked in the fever series and seems to be associated with childhood mortality.

Burial seasonality by age

The structure of causes of death, and so by inference the underlying pattern of infectious disease, thus seems to have varied substantially. According to the predictions of the HPM these changes should have been greatest in the childhood age-groups, since it is for the most part in childhood that infectious agents are first encountered, and thus it is children who bear the heaviest burden of infectious disease. Such effects are not, of course exclusive to childhood. We have already suggested that many adult immigrants might have been 'childlike' immunologically, whilst an entirely new pathogen might find native-born adults as vulnerable as any other section of the population. Nonetheless, if our hypothesis is correct, we should expect to find systematic differences in burial seasonality with respect to age,[16] and that it is in the childhood ages that this seasonality is most variable. We shall thus examine some age-specific burial data in order to test these expectations.

---

[16] The existence of age-specific seasonality differences is, of course, a necessary but not a sufficient condition for the acceptance of the high potential model, as they may arise in any of a number of different ways.

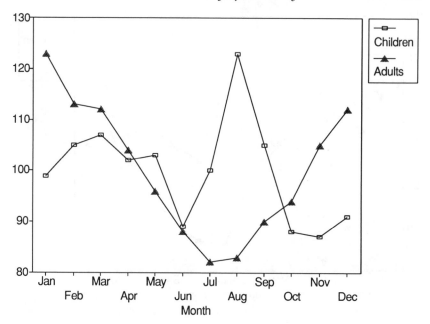

6.8 Burial seasonality, 1695–1704: restricted sample parishes

The parish register series

The Bills of Mortality provide no age-specific data until 1728, but before this we can obtain a restricted amount of age information from parish registers. The method adopted was to search the available registers for two decades, 1695–1704 and 1750–9, including in the 'main sample' all those which distinguished systematically between the burials of children and adults. Those parishes represented in the main sample for both decades were then incorporated into a 'restricted sample', and it is this sample which was used in the present analysis.[17]

The results in figures 6.8 and 6.9 confirm our expectation that child burials should be affected by changing seasonality.[18] In the initial decade there is a substantial difference between the child and adult burial seasonalities. The former display a major peak in August, together with a more restricted surplus between the months of February and May. Adult burials, by contrast show a clear winter peak, centred on January, with a deficit from May to October.

[17] See chapter 8 for further details of the sample and of the selection criteria employed.
[18] Euclidean distances between the indices for the two decades were 37, in the case of the child burials, as against only 18 for the adults.

Death and the metropolis

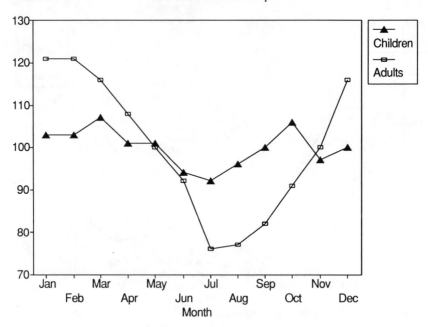

6.9 Burial seasonality, 1750–9: restricted sample parishes

In the second decade child burials show a much flatter pattern, with a modest excess in October and from January to May, and below average numbers in the summer months. The seasonality of adult burials is closer to the pattern of the first decade, although the winter excess is now larger and more broadly based. July to September MBIs decline – both for adults and children – between the two decades, with a much steeper reduction for children, but the pattern of offsetting increases differs considerably. For adults there is a relatively small and even rise spread over the months from February to June, but in the case of children the increase is concentrated in the last three months of the year – particularly October – and is correspondingly steeper.

The Bills of Mortality

A continuous age-specific monthly series was constructed using the monthly Bills' totals published in the Gentleman's Magazine from the 1730s, allowing a more detailed study of age-specific seasonality to be undertaken.[19] The indices for the period as a whole are given in figure

[19] The age-specific burial totals were derived from figures published monthly in the *Gentleman's Magazine*, which themselves were evidently constructed by aggregat-

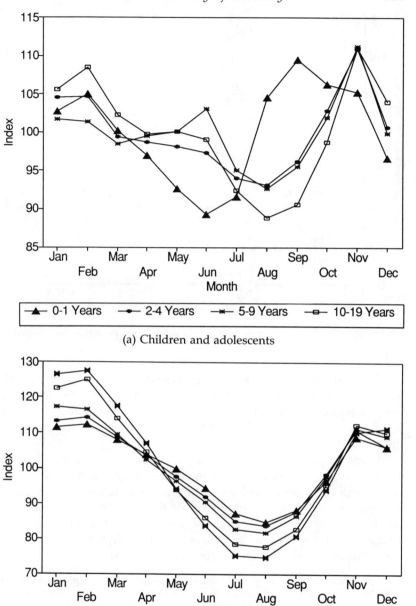

(a) Children and adolescents

(b) Adults

6.10 Age-specific burial seasonalities in London Bills

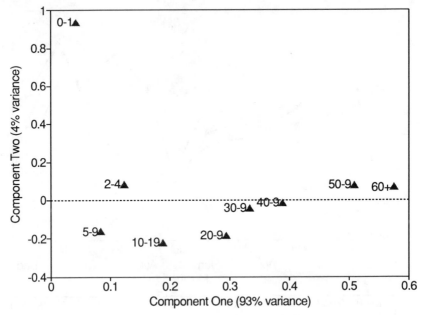

6.11 Age-specific burial seasonality in London Bills: principal component scores

6.10, for individual published age-groups up to sixty years and for all ages above this. The ratio of winter to summer indices rises in a remarkably regular manner with increasing age. This impression of regularity was confirmed by a principal components analysis (see figure 6.11).

Almost 90 per cent of the variance is accounted for by the first component, which contrasts the months of winter and early spring with those of summer and early autumn. The scores on this component – with the minor exception of the 5–9 year olds – show a regular progression with age. The second component, accounting for a little over 10 per cent of the variance, is evidently a reflection of the late summer burial peak in the youngest age-group.

ing the figures from the weekly Bills which had appeared since the previous issue of the Magazine. It was thus necessary to convert them into calendar monthly totals by determining the dates of the weekly Bills in question and assuming a linear distribution of deaths across the week. Missing values – and the 'heaping' of burials in the last week of the year – were dealt with on an analogous basis to that employed with the cause of death series (see Landers and Mouzas 1988: appendix). The methods used to construct the monthly age-specific series inevitably mean that the results are more approximate than are those obtained directly from the weekly Bills, and we have thus preferred to aggregate them into quarterly totals wherever possible.

The extent of temporal changes in the age-specific seasonalities were analysed by pooling the original data into five major age- groups and splitting the resulting series into two overlapping fifty year periods. All age-groups show a rise in the November index, although this is most marked below age twenty. There is also an increase in the February index in each age-group and a small rise in the summer indices for older age-groups. Again it is the child burial series, above two years of age, which shows the most change, although in this instance the calculated distance for the oldest age-groups is nearly as large.

Age and cause of death

The predictions of the HPM concerning the relative volatility of child burial seasonality are thus substantially borne out. Such predictions arise, however, from a broader set of assumptions concerning relationships between age-specific mortality and causes of death in metropolitan populations. We saw in chapter 3 that annual movements in the Bills age- and cause-specific burial totals suggest that these assumptions are broadly correct in the case of eighteenth-century London, but we must now determine whether they can also be sustained at the level of seasonality. The value of all such analyses is, of course, limited by the problematic nature of the Bills' cause of death categories themselves. We shall thus try to take our investigation one step further by looking at the relationship between the Bills' age-specific burial seasonalities and the Registrar-General's seasonality data employed earlier.

The Bills' causes of death

The relationship between age- and cause-specific burial seasonality in the Bills was investigated for the period 1734–83, prior to the secular decline in smallpox and fever burials. A principal components analysis was carried out on the matrix of MBIs for the five main cause of death series, and five age-categories (see figure 6.12). Some 80 per cent of the variance was explained by the first component, contrasting the months December to April with those from June to October. The scores for consumption and 'all other causes', on this component, are very similar to each other, and to the 40–59 year series, whilst the fever burials are very close to the burials below age 20. The 20–39 year olds fall midway between the two, whilst the smallpox burials and those above age 60 lie at the two extremes.

Death and the metropolis

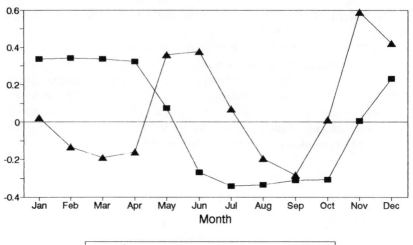

(a) Coefficients

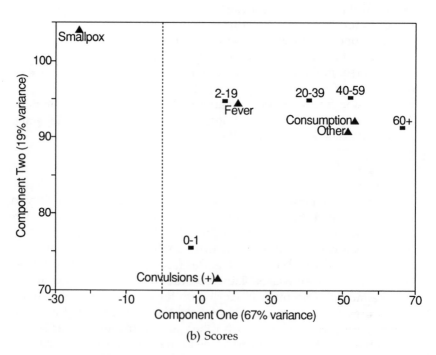

(b) Scores

6.12 Age- and cause-specific burial seasonality in London Bills: principal components analysis

The second component has strong negative coefficients for both August to September, and for the late winter/early spring months. It evidently reflects the distinctive seasonality of the convulsions and 0–1 year burials whose scores lie very close to each other.

The Registrar-General's series

Two analyses of this kind were carried out using the Registrar-General's data. The first examined the change in parish register burial seasonality between the two sample decades, whilst the second was based on the age-specific burial totals from the Bills of Mortality.

The parish register seasonalities
The logic employed in this analysis was similar to that applied to the problem of changing seasonality in the Bills' cause of death series, but in this instance principal components analysis was preferred to multiple regression as we wished to explore an entire configuration of seasonalities rather than isolate a restricted sub-set. The ratio between the parish register MBIs in each decade was thus calculated for both child and adult burials, and for the Bills' smallpox burials, and these were then correlated with the Registrar-General's cause of death seasonalities.

A principal components analysis of the resulting matrix yielded the results in figure 6.13. The first component accounted for 57 per cent of the total variance and distinguished winter from summer diseases, the autumn group falling roughly between the two. The scores for both of the parish register series fall clearly at the winter end of the spectrum on this component.

The second component splits the autumn diseases from the summer – and most of the winter – group with typhus and the respiratory conditions falling about half-way between. The child burial score is close to that of the autumn group, whereas the adult score falls at the other extreme. We should note that the smallpox score on the first component is practically identical to that for child burials, whereas on the second it is much closer to the adult score.

The Bills' seasonalities
In this case Euclidean distances were calculated between the age-specific series and each of the Registrar-General's series (together with the Bills' smallpox seasonality), and the resulting matrices subjected to a principal components analysis (see figure 6.14). The first component accounts for 82 per cent of the variance, and its

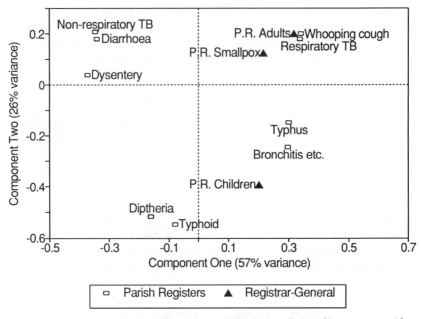

6.13 London Parish Register burials, and Registrar-General's cause-specific, mortality seasonalities: principal component coefficients

coefficients contrast the respiratory diseases, typhus and whooping cough with the remainder. The second component, accounting for 17 per cent of the variance has strongly positive coefficients for typhus and respiratory tuberculosis, together with weaker ones for smallpox and whooping cough.

The component scores show a striking pattern of age-associations. On the first of these there is a regular progression by age towards the respiratory diseases,[20] whilst the second shows a strong association between the seasonality of young adult and adolescent burials and the respiratory tuberculosis – typhus component.

Summary

The analysis of age- and cause-specific burials seasonalities in the Bills generally bears out the pattern which emerged from movements in the annual totals. Strong associations exist between the 'febrile'

---

[20] This is of course in keeping with expectations, except for the association of whooping cough with advanced age. This presumably reflects the similar seasonal pattern of the two diseases, an unavoidable shortcoming of our method which we have already encountered in the case of typhoid and diphtheria/scarlet fever.

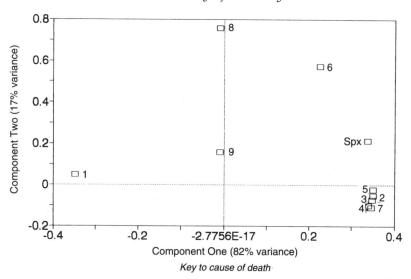

Key to cause of death

1	Bronchitis, pneumonia and influenza	6	Respiratory tuberculosis
2	Diarrhoea	7	Typhoid
3	Diphtheria and scarlet fever	8	Typhus
4	Dysentery	9	Whooping cough
5	Non-respiratory tuberculosis (scrofula and tabes mesenterica)	S	Smallpox burials in Bills of Mortality

(a) Coefficients

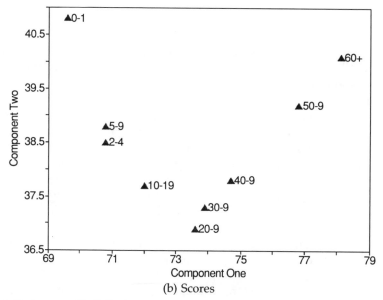

(b) Scores

6.14 Age-specific Bills' burials, and Registrar-General's cause-specific, mortality seasonalities: principal components analysis

categories (smallpox and fevers) and the younger ages, whilst consumption and the residual category are more closely linked with the older burials.

The parish register data suggest that seasonality change in the first half of the eighteenth century had at least two underlying components. The first involved a shift from the 'summer' group of water- and food-borne diseases, to the 'winter' group of airborne infections. This appears to have affected all age-groups though the effect is stronger in the adult series. Alongside this is a second movement, towards the seasonality of the 'autumn' conditions, which is apparently restricted to the child burials.

A comparison of the Bills' age-specific seasonalities with the Registrar-General's cause of death data suggests that most of the variance in the former is accounted for by a component which distinguishes the respiratory diseases – and whooping cough – from the remainder and yields scores which vary monotonically with age. This finding suggests that the secular increase in the importance of the two former conditions – implied by our analysis of the Bills' cause of death data – may reflect a change in the age composition of total burial. The second component, by contrast, clearly picks out the adolescent/ young adult age-groups, and these are strongly associated with deaths from typhus and respiratory tuberculosis.

Conclusion

The analysis of burial seasonality is relatively straightforward given the material at our disposal, since it is free of the problems of under-registration which beset the measurement of absolute mortality levels. The move from burial seasonality to the seasonality of mortality presents more difficulties, but it seems reasonable to believe that, beyond infancy at least, the former was substantially determined by the latter, with changes in the population at risk playing at most a secondary role. In principal, we cannot make this assumption where infant mortality is concerned, but the evidence suggests that any changes in birth seasonality occurring over our period were small to produce the variations we have observed at the level of burials.

Inferences concerning causes of death are more difficult to make, but the changes over our period were on a sufficiently large scale for us to be reasonably confident on a number of points. The most immediate of these was the dramatic disappearance of the excess summer mortality which had been such a feature of the seventeenth-century data. Finlay's analysis of six London parish burial registers suggests that this excess was established as early as the sixteenth century (Finlay 1976: 138), and Greatorex has found a similar pattern in a number of rural burial registers from Middlesex and Surrey (Greatorex n. d.). The elimination of the summer burial peak in the years after 1700 thus suggests the amelioration of some old-established form of gastric disease, perhaps the *cholera morbus* or the 'dry gripes' described by Sydenham,[21] as the seventeenth century gave way to the eighteenth. No evidence of significant improvement in the capital's physical environment has been put forward for this period, and Greatorex's finding of a contemporary decline in summer burials in some rural parishes around London makes such an explanation intrinsically unlikely.

The causes of the phenomenon are thus likely to have been 'exogenous' to economy and society, and two possibilities suggest themselves. The first of these is climatic. The most plausible candidate for griping in the guts seems, at this stage, to be bacillary dysentery, a condition normally associated with late summer or early autumn in temperate latitudes, since its spread is apparently impeded by the higher temperatures of mid-summer (Rowland and Barrell 1980: 23). The early part of our period, however, represents the closing decades of the 'little ice age', and August temperatures were a full centigrade degree lower in the last quarter of the seventeenth century than in the first quarter of the eighteenth.[22] It is thus possible that the unusually cool summers of this period allowed the dysentery to become established much earlier in the season than was to be the case as temperatures rose again after 1700.

The second possibility, which does not exclude the first, is that the nature of the pathogen changed, leading to the emergence of a more infective but less severe form of the disease, just as in the present century the *S. sonnei* strain has supplanted more virulent forms of dysentery in the countries of the developed world (Rowland and Barrell 1980: 22; Hornick 1983: 649). Changes of this latter kind,

---

[21] Writing of the 1660s, Sydenham said of this condition – which he distinguished from dysentery – that it 'comes almost as constantly at the close of Summer and toward the beginning of Autumn as swallows in the beginning of Spring and cuckoos towards midsummer' (Sydenham 1769: 146), but that 'it very rarely lasts longer than the month of August wherein it began' (p. 150).

[22] See Appleby 1980. Monthly temperature data for 'central England' can be found in Manley 1974. The continuing decline of the summer burial indices into the second quarter of the eighteenth century, when the rise in temperature slowed considerably, suggests that this factor is unlikely to be wholly responsible for the change in disease patterns.

whether due to mutation or to the introduction of new strains from abroad, were probably also responsible for much of the fluctuation in smallpox mortality before the 1780s, and this is almost certain to have been the case with the 'putrid sore throats' of the eighteenth century.[23]

The mysterious 'autumn disease' of the second quarter of the eighteenth century seems to have been associated with a pandemic of 'putrid sore throat' – almost certainly a form of streptococcal infection.[24] Creighton, surveying the long term development of diphtheria and scarlet fever mortality, concluded that neither disease had been a significant cause of death in seventeenth-century London. But a very serious outbreak of 'putrid sore throat' occurred in the 1730s on both sides of the Atlantic, spreading to London late in 1739, and thereafter epidemics of what may have been either scarlet fever or diphtheria occurred at intervals for the remainder of the century (Creighton 1894: 678–720). There followed, after 1800, a 'whole generation with moderate or small mortality' from scarlet fever (p. 762). Diphtheria remained unknown as a major killing disease until the pandemic of the late 1850s, but the age distribution of mortality at that time suggests near universal immunity above the childhood ages, and the history of the condition remains mysterious (Burnett and White 1972: 193–201).

The substantial rise in winter mortality over the first half of our period presents a more complex problem. Our results suggest that typhus fever increased, along with a number of respiratory conditions, after 1700, but that it declined more rapidly than the others in the last quarter of the century. Zinsser believed that louse-born typhus, as opposed to the older murine form, was a relatively new disease in the early eighteenth century, having emerged in central Europe during the wars of the sixteenth century and subsequently been disseminated by military activity.[25]

It is thus possible that the rise in typhus mortality too was associated with the introduction of a new strain of micro-organism, but we cannot afford to neglect the question of social and economic conditions when dealing with a disease so notoriously associated with poverty and overcrowding. The latter is true *a fortiori* of the other

---

[23] Mortality from scarlet fever in nineteenth-century England fluctuated markedly, in a way which does not seem to reflect changes in living conditions or medical practice. See Mercer 1986; also McKeown 1976: 82–6.

[24] See appendix 2 for some evidence on this point.

[25] See Zinsser 1935: 238, 270–9. Zinsser regarded the eighteenth century as 'par excellence the Century of Typhus' (p. 238).

members of the 'winter group',[26] but in raising such a question we are at once confronted with a paradox. As we saw in chapter 2, the evidence suggests that real wages were high in the first half of the eighteenth century – especially in the second quarter – as food prices declined, but that they fell substantially after 1760. The question of living standards, however, embraces a broader range of issues than real wages alone, and to pursue this further we must examine the extent of economic and demographic instability in eighteenth-century London.

[26] 'Typhus thrives under conditions of human misery which predispose to an increase in louse infestation, such as crowding of people, lack of fuel, lack of adequate facilities for bathing and weather so cold that the same garments are worn continuously day and night'. Snyder 1965: 105. Within the period of civil registration the incidence of the major respiratory diseases has also been associated with low socio-economic status and poor living conditions (Cronje 1984 and Goodman 1953).

7

The instability of mortality

Mortality levels in London were not only much higher than in England at large, they also varied much less from year to year. In both these respects, the capital's demography reflected the underlying characteristics of a high potential mortality regime, and, given this, it may seem odd to devote an entire chapter to the 'instability of mortality'. The importance of such instability lies not, however, simply in its absolute magnitude, or quantitative contribution to the secular level of mortality, for – as we saw in chapter 1 – historical demographers have often looked to this variable as an interpretative key to the mechanisms of secular demographic change.

The original expectations of crisis theory concerning mortality decline and 'stabilisation' may not have been borne out, but we can still hope – as Post's work (1984; 1985; 1990) implies – to gain particular insights into the internal structure of a demographic regime by studying its reaction to exceptional stress. In this context we are especially interested in the relative importance of changes in resistance and exposure to infection – and in the determinants of the latter – in generating excess mortality.

At the same time, the analysis of statistical relationships between vital series, and a variety of economic and climatic data, underlies the econometric approach to historical demography which has contributed powerfully to the establishment of neoclassical theory. Of central importance here is the conceptual distinction between high- and low-pressure demographic regimes and the attempt to identify such regimes in practice. In this chapter we shall pursue both lines of approach, beginning with some statistical time series analyses and then proceeding to the investigation of distinct 'mortality peaks'.

242

Some statistical associations

The distinction between high- and low-pressure vital regimes is central to neoclassical theory and corresponds roughly to Malthus' positive and preventive check dominated systems. It also has important implications for patterns of short-run movement in vital series. In a high-pressure regime, it is argued, mortality is high because of living standards which are so low that any further reduction will immediately push death rates still higher, resulting in significantly positive correlations between short-run movements in prices and burials.

Conversely, in a low-pressure regime, relatively high living standards permit moderate levels of secular mortality, and 'buffer' the population against all but the worst swings in prices, leading to a much weaker short-run association between the two series. By similar reasoning, low-pressure regimes should also display a weaker negative relationship between mortality and winter temperatures, since better diet, clothing and shelter would confer greater resistance to cold stress, and the population would not have to choose between purchasing food or fuel.

The distinction between the two regimes is based on the practice of 'prudential marriage'. In the case of nuptiality we should thus expect the pattern of correlations to be reversed, and a strongly negative relationship between prices and recorded marriages should emerge as the positive correlation with mortality falls away. Significant negative correlations have also been reported between food prices and conceptions (net of nuptiality effects), but their theoretical significance is less clear since they can arise, for different reasons, in either regime. In the 'high-pressure' case, the effects of famine – whether physiological, psychological or mediated by migration – might reduce marital fertility involuntarily, but the deliberate avoidance of conception in the face of dearth might also be predicted as an extension of the 'prudential' behaviour underpinning a low-pressure regime.

We shall now try to determine whether either of these two sets of associations is visible in our data, which consist of vital totals from the Bills, together with data on food prices, a series of temperature estimates for 'central England', and rainfall figures from Kew.[1] The baptism totals and the non-demographic series (collectively, the

[1] Temperature data are taken from Manley 1974 and rainfall from Wales-Smith 1971. The bread price series is based on the annual averages for the quartern loaf published by Mitchell and Deane 1962: 497–8. Calendar year prices were obtained as weighted averages of the original figures for harvest years.

'environmental' variables) were de-trended on the same basis as the burial totals. Our data allow us to work on both annual and quarterly levels, and we shall do both beginning with the former.

The annual series

The annual series were analysed using two different approaches. The first – the 'extreme value analysis' – confined attention to a restricted number of years in which extremely high, or low, values are recorded in one of the relevant series, whilst the second involved the analysis of 'co-movements' in the series as a whole.

Extreme values

The extreme value analysis was undertaken using a simple graphical technique. The annual values for each of the environmental series in turn were ranked in order of magnitude (in the case of winter temperatures and annual rainfall this was done in ascending order), and the average CMRs for each burial series were then calculated for the years ranked 1–5, 1–10, and so on through to 1–25 with the results in figures 7.1 to 7.7. These suggest that mortality in general was little affected by extreme temperatures, but that high bread prices had a major impact on mortality from smallpox and, to a lesser extent, from fever. The inclusion of CMRs for the year following the price rise – where these exceed the value for the current year – strengthens the relationship substantially in the case of the latter two burial series, but it has little effect on the others. Smallpox also stands out in its relationship to rainfall, and in this case the relationship appears to be symmetrical, since high rainfall is associated with below average smallpox mortality.

Co-movements

Many techniques are available to detect statistical relationships between time series. These include highly sophisticated econometric procedures – such as the polynomial distributed lag analysis adopted by Lee and others[2] – but we have restricted ourselves to the simpler, but more robust, Z coefficient developed by Goodman (1963) for the analysis of co-movements and already employed in chapter 3. The analyses were carried out on data for the period as a whole, and for

---

[2] For an outline of the rationale of this procedure, and its application to English data see Lee's contributions to Wrigley and Schofield (1981: 356–401, 739–40). The method has also been applied to data from the London Bills of Mortality by Galloway (1985). For alternative approaches see, for instance, Weir 1984 and Schofield 1985a.

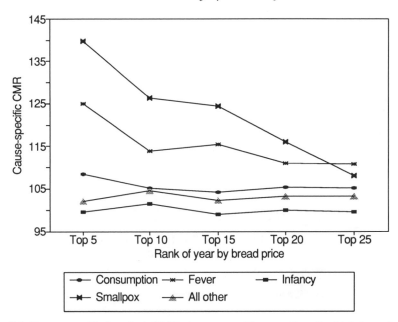

7.1 Cause-specific London CMRs in years with exceptionally high bread prices

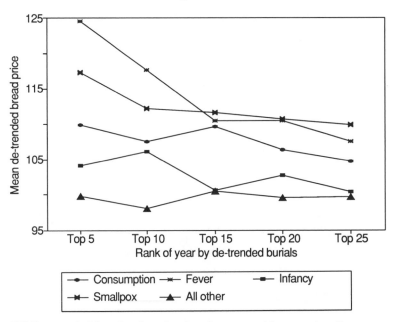

7.2 De-trended London bread prices in years with exceptionally severe mortality

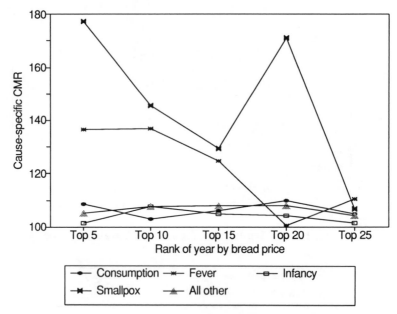

7.3 Cause-specific London CMRs in years with high bread prices (including effects lagged 1 year)

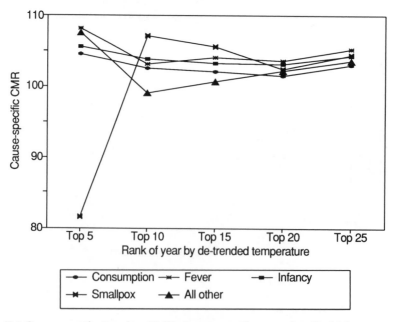

7.4 Cause-specific London CMRs in years with exceptionally high summer temperatures

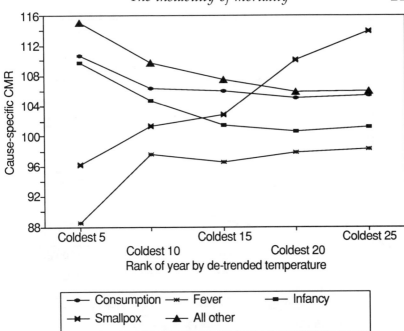

7.5 Cause-specific London CMRs in years with exceptionally low winter temperatures

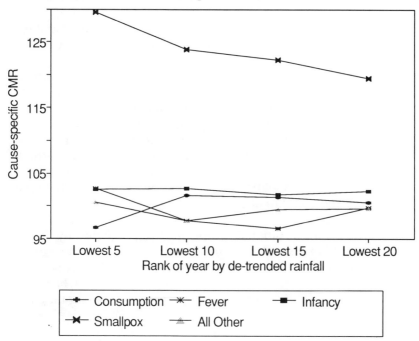

7.6 Cause-specific London CMRs in years with exceptionally low rainfall

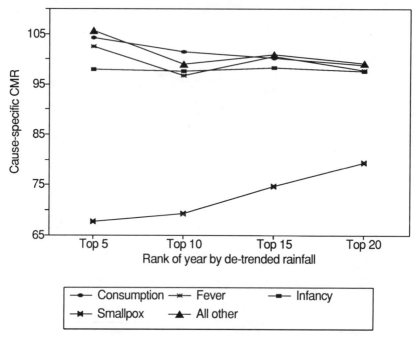

7.7 Cause-specific London CMRs in years with exceptionally high rainfall

three sub-periods of fifty years. We shall now briefly review these taking each of the environmental series in turn (see table 7.1).

Bread prices　　Taking the period as a whole, significant associations between prices and burials are restricted to the series for smallpox and the residual category, but the relationship with the first of these is very strong. Both associations are present in the first sub-period, as is one with consumption burials, but all three disappear after 1725. The link with smallpox burials reappears in the third sub-period, when a rather stronger association with infancy burials is also evident. There are no statistically significant associations between bread prices and total burials.

Summer temperatures　　Summer temperatures are significantly associated with total burials and those in the fever and infancy categories, taking the period as a whole. Where the sub-periods are concerned the only significant scores are those for the years 1725–74 when each of them – except consumption and 'all other causes' – passes the 5 per cent threshold.

Table 7.1. *Annual Z scores: burials, prices and weather*

	1675–1824	1675–1724	1725–74	1775–1824
Bread prices				
Consumption	1.62	2.09*	0.35	1.04
Fevers	0.68	0.35	0.34	0.35
Infancy	0.62	–0.95	–0.14	2.30*
Smallpox	3.11***	2.04*	1.26	1.77†
All other	1.88†	2.35*	–0.18	1.30
All burials	1.54	0.48	0.41	1.63
Summer temperatures				
Consumption	0.71	0.72	1.31	–0.64
Fevers	2.17*	0.33	2.11*	1.05
Infancy	1.76*	1.15	1.74†	0.13
Smallpox	0.72	–0.77	2.19*	–0.14
All other	0.30	1.08	0.36	–0.92
All burials	2.26*	1.35	2.14*	–0.15
Winter temperatures				
Consumption	–1.64	–1.03	–0.14	–2.24*
Fevers	0.26	–1.25	1.13	0.98
Infancy	–1.01	–0.33	0.43	–1.91†
Smallpox	–1.60	–2.27*	–1.26	0.83
All other	–3.51***	–1.71†	–1.78†	–2.99**
All burials	–0.71	–1.11	–0.16	–1.74†
	1702–1824		1725–74	1775–1824
Annual rainfall				
Consumption	0.67		1.17	1.03
Fevers	–0.19		–0.28	0.90
Infancy	–1.18		–0.40	–0.39
Smallpox	–2.82**		–2.15*	–1.00
All other	0.82		1.22	0.67
All burials	–0.98		0.23	0.0

Note: †Significant at 10 per cent confidence level
  *Significant at 5 per cent confidence level
 **Significant at 1 per cent confidence level
***Significant at 0.1 per cent confidence level

Winter temperatures   Winter temperatures show a highly significant negative association with burials in the residual category over the period as a whole, and this is also manifested at the 5 per cent level in each of the three sub-periods. There is also a statistically significant association with smallpox burials over the years 1675–1824. The remaining significant values are all found in the third sub-period when each of them – except smallpox and fevers – passes the 5 per cent threshold.

Rainfall   Movements in annual rainfall are significantly associated with only one of the burial series, smallpox, but this association is significant at the 1 per cent confidence level for the period 1702–1824, as well as at the five per cent level for the sub-period 1725–74.

Discussion

The strongest effect of bread prices on mortality is seen in the case of smallpox, and this series also stands out in its sensitivity to variations in rainfall. Exceptional prices have a large effect on fever mortality, but this does not apparently extend to the 'run of the mill' movements which dominate the calculation of the Z scores. Here it is summer temperatures which yield the only statistically significant result. The position is reversed where the residual series is concerned, since price extremes do not result in exceptional mortality, but there is a statistically significant association with price movements for the period as a whole. In this instance, however, the main influence appears to be winter temperatures, which are negatively associated with mortality in each of the three sub-periods and – at the 0.1 per cent confidence level – over the period as a whole. The total burials series shows generally very weak associations with the environmental variables. Only in the case of summer temperatures is there a statistically significant relationship over the period as a whole.

The results for the fifty year sub-periods suggest a secular shift in the pattern of dominant short-run influences. Broadly speaking, a different environmental variable stands out in each period. To begin with, bread prices dominate the picture with three significant scores, but in the second period these disappear and give way to four between burials and summer temperatures. After 1775 bread prices increase in importance, but it is winter temperatures which show the strongest associations, although these are significantly associated with at least one of the burial series in the two previous periods. We can explore these relationships further by examining the pattern visible at the quarterly level.

Quarterly data

Quarterly data permit a finer level of analysis and the detection of more immediate mortality responses, but the relationships observed at annual and quarterly levels need not be simple reflections of each other. This is so for two reasons. Firstly, the former might reflect mechanisms whose effects are 'lagged' by several months, if, for instance, much of the mortality response arose from relatively protracted causes of death, or was mediated by compositional changes in the population. In addition, it should be recalled that the Z coefficient measures the consistency of 'co-movements' between the two series rather than their absolute magnitude. Hence quarterly movements which are highly consistent, but of small magnitude, may be swamped in the annual aggregate by random factors, or by bigger responses which occur with less consistency.

The use of quarterly data requires a slightly different set of variables from that employed in the preceding section. Thus the totals for 'diseases incidental to infancy' are replaced by the modified convulsions series constructed in chapter 6, whilst the consumption and fevers totals are pooled with 'other causes' after 1775 leaving only three cause-specific series. The burial data for some age-groups were pooled, as in the last chapter, and will be considered over a single undivided period.

The London bread price series was published on an annual basis, and so we have replaced these with the monthly wheat prices assembled by Beveridge (Beveridge et al. 1939). Fortunately, our temperature and rainfall data are based on monthly figures. We shall now examine the results for each of the ecological series in turn.

Temperature
The relationship between total burials and temperature conforms to the 'expected' pattern over the period as a whole (see table 7.2). Low first quarter, and high third quarter, temperatures are associated with increased mortality, the effect of the former persisting into the following quarter. The pattern is generally reproduced in each of the subperiods, although in the last of these the negative association, at lag zero, moves from the first to the second quarter. In most cases the cause-specific burial series display significant associations with either first or third quarter temperatures, but not both.

Consumption   Consumption is the major exception to the foregoing generalisation. If we take the period 1675–1794 as a whole, there is a strong relationship between increased mortality and both low first quarter, and high third quarter, temperatures at lags zero and one. There is also a significant lagged relationship between high second quarter temperatures and increased mortality. A similar pattern of

Table 7.2. *Quarterly Z scores: burials and temperatures*

	1st quarter	2nd quarter	3rd quarter	4th quarter
1675–1813				
lag 0				
Convulsions	−1.88†	−1.40	4.79***	1.07
Smallpox	−1.54	−0.32	1.35	0.88
All burials	−3.28***	−1.25	3.52***	0.90
1675–1813				
Consumption	−2.80**	−1.22	3.55**	−0.83
Fevers	−0.71	0.18	2.90**	0.0
All other	−2.95**	0.15	0.70	−0.50
lag 1				
Convulsions	−1.47	1.73†	0.26	−0.15
Smallpox	−1.50	0.46	−0.42	−0.30
All burials	−2.83**	0.15	0.73	−1.33
1675–1793				
Consumption	−2.95**	2.49*	2.83**	1.30
Fevers	−0.86	1.78	1.76†	1.53
All other	−2.41*	0.18	2.57**	−0.33
1675–1724				
lag 0				
Consumption	−0.96	0.43	1.40	−0.19
Convulsions	−0.62	0.37	3.41***	1.81†
Fevers	1.44	−0.71	2.16*	1.30
Smallpox	−1.72†	−0.14	0.15	−0.10
All other	−2.39*	1.64	1.87†	−1.40
All burials	−2.23*	0.95	2.85**	0.93
lag 1				
Consumption	−2.56*	0.97	1.43	1.59
Convulsions	−0.73	−0.66	−0.97	−0.94
Fevers	−1.24	1.29	0.72	2.07*
Smallpox	−1.69†	0.62	−1.36	0.18
All other	−1.52	0.15	1.88†	0.14
All burials	−1.93†	−1.00	−1.17	−0.09
1725–74				
lag 0				
Consumption	−1.78†	−0.87	2.40*	−0.61
Convulsions	−1.59	−0.37	2.53*	0.21
Fevers	−1.22	0.95	1.58	−0.70
Smallpox	−2.67**	−0.14	1.60	0.60
All other	−1.99*	−0.14	0.11	−0.51
All burials	−2.40*	−0.39	3.88***	0.44

Table 7.2. *(Contd.)*

	1st quarter	2nd quarter	3rd quarter	4th quarter
lag 1				
Consumption	−1.02	1.83†	1.66†	0.14
Convulsions	0.12	0.96	0.84	−0.15
Fevers	−0.18	0.93	1.36	0.30
Smallpox	−2.05*	−0.42	0.36	−0.58
All other	−1.66†	0.65	0.61	−0.50
All burials	−1.54	−0.18	1.19	−0.50
1764–1813				
lag 0				
Convulsions	−1.13	−2.96**	2.06*	−0.12
Smallpox	1.21	0.14	0.20	1.00
All other	−1.98*	−2.76**	−1.43	0.85
All burials	−1.10	−2.81**	0.42	0.34
lag 1				
Convulsions	−2.19*	2.67**	0.94	0.67
Smallpox	0.40	1.25	−0.22	0.13
All other	−2.33*	−1.21	1.54	−2.40*
All burials	−1.96*	1.05	0.89	−1.77†

Note: †10% significance
  *5% significance
  **1% significance
  ***0.1% significance

scores is visible in each sub-period, but they do not generally become significant until the second of these and remain relatively weak.

Convulsions Over the period as a whole convulsions also displays significant temperature associations in both first and third quarters, but only the second of these is significant in either of the first two sub-periods. The results for the years 1764–1818 reveal a more complicated pattern, combining a strong negative association between second quarter temperatures and mortality, an offsetting positive relationship between second quarter temperatures and third quarter mortality, and a negative association between first quarter temperatures and second quarter mortality. The effect of cold weather over the first half of the year is thus to increase mortality in the spring but then to reduce it somewhat in the summer.

Fevers Fever mortality seems to have been chiefly affected by warm

summers over the period as a whole. If, however, we look at the two
sub-periods for which data are available, we find that significant
temperature associations are confined to the first. These include a
positive third quarter association at lag one, suggesting that warm
autumn temperatures were associated with increased mortality the
following winter. The fever series is unusual in displaying a reduced
sensitivity to warm summers between the first and second
sub-period.[3]

Smallpox   In the first two of the sub-periods there are significant
negative associations between first quarter temperatures and both
first and second quarter smallpox mortality. But these disappear in
the third sub-period, and they are not reflected in the results for the
period as a whole. In general smallpox burials seem to be the least
affected by temperatures.

All other causes   Burials in the residual category are negatively associated with first quarter temperatures over the period to 1793, and
there are also lagged associations – in the 'expected' direction – in
both first and third quarters. The first quarter relationship is displayed in both sub-periods, but the third quarter relationship is only
seen in the first of these, as was also the case with fever burials.[4]

These results suggest that the annual burial totals' heightened sensitivity to summer temperatures in the central decades of the
eighteenth century arises partly from changes in the quarterly lag
structure. In the first sub-period low first quarter temperatures are
generally associated with increased mortality throughout the first half
of the year. After 1725 these lagged effects weaken or disappear
entirely – except for smallpox and all other causes – although the

---

[3] The fact that this series becomes less responsive to hot summers at this time tells
against the climatic change explanation for the disappearance of the summer
mortality peak offered above. The reduction in the scores is also apparent at the
monthly level (see below) – the sole exception being the zero lag score for August.

	1675–99		1725–94	
Month	lag 0	lag 1	lag 0	lag 1
June	2.20*	2.75**	0.97	0.59
Jul	3.20**	2.36*	2.86**	2.30*
Aug	1.58	0.26	2.18*	1.65
Sep	1.05	1.05	0.78	1.17

[4] After 1775, when fever and consumption burials are added to this category the
pattern of negative associations becomes more widespread and excludes only the
third quarter.

immediate (zero lag) impact of low temperatures is increased. At the same time, the effect of warm summers on autumn and early winter mortality also increases.[5]

The series differ as far as the immediate effects of third quarter temperatures are concerned. Consumption – and to a lesser extent smallpox – show a stronger relationship after 1725 than they do before, but the opposite is true of convulsions and fevers, whilst the relationship effectively disappears in the case of all other causes. This divergence may reflect changes in the underlying cause of death structure, associated with the decline of the mid-summer mortality peak and the disappearance of 'griping in the guts', for both convulsions and all other causes were allocated a proportion of these deaths in the seventeenth century. Similarly, the character of 'fevers' seems to have altered appreciably from the seventeenth to the eighteenth century as we have already indicated.[6]

The weaker relationship between summer temperatures and annual burial totals after 1775, however, seems to be 'genuine' in the sense that it cannot be explained by changing lag structures. The effect is equally apparent at the quarterly level. The contemporary increase in the strength of the association between winter temperatures and annual mortality, by contrast, is not reflected in the immediate first quarter effect. Rather it seems to be second quarter burials which became increasingly sensitive to cold weather in winter and late spring.

Wheat prices
The wheat price data begin in 1683 and so the de-trended series runs from 1688.[7] Over the period as a whole the total burial series shows a

---

[5] It is of course the case that a number of these first order lag scores are not statistically significant, but we are not concerned in this context with the reasons why the observed quarterly relationships should exist (whether random or not) but simply with their effects on the behaviour of the annual series.

[6] The suggestion here is that the seventeenth-century burial totals, for these series, incorporate deaths from a cause of death which was highly sensitive to hot summers, but which had effectively disappeared from London by the central decades of the eighteenth century.

[7] The data are taken from Beveridge's series based on prices paid for naval victualling (Beveridge et al. 1939: 566–9, 584–7). In the case of years with incomplete data, the missing values were estimated by applying the profile of monthly prices in complete years to that year's annual average, which is given separately for all years. It should be borne in mind when interpreting the results that 73 per cent of the years for which prices were available had at least one missing month, 31 per cent had at least four, whilst 16 per cent had six or more. The incidence of missing values in the independent variable was a further reason underlying the choice of a non-parametric measure.

Table 7.3. *Quarterly Z scores: burials and wheat prices*

	1st quarter	2nd quarter	3rd quarter	4th quarter
1688–1813				
lag 0				
Convulsions	1.45	−0.99	−2.64**	−1.15
Smallpox	0.81	−0.09	−0.94	0.44
All burials	2.91**	−0.45	−1.79†	−2.05*
1688–1793				
Consumption	2.18*	1.65†	−0.26	0.01
Fevers	1.23	−0.67	−1.03	−0.09
All other	2.54*	0.91	0.91	−0.81
lag 1				
Convulsions	0.44	−1.68†	−0.92	0.11
Smallpox	0.23	0.09	−0.13	1.65†
All other	1.80†	1.26	−2.55*	0.27
All burials	0.61	−0.44	−1.78†	0.43
1675–1794				
Consumption	2.35*	0.50	−0.99	−0.01
Fevers	−0.28	−0.28	−0.44	−0.09
All other	1.93†	0.91	−1.12	−0.27
1688–1737				
lag 0				
Consumption	0.44	0.44	1.06	0.67
Convulsions	−0.15	−2.10*	−1.75†	−0.75
Fevers	−0.50	−1.59	0.66	0.22
Smallpox	0.86	0.91	0.99	0.93
All other	0.90	−0.21	−0.70	−0.86
All burials	0.62	−1.60	−0.40	−0.01
lag 1				
Consumption	0.15	1.04	0.73	0.42
Convulsions	−1.83†	−0.76	−0.64	−1.24
Fevers	−0.76	1.19	0.16	0.07
Smallpox	0.70	1.46	0.96	2.11*
All other	0.19	−0.21	−0.95	−0.71
All burials	−1.32	0.66	0.45	0.55
1725–74				
lag 0				
Consumption	1.30	1.26	−0.11	−0.40
Convulsions	1.01	0.14	−0.97	−1.34
Fevers	0.98	−0.15	−0.41	−0.40
Smallpox	0.52	−0.15	0.43	−0.15
All other	1.64	1.05	1.50	0.16
All burials	1.38	0.14	−0.40	−2.10*

Table 7.3. *(Contd.)*

	1st quarter	2nd quarter	3rd quarter	4th quarter
lag 1				
Consumption	1.83†	0.15	−1.69*	−0.15
Convulsions	1.28	−1.22	−0.91	1.37
Fevers	−0.12	−0.14	−0.14	0.13
Smallpox	1.07	0.77	0.67	1.35
All other	1.58	0.70	−0.07	0.80
All burials	0.72	−0.74	−0.64	0.17
1764–1813				
lag 0				
Convulsions	2.05*	0.39	−2.14*	−1.54
Smallpox	−0.07	−0.05	−2.34*	−0.84
All other	2.01*	2.21*	0.37	−1.11
All burials	3.16**	1.05	−2.10*	−3.50**
lag 1				
Convulsions	1.61	−0.77	−0.95	0.43
Smallpox	−0.85	−1.63	−0.78	−0.18
All other	2.57**	1.74	−3.03**	0.16
All burials	1.54	−0.76	−0.313	0.46

Note: †10% significance
  *5% significance
 **1% significance
***0.1% significance

significant positive association with first quarter prices and a negative association with those in the fourth quarter (see table 7.3). Third quarter prices are also negatively associated with mortality – at the 10 per cent confidence level – and this effect persists into the fourth quarter.

If Z scores are to be comparable across sub-periods the latter must be of equal length – and if they are to attain statistical significance it is important that these should not be too short. Hence we have divided the overall period into three overlapping fifty year segments. The results for total burials suggest a secular increase in price associations between these. There are no significant scores in the first period, and in the second period only the fourth quarter score is significant, whilst in 1764–1814 the first, third and fourth quarters scores are all significant. We shall now look at the results for the cause-specific series.

Consumption   Significant associations were detected between first quarter prices and burials, both at lags zero and one, over the period as a whole. The two coefficients increase in strength from the first to the second sub-period – although the zero lag coefficient remains nonsignificant and the coefficient for lag one only reaches the 10 per cent level. The second period also sees a significant negative association between prices and burials in the second quarter.

Convulsions   The convulsions series shows a strong negative association between third quarter burials and prices, for the period as a whole. This is present in a weak form in the first sub-period, when there is a stronger negative relationship with second quarter prices, but it disappears in the years 1725–74. The third sub-period sees a return of the third quarter relationship, together with a significant positive relationship in the first quarter.

Fevers   The fevers series is conspicuous in displaying no statistically significant price association – even at the 10 per cent level – whether for the period as a whole, or for either of the relevant sub-periods.

Smallpox   The smallpox series also shows a very weak set of associations. At the 10 per cent level, there is lagged positive relationship with fourth quarter prices for the period as a whole, and – at the 5 per cent level – for the first sub-period. Otherwise the only significant score to appear in the table is a negative relationship with third quarter prices for the period 1764–1813.

This finding is unexpected given the strong relationships visible at the annual level. In the first period the discrepancy is probably due in part to the difference between magnitude and consistency of response referred to above, as the quarterly relationships all have the right sign. This is not, however, the case with the results for the third period.

Closer analysis suggests that the anomaly is mainly due to the existence of higher order lagged effects, since third and fourth quarter prices are significantly associated with burials in the second quarter of the following year. Thus the effect of high prices around harvest time and shortly afterwards appears to be felt in the following spring. This implies that the relationship detected at the annual level is – in a certain sense – spurious and reflects the fact that bread prices early in the calendar year were heavily determined by the previous harvest and thus highly correlated with the previous autumn's grain prices.[8]

All other causes   The results for all other causes show a similar pattern to those for the consumption series. There is a positive first quarter association, over the period as a whole, and this strengthens between the two sub-periods whilst failing to reach statistical significance in either of them.

The period as a whole sees the secular emergence of a pattern which combines positive relationships between prices and mortality in the first half of the year, with negative relationships in the second half. For total burials this pattern first appears in the second of the sub-periods, and becomes strongly entrenched in the third. Where convulsions are concerned, the movement is generally similar in pattern, although the second period's coefficients are non-significant.

In the case of smallpox the pattern is complicated by the existence of significant higher order lags, but – at lag zero – is restricted to the appearance of a negative third quarter association after 1764. Analysis of the remaining series is complicated by the non-availability of monthly data on fevers and consumption after 1799, but the calculation of quarterly Z scores for total burials less convulsions and smallpox, for the period 1764–1813, reveals strong positive relationships between prices and mortality in the first half of the year and rather weaker negative ones in the second half.[9]

The eighteenth-century emergence of a negative price-mortality relationship has been observed in the Wrigley–Schofield dataset, and Lee (1981) has attributed the phenomenon to the confounding influence of climate – the conditions favouring good harvests being inimical to health in other and more direct ways. Our findings lend

---

[8] Alternatively, it is conceivable that the failure to detect zero lag effects reflects a deficiency of our method. As applied here the Z scores take account of autocorrelation between the observations for the same quarter in successive years. In the case of an immunising disease like smallpox, however, the negative autocorrelation between adjacent quarters may be sufficiently powerful to offset the zero lag price relationship. A more sophisticated econometric technique – capable of taking account of autocorrelation both within and across years – would be required to resolve this question with certainty, but such an explanation is difficult to reconcile with the existence of strong effects both at lags two and three months since, on this basis, the former would be expected to suppress the manifestation of the latter.

[9] The Z scores in question are as follows:

	1st Qrt	2nd Qrt	3rd Qrt	4th Qrt
Lag 0	2.01*	2.21*	0.37	−1.11
Lag 1	2.57*	1.74+	−3.03**	0.16

Table 7.4. *Quarterly Z scores: burials and rainfall*

	1st quarter	2nd quarter	3rd quarter	4th quarter
1702–1813				
lag 0				
Convulsions	–0.82	–0.58	–1.02	–0.43
Smallpox	–1.30	–1.26	–1.78†	–2.53*
All burials	–1.50	–1.11	–0.40	–0.24
lag 1				
Convulsions	1.68	–4.36***	0.44	–0.06
Smallpox	–1.78†	–2.05*	–1.99*	–1.72†
All burials	–0.25	–3.86***	–1.82†	–1.38

Note: †10% significance
  *5% significance
  **1% significance
  ***0.1% significance

some support to Lee's interpretation suggesting as they do that prices and mortality were positively associated through the months in which the direct effects of the weather that had influenced the harvest might have persisted, but that this relationship disappeared with the onset of winter.

Rainfall

In table 7.4 we present Z scores between quarterly rainfall totals and total burials, convulsions, smallpox, and burials from all other causes for the period 1702–1813. As we would expect it is the smallpox series which displays the strongest relationships, and it is noticeable that these are generally stronger at lag one. Both the total burials and convulsions series display a very powerful relationship between low rainfall in the spring and high mortality in the summer, whilst in the case of the residual category the relationship approaches the 5 per cent confidence level.

The mechanisms underlying these rainfall effects are not entirely clear, but there are two main possibilities. The relationship may be indirect and reflect the economic consequences of drought as they affected mortality, but it is also possible that rainfall levels had direct effects, since dry air is thought to favour the transmission of droplet infections. At the same time, low rainfall would have allowed an increased accumulation of organic and other rubbish, fostering the

The instability of mortality 261

breeding of flies and so facilitating the transmission of food-borne infections.

Age-specific burials
Quarterly Z scores were calculated between the age-specific burial series and each of the environmental series for the years 1739–1813 as a whole (see table 7.5).

Temperatures The negative relationship between first quarter temperatures and mortality is most marked above the age of five – indeed the Z score between temperatures and burials in the 2–4 year age-group is not statistically significant. The older adult age-groups also show a negative association between temperatures and mortality in the second quarter. The associations between temperatures and mortality in the third quarter have a U shaped profile (above the age of 1) declining with age from the 2–4 year group, becoming non-significant between the ages of 20 and 39, and then increasing again after 40.

Wheat prices Each of the age-groups shows a positive association between mortality and prices in the first quarter and a negative association in the third. The remaining scores all fall some way short of statistical significance. In the first quarter it is the youngest age-group which shows the strongest association and the 2–4 year olds the lowest.[10] The age-groups from 5 to 60 all have scores above, or very close to, the 5 per cent confidence level, whereas that for the oldest age group is rather weaker.[11] The pattern of third quarter scores shows a clear division around the age of 20 with the younger age-groups all displaying a significant relationship to prices, whereas the results for the older ages are all non-significant.

Rainfall Only the 5–19 and 20–39 year age-groups show any statistically significant relationships between rainfall and mortality, and we have limited the results reported in the table to these. As we might expect from the behaviour of the smallpox series, it is the younger of

[10] This negative finding raises the same interpretative problem as did the quarterly coefficients for smallpox and prices, and no doubt has the same underlying cause. Annual Z scores, calculated for age-specific burials and bread prices – over the period 1733–1824 – yielded statistically significant results only for the age-groups 2–4 and 10–19, at the 5 and 10 per cent levels respectively.

[11] There is, however, a positive lagged relationship between first quarter prices and second quarter burials in the 60+ age group which is significant at the 5 per cent level. This is the only such, statistically significant, relationship between prices and any of the age-specific burial series.

Table 7.5. *Quarterly Z scores: age-specific burials, prices and weather*

1739–1814	1st quarter	2nd quarter	3rd quarter	4th quarter
Temperatures				
lag 0				
0–1	–1.76†	–1.29	1.52	0.27
2–5	–1.40	–0.30	2.54*	0.47
5–19	–2.39*	–1.12	2.49*	0.09
20–39	–2.34*	–1.77†	1.05	0.29
40–59	–3.11**	–3.30***	1.98*	0.34
60+	–2.54*	–1.93†	2.30*	–0.73
Wheat prices				
lag 0				
0–1	3.12**	1.31	–2.23*	0.13
2–5	1.33	–0.29	–1.98*	0.91
5–19	2.10*	0.11	–2.37*	–0.64
20–39	1.95†	–0.62	–1.57	1.08
40–59	2.13*	1.17	–1.69†	0.59
60+	1.84†	1.49	–1.66†	–0.60
Rainfall				
lag 0				
0–1	–0.11	–1.10	–0.38	–1.57
2–5	–0.70	–0.91	–0.15	–1.36
5–19	0.01	–1.73†	0.81	–2.18*
20–39	–0.01	1.00	–0.15	0.09
40–59	0.11	0.70	–0.35	–0.33
60+	–0.13	–0.08	0.15	0.77
lag 1				
0–1	1.49	–1.10	–0.71	–0.63
2–5	–0.03	–1.22	–0.92	–1.88†
5–19	1.35	–2.07*	–0.89	–2.15*
20–39	0.66	–0.88	–0.73	–2.00*
40–59	0.78	–1.11	–0.90	–0.43
60+	0.43	–1.07	–0.18	–1.45

Note: †10% significance
  *5% significance
  **1% significance
  ***0.1% significance

the two age-groups which displays the strongest association, but it is interesting to note that the lagged effects are generally stronger than the immediate ones. Significant Z scores are confined to the second and fourth quarter rainfall levels.

Table 7.6. *Quarterly Z scores between age-specific burials and environmental variables*

Correlation Matrix	Tem1	Tem3	Wht1	Wht3
Tem3	0.095			
Wht1	−0.052	−0.486		
Wht3	−0.447	−0.371	−0.395	
Rnf21g	0.007	−0.608	0.027	0.762

Principal Components	Cmpt. 1	Cmpt. 2	Cmpt. 3
Tem1	−0.245	0.181	0.892
Tem3	−0.492	−0.473	−0.045
Wht1	0.029	0.770	−0.022
Wht3	0.586	−0.388	−0.262
Rnf21g	0.595	0.028	0.365
% of variance explained	45.0	29.7	20.5

Key to Variables
Tem1   First quarter temperatures
Tem3   Third quarter temperatures
Wht1   First quarter wheat prices
Wht3   Third quarter wheat prices
Rnf21g   Second quarter rainfall (lagged one quarter)

The pattern of relationships revealed by the quarterly Z scores is complicated but can be simplified by a principal components analysis. We have restricted our attention to the environmental variables which yield the largest number of significant associations: first and third quarter temperatures, and prices (unlagged), and the second quarter rainfall totals at lag one. In table 7.6 we set out the correlation matrix between the Z scores for these variables, together with its first three principal components.

The first component, which accounts for nearly half the variance, captures the association of hot summers, dry springs, and cheap third quarter wheat, with high mortality. Third quarter prices do not figure strongly on the remaining components, and the pattern of coefficients strongly suggests that the negative relationship between mortality and prices at this time of year is an effect of the weather, and that the influence of rainfall on mortality is probably direct rather than mediated through food prices. The remaining two components are dominated respectively by first quarter wheat prices and temperatures. This suggests that both variables exert independent effects on mortality in the winter months, unlike the position later in the year.

Discussion

The results for the period as a whole suggest a grouping of causes of death series into three categories. Firstly there are the 'winter dominated' series – consumption and all other causes. These are significantly associated with both temperatures and prices in the first quarter of the year (although consumption is also very strongly associated with third quarter temperatures). The convulsions series is 'summer dominated', displaying a significant relationship with both third quarter temperatures and prices (together with a weaker relationship with first quarter temperatures). Fever falls under this heading as well, being significantly associated with third quarter temperatures. Smallpox falls into a category by itself since only rainfall appears to exert a significant short-term influence on mortality levels at the quarterly level.[12]

The results for the age-specific series yielded a larger proportion of significant scores than did those for causes of death – although their general pattern conformed broadly to expectations given the latter's apparent age incidence[13] – making a principal components analysis worthwhile. This reinforced the suggestion that the negative third quarter relationship between prices and mortality was a spurious effect of climate. In the first quarter, however, high prices and cold weather both appeared to increase mortality independently of each other.

Winter temperatures always have a strong influence on mortality, although after 1765 there is a tendency for this to be delayed until the spring. Summer temperatures have an important influence up until the 1770s – with a rather complicated set of changes early in the eighteenth century – but thereafter they become relatively unimportant where non-infant mortality is concerned. The deleterious effects of high wheat prices are effectively confined to the early months of the calendar year, but they increase substantially throughout our period. This, together with the strengthening of the cold weather effect, tells strongly against an explanation of mortality decline in terms of increasing resistance.

---

[12] There is, in fact, an important lagged effect of prices on smallpox mortality, with a delay of six to nine months, but in this discussion we are concerned only with relationships visible in the same or the following quarter.

[13] The relationship between convulsions burials and those in the 0–1 year age-groups is a partial exception to this generalisation, and reflects the wider range of causes of death embraced by the latter category.

Conclusions

The results we have obtained do not fit comfortably into either of the regimes encompassed by neoclassical theory, and it seems unlikely that this is due wholly to shortcomings in either our data or methodology. Mortality levels were very high for much of our period, but – in contrast to the expectations of a 'high-pressure' regime – their sensitivity to price fluctuations was relatively weak.[14] None of the Z scores calculated between annual burial totals and bread prices were statistically significant, and – even at the quarterly level – it was only as mortality declined at the end of our period that very strong relationships emerged between prices and mortality in winter and spring. Any such effect in the summer months was too weak to survive the confounding effect of climate. Indeed, at the annual level it was summer, rather than winter, temperatures which exercised the dominant short-run influence on mortality.

There was one cause of death – smallpox – which showed a very strong relationship with bread prices at the annual level, but this evidently reflected a much more complicated set of relationships than a simple pathway from prices to nutritional status, and thence to mortality by way of resistance to infection. Clinical evidence suggests that the outcome of exposure to the smallpox virus was not affected by an individual's nutritional status; and furthermore, the quarterly data show no sign of an immediate link between price rises and increased mortality of the kind that is visible in the case of consumption. Rather, the relationship is heavily lagged, and the effect of a price increase builds up over the autumn and winter suggesting that other variables mediated between prices and levels of resistance, or exposure, to infection.

Similar considerations apply to fever, where there were no signifi-

---

[14] The sensitivity of conceptions to price fluctuations is more difficult to measure with the data at our disposal, but there is clear evidence of a relationship between high prices one year and baptism totals the next. In the 'top ten' years for prices the following year's baptisms were on average only 95.6 per cent of the trend value (s = 5.04 p < .05), whilst in the 'top thirty' years the figure was 96.8 per cent (s = 4.48 p < .001). Similarly, in the ten years with the lowest de-trended baptisms, bread prices were 117.8 per cent of trend (s = 19.26 p < .01) and in the lowest thirty years they were 109.7 per cent (s = 18.9 p < .01).

The relationship was, however, asymmetrical in that low prices were not associated with significant increases in the following year's baptisms. The latter averaged only 101.2 per cent (s = 4.35) of the trend value in the years following the ten lowest de-trended prices, and 100.7 per cent following the top thirty (s = 4.06). The Z coefficient between prices and baptism totals lagged one year was thus a non-significant −.514.

cant Z scores between prices and mortality at either the quarterly or annual levels, but a very strong effect was visible in the response of mortality to extreme price rises – a result enhanced by the inclusion of lagged responses. This suggests a 'threshold' effect, by which the normal relationship, or lack of relationship, between the variables was qualitatively transformed once a certain level of prices was reached. The infections subsumed under 'fever' were, no doubt, many and various, but it is likely that typhus was a very important component for much of the eighteenth century. Here again the direct nutritional contribution to resistance seems to have been modest, and it is likely that the observed price effects reflected underlying changes in the determinants of exposure.

Mortality peaks

The analysis of co-movements thus suggests that mortality was sensitive to price and weather conditions, but that these factors did not themselves determine the short-run course of London's mortality, and that the relationships were more complex than neoclassical theory would lead us to expect. We must now turn from the statistical analysis of the series as a whole to an examination of specific configurations of historical events, and the characteristics of particular 'mortality peaks', in order to see under precisely what circumstances mortality did – and did not – respond to external stresses, and what form this response took.

Our aim here is primarily to determine the degree to which it was changes in resistance, or exposure, to infection which were the principal mediating factors in such responses, and how such changes were brought about. The necessary first step in this investigation is a review of the principal mortality peaks in London over our period, complemented by an analysis of the occasions on which mortality in the capital apparently failed to respond to external stress.

Bad weather and high prices are the sources of stress generally encountered in historical studies of crisis mortality, but – as we argued in chapter 2 – the position in London was more complex, and the city was vulnerable to a wider range of external shocks. The most important of these were linked to the alternation of war and peace, and we shall thus undertake a further examination of the short-term demographic consequences of this phenomenon.

The characteristics of crisis years

The threshold beyond which an upward movement in mortality becomes a 'crisis' is a matter of debate. We saw in chapter 3 that, in no year during our period, does the overall London Bills' CMR reach the threshold of 130 advanced by Flinn (1974) as the criterion for a regional mortality crisis. There are nonetheless several years in which the figure rises above 115 – and three in which it goes over 120 – and we shall thus take the former figure as the threshold of a – loosely defined – mortality crisis.

The annual cause-specific CMRs for each of our five main cause of death categories are given in the upper panel of table 7.7, and the percentage contributions of these to the total excess burials are set out in the lower panel. Table 7.8 repeats this analysis for the age-specific burial series in the years for which data are available, whilst monthly CMRs for the total burials, together with selected cause of death series, are given in figures 7.8 to 7.12.

1694   The 1690s was a decade of mortality crises in much of north-western Europe due to climatic instability and consequent harvest failures.[15] Against such a background the London mortality peak of 1694 is remarkable less for its occurrence than for its modest scale. Total burials were only some 15 per cent above trend, but this was still substantially above the increase seen in the English CDR which rose by a mere 5 per cent in 1694 and 10 per cent in 1695. The majority of the excess London burials were due to fevers. Smallpox contributed a further fifth, and the CMRs in both categories were around 150. Infancy burials contributed a further quarter, but the CMR in this category was relatively modest.

Bread prices in London rose steeply in the early years of the decade – the average for the harvest year 1692/3 was the highest for thirty years. The following harvest brought further increases, and prices were also high in the years 1695–8. However, 1694/5 saw a temporary respite with prices back to the levels of the 1680s following a relatively mild winter and cool summer.

The monthly CMRs for total burials place the beginning of the crisis in the late spring, after which it persisted at a roughly constant level through the summer. The peak was reached between September and

[15] See Wrigley and Schofield 1981: 101. The crises of the 1690s are best known to historical demographers through Goubert's (1952) analysis of events in the Beauvais regions; for a general account of their impact in France at large see Cabourdin et al. 1988: 204–9.

Table 7.7. *Cause-specific burials in main mortality peaks*

	1694	1740	1741	1762	1763	1772	1800
Crisis mortality ratios							
Consumption	102	112	112	124	116	114	130
Fevers	150	101	200	122	106	109	143
Infancy	112	121	114	118	110	113	109
Smallpox	161	149	96	115	157	185	161
All other	99	126	109	123	123	111	115
Allocation of excess burials (%)							
Consumption	2.7	10.6	8.6	22.3	17.0	15.0	30.5
Fevers	52.5	0.9	61.2	15.0	5.1	6.3	18.6
Infancy	26.9	39.7	22.4	30.5	18.5	24.1	11.6
Smallpox	19.9	17.6	−1.4	8.0	32.3	42.8	20.8
All other	−2.0	31.1	9.2	24.2	27.1	11.8	18.5
Total excess	3,192	5,120	6,150	4,480	4,040	4,280	4,370

Table 7.8. *Age-specific burials in main mortality peaks*

Ages	1740	1741	1762	1763	1772	1800
Crisis mortality ratios						
0–1	29.4	19.2	22.1	16.2	30.0	25.9
2–4	12.4	0.5	5.2	24.2	20.7	10.3
5–9	6.9	2.3	1.7	13.0	4.7	1.6
10–19	2.7	3.7	3.3	5.3	6.1	2.9
20–9	3.4	12.5	8.2	8.5	9.5	6.2
30–9	6.5	16.8	8.5	9.5	7.8	6.0
40–9	6.0	19.2	11.4	9.2	6.0	8.0
50–9	9.9	12.0	11.7	4.4	4.6	10.0
60–9	8.1	5.4	14.3	2.7	4.7	12.8
70–9	14.7	8.2	13.8	7.0	5.8	16.3
Allocation of surplus burials (%)						
0–1	117	114	115	110	118	123
2–4	129	101	112	149	142	122
5–9	141	116	109	164	124	109
10–19	117	128	119	128	132	122
20–9	109	138	121	119	123	121
30–9	114	143	119	119	116	115
40–9	112	147	124	117	112	118
50–9	124	135	131	110	111	126
60–9	127	121	142	107	114	141
70–9	141	127	138	117	116	150

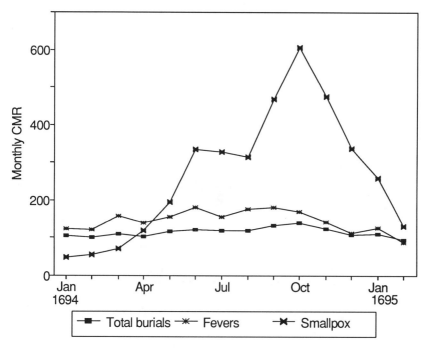

7.8 Weekly Bills of Mortality: CMRs 1694–5

November – when nearly half of the year's excess burials were recorded – before the crisis abruptly terminated with the onset of winter.

The cause-specific CMRs reveal that the autumn peak was largely due to smallpox deaths. These rose sharply in May, continuing at a substantial level throughout the summer. CMRs were above 300 from June to August and then worsened – with figures of 467, 604 and 475 for the months September to November. Fever deaths, by contrast, had already increased sharply the previous December. The monthly CMRs progressed irregularly through the winter and spring, plateauing in the summer months and declining from October.

There is thus here a clear general link between increased mortality and economic stress – a link reinforced by the de-trended baptism totals for 1694 and 1695. The former – at 10 per cent below trend – represents the largest downswing observed in our period, whilst the latter – at 8 per cent – is the seventh largest. But the relationship between prices and mortality is not an immediate or mechanical one. Movements in the fever series seem to lag prices by about six months,

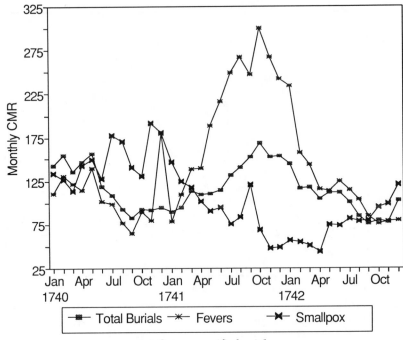

(a) Cause-specific burials

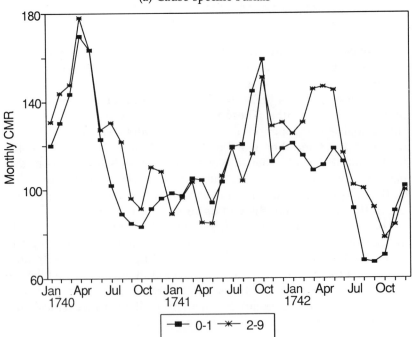

(b) Age-specific burials: children
7.9 Weekly Bills of Mortality: CMRs 1740–1

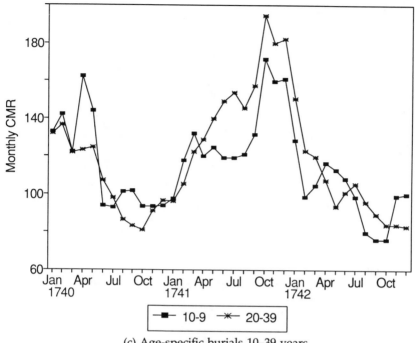

(c) Age-specific burials 10–39 years

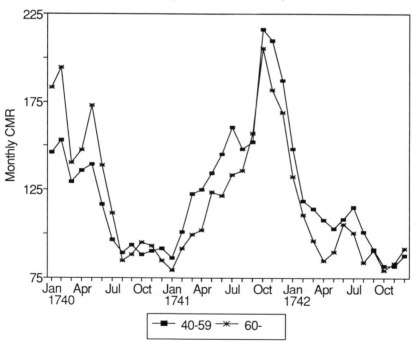

(d) Age-specific burials 40+ years

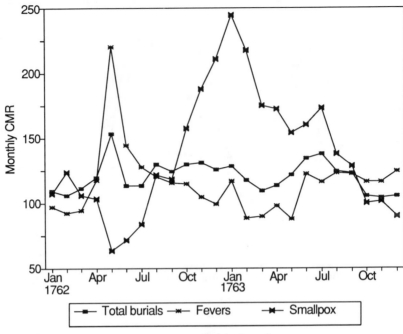

(a) Cause-specific burials

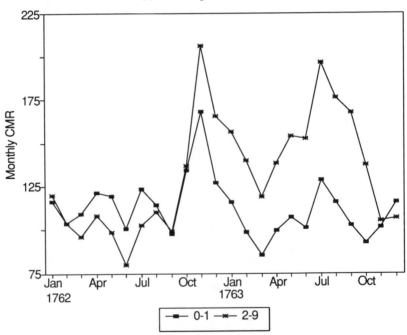

(b) Age-specific burials: children
7.10 Weekly Bills of Mortality: CMRs 1762–3

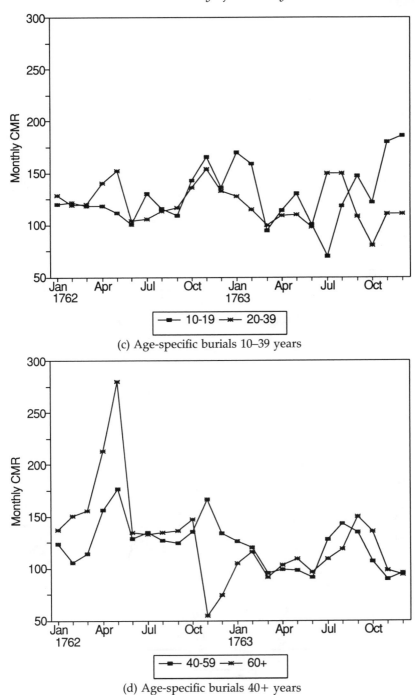

(c) Age-specific burials 10–39 years

(d) Age-specific burials 40+ years

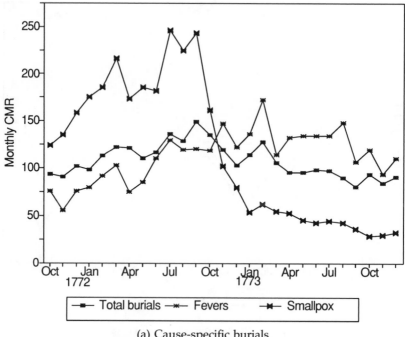

(a) Cause-specific burials

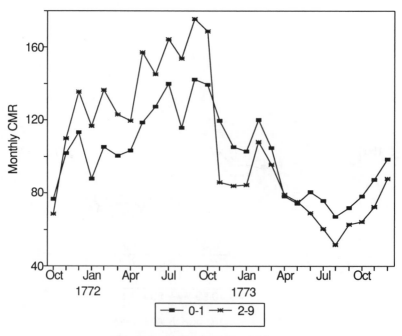

(b) Age-specific burials: children
7.11 Weekly Bills of Mortality: CMRs 1772–3

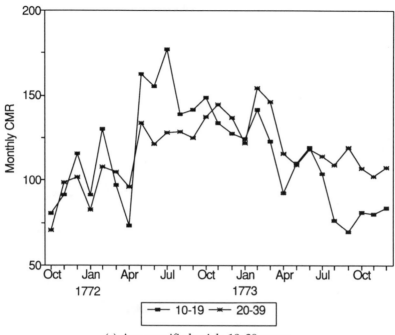

(c) Age-specific burials 10–39 years

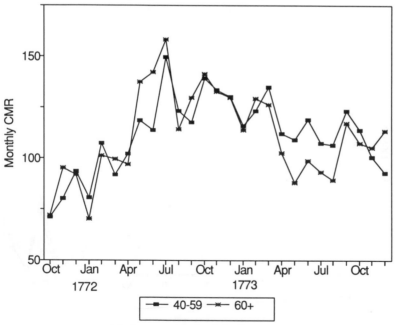

(d) Age-specific burials 40+ years

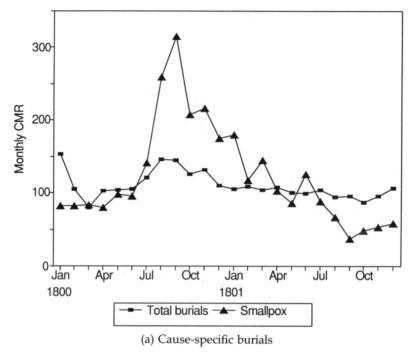

(a) Cause-specific burials

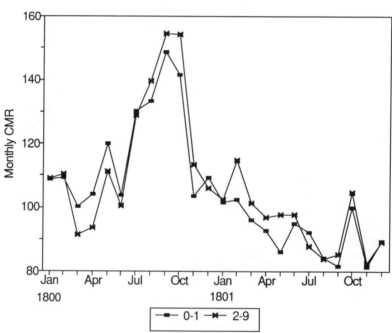

(b) Age-specific burials: children
7.12 Weekly Bills of Mortality: CMRs 1800–1

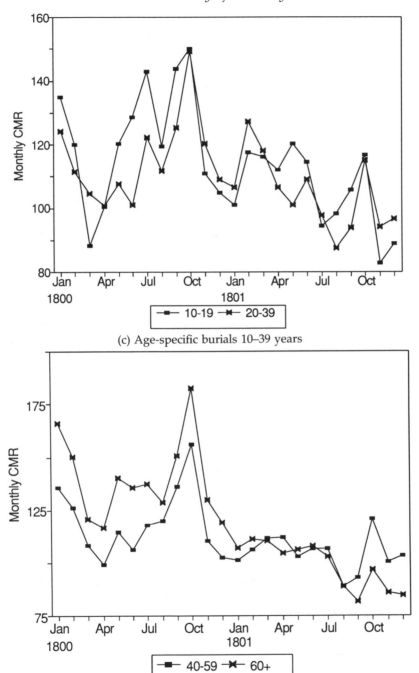

(c) Age-specific burials 10–39 years

(d) Age-specific burials 40+ years

whereas the smallpox epidemic did not begin until the eve of the price reductions which accompanied the 1695 harvest.[16]

1740–1 The excess mortality of the crisis years 1740 and 1741 – taken together – represents the worst demographic shock received by the capital at any time in our study. As in the 1690s, the episode was part of a broader mortality wave affecting much of north-western Europe and triggered by unusual weather conditions.[17] In southern England the winter of 1739/40 was dry and extremely cold, and this was followed by a very cold summer. The last quarter of 1741 was unusually dry, with temperatures only about half a degree below average, and the following summer saw a return to normal climatic conditions. The harvest years 1739/40 and 1740/41 were both marked by high bread prices. Annual averages for the quartern loaf ran at 6.2 and 6.4 pence respectively, the highest since the late 1720s and comparing with means of 5.1 and 4.3 for the adjacent quinquennia.

The burial figures for the two years reveal quite different configurations suggesting two distinct waves of mortality. In 1740 smallpox displayed the largest cause-specific CMR – although most of the excess burials were attributable to infancy and 'other causes'. The age incidence was generally U shaped, half of the excess occurring below age 10 and a further quarter or so at ages above 60. In 1741, by contrast, the excess mortality was dominated by fevers. These – together with infancy deaths – accounted for more than four-fifths of the over-all surplus, whilst the younger adults (20–49 years) were now worst affected having come off lightest the previous year.

The monthly figures also suggest two distinct episodes of exceptional mortality – the first occurring in the early months of 1740 and the second in the latter half of the following year – separated by twelve months during which the totals were close to, or below, normal. The first episode began abruptly in January and has no equivalent in the national CDR, but 1741 and 1742 both show up as crisis years in the latter series with CMRs of 121 and 128 respectively.

Smallpox mortality in London was unusually severe throughout 1740. Convulsions deaths were also above average in the first half of the year, but they had fallen to normal levels by July. Fever burials increased in the late winter and early spring of 1740, but also fell back after June. Apart from a noticeable 'spike' in December, the main epidemic did not begin until the following spring. Burials then ran at

---

[16] In fact it is likely that, by this point, some prices had already fallen on expectations of a good harvest.
[17] See Post 1985 for a detailed account.

two to three times the normal levels in each month from June 1741 to December 1742, before falling back towards the average in the winter and spring of 1742. The 'fevers' of 1741 are thought to have been primarily typhus and relapsing fever – diseases classically associated with famine conditions – and this contention is supported by the concentration of mortality in the young adult age-groups.[18]

The baptism shortfall for 1742 is second only to that of 1694 and suggests substantial economic stress. Again, however, we should note the delay between the high prices, following the harvest of 1739, and the increase in fever deaths in the spring of 1741, an increase which coincided with the abatement of the smallpox epidemic. The casualties of 1740 – those immediately associated with the high prices – were due to smallpox, the 'infant' causes of death (which probably include a number of smallpox casualties) and the 'other causes' group.[19]

1762–3 After the 1740s, the years 1762–3 form eighteenth-century London's worst mortality peak, but this time the burial totals imply a single underlying wave of excess mortality – albeit one complicated by the arrival of a smallpox epidemic in 1763. The cause-specific CMRs for 1762 show a remarkably even rise – in the vicinity of 20 per cent – for each of the burial series. An increase on this scale is also visible at all ages above 10, but the worst effects are felt by the older adults. In 1763 there is a major increase in smallpox deaths and a corresponding reduction in deaths from fevers. The older adults – together with the 0–1 year olds – now come off lightest. The CMRs for the younger adults remain much as before, but those in the childhood ages rise steeply with the increase in smallpox deaths.

The monthly totals place the beginning of the elevated mortality in the spring or summer of 1762. A sharp peak in May is followed by a recession until August, but from then until the following February the totals remain around 25–30 per cent above trend. The late winter and early spring see a short-lived remission, but high levels of mortality recur in May and persist throughout the summer and autumn. The cause-specific data reveal a sharp increase in smallpox at the end of 1762, which rises to a peak in the winter months before

---

[18] See Creighton 1894: 78–83, and Post 1985.

[19] Some of the excess mortality may also be attributable to the epidemic of 'putrid sore throat', which had ravaged New England in 1735–6 and arrived in London by the end of 1739. It claimed a number of casualties among the elite – including the two sons of Henry Pelham – but its impact on general mortality at this time is unclear, and Fothergill was inclined to minimise the effects of this earlier outbreak in comparison with that of the later 1740s (Creighton 1896: 685–93).

declining throughout the spring and summer. By contrast, the excess fever mortality is concentrated in the spring and early summer of 1762, as is that from convulsions (with the exception of a 'spike' in November).

Both years experienced unusually dry springs – particularly that of 1762 – but their outstanding climatic feature was the juxtaposition of a very hot summer in 1762, with a bitterly cold winter in 1763. Although bread prices were below average in both years, there is nonetheless evidence of substantial economic disruption, and 1762–3 saw the temporary collapse of the construction sector in the capital.[20] This was closely associated with the end of the Seven Years War – which led also to the large-scale discharge of servicemen in 1763 – a factor we shall consider at greater length below.

1772 The figures for 1772 reveal that around 40 per cent of the excess mortality was due directly to smallpox, with a further quarter falling under the infancy heading. Bearing in mind that the latter probably includes some 'fulminating smallpox' – and that a number of consumption deaths might also be linked to the disease – it seems reasonable to attribute the mortality peak of 1772 to the effects of a smallpox epidemic. This attribution is reinforced by the age-incidence of the excess mortality, since one half of the latter occurs below age 10 and nearly three quarters below 30. Correspondingly, the largest CMRs are observed in the 2–29 year age-groups – particularly amongst the 2–4 year olds and the teenagers.

The monthly burial figures, however, reveal a rather more complicated picture. Where total burials are concerned, the crisis appears to have begun in the spring of 1772 and continued throughout the summer – with a slight recession in May and June – before reaching a peak in September. It then declined throughout the autumn months, and mortality had returned to normal by December. The smallpox series displays a very similar trend – albeit in a more dramatic fashion – but the movement in fever burials is quite different. These rise above trend in midsummer 1772, remaining some 25 to 50 per cent above until the following autumn. The trend in childhood mortality generally follows that in the smallpox series, whilst the adults follow the fever trend. The teenage series reveals the impact of both of these causes of death.[21]

---

[20] The total Middlesex land registry deeds for 1761 and 1762 were 30 and 29 per cent respectively below trend (as estimated by a twenty-one point decentred moving average). These represent the eighth and ninth largest deficit of our period, and the largest before the war-related depressions of the early 1780s and late 1790s.

[21] The CMR for the 10–19 year age-group in 1772 – at 130 – is the highest observed over

The winter of 1771/2 was slightly colder than average, spring temperatures being high but not extreme, but the outstanding climatic feature of the year lay in the rainfall figures. The second and third quarters of the year were both unusually dry, with rainfall in the latter being 40 per cent below average after an unusually wet first quarter. Bread prices were high, and the annual average ties with that of 1767 as the highest since the dearth of 1709/10.[22] Unlike in 1739/40, however, this increase was not an isolated 'spike' in the price series, but one of a run of 'dear years' spanning – with some interruptions – the ten years or so after 1767, and ushering in a secular rise in food prices.

1800   The crisis of 1800 offers a classical 'Goubertian' conjunction of excess mortality and very high food prices following an exceptionally cold winter and a wet spring. Both 1800 and 1801 were years of extreme dearth and rural unrest.[23] In London, burials from smallpox, fevers, and consumption were all substantially above trend, with the latter contributing nearly a third of the overall surplus. The age profile of the latter is fairly even up to the age of 50 with burials in each age-group – apart from the 5–9 year olds – being from 15 to 25 per cent above trend, but the oldest age-groups suffered more heavily. About a third of the excess deaths occurred at ages above 60, and a similar proportion in the age-group 0–4.

The monthly burials show a severe 'spike' in January, followed by a period of moderate, or below average, mortality – the great bulk of the surplus burials occurring between July and November. The shortfall in recorded baptisms for 1801 is the third largest of our period – at 9 per cent – and indicates the extent of the economic stress experienced. Calendar year bread prices increased still further in 1801, and the general mortality wave had passed by December 1800. Fever deaths continued to increase, and 1801 saw the second highest fever CMR of our period. The age-groups worst affected were those aged 10–19, and 20–9 with CMRs of 111 and 113 respectively.

Discussion
The configuration emerging from this review is too convoluted to fit comfortably into the categories of crisis theory with its trichotomy of

our period. The annual fever CMR for 1772 was only 109 but the 1773 figure – also at 130 – was the twelfth highest of the period.
[22] See Post 1990 for an account of the European subsistence crises of the early 1770s.
[23] Ashton 1959: 26 remarked that the 'century ended in conditions verging on famine'. For a detailed account of conditions at this time see Wells 1988.

'epidemic', 'subsistence' and 'military' crises. At first sight the mortality peak of 1772 – dominated as it is by the effects of smallpox – looks like a good candidate for a straightforward 'epidemic crisis', but this attribution is complicated by the occurrence of a serious price shock.[24] The effects of high food prices are strongly implicated in the events of 1694, 1740–1 and 1800, but here too the circumstances are more complex than the classical 'subsistence crisis' model might lead us to expect.

In three of these years – 1694, 1740 and 1800 – the largest CMRs are displayed by smallpox, a disease in which nutritional factors are thought to be relatively unimportant.[25] While 1694 and 1741 stand out as the two occasions on which fever accounts for a majority of the excess deaths, 1801 is second only to the latter in the magnitude of its fever CMR. Each of these follows a year of dearth, or is the second such year in succession, and in each case the baptism totals suggest severe economic stress. The years 1694, 1742 and 1801 are the three with the largest baptism deficit of the entire period, whilst 1695 ranks sixth lowest.

High prices thus produced high levels of fever mortality – on these occasions at least – but the effect was apparently lagged by one year. The age structure data for 1741 also suggest that it was younger adults who were most at risk under these conditions, with half of the excess burials falling in the age groups 20–49. Even in the years 1694 and 1741, however, nearly half of all the excess burials are attributable to causes other than fevers, and in 1800 these account for only one fifth of the overall excess. The rise in fever deaths on these occasions was thus only one element – albeit perhaps the most important – in a larger pattern of increased mortality.

The mortality crisis of 1762–3 is the only episode of exceptional mortality which is not associated with high prices – either concurrently or in the preceding year – but in this case there is other evidence of serious economic disruption and weather conditions were extreme. The age-distributions show that 1762 – with its very hot summer and roughly even spread of cause-specific CMRs – saw the main impact fall on the oldest and the youngest age-groups. But the excess mortality of 1763 – one third of which was accounted for by

---

[24] The absence of a significant baptism deficit in 1773 does tell against the presence of serious economic stress in the capital (at 2.5 per cent below trend the 1773 total was the fortieth ranked deficit over the period), but there can be no doubt of the seriousness of the impact on a wider geographical scale (Post 1990).

[25] It is also possible, as we have already indicated, that the mortality of 1740 was further inflated by the first effects of the Atlantic 'putrid sore throat' epidemic.

smallpox – fell mainly on children and younger adults. This year also saw a bitterly cold winter, but above all the economic and social dislocation consequent on the transition from war to peace.

Crises and non-crises

The main mortality peaks in the total burial series reflected varying combinations of cause-specific peaks. Smallpox in particular was associated with five of the seven, but it is only in 1772 that the disease seems to have been directly responsible for the majority of excess deaths. The economic and other circumstances of these years also suggest that a combination of external 'shocks' was required to push the capital's demographic system into crisis. We shall consider the implications of this finding shortly, but before doing this we must complement the above review with a consideration of 'non- crises' – occasions on which the London series *failed* to respond to circumstances likely to have triggered mortality peaks. The simplest way of identifying these 'dogs that failed to bark' is to take the years in which either the London bread prices, or the Wrigley–Schofield national CDR series, displayed extreme values.

Prices
The most striking 'non-response' of mortality to extreme conditions is that of the dearth of 1709/10. In this instance the London bread price rose from an average of 4.7 pence for the harvest years 1703–8, to 7 pence in 1708/9, and then to 8.7 the following year – a level which was not reached again until the last decade of the century. The national CDR was below trend in both 1709 and 1710, and – in 1709 – so was the London total burial figure. In 1710 the CMR for the latter rose to 113, but smallpox burials increased spectacularly, and the cause-specific CMR – at 225 – was the highest observed throughout our period. The impact of the high prices was further manifested in a 9 per cent baptism deficit for 1711, the fourth largest observed in our period.

If London was worse hit than England as a whole by the eighteenth century's first major subsistence crisis, the position was dramatically reversed at the end of the following decade. Nationally, this saw the worst mortality crisis of any in our period. In 1729 the national CDR was an estimated 43 per cent above trend, having already risen by 23 per cent the previous year as bread prices increased sharply. The London price, which had averaged 5.2 pence in 1722–7, rose to 6.5 pence for the harvest year 1727/8 – the highest since 1709/10 – and fell only slightly in the following year. The impact of this dearth is evident in a baptismal deficit for 1728 – at 8 per cent, the sixth largest of the period – but burial totals remain unaffected until 1729, when they rise by a relatively modest 11 per cent. About half of this excess is accounted for by fever burials and a further 28 per cent by small-pox, both of which were about 40 per cent above trend.

The high prices of 1756/8 had a strong impact on London's baptism total for 1757, but not on the total burials nor the national CDR.[26] But both fever and smallpox burials manifested substantial upswings in London, and once again smallpox preceded fever. Smallpox CMRs were 160 and 140 in 1757 and 1758 respectively, whilst the fever CMR reached 137 in the latter year. In the nineteenth century substantial price rises occurred in both 1812 and 1816, but in neither was a response forthcoming from either the national CDR or the London total burials series.

The national death rate

The national CDR displays a number of sharp upswings which are not associated with high prices and can plausibly be labelled 'epi-demic crises'. The first of these covers the years 1679 and 1681. The national CDR was at least 20 per cent above trend in both years, although prices were close to average levels and in London the total burials rose by only five, 1 and 13 per cent respectively.[27] Smallpox – which had been 22 per cent above trend in 1679 – accounted for slightly more than half of the 1681 excess mortality, with a cause-specific CMR of 197. Fever deaths were 23 per cent above trend in 1680, falling to 13 per cent the following year.

The two remaining 'epidemic' crises are those of 1705 and 1720, both of which coincided with a run of below average bread prices. In 1705 the London total burials CMR was 104, but it had been 109 the previous year when the smallpox CMR was 153.[28] The total burials for 1720 were below trend in London, but in 1719 they had been 11 per cent above, with smallpox responsible for 40 per cent of the excess. 1720 itself saw fever burials 16 per cent above trend, the remaining categories having CMRs close to, or below, a hundred.

---

[26] The 1757 CMR for London total burials was 102, whilst the equivalent figure cal-culated from the national CDR series was only 99.

[27] London bread prices were also close to the average, although they had been 16 per cent above trend in 1678.

[28] Smallpox itself, however, only accounted for a quarter of the excess burials, with infancy, fevers, and 'other causes' claiming 27, 17 and 23 per cent respectively.

A regime under stress: mortality levels in war and peace

Once more years of high prices prove to have been associated with excess mortality from smallpox and fevers, with the former generally responding more rapidly. This remains true in general when we look at those national crises which were unaccompanied by dearth, and here there is a suggestion that the rise of smallpox in London may have anticipated the national CDR. There are, as we have seen, a number of potential pathways through which climatic, or other external, shocks might trigger an episode of exceptional mortality.

Three in particular present themselves; they are not mutually exclusive, and all work through the effect of adverse weather conditions on prices. The first is a straightforward relationship between high food prices, a decline in nutritional status, and impaired resistance to infection. But in the case of London, the causes of death most sensitive to price fluctuations were such that this pathway seems to have been, at most, of secondary importance before the nineteenth century.[29] The remaining pathways involve the proximate determinants of exposure to resistance. It is possible that economic stress might raise levels of conduction in the population by increasing the effective population density. This would occur if the redirection of expenditure towards food forced people to economise on fuel and living space, and the effect might be worsened by the direct effects of an exceptionally cold winter.

The second possibility is that the effects of economic stress outside the capital might trigger an increase in the volume of immigration. Many such migrants would, according to the high potential model, lack immunological protection to metropolitan infections such as smallpox, but it is also possible that some might bring pathogens such as typhus *rickettsiae* with them. Once in the capital, moreover, it is likely that such persons were forced to live at high densities in accommodation that was cramped and unhygienic even by the standards of eighteenth-century London, leading to further increases in the overall level of conduction.

These possibilities are very difficult to identify in practice, because it is so hard to disentangle the immediate effects of climatic extremes, and price fluctuations, from the indirect consequences which stem from the ensuing social dislocation. In London the task is made still

[29] The cause of death and age incidence of surplus mortality in 1800 raises the theoretical possibility that reduced resistance may have played an important part on this occasion, but too much depends on the interpretation of 'consumption' deaths in the Bills for the issue to be resolved with any confidence.

more difficult by the lack of quantitative data on unemployment, probably as important a constituent of economic stress as were price levels themselves. One way in which we can at least approach the problem, however, is to look at instances in which substantial dislocation occurred, without there necessarily being major price fluctuations. Such circumstances were precipitated by the transition from war to peace.

The demographic consequences of peace
Freedom from the oppression of standing armies was an ideological pillar of the restored monarchy – whether Stuart or Hanoverian. Strictly speaking, of course, this was a polite fiction, but the wars of our period nonetheless saw a dramatic expansion in the armed forces – particularly the army – and a subsequent reduction in the pool of potential subsistence migrants. Peacetime demobilisation brought a corresponding growth in the latter – a phenomenon much discussed by contemporaries, who blamed it for recurrent post-war crime waves. Creighton (1894) argued that fever mortality in the London Bills also showed such a response to the alternation of war and peace. In this section we shall examine the relationship between successive post-war demobilisations[30] and movements in the burial totals, particularly those from fever and smallpox (see table 7.9).

The Spanish Succession   The War of the Spanish Succession saw troop numbers expand from 20,000 in 1700, to 86,000 in 1702, and to a peak of 186,000 in 1711. A general peace was concluded in 1714, although the armed forces had already been cut to 46,000 the previous year. However, 1714 itself saw a substantial rise in total burials – which were 14 per cent above trend – with smallpox 45 per cent above and fevers 35 per cent.

The Austrian Succession   Britain became involved in war with Spain in 1739, and the following year the Prussian invasion of Silesia marked the beginning of the War of the Austrian Succession in continental

[30] Figures for the actual strengths of the armed forces are available only from 1774 (1776 for the navy and marines), and before this we have data only for the size of the establishments voted for by Parliament. The latter often diverged considerably from the former but should suffice to indicate the scale of the problems posed by demobilisation. For a detailed consideration of the relevant issues see Floud et al. 1990: 64–82. Our data are taken from their tables 2.1 and 2.6, except for the years 1700–14 where we have preferred Ashton's series (Ashton 1959: 187) since this incorporates the naval establishment which does not appear in the Floud series until 1715.

Table 7.9. *The consequences of peace*

Year	Bread Price[a]	Baptisms[a]	Burials[a]			Armed forces (thousands)
			Fever	Smallpox	Total	
1697	116	106	94	60	103	87
1698	124	107	102	209	99	36
1699	110	101	113	90	101	13
1712	97	105	90	108	93	153
1713	98	96	87	85	91	46
1714	100	105	135	145	114	29
1748	102	96	116	96	103	105
1749	102	97	135	145	113	75
1750	99	98	128	62	103	39
1762	87	100	122	115	120	151
1763	90	97	106	157	118	136
1764	103	107	121	97	102	48
1783	112	98	94	89	97	234
1784	110	98	80	99	90	57
1785	94	101	95	119	97	48
1802	87	102	120	115	104	274
1803	76	107	130	82	105	194
1815	76	106	126	85	102	326
1816	135	104	125	83	108	257
1817	108	106	123	143	105	203

Source: [a]As percentage of trend

Europe. Four years later a lengthy period of tension between England and France gave way to formal hostilities, and the armed forces expanded from under 40,000 in 1739, to a peak of 120,000 in 1746. Hostilities ceased in 1748, and by 1750 numbers had fallen back to 48,000. The smallpox and total burials CMRs both rose sharply in 1749, but the fever series showed a longer period of elevated mortality. This had already begun in 1747 – with a CMR of 131 – and persisted into 1750. The age-specific CMRs available for this period, show that mortality was, as we would expect, concentrated in the younger adult age-groups, with CMRs from 20 to 49 years rising between 20 and 25 per cent.

The Seven Years War   The size of the armed forces, exceeding 150,000 by the close of the Seven Years War, had fallen by more than two-thirds in 1764. This demobilisation coincided with a major mortality peak, the character of which has already been discussed above.

The American War   The next major conflict – the war for the American colonies – was unusual in that its cessation saw smallpox and fever CMRs fall below a hundred. The armed forces contracted from 230,000 in 1783, to less than 60,000 the following year, whilst the total burial CMRs for the latter two years were only 97 and 90. But if we look at the fever totals more closely, we find that the American war is the exception that proves the rule for the numbers of fever burials mounted throughout the later 1780s. The total for 1784 was unusually low – at less than 2,000 – but the annual average for the quinquennium 1785–9 was 2,670, compared with less than 2,300 for 1779–83, and the figure reached 2,880 during the three worst years, 1786–8.

The French Wars   The demographic impact of the long wars which followed the revolution in France was more complex than those we have considered so far. The wars themselves fell into two phases – the first of which ended with the Peace of Amiens in 1802, and the second at Waterloo thirteen years later – and they were contested by armed forces of an unprecedented size. From 74,000 in 1792, the British forces expanded to 482,000 by the time of the Treaty of Amiens, falling to 278,000 the following year. This contraction came on the heels of the great fever outbreak of 1801, the effects of which were still visible the following year when fever burials were 20 per cent above trend. In 1803 the fever CMR rose still further to 130, although the smallpox figure was below trend and total burials only 5 per cent above.

   The cessation of hostilities in 1815 also saw a wave of fever mortality which was around 25 per cent above trend in each of the three years 1815–7. Again, however, the rise in total burials was only moderate, with CMRs of 102, 108 and 105. Smallpox was below trend in the first two of these years, but 1817 saw a sharp rise in the burial totals – with a CMR of 143. The age-specific totals for these years show a rise of between 10 and 20 per cent in the adult age-groups above 30 years, but those for the 1815–6 period have a much more even spread across the age-groups.

Fever mortality in war and peace
Levels of mortality from both smallpox and fevers were thus highly sensitive to the social and economic dislocation associated with immediate post-war conditions – much more so, apparently, than were those from other causes of death. In the first century or so of our period it seems to have been smallpox which was the most responsive to such conditions, but this ceased to be true from the 1770s. The

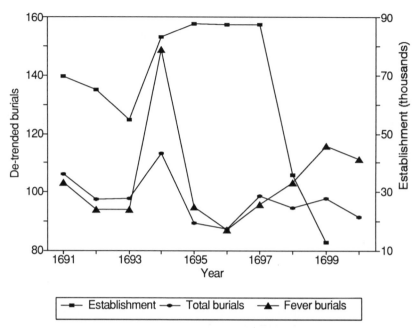

7.13 Military establishment and de-trended burials, 1691–1700

response of fever deaths continued throughout the 1790s and the early decades of the nineteenth century, but the secular decline in fever mortality meant that this had little impact on overall burial totals.

So far our analysis has been largely confined to the immediate consequences of peace, and we have used a measure – the CMR – which compares burial totals for a given year with those for the adjoining quinquennia. In the light of Creighton's observations, however, and of our findings for the later 1780s, we should also look at the possibility of somewhat longer term effects – in other words, at the possibility that runs of years with unusually high fever mortality may have occurred following the transition from war to peace. The CMRs we have been using hitherto are not well suited to this purpose, since the denominator covers too short a period of time, and we have thus constructed an alternative series using a twenty-five year moving average.

In figures 7.13 to 7.18 we plot these, together with the figures for the armed forces and similarly de-trended values for total burials, for the main wartime and post-war periods. Generally speaking the results do suggest that the rundown of military establishments was

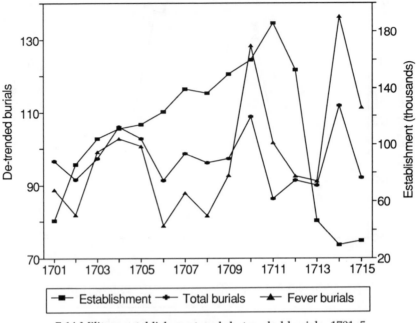

7.14 Military establishment and de-trended burials, 1701–5

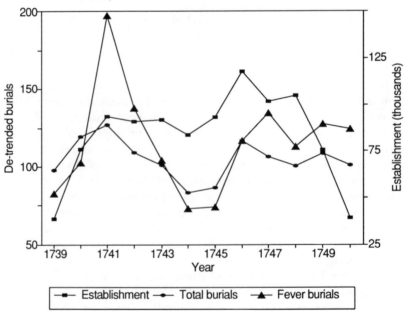

7.15 Military establishment and de-trended burials, 1739–50

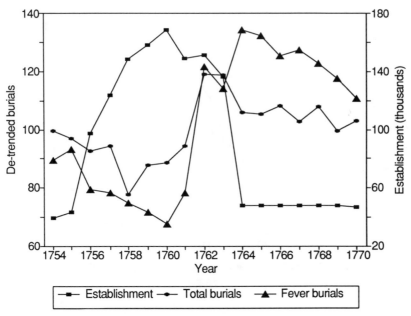

7.16 Military establishment and de-trended burials, 1754–70

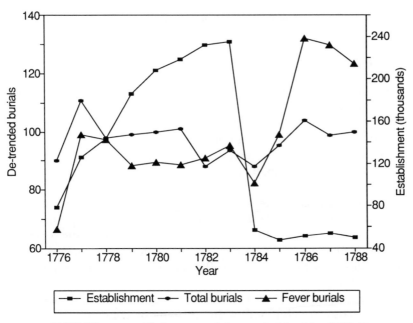

7.17 Military establishment and de-trended burials, 1776–88

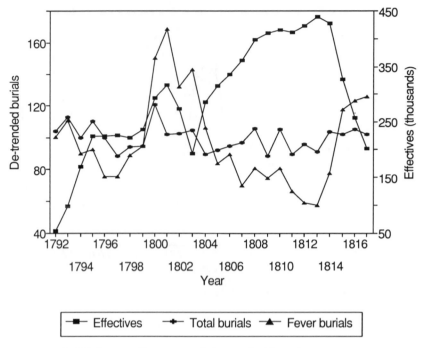

7.18 Military effectives and de-trended burials, 1792–1816

accompanied by an increase in the severity of fever mortality, although it is not in any sense a perfect correlation, and wartime conditions did not prevent major fever upsurges in 1694 and 1741. The relationship is strongest in the case of the Seven Years War, and of the wars with Napoleon. It is at its most ambiguous in the 1740s since the upswing in fever mortality at the end of the decade appears to predate the main demobilisation, but as our figures relate to establishments rather than effectives it is difficult to be sure on this point.

A further implication of our argument is that post-war increases in fever mortality should be concentrated in the age-groups most 'at risk' to military service. In figures 7.19 to 7.22 we have thus repeated the above analysis using burial totals for adolescents and younger adults, along with those for 0–9 year olds to act as a point of comparison.

The results for the 1740s indicate that the adults were rather more affected than were children by the upswing of 1746, and that it was among the 20–39 year olds that the post-war level of fever mortality

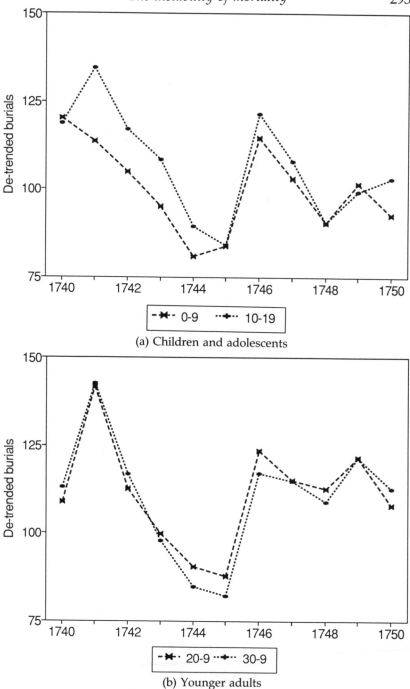

(a) Children and adolescents

(b) Younger adults

7.19 De-trended burials by age, 1740–50

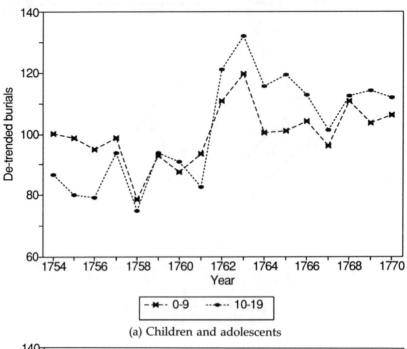

(a) Children and adolescents

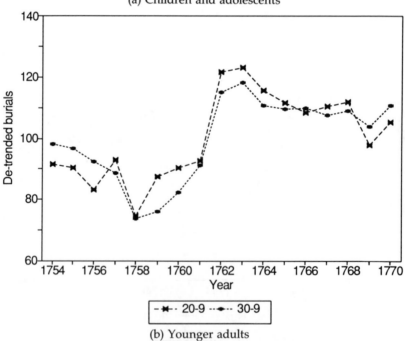

(b) Younger adults

7.20 De-trended burials by age, 1754–70

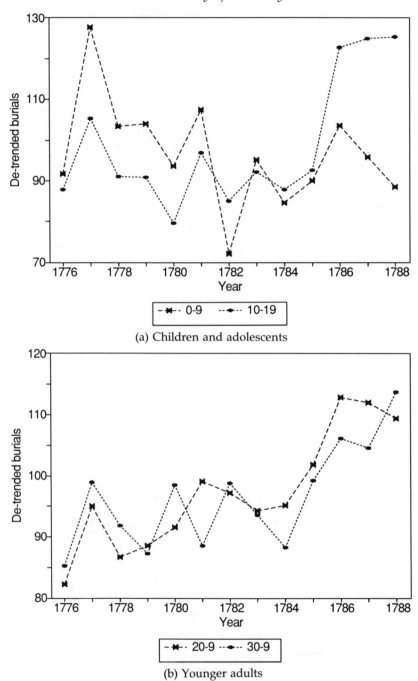

(a) Children and adolescents

(b) Younger adults

7.21 De-trended burials by age, 1776–88

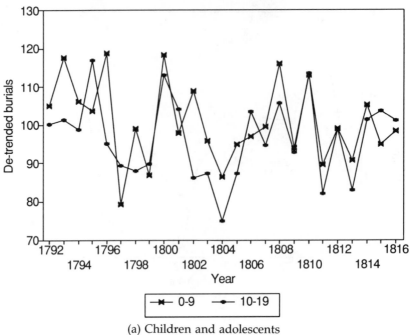

(a) Children and adolescents

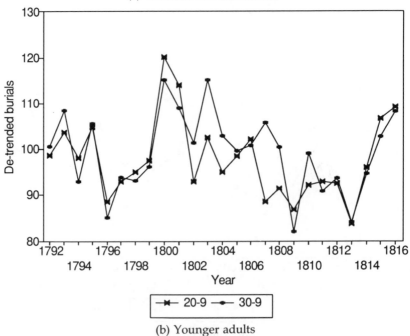

(b) Younger adults

7.22 De-trended burials by age, 1792–1816

was the highest. On this occasion the teenagers had below average mortality.[31]

After the Seven Years War there was, as we have seen, an immediate wave of mortality affecting a broad range of age-groups, but this was followed by two years, 1764 and 1765, in which the age-groups 10–29 are clearly worse affected than either the children or people in their thirties. In the latter part of the decade, however, the focus shifts to children and teenagers.

The 'lagged' response to the end of the American war is visible in the three older age-groups – particularly among the teenagers, whilst child burials are below trend for almost the whole of the period after 1782. The excess mortality of 1801 is confined to the adult age-groups, and that of 1803 effectively to those over thirty. The mortality wave after 1814 is also restricted to adults – at any rate until 1817 – but is of relatively modest proportions.[32]

Conclusions

The interpretation of these medium-term movements in fever mortality is complicated by the fact that post-war conditions were also associated with smallpox outbreaks which carried off large numbers of child casualties. Such as they are, however, the data do tend to support our hypothesis that the expansion and contraction of the armed forces affected the number of 'fever prone' individuals in eighteenth-century London, and that young adults were particularly affected by this. The relationship seems to have become much weaker, in absolute terms, in the nineteenth century, although it was still as strong relative to the secular level of fever mortality.

It was also apparently still strong in the 1780s, but this time the effect was delayed. This complicates matters, for the later 1780s witnessed a combination of economic disruption, social unrest, and Irish subsistence migration. Hence the rise in fever mortality may have reflected a wider range of factors than the presence of discharged servicemen in the population. But what is clear is that the relative importance of smallpox and fever in post-war mortality waves altered considerably in the later eighteenth century. Until the 1760s the smallpox CMRs were generally larger than those for fever,

---

[31] The 1746 mortality peak was the result of a smallpox epidemic – the smallpox CMR was almost 200 – which accounts for the upswing in child mortality. It may also account for the relatively low level of teenage mortality at the end of the decade, if an unusually high level of immunity to the disease persisted for some time as a result.

[32] In fact the main burden of mortality is felt by the older adults, whose burial totals are between 10 and 20 per cent above the 25 year mean in every year from 1815 to 1818.

Table 7.10. *Post-war crisis mortality ratios by sex*

	Females	Males
1697	102	104
1698	92	105
1699	98	105
1712	95	92
1713	91	90
1714	115	113
1748	103	104
1749	112	113
1750	103	104
1762	121	120
1763	118	119
1764	103	101
1783	96	98
1784	88	92
1785	99	96
1802	103	105
1803	108	102
1815	104	101
1816	110	105
1817	106	104

and they were manifested more rapidly. But this ceased to be the case thereafter and the response of smallpox levels at the end of the American and Napoleonic wars was delayed, relatively limited, and – particularly in the latter case – from a very much lower level than before.

It seems reasonable to assume that the post-war smallpox epidemics, like those following price shocks, reflected both the effects of social and economic dislocation on levels of exposure to infection, and the role of migration in introducing substantial numbers of non-immune individuals into the population. The close relationship between demobilisations and smallpox outbreaks before the 1780s is strong evidence for the importance of the latter, but the age-structure of mortality in these outbreaks – like those accompanying price shocks – reveals a heavy toll in the childhood deaths. The calculation of separate CMRs by sex (see table 7.10) also shows that post-war increases in female mortality were as large, or larger, than those among males. Since most of those directly affected by the demobilisation will, presumably, have been males, this provides a further evidence that the surplus deaths were not drawn only from the ranks of new arrivals, but that currents of infection set up by dislocations of this kind were able to spread more widely through the population at large.

Conclusions

The level of mortality in London was thus sensitive to short-run price movements, but this sensitivity was of a weakly 'statistical' kind and was evidently not the main determinant of short-run mortality change in the capital. The fact that such sensitivity appears to have strengthened over time does, however, tell against the attribution of secular mortality decline to improvements in nutritional status – providing we accept the neoclassical interpretation of relationships of this kind.

The analyses of annual 'co-movements' in prices and mortality revealed that the strongest relationship was to be found in the case of smallpox, and this result emerged even more strongly when we considered the demographic consequences of extreme price shocks. Fever mortality – which showed no response at the level of co-movements – also showed a noticeable sensitivity to price extremes, with a significant lagged response being evident.

The character of these two causes of death suggests that nutritional factors played little part in their response to price changes. Shifts in levels of exposure to infection and immunological resistance are likely to have been more important and to have reflected changes in population density and movement patterns. The post-war smallpox epidemics are powerful testimony to the effects of the latter where this cause of death is concerned, and it seems reasonable to assume that such a 'bounding' effect was also implicated in its sensitivity to price movements – strong lagged effects at the quarterly level providing some indirect support for this assumption.

The immunological 'naivety' of new arrivals is strongly implicated in these relationships, but the increase of childhood mortality during such 'induced' epidemics suggests that the former – 'conduction' – pathway was also implicated, and it is likely that in some way these two effects were related to each other. Perhaps the appearance of large numbers of new susceptibles allowed the more rapid spread of smallpox in the capital and thus increased the rate at which children became infected.

Fever mortality was also sensitive to price shocks, and it too increased under post-war conditions. In the early part of our period, however, the relationships seem to have been weaker than were those with smallpox, and the existence of apparent threshold and lagged effects suggests that the underlying mechanisms may have been different. Unlike smallpox, the fever totals include casualties from a variety of diseases, but it is highly likely that typhus was a major component for much of the eighteenth century.

The introduction of pathogens from outside is unlikely to have made much impact on London's pool of smallpox virus, but this may not have been as true of typhus and the other 'fevers'. The major waves of mortality from these causes may thus have owed something to changes in pathogenic load stemming from subsistence migration, as well as to the heightened vulnerability of the migrants themselves. In either case, the importance of spatial structure to an understanding of London's epidemiological regime is beyond question and it is to this topic that we must now turn.

Spatial variations in mortality

In the last chapter we argued that the proximate determinants of short-run mortality change were to be found in changing levels of exposure to infection and in aggregate shifts in the population's immunological resistance. Both of these were mediated by changes in spatial structure, and in particular by changes in housing densities and migration streams. We saw in chapter 2 that London was spatially differentiated in both these respects. Housing conditions differed substantially in different parts of the capital, and these differences widened with the development of the aristocratic districts to the west. Similarly, the distribution of recent immigrants was spatially uneven. The inner suburbs were apparently the main receiving areas for much of the period, although we have much less data on this topic and it is harder to track developments over time.

Thus, if the argument of the previous chapter is correct, we should expect mortality in different parts of London to display different levels and forms of instability. Furthermore, to the extent that housing conditions and migration patterns also influenced secular mortality patterns, we should expect London's epidemiological regime to display a more general pattern of spatial differentiation (or 'segmentation') with respect to these variables. Hitherto our population has, for the most part, been treated as though it were a single homogeneous entity, differentiated only by the demographic criteria of age, sex and migratory status. This was largely a matter of necessity forced upon us by logistical constraints and by the nature of our data, but the nature and extent of internal segmentation within London's vital regime are central questions given the explanatory model we have been developing, and in this chapter we shall try to address them by examining spatial variations in mortality patterns.

As we have seen, the London of our period was always geographi-

301

cally heterogeneous in terms of the social, economic, and migratory status of its population, and the degree of spatial segregation appears to have increased over time. The high potential model predicts that areas containing large numbers of recent immigrants will display distinctive epidemiological characteristics – which should be relatively easy to detect in the aggregate burial series – whilst other forms of local socio-economic or ecological differentiation, particularly those involving housing conditions, are also likely to have had consequences for mortality patterns.

The three dimensions of mortality with which we have been chiefly concerned – the level of mortality, its short-run instability, and the underlying pattern of causes of death – each present their own problems of measurement and analysis, and these are further compounded when we move from the metropolitan to the local level. Generally speaking, the instability of mortality is the easiest of these topics to study, and the level of mortality the most difficult. We shall thus begin with the first of these and proceed to the second by way of a consideration of causes of death.

The instability of mortality

The high potential model predicts that the districts in which recent immigrants congregated will display a greater degree of short-run instability in their recorded burial totals than will others. This is partly because the larger number of susceptible inhabitants makes them more prone to local epidemics of infectious disease, but also because of the relationships between migration, infection and economic stress which we examined in the preceding chapter. Areas with unusually poor housing conditions may have a similar predisposition owing to the higher levels of conduction they experience. In this section, then, we shall examine the extent, and overall spatial pattern, of local variations in the sensitivity of mortality to short-term stress. As a first step, however, we must try to determine how far the overall level of short-run instability varied between different areas within the capital.

Levels of instability

The Bills provide burial totals by parish throughout our period, but we cannot use them as they stand, because the level of instability in a burial series is affected by population size, and the size of the extra-

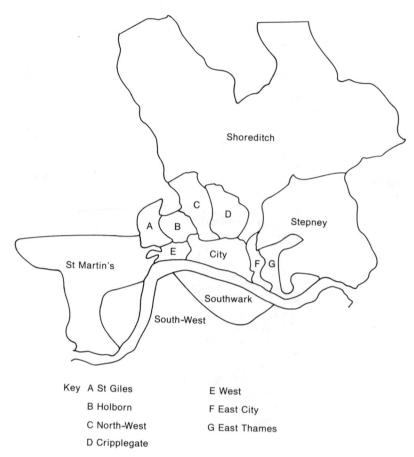

Key A St Giles   E West
     B Holborn   F East City
     C North-West   G East Thames
     D Cripplegate

8.1 Approximate boundaries of Bills' 'Districts'

mural parishes differs enormously.[1] We have thus pooled the figures
for neighbouring parishes to form 'districts', grouped so as to reduce
the long-term differences in their burial totals as much as possible
(see map 8.1 and table 8.1). The district CMR series from 1675 to 1799

---

[1] The choice of groups of parishes to form 'districts' is inevitably an arbitrary one, and
the resulting units embody substantial internal heterogeneity, as do the individual
parishes which make them up. Such internal heterogeneity is most of all a problem
with the intramural parishes, which have had to be treated as a single district, and
makes the clustering of the latter, with respect to the others, correspondingly difficult to interpret. In general, however, the failure of our spatial units to correspond to
'natural' divisions will tend to diminish any underlying variations, rather than
spuriously to enhance it.

Table 8.1. *Composition of 'districts' in London Bills of Mortality*

District	Parishes	Percentage of total burials
City	97 Intramural parishes	9.7
Cripplegate	St Giles Cripplegate	6.1
	St Luke Old Street (1733–)	
East City	St Botolph Aldgate	5.4
	St Botolph Bishopsgate	
	St Katherine by the Tower	
East Thames	St Mary Whitechapel	6.8
	St Paul Shadwell	
	St John Wapping (1694–)	
Holborn	St Andrew Holborn	5.0
	St George the Martyr (1723–)	
North-West	St Botolph Aldersgate	6.0
	St James Clerkenwell	
	St Sepulchre Middlesex	
	St John Clerkenwell (1754–)	
St Giles	St Giles-in-the-Fields	6.3
	St George Bloomsbury (1731–)	
St Martin's	St Martin-in-the-Fields	13.9
	St James Piccadilly (1685–)	
	St Anne Soho (1688–)	
	St George Hanover Square (1724–)	
Shoreditch	St Leonard Shoreditch	5.1
	St John Hackney	
	St Mary Islington	
South-West	St George Southwark	6.3
	St Mary Lambeth	
	St Mary Newington Butts	
	Christ Church Surrey	
Southwark	St Olave Southwark	9.1
	St Thomas Southwark	
	St Saviour Southwark	
	St Mary Rotherhithe	
Stepney	St Dunstan Stepney	10.5
	Christ Church Spitalfields (1729–)	
	St George in the East (1729–)	
	St Anne Limehouse (1730–)	
	St Matthew Bethnal Green (1743–)	
West	St Bride Fleet Street	4.6
	St Clement Danes	
	St Dunstan in the West	
	St Paul Covent Garden	
Westminster	St Margaret Westminster	5.2
	St John Westminster (1728–)	

(with the exception of the South-West district[2]) were then used to calculate MADs for twenty-five year periods with the results in table 8.2(a).

A two way analysis of variance reveals significant differences exist between both periods and districts, but the latter's interpretation is complicated by persisting differences in the district burial totals. In order to test whether the between-district variation in instability is simply a reflection of the latter, the districts were ranked in order of their unweighted mean MAD for the five periods, and the distribution split into 'high-', 'medium-' and 'low-' instability groups – again equalising as far as possible the numbers of burials in each group.

The results (see table 8.2(b)) reveal a very small difference in the unweighted group means for the medium and low groups, but a substantially larger difference between those for the high and medium groups. Average burial totals in the second of these are slightly higher than in the first, but this is unlikely to explain the differences in instability. Totals in the low- instability districts, however, are substantially greater than those in the other two groups, and this may well account for the difference in MADs between it and the medium group.

The districts thus appear to fall into two, rather than three, 'natural' groups, with the high-instability districts standing out from the remainder. Inspection of their geographical position suggests that these are indeed the districts where immigrants tended to congregate, running in a continuous belt eastwards from St Giles, around the northern edge of the City, to Shoreditch. We should note also that the next district in the geographical sequence – Stepney – stands at the head of the medium instability group with a MAD of 8.3, despite accounting for over 10 per cent of the total recorded burials.

Mortality peaks

The burial series for certain districts thus stand out with unusually high levels of short-run instability over the whole period. We must now see how far this is reflected in the incidence of mortality peaks. We shall begin by reviewing the district level mortality experience during the five metropolitan peaks and then consider the question of

---

[2] The parishes in the South-West district were only incorporated into the built up area in the latter part of the eighteenth century, following the construction of Westminster Bridge and the development of St George's Fields. The district has thus been included in analyses for the latter part of our period only where to do so would not detract from the comparability of the results with those for earlier sub-periods.

Table 8.2. *Burial totals by district in Bills of Mortality*

(a) Mean absolute deviations from trend (in percentages)

	Periods				
District	1675–99	1700–24	1725–49	1750–74	1775–99
City	5.3	5.3	9.2	8.0	7.8
Cripplegate	7.2	7.3	11.3	7.8	10.8
St Giles	7.0	8.1	11.7	9.3	10.8
Holborn	6.2	7.9	12.3	11.1	9.1
St Martin's	7.0	6.1	7.9	9.1	6.5
Westminster	6.4	8.9	9.3	7.6	6.4
Stepney	6.8	7.1	11.1	7.6	9.1
East Thames	6.5	5.2	9.1	8.2	7.3
Shoreditch	6.9	9.8	10.2	8.9	9.6
East City	6.8	6.9	10.3	8.7	8.1
North-West	6.8	7.7	11.1	9.7	9.6
West	5.7	5.1	9.8	8.1	8.5
Southwark	6.8	5.6	9.0	8.3	6.5

F-ratios: Between rows   =   4.089 (p <0.001)
          Between columns = 29.138 (p <0.001)

(b) Mean absolute deviation and percentage contribution to total burials for 'high', 'medium' and 'low' instability districts

District	Percentage of total burials	Mean absolute deviation
Low instability		
City	9.7	7.1
Southwark	9.1	7.2
St Martin's	3.9	7.3
Mean	10.9	7.2
Medium instability		
East Thames	6.8	7.3
West	4.6	7.4
Westminster	5.2	7.7
East City	5.4	8.2
Stepney	10.5	8.3
Mean	6.5	7.8
High instability		
Cripplegate	6.1	8.9
North-West	6.0	9.0
Shoreditch	5.1	9.1
Holborn	5.0	9.3
St Giles	6.3	9.4
Mean	5.7	9.1

Table 8.3. *District crisis mortality ratios in metropolitan mortality peaks*

District	Year						
	1694	1740	1741	1762	1763	1772	1800
City	114	118	125	121	117	117	120
Cripplegate	121	131	134	128	112	131	112
East City	117	124	130	135	113	104	122
East Thames	96	110	118	126	120	106	121
Holborn	119	120	124	123	117	128	120
North-West	112	119	126	120	121	128	111
St Giles	116	125	113	119	131	117	144
St Martin's	123	113	118	115	109	126	126
Stepney	115	123	125	122	121	108	129
Shoreditch	106	120	123	116	117	129	129
Southwark	106	113	132	126	125	124	127
West	112	132	110	109	108	109	125
Westminster	118	131	141	108	121	116	105

'local crises' with effects restricted to certain districts, or groups of districts.

Metropolitan crises

The district CMRs for the seven years with the highest total burial CMRs are given in table 8.3. In each case the crisis had an uneven geographical impact, although there are few instances of districts remaining wholly unaffected. Threshold values are necessarily arbitrary, but for the purpose of the ensuing discussion we shall take a CMR of at least 115 as signifying that a district is 'affected' by a crisis, and one of 125 or more as indicating that it is 'severely affected'.

1694 The excess mortality of this year appears to be focussed on a group of districts to the north and west of the City running from Cripplegate to St Martin's, although both Stepney and the East City district are also affected. The West and North-West districts, together with the intramural parishes, fall a little way short of the 115 threshold whereas the East Thames, Shoreditch and Southwark CMRs are all close to 100. None of the districts is severely affected although Cripplegate and St Martin's both approach this threshold.

1740–1 The crisis of 1740 has a detectable impact on the burial series for each district, although three of the CMRs fall a little way below our 115 threshold. The adjacent districts of Westminster and West are both severely affected, as are St Giles and Cripplegate, although St Martin's is unaffected on our criterion. The figures for the following year suggest a slight eastward shift in the burden of excess mortality. St Giles and West are no longer affected whilst the CMRs increase in all of the districts to the east of the City itself, and three of them are close to or above the 'severely affected' threshold. Westminster and Cripplegate, however, remain severely affected and they are joined by the intramural parishes, the North-West district and Southwark, the latter having been unaffected in 1740. If we take the average CMR for the two years together we find that the East Thames district falls fractionally below the crisis threshold, whereas the East City, Cripplegate, and Westminster are all severely affected.

1762–3   The figures for 1762–3 taken together suggest a fairly even distribution of excess mortality over the metropolis as a whole, although the impact is substantially lighter in the three westernmost districts. In 1762 both West and Westminster are unaffected, and St Martin's barely reaches the 115 threshold, whilst East Thames, East City, Cripplegate and Southwark are all severely affected. St Martin's and West are both unaffected in 1763, whilst Southwark remains severely affected. Taking an average CMR for the two years, West and St Martin's both fall below 115, whilst St Giles and Southwark reach the 125 threshold.

1772   The spatial incidence of excess mortality in 1772 is the most variable of the eighteenth-century crisis years, displaying both the largest number of unaffected districts and the second largest number of severely affected ones. The latter form a belt along the northern edge of the City running westwards from Shoreditch through Cripplegate and North West to Holborn, with St Martin's forming a detached outlier on the other side of St Giles. The unaffected group, by contrast, consists of West and a block of three districts lying to the east of the City.

1800   The CMRs for 1800 show a quite different pattern from that visible in earlier crises with three districts, Westminster, Cripplegate and North-West being unaffected whilst six of the remainder, including West, are severely affected and all have CMRs in excess of 120. The most striking feature of the district CMRs is the extremely high figure for St Giles, the highest in the table.

Each crisis thus has its own spatial characteristics, but the pattern

Table 8.4. *'Affected' districts in metropolitan mortality peaks*

District	Year						Score
	1694	1740	1741	1762	1763	1772	
City	0	1	1	1	1	1	5
Cripplegate	1	1	1	1	0	1	5
East City	1	1	1	1	0	0	4
East Thames	0	0	1	1	1	0	3
Holborn	1	1	1	1	1	1	6
North-West	0	1	1	1	1	1	5
Shoreditch	0	1	1	1	1	1	5
Southwark	0	0	1	1	1	1	4
St Giles	1	1	0	1	1	1	5
St Martin's	1	0	1	1	0	1	4
Stepney	1	1	1	1	1	0	5
West	0	1	0	0	0	0	1
Westminster	1	1	1	0	1	1	5
Scores distinguishing 'severely affected' status							
City	0	1	1	1	1	1	5
Cripplegate	1	2	2	2	0	2	9
East City	1	1	2	2	0	0	6
East Thames	0	0	1	2	1	0	4
Holborn	1	1	1	1	1	2	7
North-West	0	1	2	1	1	2	7
St Giles	1	1	0	1	2	1	6
St Martin's	1	0	1	1	0	2	5
Stepney	1	1	2	1	1	0	6
Shoreditch	0	1	1	1	1	2	6
Southwark	0	0	2	2	1	1	6
West	0	2	0	0	0	0	2
Westminster	1	2	2	0	1	1	7

Note: Key to Scores
0   'Unaffected'
1   'Affected'   (CMR >=115)
2   'Severely Affected' (CMR >=125)

displayed by the last of the series is unusual. This is presumably a reflection of the changes which occurred in the city's social geography toward the end of our period. We shall thus set the data for 1800 on one side and consider the configuration displayed by the crises of 1694–1772. In table 8.4 we present a simple incidence matrix, in the upper panel of which districts are scored '1' if they were affected in a given year and '0' otherwise. The districts scoring five or more in total form a block comprising the intramural parishes and a belt running from Stepney anticlockwise to Holborn and St Giles – with Westminster as a detached outlier.

If we broaden the scoring system, to include a score of '2' for years in which districts were seriously affected we again find that the top scoring districts (with a total score of seven or more) consist of Westminster and a block to the north-west of the City. Southwark and East City have now moved into the central group (scoring six) having been severely affected in 1741 and 1762, whilst the City within the walls – which is never 'severely affected' – falls into the lower part of the distribution. It is noteworthy that East Thames and West are at the bottom of both sets of rankings. By comparison the districts affected in 1800 form a block running westwards from East Thames to St Martin's with Cripplegate and North-West, together with Westminster remaining unaffected.

Local mortality peaks
Alongside the major mortality peaks we should consider also the distribution of peaks in single districts, or groups of districts, without reference to movements in the global burial series. For this purpose a district 'mortality peak' was defined as a year in which the relevant CMR reached, or exceeded, the 115 threshold. The numbers of such years per district are tabulated in table 8.5. The ranking is generally in

Table 8.5. *Number of mortality peaks (CMR >= 115) per district*

District	N
Shoreditch	17
St Giles	16
Cripplegate	16
Holborn	15
North-West	14
City	12
Stepney	11
West	10
St Martin's	9
East Thames	9
Southwark	8
Westminster	8
East City	8

Table 8.6. *Frequency of years with N district mortality peaks*

Frequency of years	Number of peaks (N)
0	97
1	18
2	5
3	5
4	1
5	3
6	4
7	1
8	0
9	2
10	2
11	2

rough correspondence with that seen in table 8.4, but there are some noticeable exceptions. In particular, the districts of Southwark, Westminster and East City share the bottom position, suggesting that their behaviour in the six crisis years was an exceptional response to conditions of extraordinary stress on a metropolitan scale. Conversely Shoreditch now has a substantially higher ranking.

In table 8.6 we turn the question around and set out the frequency distribution of years displaying a given number of district peaks. Of the forty-three years in which at least one peak is observed, eighteen (42 per cent) are 'singletons', eleven (26 per cent) display between two and four, and seven (16 per cent) witness metropolitan crises. It is instructive to consider the remaining seven years, in which at least five districts experience mortality peaks without one being apparent in the global series.

The circumstances of three of these: 1710, 1714 and 1749 have already been considered. 1793 was a year of economic crisis, whilst 1746 saw the concentration of troops in London to meet the threat of Jacobite invasion.[3] There is no apparent stress visible in 1681, but the unusually low baptism figure for 1682 suggests economic dislocation of some kind and 1681 was a year of very high mortality in the

---

[3] According to Creighton (1896: 697), the epidemic of 'ulcerous sore throat' – apparently a form of streptococcal infection – broke out at Bromley by Bow in the winter of 1746 and continued into 1748 in London and the surrounding villages. During this time: 'So many children died, some losing all and others the greater part of their families, that people were reminded of the plague' (p. 696).

country at large. Only 1777 diverges from this pattern with no apparent economic or social dislocation. On this occasion the two cause of death series most affected are smallpox and infancy.

The cause of death CMRs for fever and smallpox indicate the important role played by both of them – particularly smallpox – in precipitating the mortality peaks. A ranking of the number of mortality peaks observed for each district in these seven years again shows a strong geographical bias. Three districts, St Giles, Cripple-gate and Holborn, account for sixteen of the forty peaks observed, whereas five; Westminster, East Thames, East City, Southwark and – surprisingly – North-West, display only six between them. The North-West district moves substantially up the ranking if we look at the mean CMRs in these years, but the other four retain their position at the bottom of the scale.

Parishes
The advantage of grouping parishes into districts is that it reduces the numbers of observations to a manageable level, and so permits us to look at entire sets of CMRs for individual crisis years. The district results suggest definite high- and low- instability regions in the capi-tal, but it is possible that we have inadvertently distorted the underly-ing pattern by lumping together parishes with diverse characteristics. An attempt was thus made to recover any 'natural' parish grouping by analysing their behaviour during the five major metropolitan crises of the eighteenth century.

The mean CMR for the years 1740, 1741, 1772, 1762 and 1763 was calculated for each of forty-two extra-mural parishes, together with the City within the walls. The parishes were ranked and then split into three groups ('high', 'medium' and 'low') with as near as poss-ible equal numbers of burials in each. The annual burial totals for each group of parishes were then pooled and the five annual CMRs recalculated for each of them as in table 8.7 (a two-way analysis of variance reveals that the between groups variance is significant at the 1 per cent confidence level).

The ranking of the high, medium and low groups is preserved in 1740, 1741, 1772, and in 1762–3 taken together (although it breaks down if these two are taken individually). The high CMR parishes – apart from St John Westminster and Bethnal Green – fall into two groups, the first of which runs in a continuous belt around the line of the old city walls, from St Brides to St Botolph Bishopsgate, and includes Holborn and Clerkenwell, whilst the second consists of the older 'core' parishes of Southwark, together with Rotherhithe. St

Table 8.7. *Crisis mortality ratios for parish groups in metropolitan mortality peaks*

Parish group	High CMR	Medium CMR	Low CMR
1740	124	118	117
1741	131	127	119
1762	122	119	120
1763	122	123	109
1772	128	118	115
Percentage of total burials 1740–72	33.0	31.1	35.9

Parish groupings:

High CMR Parishes
St Giles Cripplegate
St Mary Rotherhithe
St Brides Fleet Street
St John Westminster
Christ Church Surrey
St Botolph Bishopsgate
St George in the East
St Saviour Southwark
St Olave Southwark
St Andrew Holborn
St James Clerkenwell
St Leonard Shoreditch
St Luke Old Street
St Sepulchre Middlesex

Medium CMR parishes
St Margaret Westminster
St Mary Magdalen Bermondsey
St John Southwark
St Giles-in-the-Fields
St John Shadwell
St John Wapping
St George Hanover Square

St Mary Newington Butts
Christ Church Spitalfields
All intramural parishes

Low CMR parishes
St George Bloomsbury
St Botolph Aldgate
St Katherine by the Tower
St Mary Lambeth
St Clement Dane
St James Piccadilly
St George Southwark
St Mary Islington
St Mary Whitechapel
St Dunstan Stepney
St Botolph Aldersgate
St George Queen Square
St Anne Limehouse
St John Hackney
St Martin-in-the-Fields
St Thomas Southwark
St Ann Soho
St Dunstan in the West
St Paul Covent Garden

Margaret Westminster and Bermondsey are ranked first and second in the medium CMR group. The low CMR parishes similarly fall into two main groupings, one taking in the west end and adjoining areas, whilst the second consists of a cluster of east end parishes.

Discussion
The parish figures thus broadly confirm the pattern suggested by the districts. The impact of the major eighteenth-century crises was

Death and the metropolis

focussed on a 'high-instability belt' of parishes to the north and north west of the City, together with parts of Westminster and Southwark, whilst the areas directly to the west and east were much less severely affected. The involvement of Westminster and Southwark seems to have been a particular feature of these episodes, since the intermediate mortality peaks – in which smallpox apparently played a major part – were more narrowly focussed on the 'belt' itself. We shall now see how far this pattern is reflected in the sensitivity of mortality levels to fluctuations in temperature and prices.

Mortality, temperature and prices

Goodman Z scores were calculated between the district CMR series, and those for summer temperatures, winter temperatures, and bread prices, on the same basis as in the previous chapter (see table 8.8). The district CMRs are based on substantially smaller numbers of burials than those used before, and to obtain statistically significant results it was necessary to treat the years 1675–1814 as a single unit. This is unfortunate, given the substantial geographical changes which occurred, but nonetheless the results do reveal some significant spatial patterns.

The 'spottiest' set of results are those for the summer temperature scores, where significant values are displayed by Southwark, the City

Table 8.8. *Goodman Z scores 1675–1814*

District	Summer temperature	Winter temperature	Bread price
City	2.20*	–1.97*	3.11***
Cripplegate	1.49	–2.69**	1.92*
East City	1.24	–0.84	0.63
East Thames	2.00*	–1.95*	0.85
Holborn	1.35	–2.50**	2.44**
North-West	1.92*	–2.52**	3.65***
St Giles	1.08	–2.16*	2.65**
St Martin's	1.12	–1.78*	1.25
Shoreditch	2.54**	–0.53	2.01*
Southwark	2.23*	–1.71*	0.29
Stepney	1.36	–1.62	1.16
West	0.95	–2.68**	0.84
Westminster	1.86*	–1.95*	2.25*

Note: *5% significance
      **1% significance
      ***0.1% significance

within the walls, and two of the easterly districts – together with North-West and Westminster. Most of the districts display significant scores for movements in winter temperatures, but these are generally stronger in the high-instability belt to the north and west of the capital. The three nonsignificant values occur in a block of districts to the north-east of the City.

The degree of clustering is most marked in the case of bread prices. Here – apart from Westminster – the districts with significant scores form a block stretching from St Giles, through Holborn, eastwards as far as Shoreditch and including the intramural parishes.

Conclusions

The main finding to emerge from this analysis is the distinctive character of the high-instability belt, running around the edge of the walls from St Giles in the north-west as far as Shoreditch or Stepney. These districts are severely affected by the major mortality peaks, but also suffer from a number of upswings in mortality which do not emerge so strongly in the metropolitan totals. The exceptional character of mortality in the former years seems to lie in the spread of severe conditions further afield, into Westminster, Southwark and the East End.

The peculiarity of the high-instability belt also emerges very strongly from the analysis of co-movements. The relevant districts are generally more sensitive to winter temperatures than are the others, and they are almost unique in displaying a significant relationship between mortality and prices. Significant associations with summer temperatures are generally confined to districts outside the belt, although the North-West district – based on Clerkenwell – is an exception in this respect. For technical reasons Z scores were calculated only for the period as a whole, but the figures for the mortality peak of 1800 suggested substantial spatial changes in London's epidemiological regime over the final quarter of the eighteenth century.

Causes of death in the London Bills

We have already seen both the importance of cause of death analysis to historical epidemiology, and the severity of the problems which the Bills' data place in the way of such an analysis. These problems are compounded at the local level of analysis because the cause of death tabulations all refer to the metropolis as a whole. Since we cannot look at spatial variations directly, we must approach the problem indirectly by correlating parish burial series with movements in the global cause of death totals.

The limitations of this approach are obvious, and we can only hope to measure the relative importance of different causes in each area, rather than the associated absolute levels of mortality. There is also a risk of bias being introduced because of differences in the size of the burial totals for the different districts. Since the parish and cause of death breakdowns are both derived from the same global figure, larger divisions will tend to correlate more strongly with any given cause of death simply because they contribute a larger share of the metropolitan total, and thus – other things being equal – of any sub-totals derived from them.

It is important to bear these limitations in mind in interpreting our results which are primarily intended to establish whether there were in fact any spatial variations in the incidence of the Bills' causes of death, and whether any patterns that might be detectable changed at all over our period. Two methods of analysis were employed, each based on product-moment correlations between the district and cause-specific burial totals. The first was principal components analysis, whilst the second was based on the pairwise coefficients themselves.

Principal components analysis

The analysis was carried out on the matrix of correlation coefficients for three overlapping fifty year periods, treating the causes of death as variables and the districts as observations. In each case the analysis yielded a first component accounting for over half the total variance, and a second which accounted for approximately a further quarter (see figures 8.1 to 8.3).

1676–1724 In this period component one distinguishes fever and – to a lesser extent – both infancy and smallpox with negative co-efficients, from consumption and 'all other causes' which have positive values, but the plot of scores suggests that it largely reflects the distinctive character of the East Thames district. The second component has positive coefficients for consumption, smallpox and the residual category, while the others are close to zero. Although the district scores fall into two fairly distinct clusters it is hard to see any geographical pattern to the variation between them.

1720–69 Component one now distinguishes smallpox from con-

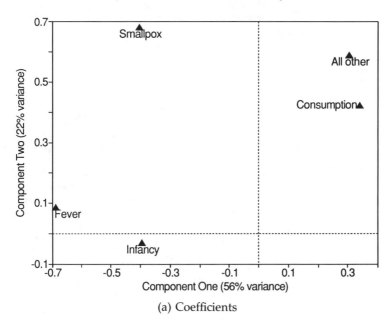

(a) Coefficients

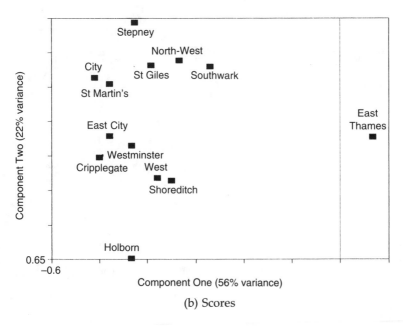

(b) Scores

8.1 Bills' burials by district and cause of death, 1675–1724: principal
components analysis

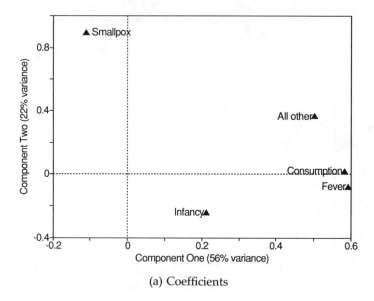

(a) Coefficients

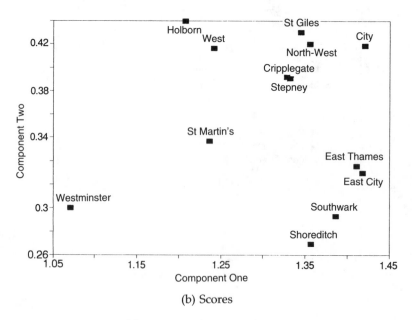

(b) Scores

8.2 Bills' burials by district and cause of death, 1720–69: principal
components analysis

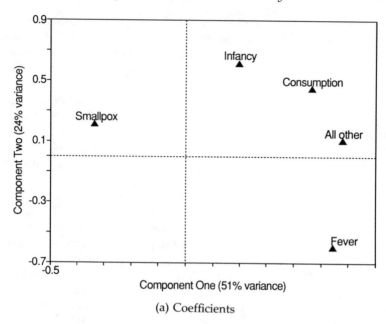

(a) Coefficients

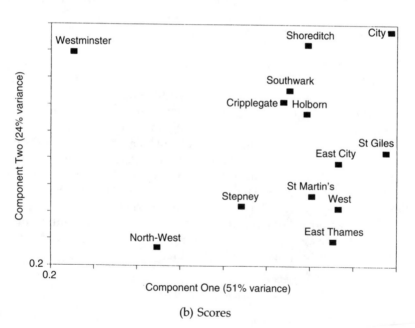

(b) Scores

8.3 Bills' burials by district and cause of death, 1760–1819: principal
components analysis

sumption, fevers and the residual category – with infancy lying roughly in the middle – and seems to reflect a contrast between adult and childhood mortality. The second component is also dominated by a positive smallpox coefficient, but in this case the infancy value is negative, and it is the residual category which is intermediate. The plot of scores reveals a striking pattern of spatial variation as the districts split into two groups on each component. The first ('adult') component divides them roughly on an east–west axis, separating a western cluster – comprising Holborn, St Martin's, Westminster and West – from the remainder, whilst East Thames, East City and the intramural parishes have the highest scores.

The second, 'smallpox', component separates St Martin's, Westminster, East Thames, Shoreditch, East City and Southwark from the others, as a result of which the observations fall into three rough groups. The loosest of these consists of the western districts and itself divides into two pairs according to the scores on component two – St Martin's and Westminster having relatively low values in contrast to Holborn and West. The second group – East Thames, East City, Southwark, and Shoreditch – is high on component one and low on component two, and the third, which contains the intramural parishes together with the bulk of the high-instability districts, score highly on both of the two components.

1765–1814 The pattern of coefficients on the first component is similar to that of the preceding period, whilst the second is dominated by the contrast between fevers – with a strong negative value – and correspondingly positive figures for infancy and consumption. As in the first period, the pattern of component scores is one of a central cluster with some outliers. Westminster, the North-West district and – to a much lesser extent – Stepney, stand out with particularly low 'adult' scores, whilst the remaining districts vary chiefly on component two. Here St Martin's, Stepney, East Thames, East City, the North-West and West districts have particularly low scores – suggesting a correlation with the fever burials – whilst the intramural parishes, Cripplegate, Holborn, Westminster, Shoreditch and Southwark display correspondingly high values.

Correlation analysis

Principal components analysis reduces the variables in a dataset to a manageable number, thus enabling its underlying structure to emerge more clearly. But in the present context we should also consider the pairwise relationships between districts and individual causes of death. This means looking at the coefficients themselves, but here we run up against the problem of differences in the numbers of burials between districts, and in order to get round this it was necessary to adopt a two stage procedure.

Firstly, correlation coefficients were calculated between districts and the consumption, fever, infancy and smallpox series, using the same fifty year periods as before. Taking each cause of death in turn, the districts were then ranked according to the strength of the correlation and the distribution split into three groups, designated 'high' (H), 'medium' (M), and 'low' (L), so as to equalise the burial totals as far as possible. The burials for the districts within each group were then pooled and converted into CMRs. In the second stage, correlation coefficients were calculated between the latter and the cause-specific series. As the three correlations in each set were based on approximately equal numbers of burials it was possible to test the differences between them for statistical significance. We shall consider the results for each of the three periods in turn (see table 8.9).

1675–1724   No systematic pattern emerges in this period, and, in the case of the fever and infancy series, only the difference between the L and M group correlations are statistically significant. For consumption burials, the L districts lie to the west of the City, whereas the H group includes the City itself and a neighbouring cluster. The districts with a low fever correlation include Southwark and a belt stretching from the Shoreditch district, through the East End districts of Stepney and East Thames. Where the infancy series is concerned there is less consistency in the distribution of the L districts which include St Giles and West, together with Westminster, but also Southwark and East Thames.

For smallpox both the H and L correlations differ significantly from that of the M group. The H group comprises City, Stepney and St Martin's, whilst the M group forms a block consisting of the adjacent Cripplegate and North-West districts together with St Giles, which is separated from them by 'low' Holborn. The districts in the L group also form two blocks. The first takes in the adjacent districts of Shoreditch, East City and East Thames, whilst the second includes Holborn, West and Westminster.

1720–69   The results for this period, as we would expect from the principal components analysis, do reveal a systematic pattern of spatial variation, and only in the case of smallpox is one of the correlation

Table 8.9. *Correlation analysis: districts with cause-specific burials*

1675–1724

Consumption		Fevers		Infancy		Smallpox	
NW[a]	0.59	Cit	0.62	E-C	0.55	Ste	0.67
E-T	0.58	W	0.55	Crp	0.47	Mar	0.59
Cit	0.48	Mar	0.52	Ste	0.46	Cit	0.56
Sk	0.48			Hol	0.43		
W	0.45	E-C	0.52	Mar	0.43	Gil	0.56
Ste	0.45	Crp	0.51	Cit	0.42	Crp	0.53
E-C	0.43	Wmr	0.51	Shr	0.41	NW	0.52
Gil	0.43	Gil	0.49	NW	0.38	Sk	0.51
		NW	0.48				
		Hol	0.44				
Mar	0.38	Shr	0.43	Gil	0.38	Wmr	0.51
Crp	0.36	Ste	0.43	Wmr	0.36	E-C	0.49
Shr	0.36	Sk	0.42	W	0.33	Hol	0.43
Wmr	0.35	E-T	0.14	Sk	0.30	Shr	0.42
Hol	0.34			E-T	0.25	W	0.40
						E-T	0.31

District groups	Correlation			Percentage of total burials		
Burial series	High	Medium	Low	High	Medium	Low
Consumption	0.61	0.51	0.43	37	30	33
Fevers	0.63	0.60	0.43	33	35	32
Infancy	0.51	0.47	0.40	28	37	35
Smallpox	0.66	0.62	0.44	37	30	33

1720–69

Consumption		Fevers		Infancy		Smallpox	
E-C	0.86	Sk	0.73	Ste	0.78	Hol	0.42
E-T	0.84	Shr	0.73	E-C	0.78	Ste	0.42
Gil	0.81	NW	0.71	E-T	0.78	NW	0.42
Cit	0.80	Cit	0.70	Crp	0.76	Gil	0.41
						Crp	0.39
NW	0.76	Ste	0.69	Cit	0.75	Cit	0.39
N	0.75	E-C	0.67	Shr	0.74	W	0.38
Mar	0.75	Crp	0.67	Mar	0.73	Mar	0.35
Sk	0.75	E-T	0.66	Wmr	0.73		
Ste	0.75	Gil	0.63	NW	0.72	Wmr	0.32
Crp	0.74	W	0.60	Gil	0.71	E-C	0.30
W	0.70	Hol	0.59	Sk	0.71	E-T	0.30
Hol	0.69	Mar	0.57	W	0.65	Shr	0.25
Wmr	0.61	Wmr	0.50	Hol	0.64	Sk	0.25

Table 8.9. *(Contd.)*

Consumption		Fevers		Infancy		Smallpox	
District groups		Correlation		Percentage of total burials			
Burial series	High	Medium	Low	High	Medium	Low	
Consumption	0.88	0.84	0.80	30	37	33	
Fevers	0.77	0.72	0.67	31	32	37	
Infancy	0.83	0.81	0.75	32	35	33	
Smallpox	0.43	0.40	0.32	36	29	35	

1765–1814

Consumption		Fevers		Infancy		Smallpox	
Cit	0.67	E-T	0.59	Cit	0.72	Sk	0.44
Shr	0.65	E-C	0.55	Shr	0.71	SW	0.43
SW	0.60	Gil	0.53	Hol	0.70	NW	0.39
		Mar	0.52	Gil	0.64	Shr	0.39
				E-C	0.62		
				Crp	0.62		
E-T	0.59	Hol	0.50	Sk	0.62	Ste	0.34
Sk	0.58	W	0.49	S-W	0.62	Wmr	0.33
Gil	0.56	Ste	0.48	Mar	0.61	Hol	0.29
Crp	0.55	Sk	0.44			E-C	0.25
Hol	0.53	NW	0.42			Crp	0.24
E-C	0.49						
W	0.46						
Ste	0.42	Shr	0.42	Wmr	0.58	Mar	0.23
Mar	0.32	SW	0.41	W	0.50	Cit	0.19
Wmr	0.31	Cit	0.39	Ste	0.48	E-T	0.16
NW	0.26	Crp	0.38	N-W	0.42	W	0.08
		Wmr	0.19	E-T	0.41	Gil	0.06

District groups		Correlation		Percentage of total burials			
Burial series	High	Medium	Low	High	Medium	Low	
Consumption	0.70	0.56	0.53	29	33	38	
Fevers	0.65	0.59	0.41	33	34	33	
Infancy	0.77	0.70	0.71	34	33	32	
Smallpox	0.49	0.35	0.21	31	30	39	

Note: [a]*Key to abbreviations*: Cit – City; Crp – Cripplegate; E-C – East City; E-T – East Thames; Hol – Holborn; NW – North-West; Gil – St Giles; Mar – St Martin's; Shr – Shoreditch; SW – South-West; Sk – Southwark; Ste – Stepney; W – West; Wmr – Westminster.

differences – that between H and M – not statistically significant. The consumption results reveal a noticeable east–west gradient, though the pattern is marred somewhat by the appearance of St Giles in the H group and Stepney in the L. The results for the fever burials reveal three well-defined blocks. The first of these – with high correlations – takes in the intramural parishes, Southwark, Shoreditch and the North-West district, whilst the M group consists of Cripplegate and the three easterly districts. The districts in the low correlation group all lie to the west and south of St Sepulchres. Where infancy burials are concerned, there is a marked divergence between easterly and westerly districts. The H group consists of the former, together with Cripplegate, whilst the L group forms a block running from the North-West through St Giles and Holborn to West, together with Southwark. St Martin's and Westminster, however, both have medium correlations.

The difference between the H and M smallpox correlations is, as we have already mentioned, statistically insignificant ($d = 1.57$), but the spatial clustering of the districts in the two groups is nonetheless interesting. The H group forms a block to the north-west of the City, with Stepney as a detached outlier, whilst the M districts form an adjacent series from the intramural parishes westward. The composition of the L group remains substantially unchanged from the previous period except that the West district has been replaced by Westminster.

The results for the fevers and smallpox series are compared in table 8.10, with the H and M groups pooled for each of the causes of death. Apart from Westminster, which falls into the L group in both cases, the districts fall into three categories. To the west of the City lie the districts which combine high, or medium, smallpox correlations with low fever coefficients – whilst Shoreditch, East Thames, East City and Southwark have the reverse characteristics. The third category, which falls into the H or M groups on both counts, consists of the City within the walls and a group of districts lying roughly to the north: Cripplegate, Stepney and North-West.

1765–1814 The data for the last of the three periods were analysed with the inclusion of the South-West district, which was incorporated into the built-up area at this time. Once more, the City appears in the H group for consumption, and the two westerly districts of Westminster and St Martin's fall in the L group, but otherwise there is no clear spatial pattern. The overall proportion of burials due to smallpox and fevers falls substantially after 1800, but significant differences in

Table 8.10. *Correlations of districts with fever and smallpox burial series 1720–69*

	Correlation Group	
District	Fevers	Smallpox
City	High/Medium	High/Medium
Cripplegate	High/Medium	High/Medium
North-West	High/Medium	High/Medium
Stepney	High/Medium	High/Medium
East City	High/Medium	Low
East Thames	High/Medium	Low
Shoreditch	High/Medium	Low
Southwark	High/Medium	Low
St Giles	Low	High/Medium
Holborn	Low	High/Medium
St Martin's	Low	High/Medium
West	Low	High/Medium
Westminster	Low	Low

the correlations of the H, M and L groups are observed in both cases. The M and L infancy correlations, however, are virtually identical – in fact the L is fractionally higher than the M.[4]

The pattern of correlation for fever burials is now quite different from that displayed in the earlier periods. Two clusters stand out in the H group: one, lying to the west of the city, includes St Martin's and St Giles (with Holborn at the head of the M districts), whilst the other takes in East City and East Thames. The M and L groups, by contrast, do not display any noticeable spatial clustering. In the case of smallpox burials the East Thames district remains in the L group, and North-West remains in the H, but the most noticeable feature is the high smallpox correlations displayed by the two districts to the south of the river. The results for infancy burials show a strong tendency for the districts circling the city to fall into the H group.

As in the principal components analysis, the clearest pattern of spatial variation emerges in the period 1720–69, when there appear to have been distinct 'regional' configurations of causes of death. We shall return to this question subsequently, but here we must consider

[4] This apparently anomalous result arises because the pooling of the different parishes within the 'M' group has evidently 'damped down' the correlated movements detectable within the individual series through a process of interference.

the extent of spatial continuity in the pattern of correlations. This is found in the case of smallpox and infant burials, the geography of fever correlations being the least stable over time. Where smallpox is concerned, six districts appear in the same group in each period, and only one features in both the H and L groups at different times. For infant burials, the relevant figures are four and four, but they are only two and two for consumption. No district appears in the same group for fevers in all of the sub-periods, and seven feature in both H and L at different points.

For both smallpox and infancy burials, the districts falling consistently into the H or M group form coherent spatial blocks. For smallpox this coincides fairly closely with the 'high-instability belt', to the north and north-west of the City, and comprises St Giles, North-West, Holborn and Cripplegate – with Stepney as a detached outlier to the north-east. The districts with H or M infancy correlations include the intramural parishes and Shoreditch together with East City and Cripplegate, both of which have H correlations in each period.

Those with consistently L or M smallpox correlations form two pairs at opposite ends of the metropolis, West and Westminster on one hand, and East City and East Thames on the other. West and Westminster also have consistently L or M correlations with infant burials – the former being in the L group in each of the three periods – as do North-West and Southwark. In the case of consumption the districts with H or M correlations form a block consisting of the City and the eastern districts of East City and East Thames, together with Southwark, and with St Giles as a detached outlier. The L/M correlation group, by contrast takes in the group of westerly districts together with Cripplegate and Stepney.

Conclusions

The geographical differences emerging from the above analyses are easier to demonstrate than they are to interpret, and almost every generalisation must be qualified in respect of at least one district. But this is scarcely surprising given the extremely 'coarse-grained' character of our materials and methods, and certain patterns recur often enough to suggest an underlying demographic reality. In the first place, there is a clear association between the 'high-instability' districts – as delineated in the previous section – and movements in the smallpox series. These districts also tend to display a sensitivity to movements in prices and winter temperatures.

A corresponding 'consumption belt' is located to the east and south of the City, and is marked by a sensitivity to summer temperatures. This finding is more difficult to interpret for the districts concerned tend to display relatively low levels of instability and smallpox correlations. It may be that mortality in this zone has a distinct character – closely associated with the diseases embraced by 'consumption' – but it is also possible that the underlying relationships prevailing here are common to the metropolis at large but are obscured elsewhere by the volatility of smallpox burials.

The clearest spatial pattern emerges during the decades of stagnation toward the middle of our period. Again, two explanations are possible in principle. It may be that the character of many districts was changing too rapidly during the early years of metropolitan expansion for any consistent structure to manifest itself, but if so it is difficult to see how continuities could emerge when the period is considered as a whole. It thus seems more likely that the relationships crystallising in the second of our sub-periods are related to the phenomenon of stagnation itself, whether at the level of cause or effect.

The fact that the fever correlations display no long-term continuities may reflect the changing character of this cause of death, and the rise of typhus mortality in the early eighteenth century. The central decades of the century, do, however, see the emergence of a clear 'fever belt'. This runs clockwise around the City from Clerkenwell to Southwark, and – between Clerkenwell and Stepney – overlaps a similar 'smallpox belt'. The principal components analysis for this period clearly picks out the districts in these two belts – with their high scores on component one – whilst the second component divides the 'pure fever' districts in the East End and Southwark (together with Shoreditch) from those in this 'mixed' zone (together with St Giles).

The implications of this pattern were pursued by looking at the matrix of correlations between districts and age-specific burials for the first fifty years in which the latter are available (1733–82). A principal components analysis of this matrix confirms that the east–west axis, visible in the 1720–69 cause of death data, reflects differences in the underlying age-pattern of mortality (see figure 8.4).

The coefficients on the first component (accounting for 56 per cent of the total variance) split the ages under 10 and over 20 into very tight groups, with the teenagers lying close to the latter. The second component, which explains 30 per cent of the variance, divides the age-groups below 20 from those above 40. This time it is the 20–39

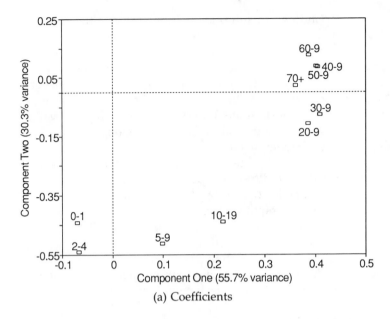

(a) Coefficients

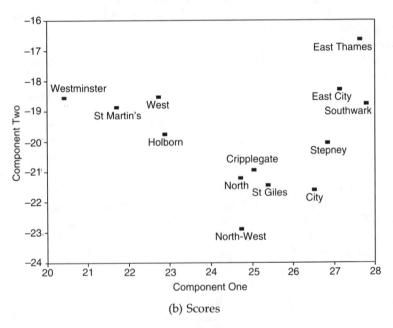

(b) Scores

8.4 Bills' burials by district and age at death, 1733–82: principal
components analysis

year olds who occupy an intermediate position, rather closer to the second of the two clusters. The pattern of scores implies that most of the short-run volatility in burial totals from Holborn westwards is due to child deaths, but that adult deaths increase in importance in South-wark and the East End – which in this respect embraces Stepney.

The behaviour of the high-instability districts from North-West to Shoreditch – together with the intramural parishes and, to a lesser extent, both Holborn and Stepney – is, however, strongly influenced by another factor, or set of closely interrelated factors. This chiefly affects the age-groups below twenty, whilst exercising a detectable influence into the twenties and thirties. This finding chimes with our observation in the last chapter that mortality waves associated with external shocks to London's epidemiological regime affected both the childhood and the adolescent/young adults age-ranges. Furthermore, the cause of death analysis suggests that both smallpox and fevers were implicated in the unusual behaviour of the high-instability parishes, and it was these causes of death which proved to be most responsive to such external shocks.

Mortality levels and seasonality

The local seasonality of burials was investigated using the parish register sample for the two decades 1695–1704 and 1750–9. The criterion for inclusion was that at least half of the entries in a register should be specifically identified as either children or adults. For this purpose child burials were those described either as a 'son' or 'daughter' – or given some more explicit label such as 'child' or 'infant' – and terms such as 'wife' or 'widow' – together with occupational descriptions – were taken to indicate an adult burial. The sample also yielded a limited amount of information on the spatial distribution of childhood mortality, and we shall consider this following our analysis of burial seasonality.

The seasonality of burials

MBIs were calculated for each parish taking child, adult burials and total burials separately, and each set of results was subjected to a principal components analysis. The child and adult burial seasonalities were analysed using the 'main sample', described above, whilst data from a number of other parishes were included in an 'extended' sample which was used to analyse the seasonality of total burials without regard to age.

The analysis of these data was complicated by two problems; substantial variations in size and thus in the scale of the burial totals, and changes in the composition of both the main and extended samples between the two decades. This latter is particularly true south of the river – where only two parishes appear in the main sample for 1750–9 – but the centre of gravity of the central parishes also moves substantially to the east as neither Holborn or St Sepulchres appear in the 1750s.

In order to deal with these problems the analyses outlined above were supplemented by two more. The parish level data were pooled to form a small number of geographical groups and the resulting burial seasonalities examined, whilst the possible effects of compositional change were investigated using two 'restricted samples' comprising parishes which appeared in the main or extended sample for both decades. Both analyses yielded a similar pattern to that seen in the main/extended sample data for individual parishes, and to avoid repetition only the latter is considered here, the supplementary results being reported in appendix 4.

The decade 1694–1705

In this decade each series yielded a first principal component with a clear seasonal pattern, although such a pattern was absent for the second and subsequent components (see figures 8.5 to 8.7). Slightly under half of the total variance among the child burial indices is accounted for by the first component, which has positive coefficients in late summer and autumn – especially August and September – and correspondingly negative values in the first four months of the year. The first component for adult burials accounts for only about a third of the variance and contrasts mortality between December and April with that from May to October. The total burials, by contrast, yield a first component explaining over half the overall variance and contrasting the months January–April with those from June to October.

8.5(b) *opposite* Scores. *Key to parishes*: 1 St Botolph Aldgate. 2 St Botolph Aldersgate. 3 St Bride's Fleet Street. 4 St Mary Magdalen's Bermondsey. 5 St Botolph Bishopsgate. 6 Christ Church Spitalfields. 7 Christ Church Surrey. 8 St Clement Dane. 9 St Giles Cripplegate. 10 St George in the East. 11 St George Hanover Square. 12 St Andrew Holborn. 13 St James Piccadilly. 14 St John Southwark. 15 St Mary Lambeth. 16 St Luke Middlesex. 17 St Margaret Westminster. 18 St Martin-in-the-Fields. 19 St Mary Newington Butts. 20 St Olave Southwark. 21 St Paul Covent Garden. 22 St Leonard Shoreditch. 23 St Anne Soho. 24 St Sepulchre Middlesex. 25 St Dunstan Stepney. 26 St Mary Whitechapel.

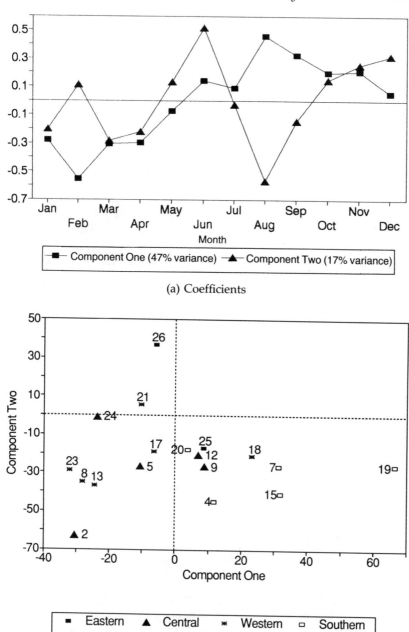

(a) Coefficients

8.5 Parish Register child burial seasonalities, 1695–1704: principal components analysis

Death and the metropolis

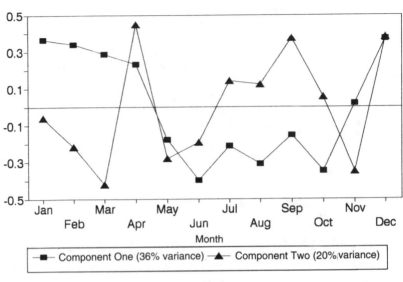

(a) Coefficients

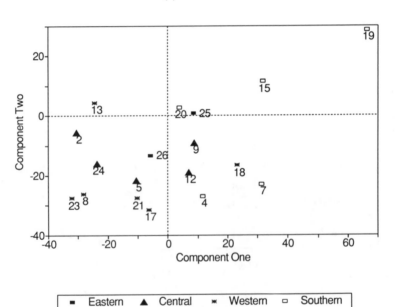

(b) Scores. For key to numbered parishes see p. 330.

8.6 Parish Register adult burial seasonalities, 1695–1704: principal components analysis

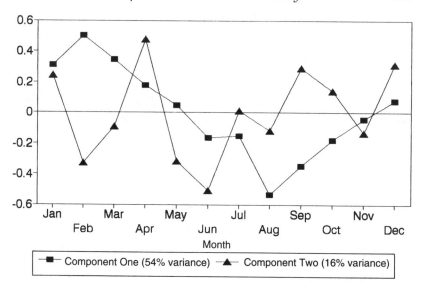

(a) Coefficients

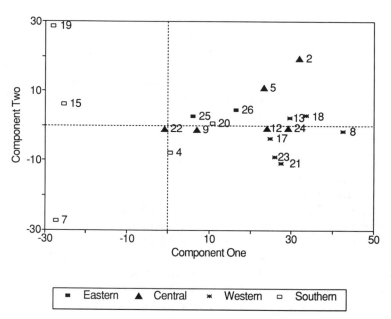

(b) Scores. For key to numbered parishes see p. 330.

8.7 Parish Register total burial seasonalities, 1695–1704: principal
components analysis

The figures also provide plots of scores for each parish on the first two principal components. The parishes have been split into four groups. Stepney and Whitechapel are paired up in 'east', whilst 'central' consists of the extra-mural City parishes including Holborn and St Sepulchres but excluding St Brides. The parishes from the latter to St Margaret's Westminster are included in 'west', and 'south' contains the parishes south of the river. In each case the scores for the first component reveal a degree of spatial clustering – those from the south and east, in particular, tending to diverge from the western parishes.

Where child burials are concerned, Whitechapel clusters with the western group, as do the central parishes apart from St Giles Cripplegate. The latter, like Stepney, falls closer to the southern parishes which form an elongated right hand 'tail' to the distribution. A similar tail of southern parishes is visible in the case of adult burials, and again it includes Stepney, although this time St Paul's Covent Garden also falls in the southern range.

The divergence of the eastern and southern parishes from the western group is particularly marked in the scores for the total burial series. Here the plot reveals three clusters. The southern parishes of Christ Church, Lambeth and St Mary Newington have particularly low scores, whilst St Olave's Southwark and Bermondsey form an intermediate cluster together with St Giles Cripplegate, Shoreditch (not included in the main sample for this period), and the eastern parishes. The remaining central parishes, and the western group, stand out with particularly high scores.

The decade 1750–9
In the second of the two decades, the child burial indices for individual parishes yielded a first component accounting for 42 per cent of the total variance, and a second for a further 21 per cent (see figure 8.8). The first of these had strong negative coefficients for the late summer and autumn, especially September and October, and positive coefficients for January and March, whilst the second had strong positive coefficients for the months from November to January. A plot of component scores shows no obvious spatial clustering on the second component, but there is a sharp divergence on component one with all of the western parishes having distinctly higher scores than those in the remaining groups.

The adult burial indices yield similar contrasts although they are less pronounced than those for the child burials. The first two components account for 31 and 23 per cent of the total variance, with the

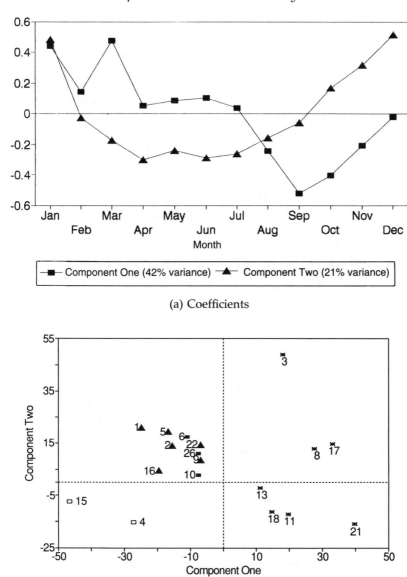

(a) Coefficients

(b) Scores. For key to numbered parishes see p. 330.

8.8 Parish Register child burial seasonalities, 1750–9: principal components analysis

coefficients on the first contrasting autumn mortality with that between April and June, and the second distinguishing between autumn and winter months (see figure 8.9). A plot of the component scores shows that the western parishes form a distinct group, with generally higher values for the winter and spring indices, but there is considerable overlap between groups in the scores on each component taken individually. We should note that St Giles Cripplegate now groups with the western parishes, whilst Aldersgate displays the 'eastern' pattern in an exaggerated form.

The results for the total burial series sharply differentiate the western parishes from the remaining groups. The first component accounts for 45 per cent of the variance and has strong negative coefficients for the autumn months (see figure 8.10). A plot of component scores shows a clear separation on this axis between the western parishes – together with Holborn – and the others, which have distinctly lower scores. A second component, with strong positive coefficients, for the months November–January accounts for a further 19 per cent of the variance, but again there is no evidence of systematic spatial clustering on this axis.

Conclusions

Most of the variation in burial seasonality, in both space and time, is to be found in the childhood ages. This is consistent with the hypothesis of varying patterns of infectious diseases, since it is at precisely these ages that the impact of 'new' diseases would be most apparent. The seasonality data suggest that the parishes north of the river fall roughly into two groups, with those from Holborn westward having a pattern quite distinct from the easterly parishes – a pattern characterised by the concentration of excess mortality in the winter and early spring. In the first of the two decades this excess is supplemented by a secondary peak in August, but the latter has entirely disappeared by the 1750s.

The seasonality of child mortality in the eastern parishes undergoes more far-reaching changes between the two decades. The initial pattern is dominated by a single August peak, but this is transformed by a substantial reduction in the August index – a reduction proportionately larger than that seen in the west – and a major rise in the figures for the last quarter. These indices also rise in the western parishes, but the increase is only appreciable in October and even here it is only about half that seen in the eastern and central parishes.

The pattern of seasonality observed south of the river is closer to that of the eastern than the western parishes, but the indices for

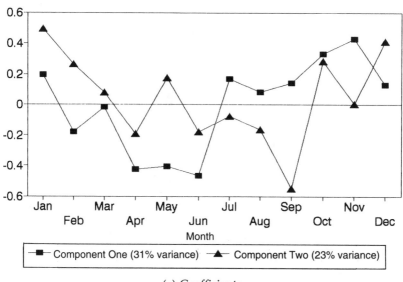

(a) Coefficients

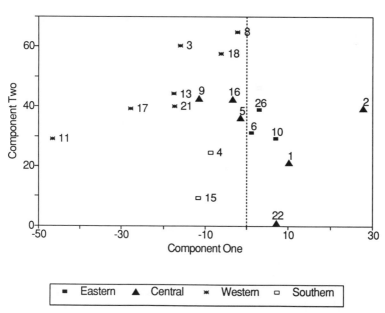

(b) Scores. For key to numbered parishes see p. 330.

8.9 Parish Register adult burial seasonalities, 1750–9: principal components analysis

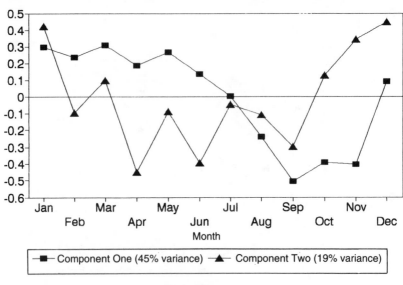

(a) Coefficients

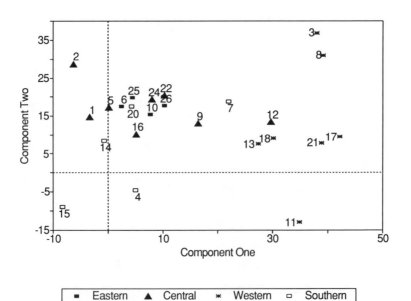

(b) Scores. For key to numbered parishes see p. 330.

8.10 Parish Register total burial seasonalities, 1750–9: principal components
analysis

August and September are generally higher than those among the former. If, as we have argued previously, seasonality variations reflect underlying differences in causes of death, then our findings imply increasing spatial heterogeneity in this regard over the first half of the eighteenth century.

The level of mortality

The investigation of spatial variation in mortality levels is hampered by the problem of differential under-registration of baptisms and burials which is likely to have varied between parishes. It is not feasible, in a study of this kind, to construct local correction factors, and – with certain specific exceptions – we have had to assume an equal level of relative baptism under-registration across the metropolitan parishes.[5] The unreality of this assumption means that results for individual parishes must be treated with caution, but comparisons between larger aggregates – comprising groups of parishes – are less likely to be seriously affected, and it is with this level of analysis that we shall chiefly be concerned. Our data are taken from the main and restricted samples for the decades 1695–1704 and 1750–9.

The decade 1695–1704
The first of the two decades furnished substantially more data than the second, particularly where the intramural parishes are concerned. The latter were pooled into three groups, each containing roughly equal numbers of baptisms, and ranked according to the ratio of recorded child burials to baptisms[6] (see table 8.11 lower panel). The extra-mural parishes were ranked in the same way, yielding the

---

[5] See appendix 1 for details of the dataset used in the analysis. The one adjustment made to the raw data was necessitated by the concentration of Huguenots in the district around Spitalfields which evidently depressed the level of Anglican baptism registration relative to that of burials. In order to deal with this, the baptism registers of the Huguenot chapels were aggregated and the totals added to the appropriate Anglican registers. The baptisms from Artillery, and from La Patente and St Jean Spitalfields, were added to the total for Christ Church Spitalfields (St Dunstan Stepney in 1695–1704). The largest chapel, Threadneedle Street, covered a bigger area, and its baptisms were allocated according to the distribution prevailing in 1700 (when the Threadneedle Street register gives residential information). 48% of the Threadneedle Street total was thus allocated to Spitalfields (or Stepney) and 23% to Shoreditch. The total additions were: 1695–1704 3,346 additional baptisms to Stepney, 1750–9 841 additional baptisms to Spitalfields and 187 to Shoreditch.

[6] It was also possible to conduct a limited analysis of socio-economic variations in the child burial baptism ratio between parishes using the proportions of 'substantial houses' recorded in the hearth tax data for 1695. For details see appendix 1.

Table 8.11. *Ratios of vital events: main Parish Register sample 1695–1704*

		Ratios			Burials of unknown age as % of total (assumed adult)
	N Baptisms	(1)	(2)	(3)	
Extra-mural parishes					
High mortality	33,614	0.76	0.58	0.76	6.9
Medium mortality	36,009	0.78	0.53	0.68	8.2
Low mortality	34,520	0.87	0.53	0.61	21.7
Intramural parishes					
High mortality	4,545	0.74	0.53	0.71	25.3
Medium mortality	4,073	0.93	0.54	0.58	19.9
Low mortality	4,112	1.06	0.46	0.44	32.6

Note: Key to ratios
  (1) Baptisms to burials
  (2) Child burials to total burials
  (3) Child burials to baptisms
See appendix 1 for composition of parish groups

results in the upper panel of table 8.11. The spread in the child burial to baptism ratio (CBBR) between the three groups is substantial – from 76 to 61 per cent – and is larger than that detected in the vital index. The 'medium group' of extra-mural parishes falls roughly half way between the 'high' and 'low' groups where the CBBR is concerned, although its vital index is close to that of the high mortality parishes.

The parish register data were also pooled into a number of geographically based 'regions' as shown in table 8.12. This grouping revealed substantial spatial variation in the CBBR – the eastern parishes having markedly higher levels than those in the intramural and west central groups. The remaining groups fell between these two extremes, with the southern parishes having somewhat lower levels than the remaining two. The spread of values between the three groups of intramural parishes is substantial. The high mortality groups have a CBBR equal to that of the eastern parishes, whilst the remaining two have a lower level than any outside the walls, and the low mortality group has a vital index above unity. In other respects the variation in vital indices generally reflects that in the CBBR.

The decade 1750–9
The proportion of parish registers furnishing the required informa-

Table 8.12. *Ratios of vital events by region: main Parish Register sample 1695–1704*

	N Baptisms	Ratios			Burials of unknown age as % of total (assumed adult)
		(1)	(2)	(3)	
Extra-mural parishes					
East	22,369	0.77	0.57	0.73	10.2
East Central	16,507	0.75	0.52	0.70	18.7
West Central	17,938	0.88	0.55	0.63	25.5
West	33,760	0.77	0.53	0.69	3.5
South	13,569	0.82	0.54	0.66	13.3
Intramural parishes	12,730	0.89	0.51	0.58	25.6

Note: Key to ratios
  (1) Baptisms to burials
  (2) Child burials to total burials
  (3) Child burials to baptisms

Parish grouping by 'regions' 1695–1704
East: SS Dunstan Stepney and Mary Whitechapel. *East Central*: SS Botolph Aldgate, Botolph Bishopsgate, Giles Cripplegate and Botolph Aldersgate. *West Central*: SS James Clerkenwell, Sepulchre Middlesex and Andrew Holborn. *West*: SS Clement Dane, Paul Covent Garden, Ann Soho, James Piccadilly, Martin-in-the-Fields, Margaret Westminster. *South*: SS Olave Southwark, Mary Magdalen Bermondsey, Mary Lambeth, Christ Church Surrey and Mary Newington Butts.

tion is smaller in the second of our two decades, although the number of data points rises due to the division of some larger parishes. In this decade the intramural parishes are weakly represented, and a substantial proportion of the recorded events are contributed by a single one – St Anne's Blackfriars. We have thus treated the latter individually, pooling the data for the others into a single group.

The results in table 8.13 contrast strikingly with those for the earlier decade. The spread of CBBRs has increased considerably, since the amelioration in child mortality is effectively confined to the low and medium groups, and the value for the high mortality regions is almost exactly equal to that obtained in 1695–1704. The ratio of high to low values has increased from 1.29 to 1.68. The divergence in vital indices is even more dramatic since the figure for the high mortality parishes actually declines by some 15 per cent of its former value, whilst the remaining two show modest increases.

The geographical coverage of the 1750–9 sample is more restricted

Table 8.13. *Ratios of vital events: main Parish Register sample 1750–9*

| | N Baptisms | Ratios | | | Burials of unknown age as % of total (assumed adult) |
		(1)	(2)	(3)	
High mortality parishes	24,743	64.4	48.1	74.7	15.7
Medium mortality parishes	27,906	85.2	48.5	56.9	9.1
Low mortality parishes	28,452	94.1	41.7	44.4	18.3

Note: Key to ratios
  (1) Baptisms to burials
  (2) Child burials to total burials
  (3) Child burials to baptisms
See appendix 1 for composition of parish groups

Table 8.14. *Ratios of vital events by region: main Parish Register sample 1750–9*

| | N Baptisms | Ratios | | | Burials of unknown age as % of total (assumed adult) |
		(1)	(2)	(3)	
Intramural	3,928	1.33	0.38	0.50	21.3
East	14,980	1.29	0.46	0.60	6.9
East Central	19,936	1.40	0.50	0.70	3.6
West	35,487	1.15	0.45	0.52	20.4
South	6,750	1.23	0.43	0.53	34.2

Note: Key to ratios
  (1) Baptisms to burials
  (2) Child burials to total burials
  (3) Child burials to baptisms

Parish grouping by 'regions' 1750–9
Intramural: St Anne Blackfriars, all other intramural (see Appendix 1 for details). *East*: SS Mary Whitechapel, George in the East and Christ Church Spitalfields. *East Central*: SS Leonard Shoreditch, Luke Old Street, Botolph Bishopsgate, Giles Cripplegate and Botolph Aldersgate. *West*: SS Bride Fleet Street, Clement Dane, George Hanover Square, Paul Covent Garden, James Piccadilly, Martin-in-the-Fields, Margaret Westminster. *South*: SS Mary Magdalen Bermondsey, Mary Lambeth.

than that for 1695–1704 (see table 8.14). The west central group is entirely unrepresented, and the southern group comprises only Bermondsey and Lambeth, but our data nonetheless reveal a clear spatial pattern. The east central parishes combine an almost unchanged CBBR with a slightly lower vital index, whilst the west and south both show substantial improvement – the CBBR falling by about one third of its original value. The behaviour of the eastern parishes is intermediate and combines a stationary vital index with a reduction of some 13 per cent in the CBBR. The CBBR of the intramural parishes is effectively unchanged, whilst the vital index falls appreciably, but the composition of the sample changes so much between the two decades that this behaviour is difficult to interpret.

Conclusions

The seasonality of burials in London varied substantially both in space and time, a variation which we have interpreted in terms of underlying differences in causes of death. If this is correct then we should expect parishes with different mortality levels also to display differences in their burial seasonality. In order to test this expectation the main sample parishes for each of the two decades were pooled into three groups, ranked according to their CBBR. MBIs were then constructed for each group, and a chi-squared statistic calculated from the 3×12 contingency tables of monthly burial totals.

The results in table 8.15 reveal highly significant results in each case although – as we might expect – the precise seasonality differences between high and low mortality parishes vary over time. In the first decade these lie mainly in the ratio of summer to winter burials – the high mortality parishes having, in particular, a much larger August peak than do those with low mortality – whereas in 1750–9 the two groups differ most in the proportion of autumn burials, especially those in October. This suggests that the high mortality of the north-eastern parishes and – to some extent – those in the East End reflected an infection, or set of infections, with a pronounced autumn peak. If our argument is correct, then this effect should be particularly marked in early childhood, when the pathogens responsible were first encountered and the specific risks and protections of infancy left behind.

We are fortunate that three of the parishes from the region in question provide age information for child burials throughout the 1750s, and in figure 8.11 we plot the resulting burial indices for three childhood age-groups, expressed as a proportion of the correspond-

Table 8.15. *Parish Register child burial seasonality indices for parishes grouped by mortality level*

	1695–1704			1750–9		
	High	Medium	Low	High	Medium	Low
Jan	94	103	96	106	98	106
Feb	103	108	109	99	107	108
Mar	103	111	107	106	104	113
Apr	100	105	106	98	104	104
May	103	103	103	102	98	101
Jun	92	88	89	94	90	94
Jul	100	99	99	89	93	94
Aug	125	119	113	93	96	96
Sep	107	105	109	97	107	93
Oct	92	84	88	111	108	95
Nov	89	86	89	102	96	93
Dec	92	91	92	103	101	102
$(1)^a$	23,894	26,162	19,359	17,160	15,866	11,488
$(2)^b$	0.762	0.676	0.532	0.746	0.569	0.446

Chi squared
1695–1704   49.1   (p <0.001)
1750–9   53.9   (p <0.001)

Note: [a]Total recorded child burials
[b]Ratio of child burials to baptisms

ing index derived from the Bills of Mortality. The seasonality of burials in the 0–1 year age-group differs little from that prevailing in London as a whole, but there is a considerable divergence in the age-group 2–4 years where the October index is nearly 40 per cent above the Bills' figure.

Conclusion

The study of spatial variations in mortality is greatly hampered by the 'coarse-grained' character of the geographical divisions. The units vary greatly in size, and they do not always correspond to 'natural' ecological or socio-economic entities. This is particularly the case for the City within the walls, but it is also true of west London where newly developed aristocratic areas might lie in close proximity to the older and less salubrious parts of Westminster and St Martin's-in-the-Fields.

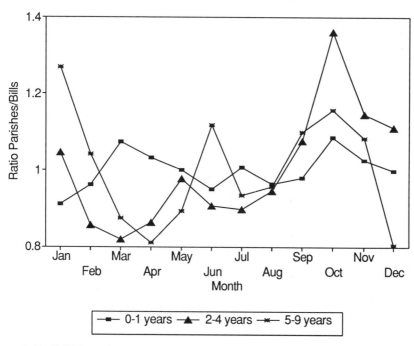

8.11 Child burial seasonality in three N.E. London parishes: as ratio to
seasonality in London Bills

Nonetheless, the results provide clear evidence of substantial
geographical variation in London's epidemiological regime over our
period, and of a structure which seems to have crystallised during the
decades of demographic–economic stagnation and high mortality.
The pattern evidently changed again in the later eighteenth, and early
nineteenth centuries, with suggestions of an emerging 'core-
periphery' opposition – mortality being higher in the latter. The
material from this period is, however, harder to interpret, as the area
documented no longer corresponds to the built-up area as a whole,
and we are seeing only a section – albeit a very large one – of a wider
metropolitan system.

The easiest dimension of mortality to study is that of short-run
instability, and here we identified a 'high-instability belt' of districts
running around the walls from Stepney westwards to St Giles, and
corresponding roughly to the 'artisanal' belt identified by Spate
(1936). This area experienced a number of 'regional' mortality peaks,
in years which did not qualify as such in the metropolitan burial
series. It also tended to be worst affected in metropolitan peak years,

but what really distinguished such years was the ability of mortality waves to break into parts of the East End, Southwark and Westminster.

The cause of death data suggest that the behaviour of the 'high-instability' districts was closely linked to movements in smallpox burials, and it is smallpox – according to the global data – which increased most during the 'regional' crises. Our principal components analysis suggested that this disease was implicated in two distinct sets of epidemiological relationships, and these seem to have borne unequally on different parts of the metropolis. The first – particularly affecting the four western districts – apparently involved childhood mortality from infancy to the age of ten, the age-range during which London-born children seem to have been first exposed to smallpox.

In principle, the childhood domination of short-run movements in burial totals could imply either that these were more volatile – relative to adult burials – in the western districts, or that the latters' totals included unusually large numbers of children. The second of these possibilities is, however, contradicted by the parish register data, and it seems safe to attribute the pattern to 'genuine' spatial differences in the relative volatility of burial totals by age.

The high-instability districts have intermediate scores on this component, but are distinguished by those on a second component, whose influence apparently runs from age two into the teenage years, and then – with progressively weaker effects – into the twenties and thirties. It seems reasonable to attribute this age-incidence to the presence of substantial numbers of non-immune adolescent and young adult immigrants in these districts, and there is also an approximate – though only an approximate – correspondence between the latter and those districts which displayed the clearest associations between burials and prices.

The geography of fever mortality appears to have changed the most over our period, but in the central decades of the eighteenth century it was particularly associated with the districts to the east and south of the high-instability belt, together with the belt itself. Movements in burial totals for the former districts – in the east and south – are less strongly related to those in the smallpox series. Consumption appears to be more important here, and it is apparently movements in adult burials which dominate the district totals. The districts in the high-instability belt itself seem to be strongly affected both by fever and smallpox mortality.

The fragmentary data we were able to assemble on mortality levels suggests an appreciable differential had developed by the 1750s. Mortality in a number of western parishes was much lower than elsewhere, whilst a number of parishes in the high-instability belt experienced exceptionally severe mortality. A clear association had also developed between the level and seasonality of mortality. The decline in the summer mortality peak seems to have been general throughout London, but the development of the autumn excess was spatially uneven. Apparently absent from the western parishes, it was manifested in a much more pronounced form in the north-east than elsewhere. Differences in the magnitude of this new autumn peak seem to explain much of the geographical variation in levels of childhood mortality.

Summary

The peculiar trend of London's mortality in the early eighteenth century was linked to a shift in its seasonal pattern, as autumn and winter levels rose sufficiently to – at least – offset the effects of an amelioration in high summer. This evidently reflected a change in the underlying cause of death structure, one element of which was the decline of an old-established gastric disease, or group of diseases. The latter seems also to have occurred in populations outside London, and so should probably not be attributed to structural change in the epidemiological regime of the capital. Climatic change might, in principle, be responsible, but the temperature sensitivity of the burial series most affected changed in a way inconsistent with the most obvious mechanism by which such an effect might have occurred, and at this stage in our knowledge spontaneous pathogenic change remains the most plausible explanation.

The early eighteenth century saw an increase in mortality from such cold weather diseases as the respiratory infections and tuberculosis, but particularly from typhus which may – at least in its louse-borne form – have been a relatively 'new' disease at this time. Smallpox mortality also rose in the early eighteenth century, but this increase too seems to have been greatest in the cooler months of the year. The Bills' burial series show substantial declines in both small-pox and fever deaths towards the end of the eighteenth century, and the seasonality data are consistent with a reduction in mortality from typhus and – possibly – respiratory tuberculosis, at this time.

Deaths in the bronchitis/influenza/pneumonia group seem to have undergone a corresponding relative increase – supporting Kunitz's interpretation (1983; 1987) of the relative importance of exposure and resistance variables in the process of mortality decline. The growing sensitivity of mortality to prices in the winter months is also consistent with an 'exposure' – rather than a 'resistance' – model of mortality decline, although we should note that typhoid mortality may have risen in the early nineteenth century.

The seasonality of mortality in the central decades of the eighteenth century was complicated by the appearance of a new condition with a marked autumn seasonality, and probably associated with a streptococcal infection spreading on a global scale in the late 1730s. The initial wave of epidemic mortality may have been fairly evenly spread across London, but the longer-term retention of pathogens was not. The evidence from the 1750s suggests that the disease remained endemic – in a severe form – in certain north-eastern parishes, but may have disappeared altogether from parts of the West End by this time. This geographical segmentation in London's epidemiological regime was, however, only part of a broader pattern of spatial differentiation which emerged strongly in the central decades of the eighteenth century.

The westerly districts of the capital seem – in certain parishes at least – to have had lower levels of mortality combined with a pattern of short-run instability dominated by childhood smallpox and by deaths in the youngest age-group. By contrast, smallpox appears to have been less important in Southwark and the East End, where correlations with deaths from consumption, fevers, and those at adult ages were more in evidence. The latter categories – especially fever – were also important in the 'high-instability' extra-mural parishes as well, but these parishes displayed a strong relationship with smallpox burials.

The age-ranges affected, however, differed from those in the west. Burials under two years of age were not implicated by the results of the principal components analysis, but the strongest relationships were observed in the 2–19 year age-group with younger adults also affected. The evidence suggests that most – if not all – of the latter would have been immigrants, and it is likely that the epidemiology of the high-instability districts was powerfully influenced by immigration. Mortality in these districts was unusually sensitive to price fluctuations – and to economic and social dislocation – as were the global smallpox figures, and it is likely that much of the latter's behaviour can be attributed to the epidemiological structure of the high-instability belt.

The mechanisms underlying the relationship between smallpox

and socio-economic stress will have involved some combination of heightened exposure to infection, and compositional changes with regard to the immunological resistance of the population. The link between demobilisation and smallpox outbreaks is evidence of the important role played by the second of these factors, but the age- and sex-specific data reveal that mortality also rose among women and children, implying an increase in the level of exposure to infection. The latter could come about – through increased conduction – in at least two ways. Economic stress – reinforced by immigration – may have led to enforced reductions in living space and thus to an increase in effective population densities. At the same time the rise in the proportion of non-immune individuals would have heightened conduction still more by providing additional channels for the smallpox virus to move through the population.

Our data suggest that processes of this kind were particularly effective in a region of the metropolis which apparently housed disproportionate numbers of recent immigrants. This 'high-instability belt' of inner suburban parishes experienced numerous smallpox outbreaks in response to a range of socio-economic shocks, but the occurrence of a major mortality wave in London as a whole depended on its success in 'breaking out' of the belt into adjacent areas such as Westminster, Southwark, and the East End. The factors determining this outcome were, no doubt, complex, but it is illuminating to consider the role of fever mortality.

Like smallpox mortality, mortality from fever showed a sensitivity to both prices and socio-economic shocks, but this appears to have taken the form of a threshold relationship and to have been somewhat 'lagged'. This may simply have been due to typhus being less infectious than smallpox, but it is likely that some of the divergence reflects underlying differences in the socio-economic and demographic mechanisms of transmission. In particular, the much closer association of typhus with destitution suggests that its spread involved a partial breakdown in the collective arrangements by which English communities – whether urban or rural – dealt with economic hardship, in a way that was not necessarily true of smallpox.

This could explain both the threshold and lag effects in terms of the ability of such arrangements to cope satisfactorily up to a certain point, and their eventual collapse in the face of unusually protracted and/or severe stress. The capital's epidemiological regime itself also seems – at the risk of anthropomorphism – to have been able to 'cope' by containing mortality waves in certain districts, but under extreme circumstances these barriers collapsed and – as in 1741 – the wave of fever mortality penetrated further afield. The responsiveness of smallpox to such circumstances apparently declined in the latter part of our period, and although that of fever mortality continued, its absolute level waned to the point at which epidemics could no longer disturb the functioning of London's demographic regime.

9

Conclusion

He who seeks conclusiveness should flee from British economic history in the
eighteenth century.   (Crafts 1981: 12)

The aim of this study has been to comprehend the structure and
dynamics of London's epidemiological regime within the framework
of intermediate variables established in chapter 1. As such, the main
lines of our conclusions emerge from the individual chapters and
sections, but at this point we must say something about two issues
which have not been directly addressed in the course of the text.
These are, first of all, the problem of mortality decline, and, secondly,
the factors ultimately determining both this latter process and the
epidemiological regime prevailing during the earlier period of very
high mortality.

The measurement of mortality levels in London is beset with too
many difficulties for any very confident statements to be made either
about its absolute level at any time, or about the precise timing of
turning points in the secular trend. But what is clear is that mortality
in the second quarter of the eighteenth century was very much higher
than it had become by the early years of civil registration. Early
eighteenth-century infant mortality was at least double the rate
prevailing in the 1840s, and the gap between London and contemporary communities elsewhere in England was of a similar order of
magnitude.

Infant mortality rates of this order were not of course unknown in
pre-transitional western Europe, being equalled in communities prac-
tising artificial feeding. But such communities generally displayed
relatively moderate levels of child mortality,[1] and this was definitely

---

[1] This is visible particularly in the results of Knodel's German village studies; see
Knodel 1988.

not true of eighteenth-century London. In fact the 'metropolitan penalty'[2] appears to have been greater in childhood than it was at other ages, but the limited information we could obtain on adult mortality suggested that death rates over the age of thirty differed much less between London and populations elsewhere.

This age-pattern of mortality provides a good fit to the high potential model of metropolitan epidemiology and underlines the importance of endemic infections. But it would be wrong to see London's mortality regime in too static a light, for substantial changes had already occurred well before the general 'mortality transition' of the later nineteenth century. Finlay's work (1978; 1981) also suggests that mortality had increased considerably between the early seventeenth century and the second quarter of the eighteenth. The chronology of this increase cannot be resolved with certainty. It may have been substantially complete by 1700, but it seems more likely that it continued into the early decades of the eighteenth century.

In any case, it is clear that these decades saw a divergence between London and other parts of the country – where mortality was improving – in the pattern of mortality experienced in the cold weather months of the year. This involved mortality from a number of conditions, but typhus is likely to have been of particular importance, and the early eighteenth-century increase in smallpox mortality also seems to have been at its worst between the months of December and May. These two diseases were, in turn, both especially implicated in the secular decline of mortality from the last years of the eighteenth century.

Some reduction in mortality levels is evident in the third quarter of the eighteenth century, but this appears to have been only a limited 'recovery' well within the range of earlier levels, and the main secular decline seems to have occurred in the half century or so after 1770. If we are to understand the reasons for this decline it is, of course, necessary to understand the earlier increase and the plateau of high mortality to which it gave rise.

We saw in chapter 1 that changes in mortality could arise from either of two sets of factors, The first of these relates to changes in the pathogenic load, as a result either of mutation or of the introduction of new strains of infectious agent. Of the diseases whose severity increased in the early decades of the eighteenth century, only typhus

---

[2] See Kearns 1988 for a discussion of the 'urban penalty' and its importance for national mortality estimates in eighteenth- and nineteenth-century England.

has any claim to be considered a 'new disease' and it may be that increased trading links, together with military action, allowed it to spread from its central European cradle.

The remaining infections are likely to have been relatively long established by the early eighteenth century, and although it is theoretically possible that new and more virulent strains arose at this time, such an explanation will hardly serve to explain the divergence between London and the rest of England. If this is to be explained we must look to the determinants of mortality potential, and in this connection – as we have indicated at a number of points in our text – the investigation of exposure potential looks more promising than does that of nutritionally based resistance.

The implication of this argument is that the environment of early eighteenth-century London deteriorated in such a way as to facilitate the transmission and retention of pathogens among its inhabitants. A deterioration of this kind needs to be considered in the light of the secular economic stagnation detectable in many of the available series for mid-eighteenth-century London – particularly that for housing. Population growth appears virtually to have ceased in the fourth and fifth decades of the century, and the numbers in 1750 probably exceeded those of 1730 by fewer than 3 per cent. The annual numbers of burials ran at an average of 25,750 from 1725 to 1749, as against 26,500 in the ten years (1715–24) before the crisis of the later 1720s.

A full explanation of this stagnation lies outside the limits of the present study, but there are some hints available in the relevant literature, in particular the important part played by luxury production, and the spending of landed income, in the economic life of the city. The period of stagnation corresponded fairly closely with that of low prices for agricultural products, and it is possible that the high real wages of the period were obtained at the expense of a fall in the demand for non-subsistence products, a slow down in economic activity, and a consequent decline in earnings for many Londoners.[3]

Whatever the explanation, however, it is clear that activity in the construction sector fell to a very low level for much of the central decades of the eighteenth century. At issue, of course, is whether such activity as continued was sufficient to meet the extent of either need or demand. Posed in these terms, the question is unanswerable with the data at our disposal – and it may be that adequate material

---

[3] Demographic stagnation, once it had set in, may itself also have intensified and prolonged the recession by reducing the volume of domestic demand.

for a detailed study does not exist – but is also somewhat unreal, for it neglects the complexity of the processes by which housing needs were met for the bulk of the population.

Accommodation – with the possible exception of parts of East London – was found not in purpose-built housing, but by a process of 'internal colonisation' with houses being divided and sub-divided as they were left behind in the westward movement of the elite and the 'middling sort'. When geographical expansion ceased, the sources of additional housing would have dried up, and the situation may well have been further worsened by the fact that much of the construction that did take place comprised the conversion of residential accommodation into warehousing. The literature suggests that many buildings were in a chronically poor state of repair and thus in need of continual maintenance. It seems unlikely that much investment was forthcoming for such a purpose in these decades and more probable that much of the housing stock decayed to the condition where it was fit only for 'such as pay no rent'. The available accommodation is thus likely to have declined in both quality and quantity – which may go far to explain the lethal impact of the price shock of the early 1740s.

These years also saw the development of geographical segmentation within London's epidemiological regime, with the emergence of a recognisably 'healthy district' in the west and a zone of unusually severe mortality around the northern edge of the intramural parishes. Mortality in this zone was not only particularly high but unusually volatile from year to year, a phenomenon that probably reflected the effects of smallpox among young adult immigrants and displayed a sensitivity to price movements. This 'high-instability belt' also seems to have been particularly affected by fever mortality, and it is likely that its demographic characteristics were heavily influenced by high levels of adolescent and young adult immigration. By contrast, burial totals in the East End, and the districts south of the river seem to have been more closely associated with movements in consumption and fever burials at older adult ages and it is possible that migration into these districts was more restricted and of a different character.[4]

The decline of mortality was associated particularly with neonatal mortality and mortality among older children, adolescents and young adults with fever and smallpox being prominent among the causes of death that declined. Although the conditions responsible for the

---

[4] In this connection it is interesting to note the close resemblance between our 'high-instability belt' and the 'artisan and industrial' zone delineated in Spate's analysis of the occupational geography of mid-eighteenth-century London (see Spate 1936: 534–6).

former cannot be identified with certainty, the decline of typhus is likely to have been pre-eminent, whilst typhoid mortality probably increased. At the same time as mortality fell, the era of economic stagnation ended decisively, and both the geographical extent and the population of the metropolis entered a new phase of expansion.

This was, of course, only a part of the broader expansion in population and economy at this time, but London's experience differed qualitatively from that of the most rapidly growing regions. If England ever had an 'industrial revolution', then London, it has been asserted, was not a part of it, being present, in Braudel's (1981) phrase, only 'as a spectator'. The true extent of London's 'de-industrialisation' at this time is as we have seen, uncertain, but it cannot be doubted that some activities were lost to the countryside and the growing towns of the north.[5]

The late eighteenth-century growth was thus associated with restructuring of the economy – although the identity of the expanding sector is unclear – and there are other signs of structural change. One of these concerns credit and finance. The problems of finance and the under-capitalisation of construction were an important theme of chapter 2, and it is possible that these were ameliorated by the growing integration of financial networks detected by Hoppitt (1987). On a national scale this came at the price of a new vulnerability to major financial crises, but the latter had long been familiar in London, and it may be that here the benefits of the new system outweighed its disadvantages.

If our analysis of housing conditions in mid-eighteenth-century London is correct, then the combination of renewed metropolitan growth and a degree of financial 'modernisation', should have alleviated some of the earlier problems and correspondingly reduced the degree of conduction and retention prevailing in the capital's epidemiological regime. The latter would have contributed to the reduction of smallpox mortality, but in this case immunological resistance is also likely to have played an important part. As we saw in chapter 3, the age-incidence of smallpox deaths seems to have shifted in the later eighteenth century – with fewer casualties in the 'teens and above – just as its responsiveness to price shocks and other disturbances also waned.

---

[5] The effects of the later eighteenth-century 'flight of production' on mortality are likely to have been complex. Whilst the loss of occupations, particularly in textiles, may have aggravated the economic insecurity of the poor it is also probable that the decline in the numbers of overcrowded workshops represented a significant reduction in an important source of exposure to infection.

The latter may have reflected a national shift in migration patterns, as other urban centres arose to form competing poles of attraction, but the growth of general inoculation in the migrants' areas of origin is also likely to have been significant. The practice of inoculation in the capital itself may have reduced mortality among London-born children, but the evidence on this point is insufficient for any definite conclusions to be reached. What does seem very likely, however, is that the decline of smallpox yielded further benefits in the shape of reduced mortality from other diseases.[6]

The reduction of typhus mortality is most likely to be explained in terms of reduced exposure to infection. Developments in the fields of housing and migration are likely to have played an important part here, as they did in the case of smallpox,[7] but the classical explanation offered by Chambers (1972: 102–6) retains much of its validity. The increased availability of cotton cloth is said to have brought a fall in the price of clothing but also enabled clothes to be boiled and lice to be eradicated. The extent to which such clothes actually were boiled, of course, is unclear,[8] and it would be unwise to take all of Place's (Razzell 1974) assertions on this point at face value – his claims for the improved physique of slum children (George 1966: 68–71), for instance, receive only equivocal support from the findings of Floud and his colleagues (1990) – but the potential for reducing mortality in this way was demonstrated by contemporary naval medicine (Mathias 1979).

The latter question brings us to the broader issue of the 'role of medicine' in eighteenth-century mortality decline. This has been held in low esteem since McKeown's (McKeown and Brown 1955) savaging of the claims of Buer (1926) and Griffith (1926), but we have already seen how medical activity – broadly interpreted – could have

[6] Any large-scale effects of inoculation in London are likely to have accrued through changes in the immunological status of immigrants, since Razzell (1977: 72–4) found little evidence for its practice among the population as a whole before the end of the eighteenth century. The 'knock-on' benefits of smallpox decline are stressed by Mercer (1985; 1990: chapter 3).

[7] The causal mechanisms linking migration to mortality will, however, have differed in the cases of smallpox and typhus since the characteristic relationship between migratory and immunological status was effectively confined to the former. Where typhus is concerned the important variable is likely to have been the volume of impoverished subsistence migrants, who experienced greater risks of being exposed to, and of transmitting, the infection once in London and may also have been infected on arrival (see Luckin 1984; Hardy 1988).

[8] The relationship between women's work, the domestic division of labour, and mortality decline has been little studied, except in the context of infant care and feeding, but is likely to prove of fundamental importance for the understanding both of dietary change and variations in the level of exposure to infection.

contributed to the decline of infant mortality,[9] and the effect of inoculation may also have been substantial. Similarly, the role of medical propaganda in favour of hygiene and ventilation should not be discounted. Typhus in particular, together with the fly-borne diseases and, possibly, respiratory tuberculosis, could have responded strongly to the measures advocated by contemporary medical propagandists, and it is clear that, where the totalitarian context of military and naval life enabled these to be enforced, substantial mortality gains accrued.[10]

It thus seems likely that the story of mortality decline in London was chiefly one of a general decline in levels of exposure to infection, with an important, specific, contribution being made by changes in methods of infant care and feeding. The decline in exposure was brought about by a range of factors which have yet to be fully elucidated, but they probably comprised a number of the traditional 'industrial revolution' variables, including changes in consumption patterns and the position of the capital in the national urban hierarchy, as well as the action of members of the medical profession. At the same time, however, the phenomenon should not be viewed wholly as a 'once for all' break with past experience. It occurred from a level which was itself unusually high by the standards of the preceding century, and stemmed in part from the structural characteristics of contemporary economy and finance. In this sense, the political economy of London's mortality in the Whig decades forms the essential context to an understanding of its subsequent decline.

---

[9] Fildes (1980; 1986: 81–97) stressed the importance of changing medical opinions in promoting neonatal breast-feeding and thus reducing mortality. Arguments of this kind are often difficult to accept because of the strictly limited influence which 'leading edge' medical opinion and practice are likely to have had among the population. In London, however, the position is rather different, for Fildes is able to argue that the activities of the Lying-in hospital provided a means by which the new ideas could spread among the 'respectable poor' – both directly and by example. Alongside this channel of influence, the 'overcrowding' of the London medical profession at the end of the eighteenth century (Loudon, 1986: chapter 10) meant that practitioners had to seek their livelihoods through a wider range of activities, and among a wider social range of patients, than might have been the case elsewhere. As Kunitz (1991) points out, propaganda for improvements in infant feeding and domestic hygiene fall outside McKeown's implicit model of medical practice, but must form an important element of any 'medical contribution' to mortality decline.

[10] See Mathias 1979 for a general review of the accomplishments of contemporary military and naval medicine. The most dramatic illustration of what could be achieved under fully 'controlled' conditions is provided by the experience of Australian convict voyages following the reforms of 1814. Here ship-board mortality was reduced by a factor of eight after the introduction of a strict hygienic regime under qualified medical supervision; see Shlomowitz 1989 for a detailed statistical analysis of the available data.

Appendix 1

The Parish Register sample

Parishes grouped by child burial: baptism ratio

1695–1704

Extra-mural parishes	Burials			Baptisms
	Total	Child	Adult	
High mortality				
St Giles Cripplegate	11,124	6,182	4,655	7,779
St Anne Soho	4,499	2,454	2,045	3,133
St Botolph Bishopsgate	5,008	2,819	2,035	3,612
St Dunstan Stepney	21,112	12,439	6,519	16,750
St Mary Lambeth	2,687	1,722	495	2,340
Medium mortality				
St Botolph Aldersgate	2,208	1,148	287	1,616
St Paul Covent Garden	1,976	1,076	329	1,522
St James Piccadilly	9,207	5,231	3,952	7,412
St Mary Newington Butts	1,948	1,021	271	1,493
St Mary Whitechapel	7,617	3,805	3,037	5,619
St Dunstan Stepney	8,166	3,726	4,141	5,508
Christ Church Surrey	1,505	859	540	1,278
St Martin's-in-the-Fields	13,695	7,493	5,624	11,561
Low mortality				
St Olave Southwark	6,429	3,347	3,082	5,226
St Sepulchre Middlesex	5,880	3,306	693	5,166
St Mary Magdalen Bermondsey	3,979	2,056	960	3,232
St Andrew Holborn	9,414	5,169	1,751	8,202
St James Clerkenwell	3,327	1,775	1,178	2,954
St Botolph Aldgate	6,029	2,976	143	5,116
St Clement Dane	4,620	2,483	2,137	4,624

Intramural parishes	Burials			Baptisms
	Total	Child	Adult	
High mortality				
Allhallows Bread Street	171	90	58	86
St Andrew by the Wardrobe	676	438	172	534
St Benet Paul's Wharf	458	239	44	382
St Edmund Lombard Street	260	151	45	200
St Katherine Cree	647	339	148	486
St Lawrence Pountney	164	96	48	148
St Magnus the Martyr	513	304	30	386
St Margaret Pattens	161	81	25	101
St Mary Aldermary	253	132	76	190
St Michael-Crooked Lane	230	109	58	176
St Matthew Friday Street	228	124	63	174
St Michael Queenhithe	386	189	124	248
St Mildred Bread Street	180	99	44	117
St Stephen Coleman Street	1,307	548	251	885
St Vedast Foster Lane	310	172	118	259
Trinity the Less	184	108	52	73
Medium mortality				
Allhallows Honey Lane	318	189	109	327
St Alban Wood Street	240	129	95	243
St Andrew Undershaft	411	185	139	354
St Anne Blackfriars	1,205	748	108	1,211
St Benet Fink	204	98	44	163
St Helen Bishopsgate	321	136	84	260
St Katherine Coleman	482	254	166	457
St Mary Woolnoth	348	164	167	298
St Michael Le Querne	157	96	55	162
St Michael Pattens	182	87	28	147
St Peter Cornhill	320	170	137	285
St Peter Paul's Wharf	188	101	18	166
Low mortality				
St Anne Aldersgate	404	128	88	318
St Dionis Backchurch	353	198	131	550
St Ethelburga	290	108	115	229
St Faith	456	180	85	502
St Gabriel Fenchurch Street	95	54	16	132
St Gregory by St Paul	744	334	114	770
St Martin Pommeroy	59	30	17	67
St Martin Vintry	281	173	40	370
St Mary Abchurch	246	130	66	272
St Michael Bassishaw	282	136	38	261
St Olave Jewry	141	64	26	130
St Swithin	282	131	73	263
Trinity Minories	243	127	9	248

Appendix 1. *(Contd.)*

1750–9

| | Burials | | | |
All parishes	Total	Child	Adult	Baptisms
High mortality				
St Botolph Aldersgate	2,076	1,149	89	1,111
St Luke Middlesex	9,825	4,926	4,899	5,087
St Anne Blackfriars	1,133	619	503	808
Christ Church Spitalfields	5,669	2,811	2,775	3,802
St Paul Covent Garden	2,194	833	673	1,206
St Margaret Westminster	8,031	3,645	0	5,477
St Mary Whitechapel	9,459	4,483	4,939	7,232
Medium mortality				
St Martin's-in-the-Fields	8,535	4,411	4,124	7,418
St Leonard Shoreditch	7,853	3,875	3,883	6,602
St Botolph Bishopsgate	3,916	2,067	1,836	3,624
St Giles Cripplegate	4,154	1,940	2,166	3,512
St Mary Magdalen Bermondsey	4,241	1,931	1,396	3,603
St Mary Lambeth	4,036	1,642	478	3,147
Low mortality				
St James Piccadilly	10,011	4,441	4,650	8,850
St George Hanover Square	7,102	3,374	3,604	6,864
Intramural Parishes	4,076	1,340	1,639	3,120
St George in the East	4,246	1,687	1,343	3,946
St Bride Fleet Street	1,643	575	856	1,654
St Clement Dane	3,165	1,209	0	4,018

| | Burials | | | |
Intramural parishes	Total	Child	Adult	Baptisms
St Katherine Coleman	347	173	160	236
St Michael Queenhithe	218	107	110	168
St Mary Mountshaw	128	60	28	121
St Mary Somerset	239	107	97	124
Trinity the Less	142	63	77	84
St Gregory by St Paul	1,665	288	82	426
St Edmund Lombard Street	106	44	9	66
St James Duke's Place	152	62	86	67
St Michael Le Querne	50	20	0	66
St Michael Bassishaw	233	92	134	160
St Olave Silver Street	215	81	25	216
St Vedast	213	80	20	196
St Nicholas Acon	32	12	1	62

Appendix 1. *(Contd.)*

All parishes	Burials			Baptisms
	Total	Child	Adult	
St Peter Paul's Wharf	177	63	4	155
St Mary Abchurch	134	47	87	149
St Alban Wood Street	208	72	2	185
St Margaret Pattens	66	22	9	53
St Benet Sherehog	111	37	72	91
St Andrew by the Wardrobe	480	157	316	304
St Mary Wood Street	160	52	21	191

The construction of 'child' burial totals

'Child' burial totals were identified as those in which the term 'son', 'daughter', 'child' or 'infant' appeared in the register, whereas 'adults' were those with an occupational or residential 'addition', or who were described as a wife or widow. This raises obvious difficulties of interpretation. In particular, it is unclear exactly at what age individuals ceased to be described as 'children', and local practice may have varied somewhat. Such uncertainty makes the absolute values of the child burial/baptism ratios difficult to interpret, but it is unlikely to have a major effect on the comparability of the results for different parishes. This is because the effective 'cut-off' was almost certainly somewhere in the early to mid-'teens, and mortality in this age-group is so low, relative to that in infancy and childhood, that small local variations can have had only marginal effects on the totals. Were the effect substantial, then we would expect to find a strong positive correlation between the child burial/baptism ratio for a given parish, and the proportion of non-child burials which are described as adults, since both would be influenced by the numbers of 'true' child burials which are not described as such in the register and have been added to the 'unknown' total. In fact the correlations (taking the extra-mural parishes individually and grouping the intra-mural parishes as above) are only a non-significant 0.298 for the decade 1695–1704, and 0.064 for 1750–9.

Mortality and 'substantial households', 1695–1704

The proximity of the 1690 Hearth Tax returns to the first of our two sample decades provides the basis for a very approximate analysis of socio-economic variations in the child burial:baptism ratio for parishes falling within the limits of the City. For this purpose we have ranked the parishes by the proportions of 'substantial houses' (where these are available) and split them into five groups so as to minimise between-group variations in the numbers of baptisms. The results (see below) reveal a definite mortality gradient, according to this measure of socio-economic status, with the exception of the low figure for the middle group. Pooling the top two and bottom two groups yield child baptism ratios of 56.7% and 61.3% respectively, a difference which is small but statistically significant. The practice of sending children to nurse in the countryside[1] may have differentially lowered the ratio somewhat in favour of the richer parishes, but it is most unlikely to be responsible for the whole of the difference, since the proportion of child burials in the two groups is almost identical at 53.1% and 54.2% respectively. Even if we make the unrealistically severe assumption that the 'true' proportions are equal, and that the former is artificially deflated by the unregistered deaths of nurse children, then the adjusted child burial:baptism ratio in the richer parishes would only be raised to 59.2%, leaving nearly half the difference intact.

Group	Burials	Baptisms	Child burials/ baptisms (%)	'Substantial households' (%)
1	2,011	1,933	56.3	50.3
2	2,333	2,133	57.2	33.2
3	2,467	2,184	52.4	25.0
4	2,250	1,941	58.8	18.8
5	2,285	2,063	63.7	4.0

[1] Quantitative data on the extent of wet-nursing in London are relatively scarce. In the course of the seventeenth century it appears to have become widespread in the upper reaches of society, although it never acquired the kind of popular basis which it did in France and declined substantially from the early eighteenth century: see Fildes 1988: 79–100; Clark, G. 1987.

Appendix 2

The Autumn diseases and the 'putrid sore throat'

The increased importance of the 'Autumn diseases' (see chapter 7) in the seasonality of mortality during the central decades of the eighteenth century coincides with the epidemics of 'putrid sore throat' described by a number of contemporary physicians. These appear to have been part of a regional pandemic which affected much of the Atlantic world from its appearance in New England in 1735–7 (Dobson 1989b: 282). As described by Creighton (1894: 698–9) it first struck England late in 1739, but was not associated with severe excess mortality until the outbreak of 1746[1], after which it continued throughout the 1750s before disappearing in the subsequent decade.

The exact nature of the condition remains obscure, but contemporary descriptions, such as that of Fothergill (quoted in Creighton 1894: 698–9), strongly suggest that it was a form of streptococcal throat infection[2]. This possibility can be investigated to a limited degree using the cause-specific burial totals from the annual Bills of Mortality. Since the streptococci in question are also responsible for puerperal fever (Loudon 1987), the hypothesis would lead us to expect a closer relationship between maternal mortality and fever mortality (the cause of death series whose seasonality seems to have been most affected) during the decades 1730–59 than either before or after.

The results of a principal components analysis carried out on the

---

[1] I am grateful to Dr Irving Loudon for drawing my attention to this point, as well as suggesting the analysis which follows.

[2] This judgement is based on Fothergill's account, which was accepted by Creighton, but the evidence of the weekly Bills suggests that the former may have understated the seriousness of the earlier outbreak. The quarterly CMRs for the first quarter of 1740 were 131, 140 and 137, for the age-groups 0–1, 2–4 and 5–19 respectively. This amounts to a total absolute surplus of approximately 1,110 deaths, of which the concurrent smallpox excess can account for only 60, suggesting the presence of an additional mortality factor of some severity.

Appendices

correlation matrix of cause-specific CMRs (see below) lend some support to this hypothesis. In each case the first component has positive coefficients for each series (with the partial exception of smallpox) and apparently reflects the overall level of mortality in a given year. The second component, however, distinguishes between the cause of death series. In the first and third sub-period consumption and 'all other causes' (together with infancy in 1700–29), are distinguished from the remainder. But in the decades 1730–49 the coefficient for maternal mortality lies at the extreme negative end of the distribution, fever being the only other series with a negative coefficient.

	1700–29		1730–59		1760–99	
Cause of death	Cmpt 1	Cmpt 2	Cmpt 1	Cmpt 2	Cmpt 1	Cmpt 2
Maternal	0.32	–0.31	0.37	–0.41	0.25	–0.41
Consumption	0.46	0.36	0.49	0.12	0.55	0.15
Fevers	0.34	–0.47	0.43	–0.17	0.38	–0.13
Infancy	0.48	0.25	0.45	0.24	0.47	–0.22
Smallpox	0.25	–0.65	0.05	0.86	0.04	–0.77
All other	0.53	0.25	0.48	0.04	0.52	0.40
Percentage of variance explained	41	20	54	19	43	22

Appendix 3

Parish boundaries

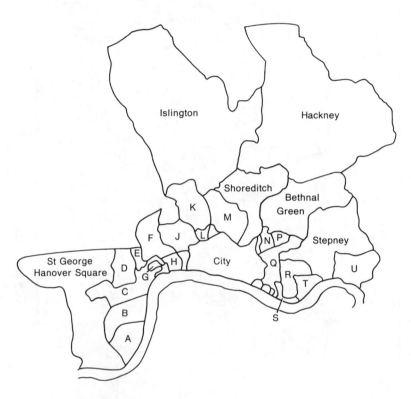

A St John Westminster
B St Margaret Westminster
C St Martin-in-the-Fields
D St James Piccadilly
E St Ann Soho
F St Giles-in-the-Fields
G St Paul Covent Garden
H St Clement Dane
J St Andrew Holborn
K St James Clerkenwell

L St Sepulchre
M St Giles Cripplegate
N Christ Church Spitalfields
P St Dunstan Stepney (detached)
Q St Botolph Bishopsgate
R St George in the East
S St John Wapping
T St Paul Shadwell
U St Anne Limehouse

A3.1 The metropolitan area – northern parishes (For southern parishes see Map 4.1)

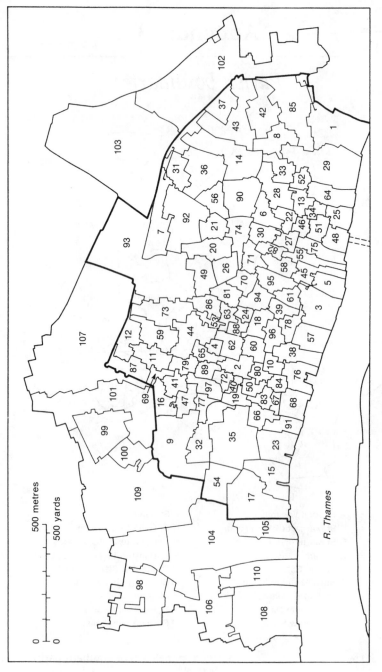

A3.2 City of London parishes

R. Thames

500 metres
500 yards

Key

Parishes within the walls

1 Allhallows Barking
2 Allhallows Bread Street
3 Allhallows the Great
4 Allhallows Honey Lane
5 Allhallows the Less
6 Allhallows Lombard Street
7 Allhallows London Wall
8 Allhallows Staining
9 Christ Church
10 Holy Trinity the Less
11 St Alban Wood Street
12 St Alphage Cripplegate
13 St Andrew Hubbard
14 St Andrew Undershaft
15 St Andrew by the Wardrobe
16 St Anne Aldersgate
17 St Anne Blackfriars
18 St Antholin
19 St Augustin by St Paul's
20 St Bartholomew by the Exchange
21 St Benet Fink
22 St Benet Gracechurch
23 St Benet Paul's Wharf
24 St Benet Sherehog
25 St Botolph Billingsgate
26 St Christopher Le Stocks
27 St Clement Eastcheap
28 St Dionis Backchurch
29 St Dunstan in the East
30 St Edmund Lombard Street
31 St Ethelburga
32 St Faith's under St Paul's
33 St Gabriel Fenchurch Street
34 St George Botolph Lane
35 St Gregory by St Paul
36 St Helen Bishopsgate
37 St James Duke Place
38 St James Garlickhithe
39 St John the Baptist
40 St John the Evangelist
41 St John Zachary
42 St Katherine Coleman
43 St Katherine Cree
44 St Lawrence Jewry
45 St Lawrence Pountney
46 St Leonard Eastcheap
47 St Leonard Foster Lane

48 St Magnus the Martyr
49 St Margaret Lothbury
50 St Margaret Moses
51 St Margaret New Fish Street
52 St Margaret Pattens
53 St Martin Ironmonger Lane
54 St Martin Ludgate
55 St Martin Orgar
56 St Martin Outwich
57 St Martin Vintry
58 St Mary Abchurch
59 St Mary Aldermanbury
60 St Mary Aldermary
61 St Mary Bothaw
62 St Mary le Bow
63 St Mary Colechurch
64 St Mary at Hill
65 St Mary Magdalen Milk Street
66 St Mary Magdalen Old Fish Street
67 St Mary Mountshaw
68 St Mary Somerset
69 St Mary Staining
70 St Mary Woolchurch
71 St Mary Woolnoth
72 St Matthew Friday Street
73 St Michael Bassishaw
74 St Michael Cornhill
75 St Michael Crooked Lane
76 St Michael Queenhithe
77 St Michael Le Querne
78 St Michael Paternoster Royal
79 St Michael Wood Street
80 St Michael Bread Street
81 St Mildred Poultry
82 St Nicholas Acon
83 St Nicholas Cole Abbey
84 St Nicholas Olave
85 St Olave Hart Street
86 St Olave Old Jewry
87 St Olave Silver Street
88 St Pancras Soper Lane
89 St Peter Westcheap
90 St Peter Cornhill
91 St Peter Paul's Wharf
92 St Peter le Poor
93 St Stephen Coleman Street
94 St Stephen Walbrook
95 St Swithin

Key *(Contd.)*
  96 St Thomas the Apostle
  97 St Vedast Foster Lane

Out parishes
  98 St Andrew Holborn
  99 St Bartholomew the Great
  100 St Bartholomew the Less
  101 St Botolph without Aldersgate

  102 St Botolph without Aldgate
  103 St Botolph without Bishopsgate
  104 St Bride Fleet Street
  105 Bridewell Precinct
  106 St Dunstan in the West
  107 St Giles without Cripplegate
  109 St Sepulchre
  110 Whitefriars Precinct

Appendix 4

Burial seasonality from Parish Registers

The pooled series

The data on which this section is based were obtained by pooling the monthly burial totals for the geographical parish groups featured in chapter 8 figures 5–10.

1695–1704

Figures A4.1–3 present sets of MBIs for the parish groups in the first of the two decades. The child burial seasonalities reveal a marked divergence – between the western parishes, on the one hand, and the south and east groups on the other – in the indices for the first four months of the year. In the south and east the average January–April index (weighted by the numbers of observations) is 98 as against 110 for the western group. The August index displays a similar contrast with corresponding figures of 129 and 114.

There are thus two distinct patterns of seasonality present in the child burial data. The first of these is common to the eastern and southern parishes and displays a clear August peak. The western pattern is bimodal, with maxima in both February/March and August, whilst the figures for the central group are intermediate. The contrast is underlined by the principal components analysis which revealed that 88 per cent of the total variance was accounted for by a single component with negative coefficients for the late summer and autumn, correspondingly positive values between January and April (see figure A4.4).

The adult burial indices show less spatial variation although – compared with the western and central groups – the southern parishes have noticeably lower first quarter indices with correspondingly higher values in August and September. The eastern group's pattern falls between these two. The principal components analysis yielded a first

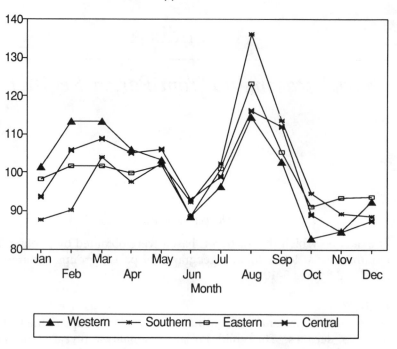

A4.1 Child burial seasonality by parish group, 1695–1704

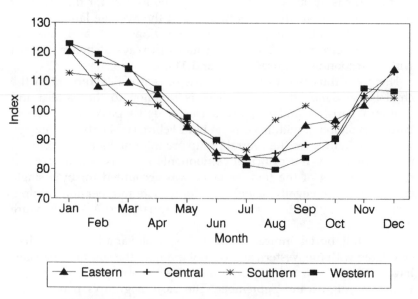

A4.2 Adult burial seasonality by parish group, 1695–1704

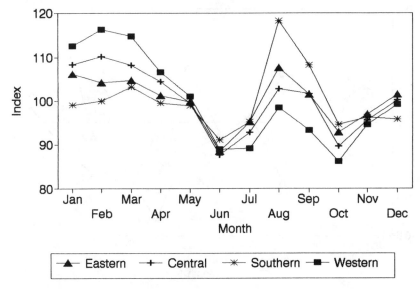

A4.3 Total burial seasonality by parish group, 1695–1704

component explaining three-quarters of the variance and contrasting the August and September indices with those for the first quarter. The component scores for the central and western parishes are similar to each other, whilst the eastern score is intermediate between these and the score for the southern group (see figure A4.5).

The monthly indices for total burials, as we might expect, display entirely different seasonal profiles in the western and southern groups. The first of these displays a maximum between January and March with burial deficits from June onwards. The southern parishes have a clearly defined August peak with most of the remaining indices at or below one hundred. The central and eastern groups fall between these two extremes, the former tending towards the western pattern and the latter the southern. A principal components analysis revealed that 95 per cent of the variance was accounted for by the first component. This – as we would expect – contrasts burials in the months August–October with those in the first quarter, and the scores on this component show a regular progression from the western, through the central and eastern, to the southern parishes (see figure A4.6).

1750–9
The indices for the pooled series bear out the substantial contrast between the western parishes, on the one hand, and those in the

Appendices

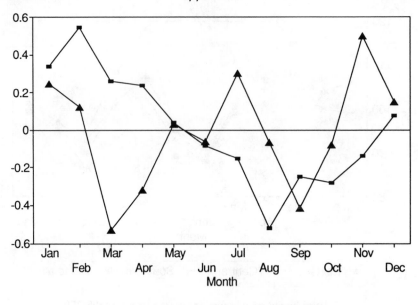

(a) Coefficients

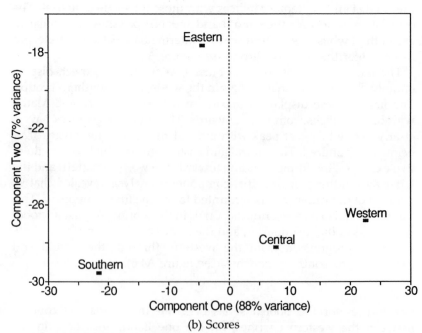

(b) Scores

A4.4 Child burial seasonality by parish group, 1695–1704: principal
components analysis

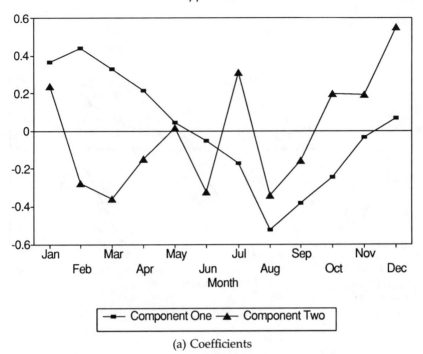

(a) Coefficients

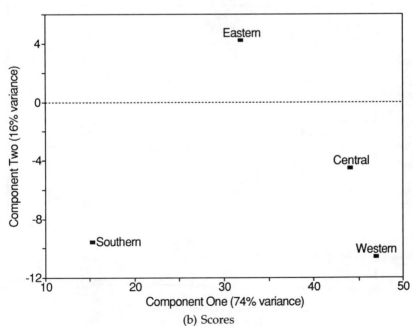

(b) Scores

A4.5 Adult burial seasonality by parish group, 1695–1704: principal components analysis

Appendices

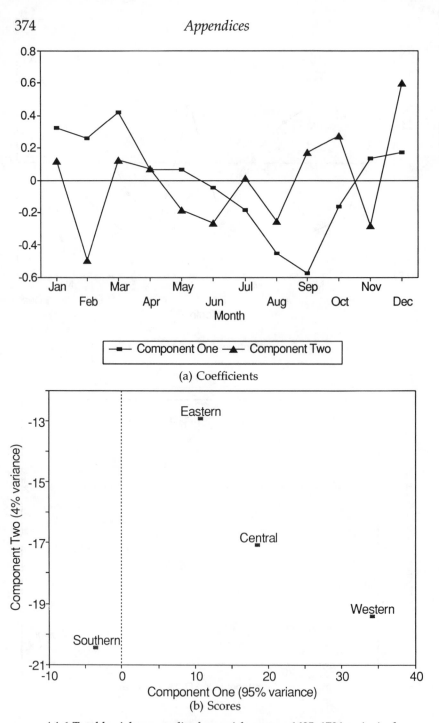

(a) Coefficients

(b) Scores

A4.6 Total burial seasonality by parish group, 1695–1704: principal
components analysis

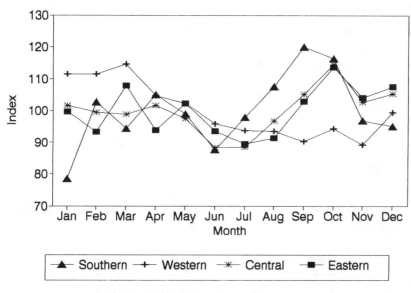

A4.7 Child burial seasonality by parish group, 1750–9

eastern and central groups on the other. The two sets of seasonal profiles for child burials are now entirely different from each other (see figures A4.7–9). The eastern and central groups display excess mortality between September and December, with a marked peak in October, whereas the western parishes have a broad plateau of excess mortality throughout the first quarter – the indices from June to December all falling below one hundred. The two southern parishes have a variant of the 'eastern' pattern, the excess mortality peaking in September and persisting into October.

The seasonal mortality profile for adults also differs between the western parishes and the remaining groups. In the eastern and central parishes excess mortality begins earlier than it does in the west – in November rather than December – and it falls away more rapidly in the spring, returning to negligible levels by April. The southern parishes resemble the western group as far as the timing of the excess is concerned, but its scale is much smaller, and this results in a much flatter seasonal profile. The excess period for total burials stretches from October, to March or April, in the eastern and central parishes, but from December to May in the west. The southern parishes have a much broader and flatter mortality plateau, stretching from September to April, and lacking any clear internal maximum.

Principal components analyses carried out on each set of indices

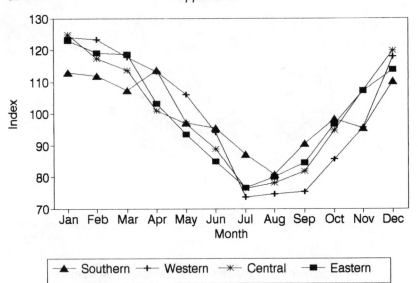

A4.8 Adult burial seasonality by parish group, 1750–9

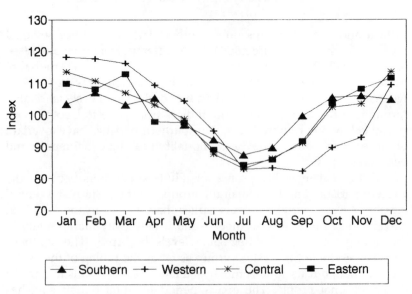

A4.9 Total burial seasonality by parish group, 1750–9

revealed that nearly all the variance in each of them could be accounted for by the first two components (see figures A4.10–12). For child burials, the first component explained three-quarters of the total and contrasted the indices for the first quarter with those for the late

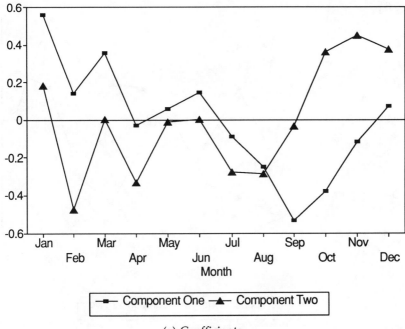

(a) Coefficients

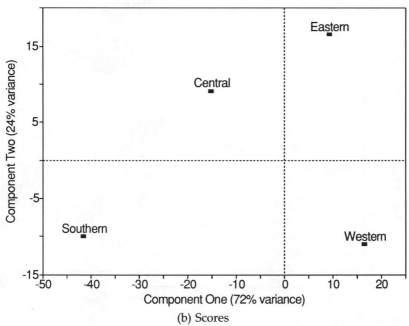

(b) Scores

A4.10 Child burial seasonality by parish group, 1750–9: principal
components analysis

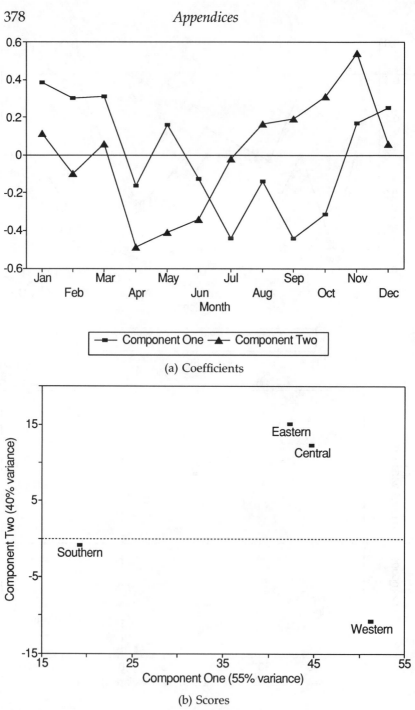

(a) Coefficients

(b) Scores

A4.11 Adult burial seasonality by parish group, 1750–9: principal components analysis

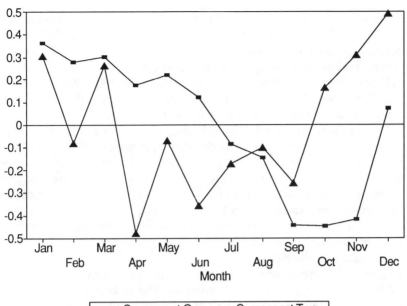

(a) Coefficients

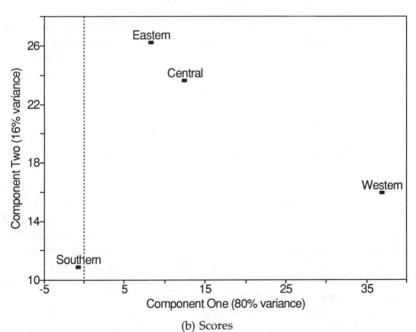

(b) Scores

A4.12 Total burial seasonality by parish group, 1750–9: principal
components analysis

summer and autumn, whilst the second component accounted for nearly all the remaining variance and was dominated by strong positive coefficients for the last quarter. A plot of scores shows the central and eastern groups close together on component one – about half way between the western and southern scores. On component two, however, they are sharply distinguished from the latter two groups which have similar, much lower scores.

The scores from the adult burial series produce a similar grouping, although the pattern of monthly coefficients is rather different, and the two components are closer to each other in the amount of variance they explain – 55 and 41 per cent respectively. In this case the first component contrasts burials in the cold weather months with those in the summer and autumn, and the second reflects the balance between the months of the second quarter and those of October and November. Here the southern score is roughly intermediate between the western group and the other two.

In the total burials series 80 per cent of the variance is accounted for by the first component, which contrasts the indices in the autumn months with those in the first half of the year, and particularly the first quarter. On this component the score for the western group stands out sharply from those of the other three which are relatively similar to each other, and substantially lower than the former. The second component, accounting for 16 per cent of the variance, separates the east–central pair from the south, with the western score falling roughly half-way between the two. Its coefficients distinguish burials in the central six months of the year from those in the first and fourth quarters.

The restricted samples

The monthly burial indices reveal a pattern generally similar to those seen in the main and extended samples – although the omission of Holborn and St Sepulchre from the 1695–1704 sample moves the central group's child burial seasonality substantially towards the 'eastern' pattern (see figures A4.13–15). Each of the groups displays a substantial reduction in the August child burial index between the two decades, the fall being rather greater in the east and south. Each group also shows an increase in the indices for the months of the last quarter, but this increase is much smaller in the west than it is elsewhere. The changes in the indices for adult burials show less in the way of systematic spatial variation, the general tendency being for values to decline in the summer and autumn, with corresponding increases

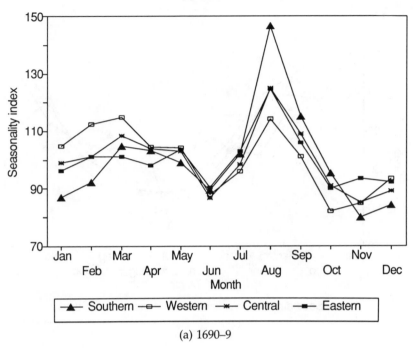

(a) 1690–9

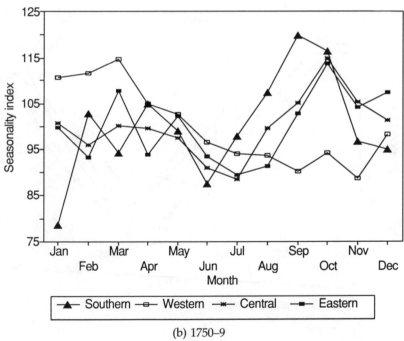

(b) 1750–9

A4.13 Restricted samples parishes, Child burials

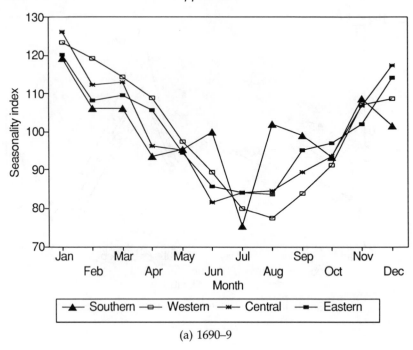

(a) 1690–9

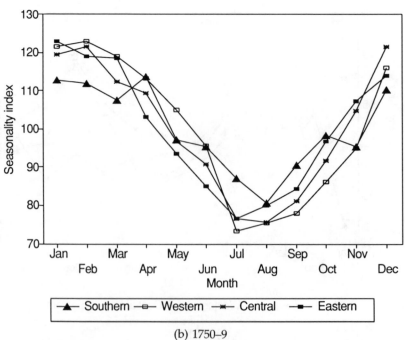

(b) 1750–9

A4.14 Restricted sample parishes, Adult burials

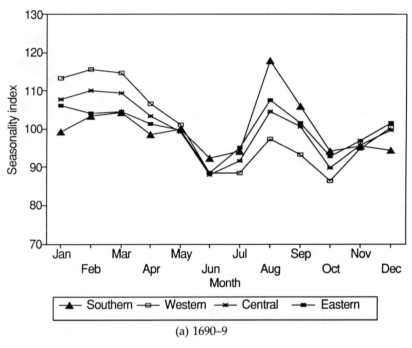

(a) 1690–9

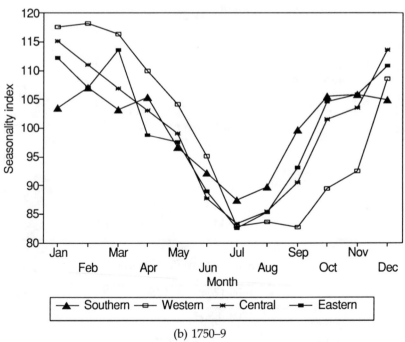

(b) 1750–9

A4.15 Restricted sample parishes, Total burials

Appendices

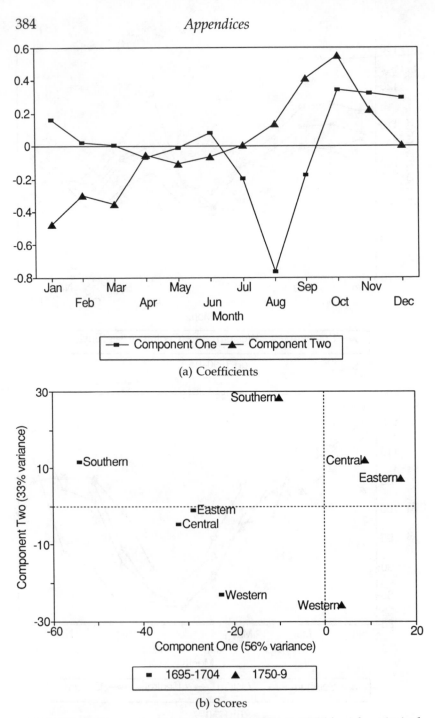

(a) Coefficients

(b) Scores

A4.16 Restricted sample parishes, 1695 and 1750–9: Child burials, principal components analysis

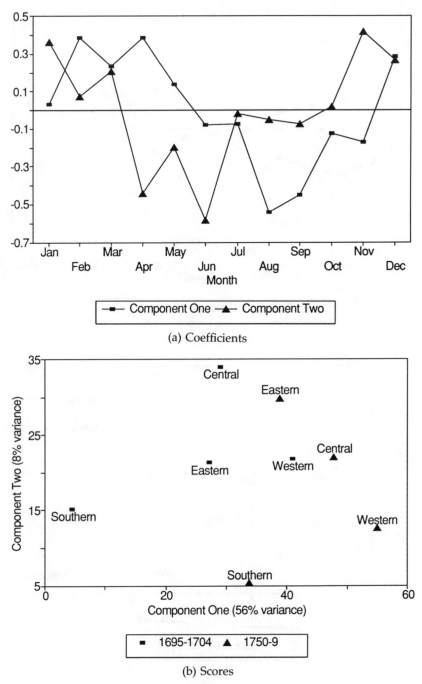

(a) Coefficients

(b) Scores

A4.17 Restricted sample parishes, 1695 and 1750–9: Adult burials, principal components analysis

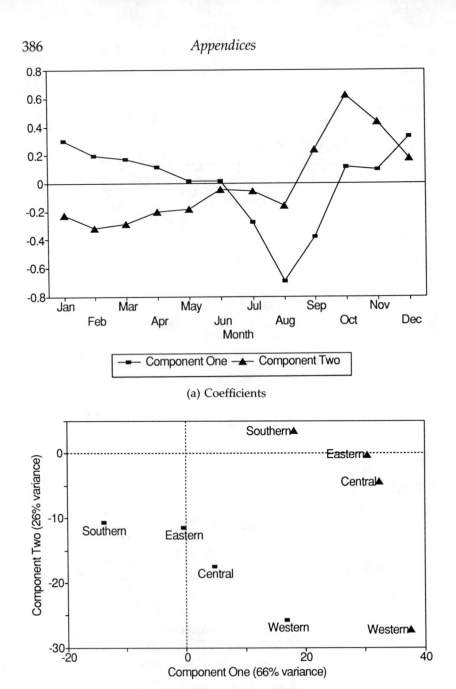

(a) Coefficients

(b) Scores

A4.18 Restricted sample parishes, 1695 and 1750–9: Total burials, principal components analysis

elsewhere in the year. The behaviour of the total burial series generally resembles that of the indices for child burials.

These patterns were examined further by another set of principal components analyses, in which the two decadal sets of indices for each group of burials were analysed jointly (see figures A4.16–18). In the case of the child and total burial series the first two components accounted for around 90 per cent of the variance. In each case the first component had negative coefficients for the months from July to September, the August value being particularly large. The first component for child burials had correspondingly positive values for the last quarter, whereas, in the case of total burial, these were spread more broadly through the winter and spring. The second component was similar for both series, accounting for around 30 per cent of the variance, and having positive coefficients for the autumn months combined with negative values between January and May.

A plot of the component scores reveals that, in each category of burials, the interval between the two decades sees all of the groups move a substantial distance along the axis of the first component. The western group, however, moves only about two-thirds of the distance travelled by the other three. This divergence is stronger in the case of the second, 'autumn', component, for here the western score actually declines, whilst those of the other three groups rise. The adult series yields less clear cut results. Here the first component accounts for only 55 per cent of the variance and the second for a further 20 per cent, whilst the clusters of component scores for the two decades partially overlap.

The coefficients of the first component contrast burials in the later summer and autumn – particularly August and September – with those in the winter and spring, and in this case it is the southern group which shows the largest differences in scores between the two decades. The second component has positive coefficients for the months between November and January, and negative values from April to June. Here the eastern group stands out with an increased score, whereas the other three show a roughly equal reduction over the period.

Bibliography

Anderson, M. 1988. *Population Change in North-Western Europe, 1750–1850*. London, Macmillan.

Anderton, D. L. and Bean, L. L. 1985. 'Birth spacing and fertility limitations: a behavioural analysis of a nineteenth-century frontier population', *Demography*, 22: 169–83.

Appleby, A. B. 1975. 'Nutrition and disease: the case of London, 1550–1750', *Journal of Interdisciplinary History*, 6: 1–22.

1980. 'The disappearance of the plague: a continuing puzzle', *Economic History Review*, 2nd ser., 33: 161–73.

Ardener, E. 1974. 'Social anthropology and population'. In Parry, H. B. (ed.), *Population and its Problems: A plain man's guide*, pp. 25–50. Oxford, Clarendon Press.

Ashton, T. S. 1959. *Economic Fluctuations in England 1700–1800*. Oxford, Clarendon Press.

Beattie, J. M. 1986. *Crime and the Courts in England 1660–1800*. Oxford, Clarendon Press.

Beck, W. and Ball, T. F. 1869. *The London Friends Meetings*. London.

Beier, A. L. 1986. 'Engine of manufacture: the trades of London'. In Beier and Finlay, *London 1500–1700*.

Beier, A. L. and Finlay, R. A. P. 1986. *London 1500–1700: The making of the metropolis*. London, Longman.

Benedictow, O. J. 1987. 'Morbidity in historical plague epidemics', *Population Studies*, 41(3): 401–32.

Bengtsson, T., Fridlizius, G., Ohlsson, R. 1984. *Pre-Industrial Population Change*. Stockholm, Almqvist and Wiksell.

Berkner, L. K. and Mendels, F. F. 1978. 'Inheritance systems, family structure, and demographic patterns in western Europe, 1700–1900'. In Tilly, *Historical Studies of Changing Fertility*, pp. 209–24.

Berry, B. M. and Schofield, R. S. 1971. 'Age at baptism in pre-industrial England', *Population Studies*, 25: 453–63.

Beveridge, W. H. et al. 1939. *Prices and Wages in England*, vol. 1, *Price tables: Mercantile era*. London.

Biraben, J-N. 1977. 'Current medical and epidemiological views on plague'. In *The Plague Reconsidered (Local Population Studies* supp.), pp. 25–36.

Blayo, Y. and Henry, L. 1967. 'Données démographiques sur la Bretagne et l'Anjou de 1740 à 1829', *Annales de Démographie Historique*, pp. 142–71.

Bongaarts, J. 1978. 'A framework for analyzing the proximate determinants of fertility', *Population and Development Review* 4(1): 105–32.

Bongaarts, J., Frank, O. and Lesthaeghe, R. 1984. 'The proximate determinants of fertility in sub-Saharan Africa', *Population and Development Review* 10(3): 511–37.

Bourgeois-Pichat, J. 1951. 'La mesure de la mortalité infantile', *Population*, 6: 233–48.

Bowler, P. J. 1976. 'Malthus, Darwin and the concept of struggle', *J. Hist. Ideas*, 37: 631–50.

Bradley, D. J. 1974. 'Water supplies: the consequences of change'. In *Human Rights in Health*, Ciba Foundation Symposium no. 23.

Brändström, A. 1988. 'The impact of female labour conditions on infant mortality: a case study of the parishes of Nedertorneåa and Jokkmok, 1800–96', *Social History of Medicine*, 1: 329–58.

Brändström, A. and Tedebrand, L-G. 1988. *Society, Health and Population During the Demographic Transition*. Stockholm, Almqvist and Wiksell.

Brass, W. 1971. 'On the scale of mortality'. In Brass, W. (ed.), *Biological Aspects of Demography*, pp. 69–110. London, Taylor and Francis.

Braudel, F. 1980. 'History and the social sciences: the *longue durée*', in *On History*, pp. 25–54. London, Weidenfeld and Nicolson.

1981. *The Structures of Everyday Life*. London, Collins.

Brett-James, N. G. 1935. *The Growth of Stuart London*. London, George Allen and Unwin.

Brownlee, J. 1925. 'The health of London in the eighteenth century', *Proceedings of the Royal Medical Society*, 18: 73–84.

Buchan, A. and Mitchell, A. 1875. 'The influence of weather on mortality from different diseases and at different ages', *Journal of the Scottish Meteorological Society*, 4: 185–263.

Buer, M. C. 1926. *Health, Wealth and Population in Eighteenth-Century England*. London, Routledge.

Burnett, M. and White, D. O. 1972. *Natural History of Infectious Disease*, 4th edn. Cambridge, Cambridge University Press.

Byers, E. 1982. 'Fertility transition in a New England commercial center: Nantucket Massachusetts', *Journal of Interdisciplinary History*, 13: 17–40.

Cabourdin, G., Birabën, J-N., Blum, A. 1988. 'Les crises démographique'. In Dûpaquier, J. et al., *Histoire de la population Francaise*, vol. 2, pp. 175–220. Paris, Presses Universitaires de France.

Cain, M. 1982. 'Perspectives on family and fertility in developing countries', *Population Studies*, 36: 159–75.

Caldwell, J. C. 1976. 'Towards a restatement of demographic transition', *Population and Development Review*, 2: 321–66.

1982. *The Theory of Fertility Decline*. London, Academic Press.

Caldwell, P. and Caldwell, J. C. 1981. 'The function of child-spacing in traditional societies and the direction of change'. In Page, H. and Lesthaeghe, R. (eds.), *Child Spacing in Tropical Africa*. London, Academic Press.

Carlsson, G. 1966. 'The decline of fertility: innovation or adjustment process?', *Population Studies*, 20: 149–74.

Chambers, J. D. 1972. *Population, Economy and Society in Pre-Industrial England*. Oxford, Oxford University Press.

Charbonneau, H. and Larose, A. (eds.), 1979. *The Great Mortalities: Methodological studies of demographic crises in the past*. Liège, Ordina.

Chartres, J. 1986. 'Food consumption and internal trade'. In Beier and Finlay, *London 1500–1700*, pp. 168–96.

Cipolla, C. M. 1962. *The Economic History of World Population*. Harmondsworth, Penguin.

Clark, G. 1987. 'A study of nurse children, 1550–1750', *Local Population Studies*, 39: 8–23.

Clark, P. 1987a. 'Migration in England during the late seventeenth and early eighteenth centuries'. In Clark and Souden, *Migration and Society*, pp. 213–52.

   1987b. 'Migrants in the city: the process of social adaptation in English towns, 1500–1800'. In Clark and Souden, *Migration and Society*, pp. 267–91.

   1988. 'The "Mother Gin" controversy in the early eighteenth century', *Transactions of the Royal Historical Society*, 5th ser., 38: 63–84.

Clark, P. and Slack, P. 1972. *Crisis and Order in English Towns*. London, Routledge and Kegan Paul.

Clark, P. and Souden, D. 1987. *Migration and Society in Early Modern England*. London, Hutchinson.

Cleland, J. and Wilson, C. 1987. 'Demand theories of fertility and the fertility transition: an iconoclastic View', *Population Studies*, 41: 5–30.

Coale, A. J. 1973. 'The demographic transition reconsidered'. In *International Population Conference, Liège* 1: 53–72. Liège, Ordina.

Coale, A. J. and Demeny, P. 1983. *Regional Model Life Tables and Stable Populations*, 2nd edn. London, Academic Press.

Coale, A. J. and Kisker, E. E. 1986. 'Mortality crossovers: reality or bad data?', *Population Studies*, 40: 389–402.

Coale, A. J. and Treadway, R. 1986. 'A summary of the changing distribution of overall fertility, marital fertility, and the proportion married in the provinces of Europe'. In Coale and Watkins (eds.), *The Decline of Fertility in Europe*, pp. 31–181.

Coale, A. J. and Trussel, T. J. 1974. 'Model fertility schedules: variations in the age structure of childbearing in human populations', *Population Index*, 40: 185–258.

   1978. 'Technical note: finding the two parameters that specify a model schedule of marital fertility', *Population Index*, 44: 203–13.

Coale, A. J. and Watkins, S. C. (eds.), 1986. *The Decline of Fertility in Europe*. Princeton, Princeton University Press.

Coleman, D. and Schofield, R. S. (eds.), 1986. *The State of Population Theory: Forward from Malthus*. Oxford, Basil Blackwell.

Corfield, P. 1982. *The Impact of English Towns 1700–1800*. Oxford, Oxford University Press.

Crafts, N. F. R. 1981. 'The eighteenth century: a survey'. In Floud, R. and McCloskey, D. *The Economic History of Britain Since 1700*. Cambridge, Cambridge University Press, pp. 1–16.

   1989. 'Duration of marriage, fertility and women's employment opportunities in England and Wales in 1911', *Population Studies*, 43: 325–35.

Creighton, C. 1894. *A History of Epidemics in Britain*, vol. 2, *From the extinction of plague to the present time.* Cambridge, Cambridge University Press.

Cronje, G. 1984. 'Tuberculosis and mortality decline in England and Wales, 1851–1910'. In Woods, R. I. and Woodward, J. (eds.), *Urban Disease and Mortality in Nineteenth-Century England*, pp. 79–101.

Darby, H. C. 1976. 'The age of the improver: 1600–1800', in *A New Historical Geography of England After 1600*, pp. 1–88. Cambridge, Cambridge University Press.

Darwin, C. 1968. *The Origin of Species*, (first published 1859). Harmondsworth, Penguin.

Daunton, M. J. 1978. 'Towns and economic growth in eighteenth-century England'. In Abrams, P. and Wrigley, E. A. (eds.), *Towns in Societies: Essays in economic history and historical sociology*, pp. 245–78. Cambridge, Cambridge University Press.

David, P. and Sanderson, W. C. 1986. 'Rudimentary contraceptive measures and the American transition to marital fertility control, 1855–1915'. In Engerman, S. L. and Gallman, R. E. (eds.), *Long-Term Factors in American Economic Growth*, pp. 307–79. Chicago, University of Chicago Press.

Davis, K. 1950. *The population of India and Pakistan*. Princeton, Princeton University Press.

Davis, K. and Blake, J. 1956. 'Social structure and fertility', *Economic Development and Cultural Change*, 4: 211–35.

De Vries, J. 1984. *European Urbanisation 1500–1800*. London, Methuen.

Demeny, P. 1972. 'Early fertility declines in Austria–Hungary: a lesson in demographic transition'. In Glass and Revelle, *Population and Social Change*, pp. 153–72.

Dietz, B. 1986. 'Overseas trade and metropolitan growth'. In Beier and Finlay, *London 1500–1700*, pp. 115–40.

Dobson, M. 1980. ' "Marsh fever": a geography of England', *Journal of Historical Geography*, 6: 357–89.

1989a. 'The last hiccup of the old demographic regime: population stagnation and decline in late seventeenth- and early eighteenth-century southeast England', *Continuity and Change*, 4(3): 395–428.

1989b. 'Mortality gradients and disease exchanges: Comparisons from old England and colonial America', *Social History of Medicine*, 2(3): 259–298.

Dûpaquier, J. 1979. 'L'analyse statistique des crises de mortalité'. In Charbonneau and Larose, *The Great Mortalities*, pp. 83–112.

1989. 'Demographic crises and subsistence crises in France, 1650–1789'. In Walter and Schofield, *Famine Disease and the Social Order*, pp. 189–200.

Dûpaquier, J. and Lachiver, M. 1969. 'Sur les débuts de la contraception en France ou les deux malthusianismes', *Annales: économies, sociétés, civilisations*, 24: 1391–406.

Dûpaquier, J., Fauve-Chamoux, A. and Grebenik, E. (eds.), 1983. *Malthus Past and Present*. London, Academic Press.

Durand, J. 1967. 'The Modern Expansion of World Population', *Proc. Amer. Phil. Soc.*, 111(3): 136–59.

Dyos, H. J. 1961. *Victorian Suburb: A Study of the Growth of Camberwell*. Leicester, Leicester University Press.

Earle, P. 1989a. *The Making of the English Middle Class: Business, society and family life in London, 1660–1730*. London, Methuen.

1989b. 'The female labour market in London in the late seventeenth and early eighteenth centuries', *Economic History Review*, 2nd ser., 42(3): 328–53.

Elliott, V. B. 1981. 'Single women in the London marriage market: age, status and mobility, 1589–1619'. In Outhwaite, *Marriage and Society*, pp. 81–100.

Everitt, B. S. and Dunn, G. 1983. *Advanced Methods of Data Exploration and Modelling*. London, Heinemann Educational Books.

Eversley, D. E. C. 1966. 'Aggregative analysis'. In Wrigley, *Introduction to English Historical Demography*, pp. 44–95.

1981. 'The demography of the Irish Quakers 1650–1850'. In Goldstrom, J. M. and Clarkson, L. A. (eds.), *Irish Population, Economy and Society*, pp. 57–88. Oxford, Clarendon Press.

Fildes, V. 1980. 'Neonatal feeding practices and infant mortality during the eighteenth century', *Journal of Biosocial Science*, 12: 313–24.

1986. *Breasts, Bottles and Babies: A history of infant feeding*. Edinburgh, Edinburgh University Press.

1988. *Wet Nursing: A history from antiquity to the present*. Oxford, Basil Blackwell.

Finlay, R. A. P. 1978. 'The accuracy of the London parish registers 1580–1653', *Population Studies*, 32: 95–112.

1981. *Population and Metropolis*. Cambridge, Cambridge University Press.

Finlay, R. A. P. and Shearer, B. 1986. 'Population growth and suburban expansion'. In Beier and Finlay, *London 1500–1700*, pp. 37–59.

Fisher, J. 1935. 'The development of the London food market, 1540–1640'. *Economic History Review*, 5: 46–64.

1948. 'The rise of London as a centre of conspicuous consumption', *Transactions of the Royal Historical Society*, 4th ser., 30: 37–50.

1971. 'London as an engine of economic growth'. In Bromley, J. S. and Kossmann, E. H. (eds.), *Britain and the Netherlands*, vol. 4, pp. 3–16. The Hague.

Flinn, M. W. 1970. *British Population Growth, 1700–1850*. London, Methuen.

1974. 'The stabilisation of mortality in pre-industrial western Europe', *Journal of European Economic History*, 3: 285–318.

1979. 'Plague in Europe and the Mediterranean countries', *Journal of European Economic History*, 8: 139–46.

1981. *The European Demographic System, 1500–1820*. Brighton, Harvester.

1982. 'The Population History of England, 1541–1871'. *Economic History Review*, 2nd ser., 35: 433–57.

Floud, R., Wachter, K. and Gregory, A. 1990. *Heights, Health and History: Nutritional status in the United Kingdom, 1750–1980*. Cambridge, Cambridge University Press.

Forbes, T. R. 1974. 'The searchers', *Bulletin of the New York Academy of Medicine*, 2nd ser., 1: 1031–8.

Fothergill, R. 1821. 'Reports on the diseases of London'. In Willan, R. (ed.), *Miscellaneous Works*. London.

Fridlizius, G. 1979. 'Sweden'. In Lee, W. R., *European Demography and Economic Growth*, pp. 340–405.

Frost, J. W. 1973. *The Quaker Family in Colonial America*. London, St James Press.

Galliano, P. 1966. 'La mortalité infantile dans la banlieu sud de Paris à la fin du xviii siècle (1774–94)', *Annales de Démographie Historique*, pp. 137–77.

Galloway, P. R. 1985. 'Annual variations in deaths by age, deaths by cause, prices and weather in London 1670–1830', *Population Studies*, 39: 487–505.

1986. 'Differentials in demographic responses to annual price variations in pre-revolutionary France: a comparison of rich and poor areas in Rouen, 1681–1787', *European Journal of Population* 2: 269–305.

1988. 'Basic patterns in annual variations in fertility, nuptiality, mortality, and prices in pre-industrial Europe', *Population Studies*, 42(2): 275–302.

Garrett, E. M. 1990. 'The trials of labour: motherhood versus employment in a nineteenth-century textile centre', *Continuity and Change*, 5: 121–54.

George, D. 1966. *London Life in the Eighteenth Century*. London, Penguin. First published 1925 by Kegan Paul, Trench, Trubner and Co. Ltd.

Glass, D. V. 1969. 'Socio-economic status and occupations in the City of London at the end of the seventeenth century'. In Hollaender, A. E. J. and Kellaway, W. (eds.) *Studies in London History*, pp. 373–92. London, Hodder and Stoughton.

1972. 'Notes on the demography of London at the end of the seventeenth century'. In Glass and Revelle, *Population and Social Change*, pp. 275–86.

Glass, D. V. and Eversley, D. E. C. 1965. *Population in History*. London, Edward Arnold.

Glass, D. V. and Revelle, R. 1972. *Population and Social Change*. London, Edward Arnold.

Goldstone, J. 1986. 'The demographic revolution in England: a re-examination', *Population Studies*, 40: 5–33.

Goodman, L. A. 1963. 'Tests based on the movements in and the comovements between *m*-dependent time series'. In Christ, C. F. et al. (eds.), *Measurement in Economics*, pp. 253–69. Stanford, Stanford University Press.

Goodman, N., Lane, R. E. and Rampling, S. B. 1953. 'Chronic bronchitis: an introductory examination of existing data', *British Medical Journal*, 2: 237–43.

Goubert, P. 1952. 'En Beauvaisis: problèmes démographiques du XVII siècle', *Annales, E. S. C.*, 7: 453–68.

1960. *Beauvais et le Beauvaisis de 1600 à 1730*. Paris.

Greatorex, I. (n.d.). 'Burial seasonality in early-modern England'. Unpublished MS in library of ESRC Cambridge Group.

Griffiths, T. 1926. *Population Problems of the Age of Malthus*. Cambridge, Cambridge University Press.

Hajnal, J. 1983. 'Two kinds of pre-industrial household formation system'. In Wall, *Family Forms in Historic Europe*, pp. 65–104.

Hardy, A. 1983. 'Smallpox in London: factors in the decline of the disease in the nineteenth century', *Medical History*, 27: 111–38.

1984. 'Water and the search for public health in London in the eighteenth and nineteenth centuries', *Medical History*, 28: 250–82.

1988. 'Diagnosis, death and diet: the case of London 1750–1909', *Journal of Interdisciplinary History*, 18: 387–401.

1988. 'Urban famine or urban crisis? Typhus in the Victorian city', *Medical History*, 32: 333–57.

Harrison, G. A., Weiner, J. S., Tanner, J. M. and Barnicot, N. A. 1977. *Human Biology: An introduction to human evolution, variation, growth, and ecology* 2nd edn. Oxford, Oxford University Press.

Hay, D. 1982. 'War, dearth and theft in the eighteenth century: the record of the English courts', *Past and Present*, 95: 117–60.

Helleiner, K. 1957. 'The vital revolution reconsidered', *Canadian Journal of Economics and Political Science*, 23: 79–86.

  1967. 'The population of Europe from the black death to the eve of the vital revolution'. In *Cambridge Economic History of Europe*, vol. 4, ch. 1. Cambridge, Cambridge University Press.

Henry, L. 1953. 'Fondements théoriques des mesures de la fecondité naturelle', *Revue Institut International de Statistique*, 21: 131–51.

  1961. 'Some data on natural fertility', *Eugenics Quarterly*, 8: 81–91.

  1976. *Population – analysis and models*. London, Edward Arnold.

Hill, A. G. 1990. 'Understanding recent fertility trends in the third world'. In Landers and Reynolds, *Fertility and Resources*, pp. 146–63.

Hollingsworth, T. H. 1964. 'The demography of the British peerage', *Population Studies*, 18: supplement.

  1976. *Historical Demography*. Cambridge, Cambridge University Press.

  1979. 'A preliminary suggestion for the measurement of mortality crises'. In Charbonneau and Larose, *The Great Mortalities*, pp. 21–8.

Hoppitt, J. 1986. 'Financial crises in eighteenth-century England', *Economic History Review*, 2nd ser., 39(1): 39–58.

  1987. *Risk and Failure in English Business 1700–1800*. Cambridge, Cambridge University Press.

Hornick, R. B. 1983. 'Shigellosis'. In Hoeprich, P. D. (ed.), *Infectious Diseases*, 3rd edn, pp. 649–54. Philadelphia, Lippincott.

Houlding, J. A. 1981. *Fit for Service*. Oxford, Oxford University Press.

Innes, J. and Styles J. 1986. 'The crime wave: recent writing on crime and criminal justice in eighteenth-century England', *Journal of British Studies*, 25: 380–435.

James, P. 1979. *Population Malthus: His life and times*. London, Routledge and Kegan Paul.

Johansson, S. R. and Mosk, C. M. 1987. 'Exposure, resistance and life expectancy: disease and death during the economic development of Japan, 1900–1960', *Population Studies*, 41: 207–36.

John, A. H. 1954–5. 'War and the English economy, 1700–63', *Economic History Review*, 2nd ser., 7: 329–44.

Jones, E. 1986. 'London in the early seventeenth century: an ecological approach', *London Journal*, 6: 123–33.

Jones, D. W. 1988. *War and Economy: In the age of William III and Marlborough*. Oxford, Basil Blackwell.

Jones, P. E. and Judges, A. V. 1935. 'London population in the late seventeenth century', *Economic History Review*, 6: 45–63.

Jones, R. E. 1980. 'Further evidence of the decline in infant mortality in pre-industrial England: N. Shropshire 1561–1810', *Population Studies*, 34: 239–80.

Kearns, G. 1988. 'The urban penalty and the population history of England'. In Brändström and Tedebrand, *Society, Health and Population*, pp. 213–36.

Kennedy, P. 1989. *The Rise and Fall of the Great Powers*. New York, Vintage Books.

Kitch, M. J. 1986. 'Capital and kingdom: migration to later Stuart London'. In Beier and Finlay, *London 1500–1700*, pp. 224–51.

Knodel, J. 1967. 'Law, marriage and illegitimacy in nineteenth-century Germany', *Population Studies*, 20: 279–94.

    1968. 'Infant mortality and fertility in three Bavarian villages: an analysis of family histories from the 19th century', *Population Studies*, 22: 297–318.

    1974. *The Decline in Fertility in Germany 1871–1939*. Princeton, Princeton University Press.

    1977. 'Age patterns of fertility and the fertility transition: evidence from Europe and Asia', *Population Studies*, 31: 219–49.

    1988 *Demographic Behavior in the Past*. Cambridge, Cambridge University Press.

Knodel, J. and Van de Walle, E. 1979. 'Lessons from the past. Policy implications of historical fertility studies', *Population and Development Review*, 5: 217–45.

Knodel, J. and Wilson, C. 1981. 'The secular increase in fecundity in German village populations: an analysis of reproductive histories of couples married 1750–1899', *Population Studies*, 35: 53–84.

Kreager, P. 1986. 'Demographic Regimes as Cultural Systems'. In Coleman and Schofield, *The State of Population Theory*, pp. 131–55.

Kunitz, S. J. 1983. 'Speculations on the European mortality decline', *Economic History Review*, 2nd ser., 36: 349–64.

    1987. 'Making a long story short: a note on men's heights and mortality in England from the first through the nineteenth centuries', *Medical History*, 31: 269–80.

    1991. 'The personal physician and the decline of mortality'. In Schofield et al., *The Decline of Mortality in Europe*, pp. 248–62.

Kussmaul, A. 1981. *Servants in Husbandry in Early Modern England*. Cambridge, Cambridge University Press.

Ladurie, E. Le Roy, 1981. 'A concept: the unification of the world by disease (fourteenth to seventeenth centuries)', in *The Mind and Method of the Historian*, pp. 28–83. Brighton, Harvester.

Landers, J. 1984. *Some Problems in the Historical Demography of London 1675–1825*. Unpublished Ph.D. thesis, University of Cambridge.

    1986. 'Mortality, weather and prices in London 1675–1825: a study of short-term fluctuations', *Journal of Historical Geography*, 12: 347–64.

    1987. 'Mortality and metropolis: the case of London 1675–1825', *Population Studies*, 41: 59–76.

    1990. 'Fertility decline and birth spacing among London Quakers'. In Landers and Reynolds, *Fertility and Resources*, pp. 92–117.

    1990. 'Age patterns of mortality in London during the "long eighteenth century": a test of the "high potential" model of metropolitan mortality', *Social History of Medicine*, 3: 27–60.

Landers, J. and Mouzas, A. J. 1988. 'Burial seasonality and causes of death in London 1670–1819', *Population Studies*, 42: 59–83.

Landers, J. and Reynolds, V. 1990. *Fertility and Resources*. Cambridge, Cambridge University Press.

Laslett, P. 1977. 'Characteristics of the Western family considered over time', in *Family Life and Illicit Love in Earlier Generations*, pp. 12–49. Cambridge, Cambridge University Press.

Lawton, R. 1978. 'Population and society 1730–1900'. In Dodgshon R. A. and Butlin R. A. (eds.), *An Historical Geography of England and Wales*, pp. 313–66. London, Academic Press.

Lee, R. D. 1973. 'Population in pre-industrial England: an econometric analysis', *Quarterly Journal of Economics*, 87: 581–607.

 1978. 'Models of preindustrial dynamics with applications to England'. In Tilly, *Historical Studies of Changing Fertility*, pp. 155–208.

 1981. 'Short-term variation: vital rates, prices, and weather'. In Wrigley and Schofield, *The Population History of England*, ch. 9.

 1986. 'Population homeostasis and English demographic history'. In Rotberg and Rabb, *Population and Economy*, pp. 75–100.

Lee, R. D. (ed.), 1977. *Population Patterns in the Past*. New York, Academic Press.

Lee, R. D. and Lam, D. 1983. 'Age distribution adjustments for English censuses 1821 to 1931', *Population Studies*, 37: 445–64.

Lee, W. R. (ed.), 1979. *European Demography and Economic Growth*. London, Croom Helm.

Leridon, H. and Menken, J. 1979. *Natural Fertility*. Liège, Ordina.

Lesthaeghe, R. 1980. 'On the social control of reproduction', *Population and Development Review*, 6: 527–48.

 1986. 'On the adaptation of sub-saharan systems of reproduction'. In Coleman and Schofield, *The State of Population Theory*, pp. 212–38.

Levine, D. 1977. *Family Formation in an Age of Nascent Capitalism*. London, Academic Press.

Lewontin, R. 1974. *The Genetic Basis of Evolutionary Change*. New York, Columbia University Press.

Lindert, P. 1983. 'English living standards, population growth and Wrigley–Schofield', *Explorations in Economic History*, 20: 134–49.

Linebaugh, P. 1975. 'The Tyburn riot against the surgeons'. In Hay, D., Linebaugh, P., Rule, J. G., Thompson, E. P. and Winslow, C., *Albion's Fatal Tree*. London, Peregrine.

Livi-Bacci, M. 1977. *Two Centuries of Italian Fertility*. Princeton, Princeton University Press.

 1978. *La Société Italienne devant les Crises de Mortalité*. Florence.

 1986. 'Social-group forerunners of fertility control in Europe'. In Coale and Watkins, *The Decline of Fertility in Europe*, pp. 182–200.

 1991. *Population and Nutrition*. Cambridge, Cambridge University Press.

Lloyd, A. 1950. *Quaker Social History 1669–1738*. London, Longman.

Longstaff, G. B. 1884–5. 'The seasonal prevalence of continued fevers in London', *Transactions of the Royal Epidemiological Society*, p. 78.

Loudon, I. 1986. *Medical Care and the General Practitioner 1750–1850*. Oxford, Clarendon Press.

 1987. 'Puerperal Fever, the streptococcus and the sulphonamides, 1911–45', *British Medical Journal* (ii), pp. 485–90.

Luckin, W. 1980. 'Death and survival in the city: approaches to the history of disease', *Urban History Yearbook*, pp. 53–62.

 1984. 'Evaluating the sanitary revolution: typhus and typhoid in London,

1851–1900'. In Woods and Woodward, *Urban Disease and Mortality*, pp. 102–119.

Lunn, P. G. 1991. 'Nutrition, immunity and infection'. In Schofield et al., *The Decline of Mortality in Europe*, pp. 131–45.

MacFarlane, A. 1978. *The Origins of English Individualism: The family, property, and social transition*. Oxford, Basil Blackwell.

Maitland, W. 1756. *The History and Survey of London*, 2 vols. London.

Manley, G. 1974. 'Central England temperatures: monthly means 1695 to 1973', *Quarterly Journal of the Royal Meteorological Society*, 100: 389–405.

Marshall, J. 1832. *The Mortality of the Metropolis*. London.

Mathias, P. 1979. 'Swords and ploughshares: the armed forces, medicine, and public health in the late eighteenth century', in *The Transformation of England*, pp. 265–85. London, Methuen.

McAlpin, M. B. 1985. 'Famines, epidemics and population growth: the case of India'. In Rotberg and Rabb, *Hunger and History*, pp. 153–68.

McKendrick, M., Brewer, J. and Plumb, J. H. 1983. *The Birth of a Consumer Society*. London, Hutchinson.

McKeown, T. R. 1976. *The Modern Rise of Population*. London, Edward Arnold.

McKeown, T. R. and Brown, R. G. 1955. 'Medical evidence relating to English population changes in the eighteenth century', *Population Studies*, 9: 115–41.

McKeown, T. R. and Record, R. G. 1962. 'Reasons for the decline of mortality in England and Wales during the nineteenth century', *Population Studies*, 16: 94–122.

McNeill W. H. 1977. *Plagues and Peoples*. Oxford, Basil Blackwell.

1980. 'Migration patterns and infections in traditional societies'. In Stanley, N. F. and Joske, R. A., *Changing Disease Patterns and Human Infections*, pp. 27–36. London, Academic Press.

Mendels, F. 1972. 'Proto-industrialisation: the first phase of the industrialisation process', *Journal of Economic History*, 32: 241–61.

Mercer, A. J. 1985. 'Smallpox and epidemiological-demographic change in Europe: the role of vaccination', *Population Studies*, 39: 287–308.

1986. 'Relative trends in mortality from related respiratory and airborne infectious diseases', *Population Studies*, 40: 129–45.

1990. *Disease, Mortality and Population in Transition: Epidemiological-demographic change in England since the eighteenth century as part of a global phenomenon*. Leicester, Leicester University Press.

Meuvret, J. 1946. 'Les crises de subsistances et la démographie de la France de l'Ancien Régime', *Population*, 1: 643–50.

1965. 'Demographic crisis in France from the sixteenth to the eighteenth century'. In Glass and Eversley, *Population in History*, pp. 507–22.

Mitchell, B. R. and Deane, P. 1962. *Abstract of British Historical Statistics*. Cambridge, Cambridge University Press.

Mols, R. 1974. 'Population in Europe 1500–1700'. In Cipolla, C. M. (ed.), *The Fontana economic history of Europe*, vol. 2, *The sixteenth and seventeenth centuries*, pp. 15–82. London, Fontana.

Mosley, W. H. and Chen, L. C. 1984. 'An analytical framework for the study of child survival in developing countries'. In Mosley, W. H. and Chen, L. C. (eds.), *Child Survival: Strategies for research*, pp. 25–48, (Supplement to *Population and Development Review*, vol. 10).

Murchison, C. 1858. 'Contributions to the etiology of continued fever', *Medico-Chirurgical Transactions of the Royal Medical and Chirurgical Society of London*, 41: 1–26.

Notestein, F. W. 1945. 'Population: the long view'. In Schulz, T. W. (ed.), *Food for the World*, pp. 36–57. Chicago, University of Chicago Press.

O'Brien, P. 1988. 'The political economy of British taxation, 1660–1815', *Economic History Review*, 2nd ser., 41: 1–32.

Ogle, W. 1892. 'An enquiry into the trustworthyness of the old Bills of Mortality', *Journal of the Royal Statistical Society*, 55: 437–60.

Olsen, D. J. 1976. *The Growth of Victorian London*. London, Peregrine.

Omran, O. R. 1971. 'The epidemiologic transition', *Millbank Memorial Fund Quarterly*, 49: 509–38.

Ormsby, H. 1928. *London on the Thames*. London, Studies in Economic and Political Science.

Outhwaite, R. B. (ed.), 1981. *Marriage and Society: Studies in the social history of marriage*. London, Europa.

Patten, J. H. C. 1977. 'Urban occupations in pre-industrial England', *Transactions of the Institute of British Geographers*, new ser., 2: 296–313.

Perrenoud, A. 1984. 'Mortality decline in its secular setting'. In Bengtsson et al., *Pre-Industrial Population Change*, pp. 41–69.

  1985. 'L'inegalité devant la Mort à Geneve Au XVIIème Siècle', *Population*, 30: (num. spec.) 221–43.

  1991. 'The attenuation of mortality crises and the decline of mortality'. In Schofield et al., *The Decline of Mortality in Europe*, pp. 18–37.

Phelps Brown, E. H. and Hopkins, S. V. 1962. 'Seven centuries of building wages'. In Carus-Wilson, E. M. (ed.), *Essays in Economic History II*, pp. 179–96. London, Arnold.

Phillips, H. 1964. *Mid-Georgian London: A topographic and social survey of central and west London around 1750*. London, Collins.

Post, J. D. 1984. 'Climatic variability and the European mortality wave of the early 1740s', *Journal of Interdisciplinary History*, 15: 1–50.

  1985. *Food Shortage, Climatic Variability and Epidemic Disease in Pre-Industrial Europe: The mortality peak of the early 1740s*. Ithaca and London, Cornell University Press.

  1990. 'Nutritional status and mortality in eighteenth-century Europe'. In Newman, L. (ed.), *Hunger in History: Food shortage, poverty, and deprivation*, pp. 241–80. Oxford, Basil Blackwell.

Power, M. J. 1972. 'East London housing in the seventeenth century'. In Clark and Slack, *Crisis and Order in English Towns*, pp. 237–62.

  1978. 'The east and west in early modern London'. In Ives, E. W., Knecht, R. J. and Scarisbrick, J. J. (eds.), *Wealth and Power in Tudor England: Essays presented to S. T. Bindoff*, pp. 167–85. London, Athlone Press.

  1986. 'The social topography of Restoration London'. In Beier and Finlay *London 1500–1700*, pp. 199–223.

Preston, S. H. 1976. *Mortality Patterns in National Populations*. New York, Academic Press.

Preston, S. H. and Van de Walle, E. 1978. 'Urban French mortality in the nineteenth century', *Population Studies*, 32: 275–97.

Razzell, P. E. 1965. 'Population change in eighteenth-century England: a reappraisal', *Economic History Review*, 2nd ser., 18: 312–32.

1974. 'The interpretation of the modern rise of population – a comment', *Population Studies*, 28: 5–17.

1977. *The Conquest of Smallpox*. Firle Sussex, Caliban.

Reay, B. 1980. 'The social origins of the early Quakers', *Journal of Interdisciplinary History*, 11: 55–72.

Reddaway, T. F. 1940. *The Rebuilding of London After the Great Fire*. London, Jonathan Cape.

Risse, G. B. 1985. ' "Typhus" fever in eighteenth-century hospitals: new approaches to medical treatment', *Bulletin of the History of Medicine*, 59: 176–95.

Rotberg, R. I. and Rabb T. K. (eds.), 1985. *Hunger and History*. Cambridge, Cambridge University Press.

1986. *Population and Economy*. Cambridge, Cambridge University Press.

Rowland, M. G. M. and Barrell R. A. E. 1980. 'Ecological factors in gastroenteritis'. In Clegg, E. J. and Garlick, J. P. (eds.), *Disease and Urbanization*, pp. 21–36. London, Taylor and Francis.

Rowntree, J. 1902. *The Friends' Registers of Births, Deaths and Marriages 1650–1900*. Leominster.

Rudden, B. 1985. *The New River: A legal history*. Oxford, Clarendon Press.

Rudé, G. 1971. *Hanoverian London*. London, Secker and Warburg.

Ryder, N. B. 1986. 'Observations on the history of cohort fertility in the United States', *Population and Development Review*, 12: 617–44.

Schofield, R. S. 1970. 'Age-specific mobility in an eighteenth-century rural English parish', *Annales de Démographie Historique*, pp. 261–74.

1984. 'Population growth in the century after 1750: the role of mortality decline'. In Bengtsson et al., *Pre-Industrial Population Change*, pp. 17–39.

1985a. 'The impact of scarcity and plenty on population change in England, 1541–1871'. In Rotberg and Rabb, *Hunger and History*, pp. 67–94.

1985b. 'English marriage patterns revisited', *Journal of Family History*, 10: 2–20.

1989. 'Family structure, demographic behaviour, and economic growth'. In Walter and Schofield, *Famine Disease and the Social Order*, pp. 279–304.

Schofield, R. S. and Wrigley, E. A. 1979. 'Infant and child mortality in the late Tudor and early Stuart period'. In Webster, C. (ed.), *Health, Medicine and Mortality in the Sixteenth Century*, pp. 61–96. Cambridge, Cambridge University Press.

Schofield, R. S., Reher, D. and Bideau, A. 1991. *The Decline of Mortality in Europe*. Oxford, Oxford University Press.

Schwarz, L. D. 1985. 'The standard of living in the long run: London, 1700–1860', *Economic History Review*, 2nd ser., 38: 24–41.

1992. *London in the Age of Industrialisation. Economy and society in the capital, 1700–1850*. Cambridge, Cambridge University Press.

Scott Smith, D. 1977. 'A homeostatic demographic regime: patterns in west European family reconstitution studies'. In Lee (ed.), *Population Patterns in the Past*, pp. 19–52.

Sharlin, A. 1978. 'Natural decrease in early modern cities: a reconsideration', *Past and Present*, 79: 126–38.

Sheppard, F. 1971. *London 1801–1870: The infernal wen*. London, Secker and Warburg.

Sheppard, F., Belcher, V. and Cottrell, P. 1979. 'The Middlesex and Yorkshire

Deed Registries and the Study of Building Fluctuations', *London Journal*, 5: 176–217.

Shlomowitz, R. 1989. 'Mortality on convict voyages to Australia 1788–1868', *Social Science History*, 13: 285–313.

Slack, P. 1987. 'Vagrants and vagrancy in England, 1598–1664'. In Clark and Souden, *Migration and Society in Early Modern England*, pp. 49–76.

Smith, R. M. 1981. 'Fertility, economy and household formation in England over three centuries', *Population and Development Review*, 7: 595–622.

Smith, S. R. 1971-3. 'The social and geographical origins of the London apprentices 1630–60', *Guildhall Miscellany*, 4: 195–206.

Snyder, J. C. 1965. 'Typhus fever Rickettsiae'. In Horsfall, F. L. and Tamm, I. (eds.), *Viral and Rickettsial Infection of Man*, pp. 1059–94.

Souden, D. 1978. ' "Rogues, whores and vagabonds?" Indentured servant emigration to North America and the case of mid seventeenth-century Bristol', *Social History*, 3: 23–41.

Spate, O. H. K. 1936. 'The growth of London A.D. 1660–1800'. In Darby, H. C. (ed.), *An Historical Geography of England Before 1800*, pp. 529–48. Cambridge, Cambridge University Press.

Srikantia, S. G. 1985. 'Better nutrition and India: a comment'. In Rotberg and Rabb, *Hunger and History*, pp. 169–72.

Stedman Jones, G. 1972. 'History: the poverty of empiricism'. In R. Blackburn (ed.), *Ideology and social science*, pp. 96–115. London, Fontana.

   1976. *Outcast London: a study in the relationship between classes in Victorian society*. Oxford, Oxford University Press.

Stevens, J. 1979. *Popular Disorders in England, 1700–1870*. London, Longman.

Stone, L. A. 1979. *The Family, Sex and Marriage in England 1500–1800*. Harmondsworth, Penguin.

Stuart-Harris, C. H. 1980. 'The ecology of chronic lung disease'. In Clegg, E. J. and Garlick, J. P. (eds.), *Disease and Urbanisation*, pp. 73–91. London, Taylor and Francis.

Summerson, J. 1978. *Georgian London*. London, Peregrine.

Sydenham, T. 1769. *Entire Works* (ed. Swan, J.). London.

Szreter, S. 1988. 'The importance of social intervention in Britain's mortality decline c. 1850–1914: a re-interpretation of the role of public health', *Social History of Medicine*, 1: 1–38.

Terrisse, M. 1961. 'Un faubourg du Havre: Ingouville', *Population*, 16: 285–300.

Tilly, C. 1978. 'Introduction', in *Historical Studies of Changing Fertility*, pp. 3–56.

   1981. Review of M. W. Flinn (1981), *Population and Development Review*, 34: 706–8.

Tilly, C. (ed.), 1978. *Historical Studies of Changing Fertility*. Princeton, Princeton University Press.

Vallin, J. 1991. 'Mortality in Europe from 1720 to 1914: long-term trends and changes in patterns by age and sex'. In Schofield et al., *The Decline of Mortality in Europe*, pp. 38–67.

Wales-Smith, B. G. 1971. 'Monthly and annual totals of rainfall representative of Kew, Surrey from 1697 to 1970', *Meteorological Magazine*, 100: 345–61.

Wall, R. 1983. 'Introduction', in *Family Forms in Historic Europe*, pp. 1–64.

Wall, R. (ed.), 1983. *Family Forms in Historic Europe*. Cambridge, Cambridge University Press.

Walter, J. and Schofield, R. S. (eds.), 1989. *Famine, Disease and the Social Order in Early Modern Society*. Cambridge, Cambridge University Press.

Wareing, J. 1980. 'Changes in the geographical distribution of apprentices to the London Companies 1486–1750', *Journal of Historical Geography*, 6: 241–9.

    1981. 'Migration to London and transatlantic emigration of indentured servants 1683–1775', *Journal of Historical Geography*, 7: 356–78.

Weir, D. R. 1984. 'Life under pressure: France and England 1670–1870', *Journal of Economic History*, 44: 27–47.

Wells, R. 1988. *Wretched Faces: Famine in wartime England 1793–1803*. Gloucester, Alan Sutton.

Wells, R. V. 1971. 'Family size and fertility control in eighteenth-century America: Quaker families', *Population Studies*, 25: 73–82.

Wilson, C. 1982. *Marital Fertility in Pre-Industrial England 1550–1849*. Unpublished Ph.D. thesis, University of Cambridge.

Wilson, C., Oeppen, J. and Pardoe, M. 1988. 'What is natural fertility? The modelling of a concept', *Population Index*, 54: 4–20.

Winch, D. 1987. *Malthus*. Oxford, Oxford University Press.

Woods, R. I. 1982. *Theoretical Population Geography*. New York, Longman.

    1985. 'The effect of population redistribution on the level of mortality in nineteenth-century England and Wales', *Journal of Economic History*, 45: 645–51.

    1987. 'Approaches to the fertility transition in Victorian England', *Population Studies*, 41: 283–311.

Woods, R. I. and Smith, C. W. 1983. 'The decline of marital fertility in the late nineteenth century: the case of England and Wales', *Population Studies*, 37: 207–25.

Woods, R. I. and Woodward, J. 1984. *Urban Disease and Mortality in Nineteenth-century England*. London, Batsford.

Wrigley, E. A. 1966a. 'Family reconstitution', in *Introduction to English Historical Demography*, pp. 96–159.

    1966b. 'Family limitation in pre-industrial England', *Economic History Review*, 19: 82–109.

    1967. 'A simple model of London's importance in changing English society and economy 1650–1750', *Past and Present*, 37: 44–70.

    1968. 'Mortality in England: Colyton over three centuries', *Daedalus*, 97: 546–80.

    1977. 'Births and baptisms: the use of Anglican baptism registers as a source of information about the number of births in England before the beginning of civil registration', *Population Studies*, 31: 281–312.

    1978a. 'Marital fertility in seventeenth century Colyton: a note', *Economic History Review*, 2nd ser., 31: 429–36.

    1978b. 'Fertility Strategy for the individual and the group'. In Tilly, *Historical Studies of Changing Fertility*, pp. 135–54.

    1981a. 'The prospects for population history', *Journal of Interdisciplinary History*, 12: 207–26.

    1981b. 'Marriage fertility and population growth in eighteenth-century

England'. In Outhwaite, *Marriage and Society: Studies in the social history of marriage*, pp. 137–85.

1983a. 'The growth of population in eighteenth-century England: a conundrum resolved', *Past and Present*, 98: 121–50.

1983b. 'Malthus's model of a pre-industrial economy'. In Dûpaquier et al., *Malthus Past and Present*, pp. 111–24.

1985. 'The fall of marital fertility in nineteenth-century France: exemplar or exception?', *European Journal of Population*, 1: 31–60, 141–77.

1986. 'Elegance and experience: Malthus at the bar of history'. In Coleman and Schofield, *The State of Population Theory*, pp. 46–64.

1987. 'The classical economists and the industrial revolution', in *People, Cities and Wealth*, pp. 21–45. Oxford, Basil Blackwell.

1989. 'Some reflections on corn yields and prices in pre-industrial economies'. In Walter and Schofield (eds.), *Famine, Disease and the Social Order*, pp. 235–78.

Wrigley, E. A. (ed.), 1966. *An Introduction to English Historical Demography*. London, Weidenfeld and Nicholson.

Wrigley, E. A. and Schofield, R. S. 1981. *The Population History of England 1541–1871: A reconstruction*. London, Edward Arnold.

1983. 'English population history from family reconstitution: summary results', *Population Studies*, 37: 157–84.

Young, R. M. 1969. 'Malthus and the evolutionists: the common context of biological and social theory', *Past and Present*, 43: 109–45.

Zinsser, H. 1935. *Rats, Lice and History*. London, Routledge.

Index

adults: immunological status, 90; mortality, 123, 157–9, 320, 329, 330ff., 369ff., seasonality of burials, 230

age: and cause of death, 115–20, 233–41; distributions in Bills, 98–101; -group correlations, 113–14; -specific CMRs, 109–12, 270ff.; seasonality of burials by, 228–36

aggregative analysis, 15, 102, 187

aggregative back projection, 129

American War, 78, 288, 297, 298

amplitude, 34–5

apprentices, 46, 47, 48

armed forces, 80, 82–3, 286–98

artificial feeding, 148–52

Austrian Succession, War of the, 286–9

autocorrelation, 117

Autumn diseases, 269, 363–4; see also seasonality

bankruptcy, 76–7

baptisms, 84, 89, 186, 269, 279, 284, 339–43, 358–62; delayed, 164–6; under-registration, 162–8, 191, 192, 339

Bills of Mortality, see London Bills of Mortality

biometric model, 139–42

birth rates, 84; decline of, 175, 190; see also crude birth rate (CBR)

births, seasonality of, 143

'black boxes', 113

bounding, 20, 33, 37, 38, 40, 86, 89, 125

bread prices, 244ff., 267, 281, 283–4, 314–15

bronchitis, 216, 217, 219ff., 226, 228, 236, 237, 347

bubonic plague, 17, 18, 24n, 30, 32

building industry, see construction industry

burials: age and cause of death interactions, 115–20; age distributions, 98–101, age-group correlations, 113–14; age-specific totals, 109–12, 123; annual series, 93–102, 244–50; cause of death, 94–8, 106–9, 122, 315–29; and CBBRs, 340–3, 358–62; comparison of London and national CMRs, 104–5; by district, 302–29; infant, 141–8, 169, 185–9, 207–9; instability of, 103, 302–15; related to prices, temperature and rainfall, 243–66; seasonality of, 141–8, 200, 205–15, 227–8, 369–87; seasonality of by age, 228–36; seasonality of by parish, 329–39, 343–7; smallpox, 153–4; surplus, 43, 125, 126, 129; under-registration, 162–8, 177, 187

cause of death, 94–8, 106–9, 203–4, 270ff.; and burial seasonality by age, 233–41; by district, 315–29; and extreme values, 120; interaction with age-specific CMRs, 115–20; and seasonal burials, 207–28; unreliability of data on, 200

Chambers, J. D., 24

child mortality, 121–2, 123–4, 152–6, 161, 233, 270, 272, 280, 299, 349; burial to baptism ratios (CBBRs), 340–3, 358–62; seasonality of, 228, 229–30, 235, 236, 330ff., 344, 345, 369, 370, 372, 375, 377, 380, 384, 387; spatial pattern of, 320, 329

children, 90, 356
cholera, 30, 36
'chrisoms', 186, 208, 209
Clark, P., 44–5, 72
climate, 20, 21, 24n, 75, 239, 249, 260,
    263, 278, 347; *see also* temperatures
clothing, 356
Coale's index, 176
coefficients, 114–19, 206, 207, 256ff.,
    320–6
co-movements, 117–19, 244–50, 299, 315
conduction, 13–14, 20, 29, 33, 36, 37, 38,
    40, 86, 87, 89, 125, 152, 285, 299, 302,
    355
construction industry, 59–61, 86, 87, 125,
    353–4
consumption: age and cause of death
    correlations, 119, 120; burials by
    district, 320–7, 346; burials correlated
    with prices and temperatures, 245–9,
    251, 252, 253, 255ff.; as cause of
    death, 94–7, 106; definition of, 113,
    121, 204; seasonality of deaths
    from, 209, 210–11, 213, 214, 218, 221,
    224, 233, 234; and wheat prices, 258
convulsions, 204, 208, 209, 210, 218, 219,
    226, 234, 251, 252, 253, 255ff.; burials
    by district, 320; in crisis years, 278;
    and wheat prices, 258
correlation analysis, 114–17, 320–6
Creighton, C., 95, 96, 240, 289, 311n.,
    363
crime, 81–2, 286
'crisis mortality ratios' (CMRs), 15, 18,
    102ff., 244ff., 267ff., 287, 321; age-
    specific, 109–12, 270–7; cause-
    specific, 106–9, 270–7; by district,
    303–14; extreme values, 120;
    measurement of, 102
crisis theory, 14–22, 35, 201, 242, 281
crude birth rate (CBR), 130; and
    population structure, 174–6;
    reliability of, 176–80
crude death rate (CDR), 84, 103, 108, 109;
    epidemic crises in, 284; and
    population structure, 174–6;
    reliability of, 176–80

death rates, 17, 284; autonomous, 23–5;
    decline of, 175, 354–7; *see also* crude
    death rate (CDR)
Defoe, Daniel, 191
demobilisations, 80–1, 286–98, 349
demographic regimes, 25–7, 201, 242
demographic transition theory (DTT), 9,
    14, 17

diarrhoea, 30, 32, 95, 216, 217, 219ff.,
    224, 226, 236, 237
diet, 36, 38, 40, 125; *see also* nutrition
diphtheria, 30, 215n., 216, 217, 219ff.,
    224, 226, 227, 236, 237, 240
diseases, *see* infectious diseases
districts, 303–4; cause of death in, 315–
    29; levels of instability in, 203–15,
    346–50; mortality related to
    temperature and prices, 314–15,
    326–7
Dobson, Mary, 33–5
Durand, J., 28
dysentery, 20, 216, 217, 219ff., 224, 226,
    236, 237, 239

East End, 303, 348, 349, 354
economic stress, *see* stress
England, 8, 9, 26, 34, 352, 353; age
    distribution of population, 181;
    death rates, 17; decline in mortality,
    161; late marriage in, 23; life
    expectation, 11, 23, 194–5; migration
    patterns, 44–6; mortality crises, 283–
    4; population structure, 42, 43;
    spatial structure of mortality in, 33
environment, 12, 13, 261–3
epidemics, 16, 20–1, 34, 282, 284, 311n
epidemiological regimes, 33, 37, 199–201
Europe, 8, 14, 16, 17, 20, 23, 26, 28, 129,
    137–9, 148, 199–200, 267, 278
exposure, *see* high potential model of
    exposure
extreme values, 120, 244

family reconstitution, 129–30, 134, 137,
    153, 157
famine, 17, 243, 279
female mortality, 298, 349
fertility, 3, 4, 26, 124, 194; measurement
    of, 175–6
fever mortality, 20, 117, 122, 286, 300,
    348, 349–50, 354; age and cause of
    death correlations, 119, 120; as cause
    of death, 94–7, 106, 108; in child
    mortality, 123–4, 126; correlated with
    prices and temperature, 244–50,
    252ff., 299; in crisis years, 269–82;
    312; definition of, 113, 121, 204; and
    demobilisations, 288–97; by district,
    320, 322; and extreme conditions,
    201; seasonality of, 211, 212, 214,
    218, 228, 233, 234; spatial pattern of,
    328–9, 346
Finlay, R. A. P., 41, 42, 130, 138, 185,
    186, 188, 193, 239, 352

Cambridge Studies in Population Economy and Society in Past Time

1 *Land, kinship and life-cycle* edited by RICHARD M. SMITH
2 *Annals of the labouring poor: social change and agrarian England 1660–1900* K. D. M. SNELL*
3 *Migration in a mature economy: emigration and internal migration in England and Wales 1861–1900* DUDLEY BAINES
4 *Scottish literacy and the Scottish identity: illiteracy and society in Scotland and Northern England 1600–1800* R. A. HOUSTON
5 *Neighbourhood and society: a London suburb in the seventeenth century* JEREMY BOULTON
6 *Demographic behavior in the past: a study of fourteen German village populations in the eighteenth and nineteenth centuries* JOHN E. KNODEL
7 *Worlds within worlds: structures of life in sixteenth-century London* STEVE RAPPAPORT
8 *Upland communities: environment, population and social structure in the Alps since the sixteenth century* PIER PAOLO VIAZZO
9 *Height, health and history: nutritional status in the United Kingdom 1750–1980* RODERICK FLOUD, KENNETH WACHTER and ANNABEL GREGORY
10 *Famine, disease and the social order in early modern society* edited by JOHN WALTER and ROGER SCHOFIELD*
11 *A general view of the rural economy of England, 1538–1840* ANN KUSSMAUL
12 *Town and country in pre-industrial Spain: Cuenca 1540–1870* DAVID REHER
13 *A stagnating metropolis: the economy and demography of Stockholm 1750–1850* JOHAN SODERBERG, ULF JONSSON and CHRISTER PERSSON
14 *Population and Nutrition: an essay on European demographic history* MASSIMO LIVI-BACCI*
15 *Istanbul households: marriage, family and fertility 1880–1940* ALAN DUBEN and CEM BEHAR
16 *A community transformed: the manor and liberty of Havering-atte-Bower 1500–1620* MARJORIE KENISTON McINTOSH
17 *Friends in life and death: the British and Irish quakers in the demographic transition* RICHARD T. VANN and DAVID EVERSLEY
18 *A rural society after the Black Death: Essex 1350–1525* L. R. POOS
19 *London in the age of industrialisation: entrepreneurs, labour force and living conditions, 1700–1850* L. D. SCHWARZ
20 *Death and the metropolis. Studies in the demographic history of London 1670–1830* JOHN LANDERS

Titles available in paperback are marked with an asterisk